Mystery
Parables
of the Kingdom

By Kevin J. Conner

CONNER
MINISTRIES

Published by Conner Ministries Inc

WEB: kevinconner.org
Email: kevin.conner321@gmail.com

Visit www.amazon.com/author/kevinjconner for a
list of other books by Kevin Conner.

About the Author

Born in Melbourne, Australia in 1927 and saved at the age of 14, Kevin Conner served the Lord in the Salvation Army until the age of 21. At this time he entered into pastoral ministry for a number of years. After that, he was involved in teaching ministry in Australia, New Zealand and for many years at Bible Temple in Portland, Oregon. After serving as Senior Minister of Waverley Christian Fellowship for eight years (1987-1994), he continued to serve the church locally as well as ministering at various conferences and the continued writing of textbooks.

Kevin is recognized internationally as a teaching-apostle after his many years in both church and Bible College ministry. His textbooks have been used by ministers and students throughout the world. He has been in great demand as a teacher and has travelled extensively. Kevin lives in Melbourne, Australia with his wife Rene.

TABLE OF CONTENTS
FOREWORD
PART ONE
PRINCIPLES OF INTERPRETATION

CHAPTER

PART TWO
PARABLES IN THE GOSPEL OF MATTHEW

PART THREE
PARABLES IN THE GOSPEL OF MARK

PART FOUR
PARABLES IN THE GOSPEL OF LUKE

SUPPLEMENTAL SECTION

FOREWORD

Any author who undertakes to write a book generally has to ask himself several important questions. Why is he writing the book? Who is he trying to reach? What is he endeavouring to accomplish? And what does he hope to have done with the book? The answers to these questions generally determine the style and format of the book. The answers to these questions have determined the style and format of this present textbook, **"The Mystery Parables of the Kingdom".**

The textbook is designed to reach the Body of Christ as a whole, but more especially leaders; those who are preachers and teachers of the inexhaustible Word of God. The text is designed to accomplish a sound interpretation and exposition of the parables. The author has designed the style and format of the book, not only to be read as a book, but, hopefully, to be used by teachers and preachers as a Teaching-Manual from which people can be instructed.

Any one who sets out to expound the parables of Scriptures leaves himself open to possible criticism. Why? Because Church History has proven that many expositors lapse into the great dangers of allegorizing the sacred Scriptures, and especially when it comes to the interpretation of the parables. Many of the early Church Fathers lapsed into allegorization. Because of this, there is a certain amount of hesitancy, much caution and fear for some preachers and teachers to even teach on the parables.

The writer believes that there are two major safeguards needed in order to properly expound the parables. These are (1) **Sound theology** and (2) **Sound hermeneutics**. Sound theology and sound hermeneutics may be liked to two sides of the same coin. You cannot have one without the other. Destroy one, you destroy the other. Or, sound theology and sound hermeneutics may be likened to the banks of a river which are needed in teaching through the various books of the Bible. The river under consideration here is the river of Divine truths seen in the parables, both Old and New Testament. It is absolutely necessary to stay within the banks of the river – sound theology and sound heremeneutics!

As will be seen, the word "parable" is a word that almost defies precise definition. The word seems to include in itself certain ingredients that overlap into other Figures of Speech, yet none of the ingredients on their own are a parable but together constitute the parable, some more and some less.Of all the definitions provided by various expositors of the parables, the simplest and most concise definition – even if not the most exact and balanced – is, **"A parable is an earthly story with a heavenly meaning"**.

The writer trusts that he has stayed within the two banks of the river, sound theology and sound heremeneutics, in the interpretation and exposition of the great truths of God flowing through the river of Divine parables.

In the Bibliography, the writer has listed reference books that are recommended to the reader of this textbook. Generally speaking, they provide much rich information on the parables in the Bible, some more, some less.

May teachers and preachers find the format of this book easy to teach from, and find as much joy in teaching and preaching these truths to the Body of Christ as the author has in the years of his own ministry.

Kevin J. Conner
P.O. Box 300
Vermont, Victoria, 3180
AUSTRALIA
1996

PART ONE

Principles
of
Interpretation

CHAPTERS 1 – 6

CHAPTER ONE
THE JEREMIAH PRINCIPLE

In approaching a study of the parables, as with other areas of Scripture interpretation, it seems that, what has been spoken of as "the Jeremiah principle", needs to be applied.

In Jeremiah 1:10 we have the Lord's commission of Jeremiah as a prophet to Judah. The Lord says, "See, I have this day set you over the nations and over the kingdoms, to root out, and to pull down, and to destroy, and to throw down, to build and to plant".

Jeremiah's ministry was twofold:

1. To root out, to pull down, to destroy and to throw down,
2. To build, to plant.

It is this "Jeremiah principle" which needs to be applied to the exposition and teaching of the parables. Certain concepts have to be rooted out, pulled down, destroyed and thrown down before one can build and plant the truth as seen in the parables. This principle may be applied in the following areas.

A. Rooting Out

The first phase of Jeremiah's ministry was the "rooting out" phase. Following are several areas that the author believes need to be rooted out before building and planting.

1. Problem of Allegorization

Extreme allegorization of the Scriptures became one of the greatest problems of the early church fathers. Church history has shown the dangers of this method of interpreting the parables, as well as other Scriptures.

As dealt with in **"Interpreting the Scriptures"** (Conner/Malmin), the allegorical method of interpretation arose through the union of Greek philosophy and religion. With the rise of philosophy, the Greeks began to realize that they could not interpret their religious writings literally and still hold to their philosophy. If both were taken literally, then they would be contradictory. Because of their new found loyalty to philosophy they had to conclude, in order to reconcile the two, that their religious writings meant something other than what they literally said. The method they created to do this is known as allegorism.

The allegorical method presumes that beneath the plain obvious sense of Scripture lies its true meaning. It believes that what the words of Scripture literally say are only external "chaff" which hides the true spiritual "wheat" of the Word. In allegorization, a passage with obvious literal meaning is interpreted using a point by point comparison, which brings out a hidden spiritual meaning not evident in the plain language of the passage. This method has been applied to the whole of Scripture by allegorists ancient and modern.

As an example of allegorism, Tan (p.38) cites Pope Gregory the Great's interpretation of the Book of Job, saying, "The patriarch's three friends denotes the heretics; his seven sons are the twelve apostles; his seven thousand sheep are God's faithful people; and his three thousand hump-backed camels are the depraved Gentiles."

Centuries have proven the allegorical method to be quite inadequate in the interpretation of Scripture. The error of this method begins at its foundational assumption: that what God said in plain language is not really what He meant. It is a dangerous method in that there are no Scriptural boundaries to guide its implementation. Undoubtedly, this is the reason for the great variety of contradictory theological positions among allegorists. Through the allegorical method Scripture is interpreted apart from its grammatical-historical meaning. What the author was trying to plainly communicate is almost totally ignored and what the interpreter desires to say is forced upon it. Allegorism obscures both the literal and figurative elements in Scripture. By exalting the interpreter's intentions and ignoring the author's intended meaning, the allegorical method fails to reach the basic goal of interpretation and therefore, must be set aside.

Extreme typology borders on allegorization. However, it must be recognized that these two are not synonymous. The difference, as cited by Mickelsen (p.238) quoting K.J.Woolcombe, is that typology is "the search for linkages between events, persons or things within the historical framework of revelation, whereas allegorization is the search for secondary and hidden meaning underlying the primary and obvious meanings of a narrative.

The interpreter must also be careful not to confuse the practice of allegorization with the figure of speech called allegory. In a class of its own is Paul's "allegory of the two covenants" in Galatians 4:21-31. This passage is not an allegory as defined above, but rather is the only example in Scripture of inspired allegorization. In contrasting the Old and New Covenants, Paul allegorizes certain Old Testament historical realities for the sake of illustration and emphasis. Because of this passage, some have misconstrued Paul as a fanciful allegorist, while others have used him to justify their own allegorical abuse of Scripture. Both need to recognize that Paul himself indicated that this was an exceptional use of the Old Testament for illustration, that this is the only example of such in his writings, and that Paul fully supported the validity and literal meaning of the historical events. The following shows that Paul used the grammatical-historical actual account of Abraham, Sarah and Isaac with Hagar and Ishmael.

Character	Factual	Allegorical
1. Abraham	The Father	God the Father
2. Sarah	The Free Mother	Jerusalem above
3. Isaac	Covenant Promised Son	New Covenant Sons
4. Hagar	Bondwoman	Jerusalem below
5. Ishmael	Bondson of the Flesh	Old Covenant Sons
6. Isaac/Ishmael	Persecution	Judaizers/Believers
7. Hagar/Ishmael	Cast out	Abolished
8. Isaac	The Heir of Promise	Believers are Heirs

Paul is not distorting in any way the historical facts pertaining to Abraham, Sarah and Isaac or Hagar and Ishmael, as do allegorists. The historical facts remain the same. If he was distorting the characters of the people involved to be something or someone they were not, then that would be allegorization. Paul is drawing some lessons from the historical account of the conflicts in Abraham's household over the two sons, Ishmael and Isaac.

Therefore, the interpreter must not confuse allegory with allegorization. Allegory is a legitimate way of teaching and illustrating truth by way of comparison. Allegorization forces a passage to communicate things not intended by the original author through use of a point by point comparison. In the allegorical method, a text is interpreted apart from its grammatical-historical meaning. What the original writer is saying is ignored, and what the interpreter wants to say becomes the only important factor. Allegorization is the arbitrary assigning of meaning to Scripture.

Fear of allegorization keeps many teachers from teaching on the parables. It is a good and healthy fear, but it can also rob the people of God of much valuable truth. As will be seen in the definition of parables, there is a fine line between parable and allegory. They often overlap and parables and allegories have to be distinguished. However, by following sound theology and sound hermeneutics, the expositor of the parables does have safeguards that, if followed, can prevent him from the dangers of allegorization.

2. Problem of Traditional Interpretations

The next thing that needs to be "rooted out, pulled down, thrown down", in order "to build and to plant", is the traditional interpretations of many of the parables. This will be dealt with in the appropriate chapter, but the following illustrates the point here.

A persons understanding of **"the kingdom"** affects their understanding and interpretation of the parables, especially the parables of Jesus. Traditional interpreters teach that "the kingdom" is a nationalistic or Jewish kingdom and has absolutely nothing to do with the church. Therefore, on the basis of this, the "mystery parables of the kingdom" have nothing to do with the church, nothing to say to the church, and are given primarily to the Jews in Christ's time.

While it is to be admitted, that the cultural, historical, national and personal setting of the parables, as given, has to be taken into account, the kingdom of God is not a Jewish thing. All truly born again believers are "born again" into the kingdom of God and are therefore subjects of the kingdom, here and now, and not just in the future aspect of the kingdom (John 3:1-5; Colossians 1:13-14).

There are many lessons for kingdom citizens in the parables of the kingdom of which Jesus is here and now the heavenly king, after the order of Melchisedek (Hebrews 7 with Acts 17:7). To allocate the parables of Jesus to Judaism only is to allow traditional interpretations to rob the people of God of much truth!

3. Problem of Interpretation and Application

Another traditional concept that needs the Jeremiah principle – rooting out, pulling down, destroying and throwing down, in order to build and plant – is that which pertains to **interpretation** and **application** of parabolic truth.

This method of interpretation says that there is only "one interpretation" and only "one application" of any parable. It says that there is only "one moral, one truth" in any given parable. This one moral is to be discovered only if it has not been given by the Lord or any New Testament writer. Therefore, the application can only be to those to whom the Lord spoke the parable, and nobody else.

The writer would say that there is indeed "one interpretation" of the parable, but "many applications" of the truth of that parable. However, proper interpretation of a parable must precede proper application of the truth of the parable.

An example of this can be seen in the historical-prophetical "Parable of the Wicked Vinedressers" (Matthew 21:33-46).

A glance over the contents of the parable shows that it reaches from Old Testament times of the prophets through to the coming of the Son, the Messiah, and on to the kingdom of God being taken from Jewry and given to the holy nation, which is the New Testament church.

The **interpretation** is basically clear. The **application** is evident when the chief priests and Pharisees perceived that Jesus was speaking of them. Yet surely, the truth of the parable is **applicable** in and to every generation. The fact of the matter is, truth is eternal. What was truth then is truth now. Truth is always truth. Though the **interpretation** and **application** of the parable was originally given to Jewry and to the religious leaders of Christ's day, is the truth not **applicable** to religious leaders in every generation if they fail to bring forth fruits of the kingdom?

This is true of all the parables of Christ. Discover the interpretation and the original application of the truth of the parable. Once discovered, such truth is applicable in all ages. Therefore, we may safely say, one interpretation as originally meant, and one application to the hearers, but on-going applications of the truth to all believers or unbelievers of all ages, in every generation. If this is not so, then the expositor limits the parabolic teaching to the Jewish nation of Christ's time.

It is important for the teacher of parables to understand the relationship of interpretation and application, both then and now.

Also, various expositors insist that any parable has only one truth in its interpretation, that there cannot be more than one truth (or moral) to any parable.

In comments like these, we need to realize that truth in itself is multi-faceted. In some of the extended parables of Jesus, even though there may be one major truth in the parable, there are certainly and unquestionably complementary or supplemental truths.

One example of this is "The Parable of The Sower and Seed". The one major truth may be seen as the Gospel of the Kingdom is sown in all kinds of soil. However, surely the wayside soil, the stony ground, the thorny ground and the good ground all supply supplemental truths about the conditions of the hearts of all who hear the Gospel of the Kingdom (Matthew 13). To limit the parable to but one moral, one truth, is indeed to rob the parable of the fulness of truth that is contained within its framework. One proper interpretation, and application to Christ's generation, but also ongoing truth and application in every generation!

4. **Problem of The Parable and Its Parts**

    Perhaps one final problem to be "rooted out", "pulled down", "destroyed" or "thrown down", before being able "to build and to plant", is that which pertains to the parable and its parts.

Through fear of allegorization and extreme and fanciful interpretations, many expositors say that one must not take all the parts of a parable and seek to deduce truths from them. Many feel that the parts of the parable are peripheral and are just there "to make up the story", and nothing more. It is the one major spiritual lesson or moral of the story that counts. They say that one should not make something out of every point or the major points.

The problem here is that one can make too much or too little of the story. All we should seek to do is get out of the parable what is in the parable; no more, no less.

The Lord Jesus Himself actually gives us the "key" for interpreting the parables. This is especially seen in the longer or more extended parables of Jesus.

In the parables of "The Sower and Seed", and "The Wheat and the Tares", Jesus takes virtually all the major parts of the parable and uses them to teach truth. There may be one dominant truth, but there are also supplementary truths. Jesus gave the example.

Because these parables will be interpreted more fully in their appropriate chapters, the demonstration of what has just been written is brief.

The Parable (Matthew 13:24-30) **Wheat and Tares**	**The Interpretation** (Matthew 13:36-43) **The Truths**
1. The Man who sowed seed -------------	The Son of Man, the Sower
2. In the field	The field is the world
3. Good seed	Children of the Kingdom
4. Bad seed	Children of the Wicked One
5. The enemy	The Devil
6. Wheat & Tares grow together	Righteous and Wicked in earth
7. The harvest time	End of the Age
8. Separation of Wheat and Tares	Angels separate Righteous and Wicked

Undoubtedly, the dominant truth is "the mixture in the kingdom". However, that is not the only truth in the parable. There are other truths which add to the picture.

The Son of Man and the Devil both sow seed: children of the kingdom and children of the wicked one. The two kinds stay together in the field until the end of this age. Then comes the great separation. The wicked are gathered together and burnt in the fire. The righteous shine forth as the sun in the kingdom of their Father. There is no sound reason to discard these supplemental truths.

This approach is in reality, what has been called, "the hermeneutical circle", in which one works from part to whole and whole to part. All the major parts of the parable find their significance in relation to its central lesson. Each of the parts are like supplemental truths that strengthen and support the central truth of the parable.

Or, to use another illustration, it is like putting together a jig-saw puzzle. All the parts together make up the whole puzzle. Putting the puzzle together, one has to work from part to whole and whole to part. One cannot leave parts out or else there are holes in the puzzle. None of the parts are peripheral but each are part of the whole. There is indeed but one picture in the puzzle, but all the parts of the puzzle make up the one picture. So we believe it is with the interpretation of parables. We work from part to whole and whole to part and gain the full picture of what Christ had in mind in the parabolic story.

In Kenneth E.Bailey's excellent book, **"Through Peasant Eyes"** (Introduction, p.xxi), he writes:

"Because of the irresponsible extravangances of the past, a number of scholars moved to the other extreme and rejected **all** allegory, insisting that there is only one teaching on each parable. It is our view that parables have in them more than a single theme and that these schemes can be understood without either destroying the unity of the parables or falling into allegorizations of the past.

It is instructive to remember David and Nathan. Nathan tells a story to David about a rich man, a poor man, and a lamb (2 Samuel 12:1-6). David had stolen another man's wife and had had her husband killed. Nathan's story to David has three symbols:

1. The rich man symbolizes David.

2. The poor man symbolizes Uriah.

3. The lamb symbolizes Bathsheba.

Two separate aspects of this parable must be observed with care. The first is this set of symbols that David (the original listening audience) understood instinctively. These (mentioned above) are **symbols**, not allegorizations. A symbol **represents** something else, an allegory is something else and has no other existence. These three symbols function in the story and without them the parable is pointless. By having identified the three symbols that **the original audience** (David) instinctively identified, we are **not** free thereby to start making other symbolical identifications. That is, we could take the city, the flocks and herds, the cup, the traveller, and the morsel and assign them meanings of one kind or another, and in the end make the parable mean whatever we might want. Yet there are symbols in the parable... **The symbols to look for are the ones the original teller puts in the story for the purpose of communicating with the original audience.** The storyteller, in the telling of the parable, skillfully uses these symbols to press the original listener to make a decision/response. In the case of the above, David is pressed to understand "I am the man." It is in that single response that the unity of the parable is to be found." (Emphasis K.E.Bailey)

B. Build and Plant

The second phase of Jeremiah's ministry was "to build and to plant". Once the wrong concepts of interpretation of the parables are "rooted out and pulled down", then one can "build and plant".

In the writer's understanding, there are two major qualifications required for sound interpretation of the parables in Scripture. As already mentioned in the Foreword, these two qualifications are (1) Sound Theology, and (2) Sound Hermeneutics.

1. Sound Theology

The first important safeguard for a proper interpretation and exposition of the parables of Jesus is sound Biblical theology. Some of the interpretations of parables that this writer has either read or heard preached on over the years shows a lack of sound theology. Biblical doctrine will help safeguard one from heretical interpretations.

Although doctrines cannot be founded on parables, parables can illustrate doctrine. However, the doctrine must be sound first of all, otherwise parables can be made to say anything the expositor wants them to say.

Although referred to later in the text, there are those interpreters who use "The Parable of the Woman and the Leaven" to teach the doctrine of Universalism – that is, that all divisions of mankind (Three Measures of Meal) will be saved by the leavening influence of the Gospel (Matthew 13:33).

This is an example of unsound doctrine, unsound theology. In interpreting the parable as a whole, both as to its major moral lesson, and its relevant parts, nothing will be used as interpretation that contradicts or violates, sound Biblical theology.

Kenneth E. Bailey, in **"Poet and Peasant"** (p.37) has some excellent words to say about parables.

"In this section we shall attempt to show that a parable has three basic elements. First, the parable has one or more points of contact (referents) within the real world of the listener, which can be called **"symbols."** The second element in a parable is the **"response,"** that the original listener is pressed to make to the original telling of the story. The third element is a combination of theological motifs in the parable that together pressed the original listeners to make that response. This combination we choose to call the **"theological cluster."** Thus, one or more symbols with corresponding referents in the life of the listener impel him to make a single response which has in view a cluster of theological motifs."

In **"Through Peasant Eyes"** (Introduction, p.xxii), he says:

"In this study we will try to identify the original listener and attempt to discover what Jesus was trying to get him to understand and do. Then, through the analysis of that initial response/decision, we will be able to see what the text says to us. We will attempt to discern the multiplicity of theological themes in a parable (where they exist) without destroying its unity and without allegorizing its details."

Sound theology, therefore, is one of the major safeguards for a proper interpretation of the parables.

2. Sound Hermeneutics

The next important safeguard and qualification for proper interpretation of parables is sound hermeneutics, sound principles of interpretation of the sacred Scriptures.

In the text, **"Interpreting the Scriptures"** (Conner/Malmin, pps 139-165), the authors deal with some of the specialized principles of interpretation designated as "The Figures of Speech Group of Principles". These principles include:

* The Symbolic Principle
* The Numerical Principle
* The Typical Principle
* The Parabolic Principle
* The Allegorical Principle.

As will be seen in the definition of "parables", most writers see some overlapping, as it were, or interplay in these hermeneutical principles. Parables interplay with allegory. Parables have symbols in them oftentimes and these need to be interpreted in order to understand the parable. Sometimes numbers are used in parable and allegory. Some expositors see various parables as having typical import. All belong to these specialized group of principles and require the skill of the interpreter.

Under "Qualifications for Interpretation of Parables", these things are dealt with more fully and further safeguards are provided. The issue is, the interpreter of parables must have and must use sound principles of interpreting the Scriptures, or, sound hermeneutics, otherwise extreme or even heretical interpretations result.

The author of this text has endeavoured to interpret the parables within the boundaries of sound Biblical theology and sound Biblical hermeneutics. But this brings us to the chapter on The Definition of a Parable and the Parabolic Principle.

CHAPTER TWO
DEFINITION OF A PARABLE

Hermeneutically, the Parabolic Principle has been defined as "that principle by which any parable is interpreted by discerning its moral and interpreting its parts" (Conner/Malmin). However, the defintion of a parable itself is far more complex and comprehensive as the following definitions show.

Various expositors have attempted to provide a full and complete defintion of the word "parable". Some have given a concise definition of the word. Others see the word to be quite a comprehensive word embracing a variety of elements in its definition, and because of this, there seems to be little agreement on what exactly is a parable. Following are some of the defnitions from various sources.

A. Strong's Concordance
1. Old Testament Hebrew
The Hebrew word "**Mashal**: (SC 4912) is defined as" properly a pithy maxim, usually of a metaphorical nature, hence a simile; a proverbial saying, parable, similitude, resemblance (as an adage, poem, discourse). It is translated:-

Parable – Numbers 23:7,18; 24:3,15,20,21,23; Job 27:1; 29:1; Psalms 49:4; 78:2; Ezekiel 17:2; 20:49; 24:3; Micah 2:4; Habakkuk 2:6.

Proverb – Deuteronomy 28:37; 1Samuel 24:13; 1Kings 4:32; 2Chronicles 7:20; Psalm 69:11; Proverbs 1:1,6; 25:1; Ecclesiastes 12:9; Isaiah 14:4; Jeremiah 24:9; Ezekiel 18:2,3.

Byword – Psalm 44:14

Like – Job 13:12.

2. New Testament Greek
The New Testament Greek word **"Parabole"** (SC 3850) is defined as "a similitude, ie., symbol, a fictious narrative of common life conveying a moral. It is translated:-

Comparison – Mark 4:30

Figure – Hebrews 9:9; 11:19

Proverb – Luke 4:23

Parable(s) – Matthew 13; 15:15; 21:33,45; 22:1; 24:32; Mark 4:13; 7:17; Luke 5:36; 6:39; 12:16,41; 18:19; 19:11; 20:9,19; 21:39.

The word **"Parabole"** comes from **"Parabollo"** (SC 3846), meaning, "to throw alongside, ie (reflex.) to reach a place, or (fig) to liken:- arrive, compare.

Dan Seagren, in **"The Parables"** (p.19) says, "The Greek word" **"Parabole"** in the New Testament is a compound word, made up of **"Para"** (a preposition, meaning, near, beside, with, in), and **"Ballo"**, to throw, rather vigorously.

These words together mean, "to throw something with force at someone", a "placing something alongside another", or "something which resembles or has a likeness for the purpose of comparison".

B. Vine's Expository Dictionary

Vine says, **"Parabole"** (SC3850) literaly denotes **"a placing beside"** (akin to **"Parabollo"**, "to throw" or "lay beside, to compare").

It signifies "a placing of one thing beside another" with a view to comparison (Some consider that the thought of comparison is not necessarily contained in the word).

In the New Testament it is found outside the Gospels, only in Hebrews 9:9 and 11:10. It is generally used of a somewhat lengthy utterance or narrative drawn from nature or human circumstances, the object of which is to set forth a spiritual lesson; eg., those in Matthew 13 and the Synoptic parallels; sometimes it is used of a short saying or proverb; eg., Matthew 15:15; Mark 3:23; 7:17; Luke 4:23; 5:36; 6:39.

It is the lessen that is of value; the hearer must catch the anaology if he is to be instructed (this is also true of a proverb). Such a narrative or saying, dealing with earthly things with a spiritual meaning, is distinct from a fable, which attributes to things what does not belong to them in nature.

Christ's "parables" most frequently convey truths connected with the subject of the kingdom. His withholding the meaning from His hearers was a Divine judgment upon the unworthy.

Two dangers are to be avoided in seeking to interpret the "parables" in Scripture; that of ignoring the important features, and that of trying to make all the details mean something."

C. Noah Webster's Dictionary (1828 Edition)

Parable, from Parabole; to throw forward or against, to compare; to set together, or one thing with another.

A fable or allegorical relation or representation of something real in life or nature, from which a moral is drawn for instruction; such as the parable of the trees choosing a king (Judges 9); the parable of the poor man and his lamb (2Samuel 12); the parable of the ten virgins (Matthew 25:1-13).

D. Arden L. Chitwood

In **"Parables of the Kingdom"** (Foreword, p.7), Arden L.Chitwoord says: "The word "parable" is a transliteration of the compound Greek word "parabole", which means "to cast alongside". Used in this sense, a parable is one truth cast alongside a previous truth to help explain the previous truth".

E. A.R. Fausett

On "Parables" (pp.538-539), Fausett has this to say. "Hebrew word "MASHAL", Greek word "PARABOLE", is a placing side by side or comparing earthly truths, expressed, with heavenly truths to be understood.

The basis of parable is that man is made in the image of God, and that there is a law of continuity of the human with the Divine. The force of the parable lies in the real analogies impressed by the Creator on His creatures, the physical typifying the higher moral world.

Quoting Lisco, A.R.Fausett says: "Both kingdoms develop themselves according to the same laws; Jesus parables are not mere illustrations, but internal analogies, nature becoming a witness of the spiritual world, whatever is found in the earthly also exists in the heavenly kingdom. The parables, earthly in form, heavenly in spirit, answer to the parabolic character of His own manifestation.

Fausett also seeks to make the distinction between Fables, Parables, Allegory and Proverbs, which is adapted for the purpose here.

Fables – introduces brutes and transgresses the order of things natural, introducing improbabilities resting on fancy (ie., animals, trees speaking, representing mankind).

Parables – do not bring in brute beasts, but has a loftier significance; resting on the imagination, introducing only things probable.

Allegory – personifies directly ideas or attributes. The thing signifying and the thing signified are united together, the properties and relations of one being transferred to the other; instead of being kept distinct side by side, as in the parable. It is a prolonged metaphor, or extended simile; it never names the object itself; it may be about other than religious truth, but the parable only about religious truth.

Proverb – is a condensed parable while the parable is often an expanded proverb. The parable is longer carried out than the proverb, and not merely by accident or occasionally, but necessarily, figurative and having a similitude. The parable expresses some particular fact, which the simile does not.

F. New Bible Dictionary

From pages 877-879, on "Parables", the New Bible Dictionary says "Parable is ultimately derived from the Greek "parabole", literally 'putting side by side'. Etymologically it is thus close to 'allegory', which by derivation means 'saying things in a different way'. Both parables and allegories have usually been regarded as forms of teaching which present the listener with interesting illustrations from which can be drawn moral or religious truths.

Parable is somewhat protracted simile or short descriptive story, usually designed to inculcate a single truth or answer a single question, while allegory denotes the more elaborate tale in which all or most of the details have their counterparts in the application. The line between parables and allegories is obviously a fluid one, and both forms are found in the Gospels.

There is, however, a more basic difference than that of amount of detail present. While the developed allegory is essentially derived from the application, many of the parables of Jesus are not merely illustrations of general principles; rather they embody messages which cannot be conveyed in any other way. The parables are the appropriate form of communication for bringing men the message of the kingdom, since their function is to jolt them into seeing things in a new way. They are means of enlightenment and persuasion, intended to bring the hearers to a point of decision. Jesus, as it were, stands where His hearers stand, and uses imagery familar to them to bring new and unfamiliar insights to them.

Then under Section II, the Dictionary continues: "In the New Testament the actual word "parable" is used with the same broad variety of meaning as the Hebrew word "pashal" to refer to almost any kind of non-literal utterance. What we should normally call a proverb can be termed a parable (Luke 4:23). The "parable" in Matthew 15:15 has almost the nature of a conundrum. The simple illustration that leaves on a tree are signs of the approach of summer, is a parable (Mark 13:28). The more elaborate comparison between children at play and the reaction of Jesus' contemporaries to John the Baptist and Himself is usually spoken of as 'the parable of the children's game' (Luke 7:31). On the other hand, the parables of the sower and the tares are both given detailed allegorical interpretations (Matthew 13:18-23,36-43), and the parables of the drag-net (Matthew 13:47-50), the wicked husbandmen (Mark 12:1-12), the marriage feast (Matthew 22:1-14), and the great supper (Luke 14:16-24) obviously contain details with allegorical significance.

Further on it says: "But it is in reality impossible to draw a clear-cut distinction between parable and allegory in the stories told by Jesus. Some of His stories were clearly intended to illustrate several lessons, as in the parable of the prodigal son, where stress is laid on the joy which God as Father has in forgiving His children, the nature of repentance, and the sin of jealousy and self-righteousness (Luke 15:11-32)".

G. Dan Seagren – "The Parables"
On pages 16-17 Dan Seagren admits that parables almost defy full definition. Parables are complex, since so many of the parables are strengthened by various figures of speech. On these pages he lists 14 figures of speech, concluding that parables contain any or some of these figures. All of this variously makes it difficult to give a perfectly simple definition of a parable. If the interpreter realizes this, then exactitude will not be so problematical.

Allegory – a story, poem, or word-picture in which a spiritual or poetic meaning is conveyed symbolically.

Analogy – a comparison of two unlike things which share certain similarities.

Anecdote – an account of a happening which is told to make or illustrate a point or to evoke a response (humour, pathos, anger, rapport, etc.).

Fable – an imaginative story designed to convey a moral, often employing animals or objects as communicating characters.

Idiom – a mode of expression whereby the real meaning is not understood by a normal understanding of the words (e.g., shoot the breeze).

Illustration – a story or an example used to clarify, enrich, reinforce, or possibly help prove a certain idea or pattern of thought.

Metaphor – a word or a phrase used to convey another meaning (e.g., a copper sky, a burning temper,etc.).

Myth – a legendary or traditional attempt to explain or account for events in nature, history, and religion, particularly as they relate to the supernatural.

Narrative – a series of connected details used in story-telling, poetry, and drama to describe or explain.

Proverb – a short local or universal saying which has stood the test of time and contains special truth or wisdom.

Rhetorical Question – a question which is raised in order to evoke a response without expecting or receiving an answer.

Riddle – a puzzling question, statement, or problem which requires an answer or a solution.

Simile – a figure of speech in which two essentially unlike things are compared (such as smart as a whip, cheeks like roses, etc.).

Story – a relating of an event (or a series of events), fictional or true, usually in a detailed manner.

As Seagren says, Parables can contain any of these elements of these figures of speech, though no one of them alone are necessarily parables. It is this that makes parables hard to define, or provide a perfectly single definition of a parable.

H. Gordon D. Fee

In **"How to Read the Bible for all its Worth"** (pp.1224-125), Gordon Fee has this to say. "One of the keys to understanding them (the parables) lies in discovering the original audience to whom they were spoken; as we noted, many times they came down to the evangelists without a context.'

If the parables, then, are not allegorical mysteries for the church, what did Jesus mean in Mark 4:10-12 by the mystery of the kingdom and its relationship to parables? Most likely the clue to this saying lies in a play on words in Jesus' native Aramaic. The word **methal** which was translated **parabole** in Greek was used for a whole range of figures of speech in the riddle, puzzle, parable category, not just for the story variety called "parables" in English. Probably verse 11 meant that the meaning of Jesus' ministry (the secret of the kingdom) could not be perceived by those on the outside; it was like a methal, a riddle, to them. Hence His speaking in mathelin (parables) was part of the methal (riddle) of His whole ministry to them. They saw, but they failed to see; they heard- and even understood- the parables, but they failed really to appreciate the whole thrust of Jesus' ministry."

I. J. Jeremias

In **"The Parables of Jesus"** (p.20), J. Jeremias defines the word "parable" in the following way:

"This word (parable) may mean in the common speech of post-Biblical Judaism, without restoring to a formal classification, figurative forms of speech of every kind: parable, similitude, allegory, fable, proverb, apocalyptic revelation, riddle, symbol, pseudonym, fictitious person, example, theme, argument, apology, refutation, jest."

In summary of the various commentaries and expositors definitions of parables we would say:

1. A parable is a pithy maxim, usually of a metaphorical nature, hence a simile; a proverbial saying, similitude, resemblance.

2. A parable is a similitude, a symbol, a fictitious narrative of common life conveying a moral.

3. A parable is one truth cast alongside a previous truth to help explain the previous truth.

4. A parable is a placing side by side or comparing earthly truths, expressed with heavenly truths to be understood.

5. A parable, theologically speaking, is a fictitious, but true to human life, story that is designed to illustrate, by way of comparison, some spiritual truth.

6. A parable is a short (or longer) story from which a moral lesson (or lessons) may be drawn.

7. A parable is a story in earthly form but heavenly in spirit.

8. A parable is a placing of one thing beside another; a comparison of one thing wth another; a short discourse that makes a comparison. It expresses a single complete thought.

9. A parable is a narrative, fictitious but agreeable to the laws and usages of human life, by which either the duties of men or the things of God, particularly the nature and history of God's kingdom, are figuratively displayed.

10. A parable is a earthly story with a heavenly meaning.

11. A true parable is a story, pure and simple, with a beginning and ending.

12. A parable is an ingenious (picturesque) figure of speech, usually a short story of everyday life, which teaches a singular truth, as well as suggesting subordinate truths.

13. A parable can be a complexity of ingredients of other figures of speech which have to be interpreted in order to understand the truth of the parable.

14. A parable is a picturesque form of speech created to make an impact upon the listener.

15. A parable is a true to life story, in a familiar setting, given to teach a lesson, but which the hearers may understand the natural story and miss the spiritual lesson.

16. A parable can have allegorical elements in it without becoming an allegory.

That is exactly what parables did in the time of Christ and can still do today to those who have "ears to hear" and a "heart to perceive" what the Lord can say to His people in our generation.

CHAPTER THREE
CLASSIFICATION, SOURCES, GROUPINGS

A. Classification of Parables

There is much difference of opinion among Bible scholars over the definition and classification of the parables of Scripture. Though a few accept only those parables designated by Scripture as such, most scholars allow for a broader definition, as we have seen in the previous chapter. Most all agree that a parable is an extended simile, but there is disagreement over where the boundary line should be placed between simile and parable. Thus, in tabulating parables, there is among scholars a wide range of numbers. Although various scholars have suggested several ways of classifying parables, for the sake of simplicity, we will classify them as follows: (1) Short Parables and (2) Extended Parables.

1. Short Parables

A short parable can be easily confused with a simile. For the purposes of distinction, the simile will be viewed as generally only having one pair of details that can be compared, while a short parable will be seen as having several such pairs.

For example, "He was led **as** a sheep to the slaughter" (Acts8:32; Isaiah 53:7), is a simile. "His eyes were as a flame of fire" (Revelation 1:14), is a simile, "My Beloved is **like** a roe" (Song of Solomon 2:9), is also a simile.

On the other hand, "Another parable put He forth unto them, saying, The kingdom of heaven is like a grain of mustard see, which a man took, and sowed in his field: Which is indeed the least of all seeds, but when it is grown, it is the greatest among herbs, and becometh a tree, so that the birds of the air come and lodge in the branches thereof" (Matthew 13:31,32), is designated a short parable.

"Either what woman having ten pieces of silver, if she lose one piece, doth not light a candle, and sweep the house, and seek diligently until she find it? And when she hath found it, she calleth her friends and her neighbours together, saying, Rejoice with me; for I have found the piece which I had lost" (Luke 15:8,9), is an undesignated short parable.

And, "There was a little city, and few men within it; and there came a great king against it, and beseiged it, and built great bulwarks against it. Now there was found in it a poor wise man, and he by his wisdom delivered the city; yet no man remembered the same poor man" (Ecclesiastes 9:14,15), is an undesignated short parable.

2. Extended Parables

An extended parable differs from a short parable primarily in its length and in the number of pairs of details which can be compared. A short parable will generally include from two to five such pairs, while an extended parable will include more.

An extended parable must also be distinguished from an allegory, although, as seen in our previous chapter, there seems to be some overlap. Some examples of extended parables are: The Parable of the Sower (Matthew 13:1-8), a designated extended parable; The Parable of the Prodigal Son (Luke 15:11-31), an undesignated extended parable; The Parable of the Vineyard (Isaiah 5:1-6), an undesignated parable (Refer to **"Interpreting The Scriptures"** (Conner/Malmin).

Because this textbook deals with a number of the parables, the truth of "short parables" and "extended parables" will be demonstrated in the appropriate chapters, as well as whether they are designated or undesignated parables.

B. Sources of Parables

Jesus took His parables from primarily two major sources:

1. The Realm of Creation

Jesus used symbols in His parables, taken from the realm of nature, the realm of creation. Such included things like seed, bread, wheat and tares, fish and fishermen, leaven, pearls, vineyards, sheep and shepherds, as well as numerous other things. The symbol needs to be interpreted to properly interpret the parable.

2. The Realm of Human Relationships

Jesus also used human relationships in many of His parables. We have kings and kingdoms, fathers and sons, masters and servants, bride and bridegroom, weddings, virgins, friends, shepherds, as many others. All have to be interpreted to interpret the parable properly. Jesus used the human relationships to illustrate Divine relationships in His parables.

C. Groupings of Parables

Most expositors of the parables realize it is not really possible to make an exact listing of parabolic groupings or parabolic sayings of Jesus. Many times there is overlapping of truths in the parable which makes it difficult to be exacting in groupings. However, for the purpose of this chapter, we group as suitable and possible, the parables that are dealt with in this text.

1. Kingdom Parables

These parables of the kingdom generally begin with, "The kingdom of heaven is like unto..." They include both present and future aspect of the kingdom and most seem to have some eschatological element in them. This is especially so in the parables of the kingdom in Matthew, although alluded to in parables from Mark and Luke.

Parable of the Sower and Seed (Matthew 13:3-23; Mark 4:2-20; Luke 8:4-15).

Parable of the Wheat and Tares (Matthew 13:24-30,36-43).

Parable of the Mustard Seed (Matthew 13:31-32; Mark 4:30-32; Luke 13:18,19).

Parable of the Woman and Leaven (Matthew 13:33; Luke 13:20-21).

Parable of the Treasure his in the Field (Matthew 13:44).

Parable of the Merchant Man and Pearls (Matthew 13:45-46).

Parable of the Dragnet and Fish (Matthew 13:47-50).

Parable of the Scribe and Householder (Matthew 13:51-52).

Parable of the King and Servants (Matthew 18:23-35).

Parable of the Vineyard Labourers (Matthew 20:1-16).

Parable of the Two Sons and the Vineyard (Matthew 21:28-32).

Parable of the Vineyard and Husbandmen (Matthew 21:33-45; Mark12:1-12; Luke 20:9-19).

Parable of the Marriage of the King's Son (Matthew 22:2-14).

Parable of the Wise and Foolish Virgins (Matthew 25:1-13).

Parable of the Used and Unused Talents (Matthew 25:14-30).

Parable of the Sheep and Goats (Matthew 25:31-46).

Parable of the Kingdom Seed (Mark 4:26-29).

Parable of the Pounds (Luke 19:11-27).

2. **Nature Parables**

Several of the parables of Jesus mainly use parables of nature, or creation, each of which teach truth by way of symbol and parable.

Parable of the Lighted Lamp and City (Mark 4:21-22; Matthew 5:14-16; Luke8:16-17 with 11:33-36).

Parable of the Old and New, Garments and Wineskins (Luke 5:36-38; Matthew 9:16-17; Mark 2:21-22).

Parable of the Fig Tree – Barren, Cursed or Budding (Luke 13:6-9; 21:29-33; Matthew 24:32-44; Mark 13:28-32).

Parable of the Strait and Broad Gates (Luke 13:22-24; Matthew 7:13-14).

Parable of the Salt (Luke14:34-35; Matthew 5:13; Mark 9:50).

3. **People Parables**

Undoubtedly Luke's Gospel is particularly the "peoples parables" Gospel. Most all parables include people, but Luke has the most personal touch in the people parables than the other Gospels.

Parable of the Absent Housemaster (Luke 13:33-37).

Parable of the Wise and Foolish Builders (Luke 6:46-49; Matthew 7:24-27).

Parable of the Creditor and Two Debtors (Luke 7:36-50).

Parable of the Good Samaritan (Luke 10:30-37).

Parable of the Three Friends (Luke 11:5-13).

Parable of the Rich Fool (Luke 12:16-21).

Parable of the Watchful Servant (Luke 12:35-40; Matthew 24:42-44).

Parable of the Faithful and Wise Steward (Luke 12:42-48); Matthew 24:45-51).

Parable of the Shut Door (Luke 13:25-30).

Parable of the Wedding Feast Invitation (Luke 14:7-11).

Parable of the Great Supper (Luke 14:16-24).

Parable of the Tower Builder and Warring King (Luke 14:25-33).

Parable of the Lost and Found Sheep (Luke 15:3-7; Matthew 18:12-14).

Parable of the Lost and Found Coin (Luke 15:8-10).

Parable of the Lost and Found Son (Luke 15:11-32).

Parable of the Unrighteous and Shrewd Steward (Luke 16:1-13).

Parable of the Rich Man and Lazarus (Luke 16:19-31).

Parable of the Unprofitable Servants (Luke 17:7-10).

Parable of the Unjust Judge and the Widow (Luke 18:1-8).

Parable of the Pharisee and Publican (Luke 18:9-14).

Parable of the Pounds (Luke 19:11-27).

Jesus was indeed the Master Teacher, THE Teacher of teachers! He was able to take everything of creation, of nature, and of human relationships and teach it in parabolic form to communicate Divine and eternal truths, suitable to every age and generation.

In **"Through Peasant Eyes"** (Introduction p.xi-xii), Kenneth E. Bailey writes: "There are at least six different types of formats in which the parables of Jesus function. It is crucial for their interpretation to see how they function in these different settings. These six are:

1. The parable in a theological dialogue.

2. The parable in a narrative event.

3. The parable in a miracle story.

4. The parable in a topical collection.

5. The parable in a poem.

6. The parable standing alone.

Each of these requires brief examination.

We arrange his comments on each of these formats.

1. **A Theological Dialogue**
   An example of this is the theological discussion between Jesus and the rich ruler in Luke 18:18-30. The climax of the discussion occurs, as we will observe, in the telling of the parable of the Camel and the Needle. The parable has a crucial function in forming the climax of the entire discussion and cannot be isolated from it.

2. **A Narrative Event**
   The banquet at the house of Simon the Pharisee in Luke 7:36-50 is an example of a parable in a narrative event. The parable of the Creditor and the Two Debtors functions as part of the narrative event. There is dialogue but the dramatic actions of the silent woman are the focus of the entire scene.

3. **A Miracle Story**
   The miracle story of the healing of the woman with a spirit of infirmity in Luke 13:10-17 becomes a theological debate between the head of the synagogue and Jesus, and thus also overlaps with type one above. Yet it is a miracle story and again the parable of the Ox and Ass functions as a crucial part of the whole.

4. **A Topical Collection**
   In Luke 11:1-3 we have a topical collection on the subject of prayer. The parable of the Friend at Midnight (Luke 11:5-8) is a part of that collection. A careful distinction must be made in such a collection among the different units of tradition that are included in a collection. That is, because a number of sayings on one topic are grouped together, it is easy to fail to perceive where the paragraph breaks should come and thus misinterpret the material.

5. **A Poem**

   Occasionally, as in Luke 11:9-13, we have a very carefully composed poem on prayer. Jesus gives three striking parables in the central stanza of the poem. Their function in that climax is the key to understandind the entire poem.

6. **Standing Alone**

   Finally, a parable at times stands alone. In Luke 17:1-10 we have three topics in rapid succession, each of which has some parabolic speech. There is the parable of the Millstone, and the topic of judgment on the tempter. This is followed by the parable of the Grain of Mustard Seed and the apostles' request for faith. Then comes the dramatic parable of the Obedient Servant in vs 7-10. These three stand relatively alone with no clear connection to what surrounds them and no specific context.

   Thus in all but the last type the parable functions as a crucial part of a larger literary unit. It is the larger unit in each case that must be examined to determine what the parable is all about. With a working definition of what parables are in the New Testament and where they occur, we must then ask how they are to be interpreted."

In our expositions of the various parables in the Gospels, we will endeavour to discover the setting of each of the parables considered.

CHAPTER FOUR
QUALIFICATIONS FOR INTERPRETING THE PARABLES

Because of the dangers and pitfalls of improper interpretation of parables, and the evident lapse into allegorization of parables, there needs to be some Biblical safeguards and guidelines laid down for any exposition of parables. Following are Biblical safeguards and guidelines which the writer has constantly sought to follow in this textbook.

1. The first step in using the Parabolic Principle is to make certain that the passage under consideration is a parable, whether designated as such or not.

2. Because parables are drawn from the cultural background of their authors, the interpreter should research the (a) Manners, (b) Customs and (c) Material Culture involved in the parables he is interpreting. This is bridging the Historical, Geograhical and Cultural gaps existing between our generation and Christ's generation. The parables are far more Palestinian culture than Western culture. They must be considered in their Biblical context.

3. The interpreter should find out, if possible, who the parable was being told to, and endeavour to identify himself with what the original hearers would hear. Search out the "setting" or "stage-drop" in which the parable was given.

    Kenneth E. Bailey in **"Poet & Peasant"** (p.27) writes: "Palestinian Christians saw their own culture reflected in the parables and could thereby understand the teller/authors intent directly."

    Parables are to be seen in First Century Palestinian background.

    Again, Bailey in **"Through Peasant Eyes"** (Introduction p. xvi) writes concerning the cultural setting of the parables in Middle Eastern Bible times. "It is absolutely unacceptable to continue reading our own culture (Western or otherwise, authors comment) subconsciously into the parables once we become aware of what we are doing. In short, the parables are stories about people who lived in a particular time and place."

    "The crucial questions are those of **attitude, relationship, response and value judgment.** What is the **attitude** of a sleeping neighbour to a call for help in the night? What is the **relationship** between a landowner and his renters? What is the expected **response** from a father when his son requests his inheritance? What **value judgment** do the renters make regarding the steward when he suggests the reduction of rents?"

    It is important, therefore, to see the parables in the cultural setting in the First Century and Palestinian Bible background.

    (a) The Parable of the Lost Sheep, The Lost Coin, The Lost Son, were each given in the setting of Jesus receiving lost sinners, and was given in the hearing especially of the Scribes and Pharisees (Luke 15:1-2).

    (b) The Parable of the Good Samaritan was given to a lawyer testing Christ out on the requirements for eternal life, and then seeking to justify himself on Christ's answer to him (Luke 10:25-37).

    (c) The Parable of the Unforgiving Servant was given to Peter over the issue of how often he should forgive an offending brother (Matthew 18:21-35).

When originally spoken, the hearers, generally, were their own interpreters.

4. In interpreting the parable, the interpreter must realize that there is one major or fundamental spiritual truth therein. The interpreter should seek to discover that one central truth in the parable even though there may be (or will be) other supplemental, subservient and complementary truths in that same parable. These subservient truths will reinforce, strengthen and undergird the one central truth. This one central truth is actually "the key" to the interpretation of the parable.

For example:-

(a) The central truth of the Parable of the Virgins is given by the Lord Himself at the conclusion of the parable. That is, "Watch therefore, for you know not the day nor the hour when the Son of Man cometh" (Matthew 25:1-12, especially verse 13).

(b) The central truth of the Parables of the Lost Sheep, Lost Coin and Lost Son is "this Man receives sinners", and "there is joy in heaven over one sinner that repents" (See Luke 15:1-2,7,10). The interpretation is given at the beginning and ending of the parables.

(c) Sometimes the central truth is given at the beginning of the parable, as in the Parable of the Unjust Judge (Luke 18:1), and the Parable of the Pounds (Luke 19:11). We must pray with insistancy, and we will be accountable for that which we have been given. These are the central truths of these parables.

(d) Sometimes the central truth is given at the beginning and ending of the parable. This is seen in the Parable of the Unforgiving Servant (Matthew 18:21-35, especially verses 22,35). We must forgive one another as long as God forgives us is the major truth of the parable.

Within each of these parables one may see subservient, or supplemental and complementary truths. But all support, undergird and throw further light on the one central truth. There will be nothing contradictory in the truths therein, because ultimately all fragmentary truths are part of the one whole truth.

Myles Coverdale (AD 1535) says: "It shall greatly help you to understand Scripture, If you mark not only what is spoken or written, But of whom, and to whom, with what words, at what time, where, and to what intent, with what circumstances, Considering what goeth before and what followeth".

To interpret Scripture, and here we especially are speaking of the parables, we must therefore investigate:

* **What** – What is actually being said, not "reading between the lines".
* **Of Whom** – Who is being talked about (or to?). "Of whom speaketh the prophet? said the eunuch to the evangelist Philip (Acts8:30).
* **To Whom** – Who is being spoken to? Who was Christ speaking His parables to? To His disciples? To the religious leaders? To the multitude? To an individual?
* **With what words** – In what language? Consider why such terms are used by Jesus His parabolic teaching.
* **At what time** – When did Jesus speak His parables? At what period of His ministry was the parable(s) spoken?
* **Where** – Where was Jesus when He spoke the parables? In a house, a boat, in the temple, or the countryside?

* **To what intent** – What was Christ's purpose or reason behind His teaching the parable?
* **With what circumstances** – What were the circumstances under which Jesus spoke the parable?
* **What goeth before** – Check the preceding context; that which flows into Christ's teaching of the parable.
* **What followeth** – Check the succeeding context; that which flows out of Christ's teaching of the parable.
5. What may be called "the threefold cord" of Ecclesiastes 4:12 must not be broken. That is:

   Observation, Interpretation and Application. Observation precedes interpretation, and proper contextual interpretation precedes application.
* **Observation** – What does the parable actually say – not what you want it to say.
* **Interpretation** – What does the parable actually mean – not what you want it to mean?
* **Application** – How can the moral of the parable be applied to us in our generation?

   Observation is knowledge. Interpretation is understanding. Application is wisdom (Proverbs 1:1-6).
6. A parable, being an extended simile, has one main focal point of comparison, but it is the whole of the parable that is the comparison. It is a comparison between the natural realm and the spiritual realm. Each of the details given concerning the natural realm have their correspondence to the spiritual realm. However, they are all vitally related to the focal point of the comparison.

   A parable may be likened to a zig-saw puzzle. The puzzle has many parts to it but there is one picture. When putting a puzzle together, all the parts are necessary to make the complete or the whole picture. None of the parts are superfluous. One works from part to whole and whole to part. To leave any part, or parts, of the zig-saw puzzle out would certainly leaves 'holes' in the picture.

   Because of extreme interpretations and allegorization of parables, some expositors say that all the parts of the parable are not really significant, that there should not be a point by point comparison. Some say there is only one major point, the parts of the parable are peripheral and therefore not to be pressed into a point by point comparison. Others say all the parts are to be examined by way of extended analogy or comparison, not just the major parts.

   To refer again to the illustration: In the putting together of a puzzle, the artist knows there is but one picture, one puzzle, but all of the parts are parts of the puzzle. The artist works from part to whole and whole to part without forcing the parts or distorting the picture. To say that some or several of the parts of a parable are insignificant and throw them aside would be to destroy the parable. All the parts of the parable are necessary to make up the whole of the parable. However, the safeguard is indeed, not to "force" interpretation on the parts that would distort the parabolic picture or Biblical theology and Biblical hermeneutics.

   This may be illustrated with the kingdom of heaven parable in Matthew 13:33; the Parable of the Woman and Leaven. The following questions could be asked concerning the comparison.

Is the kingdom of heaven like leaven?

Or, is the kingdom of heaven like leaven which a woman took?

Or, is the kingdom of heaven like leaven which a woman took and hid?

Or, is the kingdom of heaven like leaven which a woman took and hid in three measures of meal?

Or, is the kingdom of heaven like leaven which a woman took and hid in three measures of meal until the whole was leavened?

There is one picture, one major or central spiritual truth, but it takes all of the parts of the parable to make the picture complete. No one part of the parable can be non-essential; all are essential parts of the one parabolic picture. The various parts of the story make up the whole story. It is fear of allegorization that causes expositors to say otherwise.

Or, to say it again, every parable is designed to provide one fundamental spiritual truth. In order to perceive the point of the parable, the significance of each of its parts must be recognized. In other words, the part cannot be interpreted apart from the interpretation each of its parts. As with all of Scripture, the interpretation of parables must move from whole to part and from part to the whole. All the details of a parable find their significance in relation to its main truth, its main point, its major moral, its spiritual truth.

In **"Poet & Peasant"** (p.41,42), Bailey quoting C.W. Smith ("The Jesus of the Parables"), writes: "It will be observed that many of the details are so apt (ie., Parable of the Prodigal Son) that, once the **central point** is grasped, **many applications** may be made and deductions drawn."

Geraint Vaughan Jones, in **"The Art & Truth of the Parables"** (p.140) states "To insist that there shall be one point and one point only, and that a parable shall be understood only as a whole, and not in relation to its part (which is supposed to turn it into an allegory), is pure dogmatism."

Bailey writes: "Who is to say that John 3:16 discusses only "love" or "the world" or "believing" or "perishing" or "eternal life"? This does not mean that there is no unity in this verse, but it does signify that the unity is found in a theological cluster of concepts."

7. Parables have a twofold purpose. They either reveal truth or conceal truth, according to the attitude of the hearers, both then and now. This is seen very clearly in the words of Jesus in answer to the question of His disciples. "Why do You speak to them in parables?" The general multitude had eyes to see and did not see, they had ears to hear and did not hear, they had hearts to perceive and did not understand. The disciples' eyes, ears and hearts were blessed with spiritual sight, spiritual hearing and spiritual perception.

    Christ's purpose was to withdraw the truth from those unworthy and unfit to receive it (Matthew 13:9-16; Mark 4:11-12; Luke 8:9-10 with Isaiah 6:10). Those who were hungry and open hearted to the Lord's word would receive the truth.

8. In interpreting the parts of a parable, the interpreter must allow Scripture to interpret Scripture by using, what has been called, "The Context Group of Principles" (ie., First Mention, Progressive Mention, Comparative Mention, and Complete Mention

Principles), along with other principles, such as, the Moral and Symbolic Principles (Refer to **"Interpreting the Scriptures", Conner/Malmin**).

The parables have a moral behind them. The parables most often have symbols in them. One must interpret properly the symbols in order to interpret the parables. The symbols often are the parts in the whole, the moral is the spiritual truth or lesson in the parable. Parables generally involve various symbols which must be properly interpreted before the lesson of the parable can be rightly discerned. Many times the key to the interpretation of the parable will be found in its immediate context. The issue is, proper principles of interpretation (Biblical Hermeneutics) must be used to properly interpret the parables.

9. The parable clothes truth in external form. Paul says that "knowledge and truth" was found in the external form of the law (Romans 2:20). So "knowledge and truth" is in the external form of the parable.

If the Lord had given straight, spiritual truth, His words may have been forgotten in the hearts and minds of His hearers. Jesus clothed truth in parabolic form by the use of symbols in the parable. The Parables of the Sower and Seed, the Wheat and Tares illustrate this fact (Matthew 13:3-8,18-23; Matthew 13:24-43). It is much easier to remember a story clothing truth than truth in abstract form.

The writer to the Hebrew believers says that the Tabernacle of Moses and all its services was a parable (Hebrews 9:9. Grk). Within this "parable" are numerous symbols, holding knowledge and truth in the external form. The symbolic/parabolic Tabernacle and its services has been abolished, passed away, but the knowledge and truth hidden in the external form remains, for truth itself is eternal. One must move from the literal/actual to the figurative, from the clear to the obscure, and never the reverse in order to remain in truth. This is a sound law of Scripture interpretation.

10. Distinctions need to be kept in mind between parable and allegory. This has been dealt with under the Definition of Parables. However, further comment is appropriate here.

R.C. Trench in **"Notes on the Parables of our Lord"** (pages3-5) makes distinctions between the following, which we adapt for our purpose here.

(a) A Parable is not a Fable

A fable is of the earth, earthy. A fable attributes reason and language to beasts and trees. A parable is of the earth, but conveys a heavenly and spiritual truth. A parable does not attribute reason and language to beasts and trees.

(b) A Parable is not a Myth

A myth is not a truth; a parable is a truth whether revealed or concealed.

(c) A Parable is not a Proverb

Some proverbs are concentrated parables, such as "the blind leading the blind" (Mathew 15:14-16). Sometimes parables and proverbs are used interchangeably (2Peter 2:22). However, a parable goes beyond being a proverb.

(d) A Parable is not an Allegory

A parable compares one thing with another. An allegory makes one thing the other. Isaiah 5:1-6 is an allegory of the vine and vineyard and the interpretation is given in verse 7. "The vineyard of the Lord of Hosts is the house of Israel, and the men of Judah His pleasant plant".

Psalm 80:8-16 is an allegory of Israel as God's vine. Some proverbs are brief allegories also. However, parables are not to be allegorized.

Dr. Gordon D. Fee, in, **"How To Read The Bible For all Its Worth"** ("The Parables", pps 123-134), says that parables almost overlap with allegories having allegorical features. However, there is always the danger of allegorization of the parables, as Church History has shown. A true allegory is a story where each of the elements in the story mean something quite foreign to the story itself.

Paul provides an allegory for us in Galatians 4:1-31 and interprets the same for us. Abraham's "two sons" are "two covenants". However, he is not allegorizing Scripture to extreme or fanciful interpretation, as seen in a previous chapter of this text.

Most expositors find difficulty in making the distinction between the parables and the allegories because of certain resemblances in both. The fine line is discerning and defining such, as there is sometimes overlapping in certain Figures of Speech.

11. Parables are not to be made sources of doctrine. Doctrine should not be founded on parabolic teaching. Parables may be used to illustrate and confirm doctrine but must not become foundations for doctrine. It has already been said that a proper safeguard for the interpretation of parables is sound theology along with sound hermeneutics.

   Parabolic interpretation must never be used to contradict Biblical theology. We remind the reader of the example in Matthew 13:33. Some expositors interpret "the three measures of meal" to represent the three divisions of mankind through the three sons of Noah. "The leaven" is interpreted to be the Gospel. And "the whole being leavened" is interpreted to be the universal salvation of all mankind (Universalism)!

   This violates Biblical hermeneutics and violates sound Biblical theology. The Bible nowhere teaches "the universal reconcilation of mankind or fallen angels". This contradicts the clearly defined teachings of Scripture and becomes heretical doctrine founded on wrong interpretation of a parable.

12. It is to be recognized that some parables have historical/prophetical import. In other words, they cover some Old Testament history, flowing on into Christ's first coming, His ministry, His crucifixion, and then they flow on into New Testament Church history.

   Drawing "a time-line" of this would show the truth of this as seen in the Parables of the Wicked Husbandmen and the Parable of the Marriage of the King's Son (Matthew 21:33-46; 22:1-14).

   In these parables we see the Old Testament inter-play of Israel's history, then the coming and rejection of their Messiah, the burning of Jerusalem in AD.70, and the coming in of the Gentiles through the Gospel of the Kingdom being preached in all the world in New Testament times. These make historical/prophetical parables.

13. The end purpose of the study of parables, as for all Scripture, is to bring the moral to bear practically on our lives. As already noted, observation leads to interpretation, and interpretation leads to practical application. The purpose of information of the mind is to lead to formation of the Christian's character. Teaching is so that the believer may be "transformed by the renewing of the mind" (Romans 12:1-2).

14. The interpreter will discover that parables fall primarily into two groupings: Interpreted parables and Uninterpreted parables.

(a) Jesus interpreted the first two parables in Matthew 13; the Parable of the Sower and Seed, and the Parable of the Wheat and Tares (Matthew 13:3-8,18-23; 24-30, 36-43).

(b) Jesus did not specifically interpret many of His other parables; those recorded in Matthew and Luke.

How then can we safely interpret the uninterpreted parables? It seems quite evident that the first parable of the sower and seed is "the key" to all parables (Mark 4:3-20; Matthew 13:3-23; Luke 8:5-15). Jesus said to His disciples, If you do not understand this parable, how will you understand all other parables?

The way Jesus gave an extended anaology of the parts of the Parable of the Sower and Seed and Wheat and Tares, and the moral of each parable, surely gives us some guidelines and safeguards for interpreting the uninterpreted parables. These parables, in a sense, become "sample-interpreted-parables", to help one interpret the uninterpreted parables.

"Through Peasant Eyes" (Introduction, p.xxiii), Kenneth Bailey provides eight basic steps to help us understand the parables of Jesus and to discern their message for today. These eight basic steps can be carried to some degree by the nonspecialist, and be pursued in much greater detail by the specialist. These steps can be briefly stated as follows:

1. Determine the audience. Is Jesus talking to the scribes and Pharisees, to the crowds, or to His disciples?

2. Examine carefully the setting/interpretation provided by the evangelists or his source.

3. Identify the "play within a play" and look at the parable on these two levels.

4. Try to discern the cultural presuppositions of the story, keeping in mind that the people in them are Palestinian peasants.

5. See if the parable will break down into a series of scenes, and see if themes within the different scenes repeat in any discernable pattern.

6. Try to discern what symbols the original audience would have instinctively identified in the parable.

7. Determine what single decision/response the original audience is pressed to make in the original telling of the story.

8. Discern the cluster of theological motifs that the parable affirms and/or presupposes, and determine what the parable is saying about these motifs."

In summary then: Within these guidelines and safeguards, and the theology of the Bible as a whole, the expositor should be able to provide sound interpretation of uninterpreted parables. Sound theology and sound hermeneutics become good foundation for sound interpretation and exposition of the parables of our Lord Jesus Christ.

(Note: In the Combined Edition of **"Poet & Peasant"** and **"Through Peasant Eyes"**, Kenneth E. Bailey deals with the Literary Structure of Scripture, applying it especially to the parables he interprets. The literary structure of Scripture and the parables is beyond the skill of the writer. The reader is referred to Bailey's excellent textbook).

CHAPTER FIVE
UNDERSTANDING THE WORD OF THE KINGDOM

It has already been drawn to our attention that one's view of "the kingdom" affects one's interpretation of Scripture. We especially think of the interpretation of the parables. The parables are primarily parables of the kingdom given by the king of that kingdom, the Lord Jesus Christ Himself.

In the very first parable given in the Matthew 13 grouping, Jesus speaks of the matter of the kingdom. "When any one any hears the **word of the kingdom** and does not understand it..." (Matthew 13:19). It is not just hearing the word, or any word, but it is hearing **"the word of the kingdom"** and not understanding it. That is when the word is taken out of the heart.

What then is this "word of the kingdom?" What do we understand by "the kingdom?" Is the kingdom past, present or future? Is the kingdom strictly a Jewish kingdom; nationally and politically pertaining to the nation of Israel?

For many years the writer was taught and believed that "the kingdom" and "the church" were distinct and separated things. "The kingdom" was for the Jew. "The church" was predominantly for the Gentiles. Ultra-dispensational teaching propagates that the kingdom was presented to Jewry by John the Baptist, then by Jesus and then by the apostles over the Gospel ministry and on into the Book of Acts.

However, the Jew rejected the kingdom and crucified the king and therefore the kingdom was postponed to the end of this age, when Jewry would have its eyes opened to their long-rejected Messiah.

In the meantime, God brought into being "the church", as a parenthetical idea in which believing Jews and Gentiles are made one. However, the church is simply a parenthesis between the first and second coming of Christ. Once Jesus returns, "the kingdom" will be brought in again and the Jews will preach the Gospel of the kingdom which had been postponed because of Jewish unbelief. The church preaches the Gospel of the grace of God. The Jew will preach the Gospel of the kingdom.

Just a brief consideration of this view shows how, holding to this concept, one's interpretation of the parables of the kingdom will be affected. Hence the importance of understanding "the word of the kingdom". It is not that all the parables of Jesus are defined as kingdom parables, but the theme of the kingdom, past, present and future is the thread of truth that runs through them all, whether designated or undesignated kingdom parables.

The following material is taken from (**"The New Testament Church"** by Kevin J.Conner), and it provides an overview of the kingdom from eternity to eternity.

One of the greatest areas of controversy and confusion is that which pertains to the distinction yet relationship between the Church and the Kingdom. Dispensationalists speak of the kingdom as being a Jewish thing, and the church as being a parenthetical plan of God after the Jews rejected the king, Jesus Christ. They teach that the kingdom was postponed during this dispensation of the Holy Spirit, and that the church is God's temporary purpose in this period of time of Jewish unbelief.

However, this is very far from the truth of Scripture as it pertains to both the church and the kingdom. Questions that can be asked: Is the church and the kingdom synonymous?

Is the church in the kingdom or is the kingdom in the church? Is the church Gentilish and the kingdom Jewish? Is the kingdom past, present or future? Materialistic, national, political, militaristic, or spiritual?

A. The Kingdom Defined

The word "kingdom" is made up of two words: "King's domain" = Kingdom. It is the territory or area over which a king rules and reigns; the king's domain. God's kingdom is the rule and reign of God, whether in heaven or in earth. It is the purpose of God – the extension of God's rule.

The Greek word "Basilea" speaks of the sway, rule, administration of a king. The royal reign of the kingdom of God is seen. One cannot separate the king and the kingdom as far as God is concerned. The word kingdom is used some 160 times in the New Testament.

1. How long has the Kingdom of God been in existence?

(a) The kingdom of God is an everlasting kingdom (Psalm 145:10,13; 103:19; Daniel 4:3). There has never been a time when the kingdom of God has not been in existence. It has neither beginning nor end.

(b) The kingdom of God is sovereign, ruling over all other kingdoms (Psalm 103:19; Revelation 11:15).

(c) The kingdom of God is all-inclusive, including within itself, its domain, the total universe, the elect angels, heaven, the fallen angels and all creatures and mankind on this earth. All are under His control and dominion. None could exist or act without His sustaining power (Psalm 103:19; Exodus 15:18; Psalm 145:10-13).

2. Is there a difference between the Kingdom of God and Kingdom of Heaven?

There is no difference between these terms; they are synonymous. A comparison of the following Scriptures shows that what is said of the kingdom of God is also said of the kingdom of heaven (Matthew 23:22).

Kingdom of Heaven	Kingdom of God
Matthew 4:7	Mark 1:14
Matthew 5:3	Luke 6:20
Matthew 10:7	Luke 9:2
Matthew 11:11	Luke 7:28
Matthew 13:11	Luke 8:10
Matthew 13:31	Luke 13:18,19
Matthew 19:14	Mark 4:30,31
Matthew 19:23,24	Luke 18:24

Matthew, writing particularly for Jewish converts, almost invariably uses the expression "kingdom of heaven", while Mark, Luke and John substitute "kingdom of God". It was customary among the Jews to use the word "heaven" for God, and in Matthew 23:22 the Lord Himself states that to swear by heaven is to swear by "the throne of God and by Him that sits thereon".

B. The Progressive Revelation of the Kingdom

In each age, as pertaining to earth, there has been a further or progressive revelation of the kingdom of God. This is the purpose of God for His kingdom to be manifested. The following provides an overview of the kingdom as pertaining to eternity, time and the earth.

1. The Kingdom of God in Heaven – Time Past

Matthew 6:6-9; Psalm 102:19; 145:10-13. The angels and the archangels were created as subjects of the heavenly kingdom in the eternity past. Sin brought confusion and originated a rebel kingdom of Satan and fallen angels there (Revelation16:10; John 8:44; 2Peter 2:4; Jude6).

2. The Kingdom of God in Eden

Genesis 1-2 chapters. God created Adam and Eve giving them dominion and rulership over the earth. In and through them God desired to rule and reign. His kingdom was to be established in the earth, in Adam's race. However, as instruments for the expression of God's kingdom, they failed, because of sin and sold their unborn generations over to Satan and the kingdom of darkness.

3. The Kingdom of God in Patriarchal Times

Noah, Abraham, Isaac and Jacob were faithful patriarchs and covenant men. In them was illustrated and demonstrated the kingdom of God in the earth. The promises of kingship and the king Messiah were preserved in these men who were instruments for the expression of God's kingdom. These men, though imperfect, knew the rule and reign of God in their hearts and lives in the midst of corrupt and apostate nations about them (Genesis 8-50 Chapters).

4. The Kingdom of God in Israel

Exodus 19:1-6. In due time God brought forth the nation of Israel, and chose it out of the midst of other nations (Deuteronomy Chapters 4-5). In this nation He established more fully His kingdom, His laws. Israel was a theocracy. God was their king (Numbers 24:5-7; Deuteronomy 6:6-8). God intended Israel to be the instrument in earth to demonstrate His rule and reign to the other nations; to give all nations the true revelation of God. Saul, (1Samuel 9-10), David (1Samuel 16; 1Chronicles 10:14), Solomon (1Kings 1:46) were the first kings to reign over a united nation. In due time, the kingdom of Israel was divided into two houses, the house of Israel and the house of Judah (1Kings11-12; Ezekiel 16; Ezekiel 23). Both houses had prophets of God sent to them to remind them of the laws of God. The tragedy is that Israel failed to be all that God intended them to be. For this reason, God allowed the captivity of both houses.The house of Israel went into Assyrian Captivity, the house of Judah into the Babylonian Captivity.

5. The Kingdom of God in the Gentile World

During the Captivity of Israel and more especially that of Judah, God used the Gentile nations to be the instrument of His rule and reign in the earth. The Book of Daniel especially shows the sovereignty of God's kingdom. He rules in the heavens and the earth and He gives the kingdom to whomsoever He will (Daniel 2; Daniel 4; Psalm 9:16; Ezra 1:1-4; Daniel 7:9-14,26,27; Psalm 22:28,29; 1Kings 2:15; 2Samuel 16:8; 2Chronicles 36:22,23; Daniel 4:17,25, 32-35).

Thus Assyrian, Babylonian, Medo-Persian, Grecian and Roman Kingdoms were given the reign, under God, over the people of God because of their failure. God rules in the heavens and in the affairs of men. God is sovereign.

6. **The Kingdom of God in Christ**

God held the house of Judah in the land of Palestine until the advent of the king, Jesus Christ. The Gospel of Matthew is particularly the Gospel of the King and the Kingdom. Jesus preached, taught and demonstrated the kingdom of God. He gave the laws of the kingdom in Matthew 5-6-7 chapters. He presented the rule and reign of God to the house of Judah (Matthew 4:17,23-25). The king was actually the personification of the kingdom of God in the earth.

* Jesus preached the Gospel of the kingdom – Matthew 4:23; Mark 1:14; Acts 1:3.

* Jesus taught the kingdom was at hand – Matthew 4:17; Mark 1:15.

* Jesus showed His ministry ushered in the next phase of the kingdom – Matthew 12:24-28; Luke 11:20; 16:16.

* Jesus told His disciples to preach the kingdom of God – Matthew 10:7; Luke 9:2; 10:9-11.

* Jesus taught His disciples to pray, "Thy kingdom come" – Matthew 6:6-9; Luke 11:2

* Jesus told some of His disciples that they would not die until they had seen the kingdom of God come with power – Matthew 16:28; Mark 9:1; Luke 9:27.

* Jesus said He would not eat and drink of the fruit of the vine until He did it anew in the kingdom – Matthew 26:29; Mark 14:28; Luke 22:16-18. This was demonstrated in the communion times He had with them after the resurrection – Acts 1:4; 10:41; John 21:13; 1Corinthians 11:23-34.

However, because the Jews had such a nationalistic and materialistic concept of the kingdom of God, they rejected their king and crucified Him (Matthew 26-27). But, contrary to the Dispensationalists, the kingdom was not postponed until the end of the age and the lifting of Jewish blindness and unbelief, nor was the church brought in as a parathentical plan. The kingdom was transferred over to the church. The kingdom was taken from Jewry and given to a nation, which was the New Testament church (Matthew 21:41-46 with 1Peter 2:5-9).

7. **The Kingdom of God in the Church**

That there is a relationship between the church and the kingdom is evident from Matthew 16:1819. Jesus said, "Upon this rock I will build My CHURCH...and I will give unto you the keys of the KINGDOM of haven..." As will be seen, the church now becomes the instrument for the declaration and demonstration of the kingdom of God in the earth. It is also the final instrument for that ministry. The church is entrusted with the administration and authority of the kingdom in earth, symbolized by the "keys of the kingdom" given to it. This will be seen more fully at the conclusion of this chapter.

8. **The Millennial Kingdom**

There is a further aspect of the kingdom of God as to its manifestation in earth and that is the 1000 years reign of Christ on earth with the saints (Daniel 2;

Daniel 7; Revelation 20:1-10). However, there is much controversy and confusion over the fact and nature of this aspect of the kingdom. It is not the purpose of this text to deal with this matter, but simply to note that this is just the final aspect of the kingdom revelation in earth after Christ's second advent.

9. The Kingdom in Eternity

The final aspect of the progressive revelation of the everlasting kingdom of God is that which takes place at the close of the 1000 year period. Paul says, "Then comes the end when He (Christ) shall have delivered up the kingdom to the Father..." (1Corinthians 15:24-28).

Here we complete the cycle. The everlasting kingdom has been expressed in its sevenfoldness in earth, reaching from eternity through time to eternity.

In Summary:

The kingdom of God is the rule and reign of God over the universe and all creatures therein, whether angelic or human. There has been and is but ONE KINGDOM of God, but the instruments through which this one kingdom has been expressed have varied. The kingdom never changes, the instruments do. The final instrument for the expression, manifestation and demonstration of the kingdom in earth is the Church! The instrument of God has changed over the centuries, but the purpose of God has never changed.

C. The Church and The Kingdom

Having defined and followed the cycle and progressive revelation of the kingdom of God eternity to eternity, through time, we consider more the relationship of the church and the kingdom.

1. Distinction and Relationship

The church and the kingdom are distinct, yet related. The kingdom is the universal reign of God over all creation and creatures and the universe of worlds, including in itself angels and men.

The church is composed of redeemed believers, out of every kindred, tongue, tribe and nation. The church does not include the angelic hosts. So we may say that the angelic hosts are in the kingdom, but only the redeemed are in the church and also in the kingdom.

The kingdom is eternal and unlimited. It is all-encompassing. The church is God's eternal purpose manifested in time. It is limited to those of mankind who are redeemed by Christ.

The church becomes the instrument for the full demonstration of the kingdom. God's kingdom, God's rule and reign, is to be established in the church. The church is in the kingdom and the kingdom is in the church. But the church is not the totality, but only a part of the kingdom of God. The kingdom of God is far more inclusive than the church.

This distinction, yet relationship, between the church and the kingdom needs to be recognized and understood in order to avoid confusing the real issues involved in both. We do not pray "Thy church come", but, "Thy kingdom come (Matthew 6:6-10). Nor do we preach "The Gospel of the church" but the "Gospel of the kingdom" (Matthew 24:14).

2. The Church and the Kingdom

The word "church" is used about 115 times in the New Testament. The word "kingdom" is used about 160 times. A study of the Book of Acts, along with other major Scriptures from the Gospels shows that the early church was indeed the channel, the instrument, the vehicle and vessel for the expression of the kingdom of God. It was through the church that the kingdom of God was extended in the earth in the hearts of men. We note some of the major truths concerning the kingdom of God in these verses.

* Christ said He would build His church and give her the keys of the kingdom – Matthew 16:18,19.

* Repentance and faith are the doorway into the kingdom – Matthew 3:2;4:17,23.

* One must be born again from above by spiritual and heavenly birth to enter the kingdom (John3:1-5). If the kingdom was postponed, then it means that no one could and no one is born again until then.

* Regeneration is a translation out of the kingdom of darkness into the kingdom of love and light – Colossians 1:13,14.

* The kingdom of God is righteousness, peace and joy in the Holy Spirit – Romans 14:17. It is the like the king – Psalm 85:10; Hebrews 7:1-3.

* The kingdom of God is not of this world system – John 18:36; Matthew 6:9,10; Luke 17:20-21.

* The Gospel of the kingdom is to be preached in all the world for a witness to all nations before the end comes – Matthew 24:14; Mark 16:15-20.

* The law and the prophets were until John; since that time the kingdom of God is preached – Luke 16:16; Matthew 5:17,18; 11:13; 12:28.

* The kingdom was taken from Jewry and given to the holy nation, which is the church – Matthew 21:42-46; 1Peter 2:5-9.

* Believers are the good seed of the kingdom, in the mystery form of the kingdom in this age – Matthew 13:37,38; Mark 4:11; Matthew8:11; Luke 13:28,29.

* We are to seek first the kingdom of God – Matthew6:33; Luke 21:31.

* The church taught and preached and demonstrated the power of the kingdom of God.

(a) Jesus spoke to the disciples of the kingdom of God – Acts 1:3-6.

(b) Philip, from the church at Jerusalem, preached the kingdom of God as an evangelist – Acts 8:1,12.

(c) Paul preached the kingdom of God, as an apostle from the church at Antioch – Acts 14:22; 19:8; 25.

(d) John and Paul, apostles of the New Testament church, believed they were then in the kingdom (Revelation 1:9; Colossians 4:11; Acts 28:23,31).

(e) Jesus Christ is the king-priest after the order of Melchisedek (Hebrews 7:1-2; Revelation15:3; 1Timothy 1:17; 6:15; Revelation 19:6). The church is also a royal priesthood after the same order (Revelation 1:6; 5:9,10; 1Peter 2:5-9; Romans 5:17,21).

(f) Believers are born into the kingdom as subjects of the kingdom (John3:1-5), and then they are added to the church as members of the new community (Acts 11:24; 2:41-47).

(g) The church preached the Gospel of the kingdom, for there is only one Gospel for both Jew and Gentile. It is spoken of as:

The Gospel of the kingdom – Mark 1:14,15; Matthew 24:14

The Gospel of Jesus Christ – Mark 1:1

The Gospel of God – Romans 1:1

The Gospel of His Son – Romans 1:9

The Gospel of the grace of God – Acts 20:24; Romans 1:16; Ephesians 2:8,9

The glorious Gospel – 1Timothy 1:11; 2Corinthians 4:3-4

The everlasting Gospel – Revelation 14:6

The Gospel of the circumcision – Galatians 2:7

The Gospel of the uncircumcision – Galatians 2:7

The Gospel – Mark 16:15-20

The Gospel according to Paul – Romans 2:16; 16:25; Galatians 1:6-9; 1Corinthians 15:1-8.

The church today is the agent for the proclamation and demonstration of the kingdom of God in the earth. Though the church and the kingdom are distinguisable, they are indivisible in the eternal purposes of God.

Undoubtedly there is significance in the fact that the Gospel of Matthew – The Gospel of the Kingdom – is the only Gospel which mentions the church. The two passages in Matthew 16:15-20 and 18:15-20 actually become the seed or root out of which the full revelation of the church grows and is developed through the Acts and the Pauline Epistles.

Whatever the interpreter's understanding of "the word of the kingdom", this will be evident in the interpreter's exposition of the parables of the kingdom, as well as other parables of Jesus. This writer's understanding of the distinction and relationship between **"the church"** and **"the kingdom"** is set out in this chapter, and therefore affects and determines his understanding of the parables in the succeeding chapters. The parables have timeless truth, applicable both to those in Christ's day and in our generation. Understand the truth of the kingdom and one will better understand the parables of the kingdom!

CHAPTER SIX
METHOD AND FORMAT OF EXPOSITION

It will be important that the reader of this textbook constantly keep in mind the writer's method and format of exposition of the parables. The format is basically fivefold, providing: The Scripture(s), The Setting, The Moral, The Exposition and The Practical Application of the parables. The reader will bear with the repetition of some things that have been mentioned in previous chapters as the format is covered in this chapter.

A. The Scriptures on the Parable

The first thing to see is the Scripture or Scriptures which deal with the parable. All Scripture is given by inspiration of the Holy Spirit and is profitable for doctrine, for reproof, for instruction in righteousness. The Scripture reference or references should be read carefully as this provides a general knowledge of the wording and language of the parable. The reader will see the various symbols that may be used in the parable which need to be interpreted, as well as realizing there is truth that needs to be discovered in the parable as a whole.

B. The Setting of the Parable

The second important step to understanding the parable is the setting of the parable. This setting may be twofold: Historical and Inspirational.

1. Historical Setting

It will be in order to "set the stage" for the parable. This can be done, generally speaking, by a consideration of the events which either preceded or followed the parable. Sometimes parables arose out of conversations with people; sometimes out of accusations of the Scribes or Pharisees; sometimes from Christ's own disciples or other individuals. Sometimes parables were given in answer to requests or questions asked of Jesus, or even in response to the thoughts of people's hearts, which Jesus Himself discerned. The circumstances in which the parables were spoken help to set the stage.

Also, part of the historical setting for the parable is to whom were the parables spoken? Sometimes the parables were spoken to His disciples, sometimes to the multitude, sometimes to individuals, or to the religious leaders, as the Scribes, Pharisees and Sadducees.

Therefore, where, what were the circumstances, and to whom were the parables spoken? These are questions which need to be answered to provide the stage, the historical backdrop for a clearer understanding and exposition of the parables.

2. Inspirational Setting

Because we believe that the Gospels, as also the whole Bible, were inspired by the Holy Spirit, we also believe that the writers each have a unique presentation of Christ's ministry, works and words.

Matthew writes his Gospel more especially to the Jews with his emphasis on Jesus as the Son of David. The parables in Matthew are especially "kingdom of heaven" parables. Mark writes more especially to the Roman world and presents Jesus as the Son of Man. Mark has few parables, but what he writes has its unique setting. Luke presents Jesus as the Son of Adam, writing more to the Greek world. Luke has parables that are unique to his Gospel and these are written in their unique setting. There is no contradiction in the Gospels, but there is inspiration. This fact has to be recognized and accepted.

Therefore, there is the historical setting for the parables, but there is also the inspired setting for the parables, in their Gospel context. Both blend together for a proper understanding, interpretation and exposition of the parables.

C. The Moral of the Parable

The next thing the writer has sought to set out is the major moral, the spiritual lesson, or the central truth of each parable. The reader will see that there are, in some parables, other supportive or supplemental truths to be seen in the details of the parable. However, there is the central truth of the parable around which these supportive truths revolve. It could be said that the central truth is "the hub" of the parable, and the other supportive or supplemental truths are like "the spokes" of the wheel that run to and from the hub in "the wheel" of the parabolic story Jesus gives.

The interpreter, this writer believes, cannot be locked into the concept that all parables have only one truth. There is the central truth, but there are also complementary truths in most parables, which make up the whole truth of that particular parable.

It is good to discover the central truth and spiritual lessons early, as this will help the expositor to maintain a sound interpretation and exposition of the parable. It is also important to remember that no one parable contains all the truth on all the truths of God in the Bible. Each have their major truth and supportive truths but no one parable is the whole truth. All present truth in fragmentary form.

As Hebrews 1:1 puts it: "In many separate revelations – each of which set forth a portion of the Truth – and in different ways God spoke of old to our forefathers in and by the prophets, But in the last of these days He has spoken to us in the person of a Son..." (Amplified New Testament). What is said here is certainly true of Christ's parabolic teaching. They set forth portions of truths, but no one parable has the whole or the complete truth. Together they constitute truth that Jesus wanted to communicate to His own. Discovering the moral of the parable is actually the use of the hermeneutical principle – The Moral Principle.

D. The Exposition of the Parable

In the writers exposition of the parables, certain guidelines have been followed in order to produce a sound Biblical exegesis of the such. Following are the guidelines that the author believes should be used and which have been used throughout this textbook.

1. Observation

First and foundational in all Bible exposition is "What does the Bible actually say? In this case, What do the Scriptures actually say on this parable? Not what the reader wants it to say, or forces it to say, but what does the Bible writer really say? What are the words used, inspired by the Holy Spirit. Because it is fundamental that one believes in the inspiration of the Scripture, words are important. Jesus said these words, the Gospel writers were inspired to write His words, and this is what is meant by plenary-verbal inspiration. The **thoughts and the words** written were inspired by the Holy Spirit. This is observation.

2. Interpretation

Not only "What does the Bible say", but also "What does the Bible mean?" In this case, What does the parable mean? What did it mean to the hearers then? What does it mean to us now? This is interpretation. It has to with sound hermeneutics, or sound principles of interpretation. In interpreting the parables, the hermeneutical principles that would have to be used would at least involve the following:

(a) Sound Hermeneutics

1. The Parabolic Principle (Refer to Chapters 2 and 5)

2. The Symbolic Principle – Because most parables have symbols in them, in order to interpret the parable, one has to properly interpret the symbols therein. It may involve symbolic objects, creatures and numbers. The New Testament is replete with the use of symbols from Old Testament, and therefore, the Old Testament can be used to help one interpret New Testament parables. One may think of leaven, oil, meal, feasts, marriages, lamps, and other things used in symbolic form. Interpreting the parables, at times, involve the total Bible. One must use Scripture to interpret the symbols in the parable or the language of parabolic illustrations to interpret the parable.

    As will be seen, Jesus interpreted the first two parables in Matthew 13 concerning the Sower and the Seed, and the Wheat and the Tares. There Jesus spoke of the sower, the wheat, the tares, the field, the enemy, the reapers and the harvest. Each and all of these parts were interpreted by Jesus Himself, as He worked from part to whole and whole to part.

3. The Typical Principle – Because some parables involve typical persons, offices and institutions, or even events, in order to interpret the parable, the typical elements will have to be properly discerned and interpreted.

4. The Comparative Mention Principle – Because the Gospel writers repeat some of the parables of Jesus, then the Gospels are to be compared as to their presentation of that particular parable. Also, the elements of the parables often can only be interpreted by comparing Scripture with Scripture, then the Comparative Mention principle has to be applied.

5. The Context Principle – Because the Bible is one inspired whole, and the parables are part of the Bible, though not the whole of the Bible, interpretation will not contradict any other parts of the Bible. Parables will be interpreted in the context of the whole Bible, and not violate any other Scripture. Therefore verse context, passage context, chapter context, book context and Bible context will all harmonize together in a proper interpretation of the parables.

6. The Moral Principle – As has been seen, the Moral Principle is also involved in the exposition of parables. What is the major spiritual lesson of the parable all about? One can make the parables say too much or too little. The interpreter must avoid extreme interpretation,

not founded in Scripture but arising out of unScriptural imagination and allegorizaton.

7. The Chronometrical Principle – Some parables have a distinct "time element" seen in them. They deal with the past, the present and the future. This is seen in parables like that of "The Parable of Vineyard and the Husbandmen". In this parable we see Israel's past; persecuting, rejecting and killing the prophets; then the rejection and crucifixion of the beloved Son, and then the transference of the kingdom to the New Testament Church. The parable covers past, present and future. It has prophetic import.

Other hermeneutical principles may also be involved, depending on the contents of the parables. Parables, therefore, may be considered from the moral, practical, dispensational and prophetical viewpoints, depending on the contents. But sound hermeneutics is absolutely important for a sound interpretation of Christ's parables.

The parables touch, as it were, "two worlds": the natural and the spiritual, the earthly and the heavenly, the geographical locally and the world universally and the temporal and the eternal. They were spoken "then" but the truths therein are applicable "now". In interpreting the parables, "one has to learn to think Palestinally, parabollically, provincially, and culturally" (Dan Seagren).

(b) Sound Theology

This point has been noted quite fully in previous chapters. However, it is vitally important to follow through in parabolic interpretation within the boundaries of sound Biblical theology. The interpreter must not interpret the parables so as to contradict sound theology. Otherwise, extreme, fanciful, allegorical and even heretical explanations and interpretations of the parables are the result. The author has endeavoured to interpret the parables within the boundaries of sound theology.

E. The Practical Application of the Parable

After consistently following the format, the end result of all observation and interpretation is application. How can the truth be applied practically to a person's life, to our generation. It has been said: There is one interpretation, but many applications. This is a sound statement after:

1. What was said to them (the hearers)

2. What it meant to them (the hearers), and,

3. How was it applied to them (the hearers) has been properly dealt with. It is then the expositor can safely see what spiritual lesson, or lessons in the parable may be applied to us in our day.

Although the parables were spoken to Christ's generation, of individuals and people, the truth is applicable in every generation. As has been seen, truth is eternal. Can we learn from the parables: What Christ said, what Christ meant by what He said, and how Christ applied the truth to them in a very practical manner? The answer is indeed in the affirmative.

Paul's principle concerning the events in the history of Israel is surely applicable to the parables and words of Christ. "All these things (Israel's history, Christ's parables), happened to them for types and examples, and are written for our admonition upon whom the ends of the age are come" (1 Corinthians 10:6,11).

The ones who responded to Christ's parabolic teaching had their lives changed by accepting the moral of the parable. The same is true for all who have responsive hearts in this day and age. Application brings to bear upon the heart and life the moral of the parable, the moral principle.

Thus, **Observation, Interpretation and Application** is indeed "a threefold cord" that should not be broken (Ecclesiastes 4:12).

PART TWO

Parables
in the
Gospel of Matthew

CHAPTERS 7 – 23

CHAPTER SEVEN
THE THIRTEENTH CHAPTER OF MATTHEW

Undoubtedly the thirteenth chapter of Matthew's Gospel seems to be the proper place to begin when it comes to a study of the parables. There are, as it were, in this chapter, foundational "keys" that are needed to be used which unlock the door into the whole treasure-house of New Testamernt parables. Although the majority of parables are found in the Gospels of Matthew and Luke, and several in Mark's Gospel, Matthew 13 gives us the real reason why Jesus spoke in parables and some keys as to their interpretation.

Therefore, before proceeding with an exposition of the parables in the Synoptic Gospels, a consideration of these master keys in the thirteenth of Matthew will be necessary.

A. The Importance of Matthew 13

Most all expositors of the parables have recognized the significance of the thirteenth chapter of Matthew's Gospel. Some of their comments are worthy of consideration.

A.W. Pink says, "...from the standpoint of prophecy, the most important chapter of all the New Testament."

A.C. Gaebelein says, "If this one chapter could be rightly understood by the professional church, the consequences would be the most rewarding."

A. Edwin Wilson says, "This chapter is fundamental and primary because it is a chronological development of Christendom from the time of our Lord's first advent until His return."

There certainly is no chapter in the New Testament noted for its uniqueness of a continuous discourse of the parables of Jesus. In this chapter there are seven or possibly eight parables. Six are especially designated as such, while the first and the eighth do maintain the theme of "the kingdom" in them, though not specifically designated as parables. This text would follow those expositors who hold for eight parables. It is indeed a unique chapter because there seems to be a definate progression given in the seven of the eight parables. This will be seen in the appropriate chapters.

B. The Setting of Matthew 13

Matthew 13:1 opens with these words: "The same day went Jesus out of the house and sat by the seaside..." Significant words indeed! As the multitudes gathered to Him, He opened His mouth and began to teach in parables, the kingdom of heaven parables.

From verses 1-34 there are four parables given to the multitude, by the seashore, and outside the house. The parables of the sower and seed, the wheat and tares, the mustard see tree and the woman and the leaven are each given to the multitude.

In verse 36 there is a change. Jesus sent the multitude away and went into the house. There His disciples came to Him and ask for the explanation of the parable of the wheat and tares, which Jesus proceeded to give them. After that, Jesus gave several more parables, but these are to His disciples, inside the house. These were the parables of the treasure in the field, the pearl of great price, the net of fish and the instructed scribe.

Therefore, we have four parables to the multitude "outside the house" and four parables to His disciples "inside the house" to His own. "Outside the house" to the crowds and "inside the house" to His own speak of a physical yet symbolic act of Jesus the Messiah.

A brief overview of the previous chapters in Matthew's Gospel will bring Matthew 13 into a sharper focus.

1. Matthew 1. The genealogy and birth of the king.
2. Matthew 2. The wise men's visit and presentation to the king.
3. Matthew 3. The king's forerunner and the King's baptism.
4. Matthew 4. The king's temptation and calling of four disciples.
5. Matthew 5,6,7. The king's sermon on the mount- the laws of His kingdom.
6. Matthew 8,9. The power and demonstration of the king's kingdom.
7. Matthew 10. The king commissions the twelve apostles.
8. Matthew 11. The king's commendation of His forerunner, John the Baptist.
9. Matthew 12. The king's rejection of the religious leaders.

Chapter 12 is a climatic chapter. It concerns the Pharisees and Scribes and their rejection of Jesus.

* The Pharisees criticize Jesus and His disciples plucking corn on the Sabbath day (verses 1-8).

* The Pharisees take council to destroy Jesus after His healing the man with the withered arm on the Sabbath day (verses9-14).

* The Pharisees charge Jesus that He cast out devils by the prince of devils, Beelzebub, after His healing of a deaf and blind man (verses 22-30).

* Jesus then warns them of the danger of the unpardonable sin, the blasphemy against the Holy Spirit (verses 31-37).

* The Scribes and Pharisees ask Jesus for a sign, to which Jesus replies that the only sign an evil and adulterous generation would get is the sign of Calvary's three days and three nights, the sign of Christ's death, burial and resurrection, the sign of the prophet Jonah (verses 38-42).

The chapter closes with the warning that "this wicked generation" will be like a house cleansed of an unclean spirit, but being left swept and empty, seven other spirits more wicked than the first will enter that house. The result? The last state will be worse than the first. So shall it be also to this wicked generation (verses 30-35).

Jesus then repudiates His brethren after the flesh and acknowledges His true brothers and sisters as those who do the will of His Father in heaven (verses 46-50).

It is in the light of all this, the events of chapter 12, that: "The SAME DAY Jesus went out of the house and sat by the seashore..." (Matthew 13:1). "Outside the house" and "inside the house" certainly suggests some significant physical/symbolical act of Jesus and truth that He intended to convey. "The house" is symbolic truth, and "the sea" is symbolic truth.

It is the same truth as seen in the cleansings of the temple at the beginning and ending of His earthly ministry. In the first cleansing, He spoke of "My Father's house" (John 2:13-22). In the final cleansing He spoke of "My house" (Matthew 21:12-17). The religious leaders, Priests, Scribes and Pharisees, reject the cleansing and Christ's last words to them are to found in Matthew 23:37-39; 24:1-2. "Your house" is left unto desolate. No longer is it "My Father's house", but "your house" devoid of inhabitant. The glory of God in Christ departed and then Jesus proceeded to prophesy of the destruction of the temple under Prince Titus and the Roman armies in AD.70 which came to pass!

The New Testament writers in the Epistles from then on speak of the church as being "the Lord's hoiuse", "whose house are we", and the church is being built into "a spiritual house" (Read Hebrews 3:1-6; 1Peter 2:1-10; 1Timothy 3:15; Ephesians 2:19-22).

Without doubt, the "house of Judah", or, Jewry as a nation, had been swept and garnished by religious Judaism, but left empty. Insteading of receiving Jesus into the house, they rejected Him and opened the way, in that generation, to evil spirits. The disciples received Jesus and they became His house, which is the church of the living God.

"Outside the house", at the seaside (symbolic of peoples), He speaks in parables to the multitude, predominantly without interpretation. "Inside the house". He speaks to His own with interpretation. In John's words, "He came unto His own, and His own received Him not, but to as many as did receive Him, He gave them the power (right, privelege) to become the sons (the children) of God, even to them that believe on His name" (John 1:11-12).

C. Why Jesus Taught in Parables

After the first parable Jesus had spoken, the parable of the sower and seed, the disciples came to Him and asked Him "WHY do You speak to them in parables?" (Matthew 13:10; Mark 4:10; Luke 8:9). It is a good question and one that Jesus answered clearly.

Up to this period of time, the teaching of Jesus had been plain and clear. As a whole, the Gospel of Matthew, shows the teaching of Jesus in the laws of the kingdom, in the sermon on the mount (Matthew 5,6,7). Though there are some simple parabolic sayings in this sermon, the teaching basically is clear. But the Scribes, the Pharisees and the Sadducees have taken council to kill Jesus. Now Jesus changes His method of teaching, and from now on the rest of Matthew's Gospel provides a number of great parables of the kingdom. Matthew 13 seems to be the great foundational chapter of Christ's parables in this Gospel.

In the answer of Jesus to His disciples "Why?", Jesus shows them the real reason. To every "why" there is a "because". "BECAUSE it is given unto you to know the mysteries of the kingdom of heaven, but to them it is not given...BECAUSE they seeing see not, and hearing they hear not, neither do they understand..." (Matthew 13:11,13).

There are several things which needs to be considered in this answer of Jesus in Matthew 13:10-17.

1. Two Companies of People

Jesus separates the multitude and the disciples into two groups of people: "to you" and "to them" in Matthew 13:11,13. "You" and "them that are without" in

Mark 4:11. "You" and "others" in Luke 8:10. People make their decision to be with the Lord's disciples or with the others. It is either within or without. The choice is theirs to make.

2. **Twofold Spiritual Condition**

In Matthew 13:13-17 Jesus speaks of a twofold spiritual condition, pertaining to the "hearing" and the "seeing", or spiritual deafness and spiritual blindness. The multitude had ears to hear and heard not, and eyes to see and saw not. The disciples were blessed as they had ears and heard, and eyes to see and saw. The Scriptures in both the Old Testament and New Testament speak of these conditions and lament this in the people of God.

(a) **Ears to Hear, Hear Not, and Eyes to See, and See Not**

Ezekiel the prophet was sent to a rebellious people, having eyes to see and seeing not, and ears to hear and hearing not (Ezekiel 12:2). Jeremiah speaks to a foolish people who have eyes to see and see not, and ears to hear and hear not (Jeremiah 5:21). They are spiritually deaf, spiritually blind, and lack spiritual understanding. Isaiah also is sent to a people who have ears to hear and hear not, and eyes to see and see not. They are dull of hearing. They have heavy eyes. They have closed their ears and shut their eyes because they do not want to hear or see or understand and be healed (Isaiah 6:9-10).

Amos the prophet also prophesied of a famine, not a famine of food or water, and not even a famine of the words of the Lord, but a famine of HEARING the words of the Lord (Amos 8:11-12).

The Lord Jesus laments the same spiritual condition in His generation, quoting to the disciples the prophecy of Isaiah, which is one of Isaiah's most quoted prophecies by the New Testament writers (Matthew 13:13-15; Mark 4:11-12; Luke 8:9-10; John 12:37-41).

Finally, the apostle Paul quotes Isaiah, realizing the sad condition of the Jews of his generation, and seeing why God turned to the Gentiles for their salvation (Acts 28:25-28 with Romans 11:8).

(b) **Healing Deaf Ears, Opening Blinded Eyes**

There is no doubt that Jesus used the physical to point to the spiritual. Jesus was anointed to unstop deaf ears and open blinded eyes (Isaiah 61:1-2; Luke 4:18-19).

Jesus took a deaf man aside from the multitude and healed him (Mark 7:31-37). His ears were opened. Note also other deaf people healed (Matthew 11:5; Mark 9:25; Luke 7:22).

Jesus also took a man who was blind and led him out of town and healed him. His eyes were opened (Mark 8:22-26). Note also other people healed of blindness (Matthew 9:27-28; 11:5; 12:22; 15:30-31; 20:30; 21:14; Mark 10:46-51; Luke 7:21-22; John 5:3; 9:1-41; 10:21; 11:37; Revelation 3:17).

The Pharisees were "blind leaders of the blind people" (Matthew 15:14; 23:16,17,19,24,26; Luke 6:39). The Pharisees boasted they could see. They could see physically but were spiritually blind to the Christ of God.

The hearing ear and the seeing eye, the Lord has made even both of them (Proverbs 20:12). The Lord's final call, even to the seven churches in Asia, is to "have an ear to hear what the Spirit says to the churches" (Revelation 2:7,11,17,29; 3:6,13,22). To the church of Laodicea Jesus challenges them to buy eyesalve to anoint their eyes that they may see (Revelation 3:18).

This spiritual lesson from the parabolic teaching of Jesus is as applicable to the church today as it was to Christ's generation.

Jesus said that many of the prophets and righteous men desired to see and hear the things that the disciples were seeing and hearing. Peter said the prophets prophesied of the grace that would come to his – and our – generation (1Peter 1:10-12). One may think of the prophets; Elijah, Elisha, Isaiah, Jeremiah, Ezekiel, Joel, Amos, Zachariah and even Moses and Samuel, as well as other righteous men – all would love to have seen their prophecies fulfilled in the Christ of God.

The ears and eyes of the disciples were blessed because they were hearing and seeing such things in the ministry and person of Christ. He that has ears to hear, let him hear.

3. **The Heart Condition**

After all, it was a HEART condition which hindered the multitudes hearing and seeing what Jesus said. "This people's HEART is waxed gross". "The HEART of this people have grown dull" (Matthew 13:15.NKJV). Their ears are hard of hearing, their eyes they have closed, lest they should see with their eyes and hear with their ears should understand with their heart..." (Matthew 13:15).

Numerous Scriptures speak of the condition of the heart. Ears and eyes are external channels to the internal or inner man of the heart. If there is heart-trouble, then the hearing and seeing is affected.

Note how the Scriptures speak of the heart. The heart of man is deceitful above all things and desperately wicked, and only the Lord knows it (Jeremiah 17:9-10). The evil things that proceed out of the heart of man are the things that defile the man (Matthew 15:18-20; Mark 7:21-27). Jewry honoured the Lord with their lips but their heart was far from Him (Mark 7:6-7). The Lord asked Israel to love Him with all the heart, soul, mind and strength (Mark 12:28-33).

Jesus came to cleanse them and give them a new heart and a new spirit, and take away the stony heart out of them, and put His Spirit within them. The prophet Ezekiel had foretold this (Ezekiel 36:25-27). But Jewry refused and hardened their hearts against the Christ, the Son of the living God. This was another reason why the Lord spoke in parabolic form.

4. **Concealing or Revealing Truth**

Another reason why Jesus spoke in parables was a twofold reason: either to conceal or to reveal truth, according to the attitude of the listeners.

Undoubtedly the multitude heard the story on the surface, and heard and saw nothing beyond that. The disciples saw there was something deeper than the surface. Mark 4:10 tells us, "When He was alone, they that were about Him with the twelve asked Him of the parable..."

To the crowds, the parable concealed truth from them. To the disciples, the parable revealed truth to them. To the crowds, the parable was veiled, a hidden secret. To the disciples the parable was unveiled, an open secret. The same parable that concealed the truth from one is the same parable that revealed truth to another. "But without a parable spake He not unto them; and when they were alone, He expounded all things to His disciples" (Mark 4:34).

D. Mysteries, Parables, Dark Sayings

In Matthew 13, Jesus uses three significant designations relative to His parabolic teachings. He uses a significant quotation from the Book of Psalms also. These designations are, Mysteries, Parables and Dark Sayings. Each are worthy of our consideration for any study of the parables.

1. Mysteries of the Kingdom

The expression, "mysteries of the kingdom" is used in Matthew 13:11; Luke 8:10; Mark 4:11.

The word "mystery" is defined in Young's Concordance as "that which can only be known to the initiated". Strong's Concordance defines the Greek word, **"Musterion"** (SC3466), as "secret or mystery, through the idea of silence imposed by initiation into religious rites:- mystery. Includes **"Muo"** – to shut the mouth".

This is not a mystery which is hidden, something concealed or secret, which cannot be known. It is in the heathen religions, with their rites of initiation into the mysteries that the counterfeit is to be seen. The mysteries of the kingdom are revealed and yet concealed, because it is Christ Himself, by the ministry of the Holy Spirit, who initiates the believer – the true disciple – into the truths of the kingdom. Such cannot be found out by reason or the logic of man's wisdom. It is "the wisdom of God in a mystery, even the hidden wisdom, which God ordained before the world unto our glory..." (1Corinthians 2:7).

The parabolic teaching of Jesus was "a mystery concealed" to the unenlightened multitude, but the same teaching was "a mystery revealed" to the initiated disciples. It takes the Holy Spirit to initiate one into the mysteries of the kingdom of heaven. There are at least seventeen "Mysteries" spoken of in the New Testament writings, which are referred to more fully in the final parable of the instructed scribe at the close of Matthew 13.

The parables are mysteries of the kingdom of heaven, known only to those who have been initiated into their secrets. If that was true then, it is also true today. Christ, by the Holy Spirit, has to initiate His own into the truths of the parables, otherwise they will not hear or see them.

All mysteries fall into either of two catergories: those pertaining to the "Mystery of Godliness" (1Timothy 3:16), or the "Mystery of Iniquity" (2Thessalonians 2:7).

2. Parables of the Kingdom

Not much needs to be added to the definition of this word as the subject of the kingdom has been covered in the earlier chapter.

Arlen L. Chitwood, in "Mysteries of the Kingdom" (p.6), explains the word "parable" as follows. The Greek word for parable means "cast alongside". It is a truth cast alongside a previous truth to help explain the previous truth. For those who had rejected the previous truth, the parable would hold little meaning. But for those who had accepted the previous truth, the parable would cast additional light upon truth already given (Matthew 13:10-17).

And **Dan Seagren,** in **"The Parables"** (p.19) defines the word "parable" by saying: A parable is an ingenious figure of speech, usually a short story of everyday life, which teaches a singular truth, as well as suggesting subordinate truths."

3. Dark Sayings of the Kingdom

In Matthew 13:34-35, it says, "All these things spake Jesus unto the multitude in parables, and without a parable spake He not unto them. That it might be fulfilled which was spoken by the prophet saying, I will open My mouth in parables, I will utter things which have been kept secret from the foundation of the world."

Jesus is actually quoting from a Psalm of Asaph. "I will open my mouth in a parable. I will utter dark sayings of old" (Psalm 78:1-2).

Mysteries, Parables, Dark Sayings or secrets – all speaking of one and the same method of Christ's teaching.

The Hebrew word for "dark saying" (SC 2420, from 2330), is "to tie a knot (ie., fig), to propound a riddle; a puzzle, hence a trick, conundrum, sententious maxim", and is translated "dark saying, sentence, speech, hard question, proverb, riddle" (Psalm 78:2; 49:4). The Psalmist says, "I will incline my ear to a parable (proverb), I will open my dark saying upon the harp". It is a Psalm of the sons of Asaph.

The Psalm of Asaph anticipates prophetically Christ's use of parables and dark sayings in the mysteries of the kingdom.

The New Testament Greek speaks of the word "secret" (SC 2928. Grk. **"Krupto"**), as meaning "to conceal (prop. by covering)". It is translated "hide self, keep secret, secret, secretly". Paul speak of his Gospel as being kept secret as a mystery from before the world began (Romans 16:25).

So the parables of Christ are like "dark sayings", puzzles, riddles, conundrums and have to be discerned as to the parts in order to discover the truth.

4. Doctrine of the Kingdom

Mark's Gospel adds one other designation in Mark 4:2. "And He taught them many thing by parables, and said unto them in His doctrine..."

The word "doctrine" simply means "teaching". The parables of Jesus were a form or method of teaching. There is doctrine or teaching of the kingdom in the parables of Jesus. It is parabolic teaching but it was Christ's method in much of His latter ministry.

This part of "all Scripture" is inspired of God and is profitable for doctrine, for reproof, for correction and for instruction in righteousness, that the man and woman of God may be perfect, thoroughly equipped for every good work (2Timothy 3:16-17).

E. Use or Lose

In concluding this introductory chapter to the parables of Matthew 13, a consideration is given to a peculiar saying of Jesus within the context of "hearing, seeing and understanding". It is a peculiar saying and it is used at least five times by Jesus in connection with His parables. Therefore there is some significance in it.

"For whosoever has, to him will more be given, and he will have abundance; but whoever does not have, even what he has shall be taken away from him" (Matthew 13:12). It is used in Mark 4:25 in connection with having ears to hear. It is also used in Luke 8:18 in connection with hearing. And it is used in Luke 19:26 in connection with the parables of the pounds, whether used or unused.

The message in this peculiar verse seems to be: Use or lose! We lose what we do not use! Hearing and seeing – use our ears to hear, and our eyes to see, or else we lose the use of them. Talents or pounds – use them for the Lord, or hide them and we lose them. We will lose what we do not use is the message.

To those who have an hearing ear, more will be given. To those who do not have any hearing ear, they will lose even what they seem to have. To those who have a faithful, servant spirit, and use their talents or pounds, more will be given. To those who are slothful, and do not use their talents or pounds they will also lose what they did not use. In the context of the this peculiar parabolic saying, Jesus said:-

1. Take heed WHAT you hear (Mark 4:24). That is, the material you listen to.

2. Take heed HOW you hear (Luke 8:18). That is, the attitude in which you listen.

Conclusion:-

Without a doubt, the truths in this great chapter are applicable, not only for Christ's generation, but this generation in which we live. The truths in this chapter become foundational and preparatory to the chapters and exposition of the parables. Christian preachers and teachers can surface-read the parables and receive little from them. Some may read and throw the exposition aside as allegorization. Others will take heed WHAT they read and HOW they read and will be enriched in their relationship with the Lord, and help other believers in the Body of Christ to a greater understanding of the things of the kingdom. We can join the crowd or be His disciples. The choice is ours! The writer believes "the keys" of interpreting the parables are to be found in Matthew Chapter 13.

CHAPTER EIGHT
THE PARABLE OF THE SOWER AND SEED

A. The Scriptures on the Parable

1. Matthew 13:3-23

And he spoke many things unto them in parables, saying, Behold, a sower went forth to sow;

And when he sowed, some seeds fell by the way side, and the fowls came and devoured them up:

Some fell upon stony places, where they had not much earth: and forthwith they sprung up, because they had no deepness of earth:

And when the sun was up, they were scorched; and because they had no root, they withered away.

And some fell among thorns; and the thorns sprung up, and choked them:

But other fell into good ground, and brought forth fruit, some an hundredfold, some sixtyfold, some thirtyfold.

Who hath ears to hear, let him hear.

And the disciples came, and said unto him, Why speakest thou unto them in parables?

He answered and said unto them, Because it is given unto you to know the mysteries of the kingdom of heaven, but to them it is not given.

For whosoever hath, to him shall be given, and he shall have more abundance: but whosoever hath not, from him shall be taken away even that he hath.

Therefore speak I to them in parables: because they seeing see not; and hearing they hear not, neither do they understand.

And in them is fulfilled the prophecy of Esaias, which saith, By hearing ye shall hear, and shall not understand; and seeing ye shall see, and shall not perceive:

For this people's heart is waxed gross, and their ears are dull of hearing, and their eyes they have closed; lest at any time they should see with their eyes, and hear with their ears, and should understand with their heart, and should be converted, and I should heal them.

But blessed are your eyes, for they see: and your ears, for they hear.

For verily I say unto you, That many prophets and righteous men have desired to see those things which ye see, and have not seen them; and to hear those things which ye hear, and have not heard them.

Hear ye therefore the parable of the sower.

When any one heareth the word of the kingdom, and understandeth it not, then cometh the wicked one, and catcheth away that which was sown in his heart. This is he which received seed by the way side.

But he that received the seed into stony places, the same is he that heareth the word, and anon with joy receiveth it;

Yet hath he not root in himself, but dureth for a while: for when tribulation or persecution ariseth because of the word, by and by he is offended.

He also that received seed among the thorns is he that heareth the word; and the care of this world, and the deceitfulness of riches, choke the word, and he becometh unfruitful.

But he that received seed into the good ground is he that heareth the word, and understandeth it; which also beareth fruit, and bringeth forth, some an hundredfold, some sixty, some thirty.

2. Mark 4:1-20

And he began again to teach by the sea side: and there was gathered unto him a great multitude, so that he entered into a ship, and sat in the sea; and the whole multitude was by the sea on the land.

And he taught them many things by parables, and said unto them in his doctrine,

Hearken; Behold, there went out a sower to sow:

And it came to pass, as he sowed, some fell by the way side, and the fowls of the air came and devoured it up.

And some fell on stony ground, where it had not much earth; and immediately it sprang up, because it had no depth of earth:

But when the sun was up, it was scorched; and because it had no root, it withered away.

And some fell among thorns, and the thorns grew up, and choked it, and it yielded no fruit.

And other fell on good ground, and did yield fruit that sprang up and increased; and brought forth, some thirty, and some sixty, and some an hundred.

And he said unto them, He that hath ears to hear, let him hear.

And when he was alone, they that were about him with the twelve asked of him the parable.

And he said unto them, Unto you it is given to know the mystery of the kingdom of God: but unto them that are without, all these things are done in parables:

That seeing they may see, and not perceive; and hearing they may hear, and not understand; lest at any time they should be converted, and their sins should be forgiven them.

And he said unto them, Know ye not this parable? and how then will ye know all parables?

The sower soweth the word.

And these are they by the way side, where the word is sown; but when they have heard, Satan cometh immediately, and taketh away the word that was sown in their hearts.

And these are they likewise which are sown on stony ground; who, when they have heard the word, immediately receive it with gladness;

And have no root in themselves, and so endure but for a time: afterward, when affliction or persecution ariseth for the word's sake, immediately they are offended.

And these are they which are sown among thorns; such as hear the word,

And the cares of this world, and the deceitfulness of riches, and the lusts of other things entering in, choke the word, and it becometh unfruitful.

And these are they which are sown on good ground; such as hear the word, and receive it, and bring forth fruit, some thirtyfold, some sixty, and some an hundred.

3. Luke 8:4-15

And when much people were gathered together, and were come to him out of every city, he spake by a parable:

A sower went out to sow his seed: and as he sowed, some fell by the way side; and it was trodden down, and the fowls of the air devoured it.

And some fell upon a rock; and as soon as it was sprung up, it withered away, because it lacked moisture.

And some fell among thorns; and the thorns sprang up with it, and choked it.

And other fell on good ground, and sprang up, and bare fruit an hundredfold. And when he had said these things, he cried, He that hath ears to hear, let him hear.

And his disciples asked him, saying, What might this parable be?

And he said, Unto you it is given to know the mysteries of the kingdom of God: but to others in parables; that seeing they might not see, and hearing they might not understand.

Now the parable is this: The seed is the word of God.

Those by the way side are they that hear; then cometh the devil, and taketh away the word out of their hearts, lest they should believe and be saved.

They on the rock are they, which, when they hear, receive the word with joy; and these have no root, which for a while believe, and in time of temptation fall away.

And that which fell among thorns are they, which, when they have heard, go forth, and are choked with cares and riches and pleasures of this life, and bring no fruit to perfection.

But that on the good ground are they, which in an honest and good heart, having heard the word, keep it, and bring forth fruit with patience.

B. The Setting of the Parable

Enough has been written on the setting of the parable in the previous chapter. Briefly, however, the setting is by the seashore. Jesus is outside of the house He has been in. Some would suggest the house from Capernaum, His own city, close to the seashore, and seaside of Galilee. He enters a boat and sat down to teach. The multitude stand on the seashore (Matthew 13:1-2; Mark 4:1-2). Luke emphasizes that many people had come out of their cities to gather to Him and hear the teaching. Jesus is sitting. The people are standing.

C. The Moral of the Parable

As dealt with previously, all parables have a major moral, or central spiritual truth, and many have subordinate truths. So it is with the parable of the sower and the seed. The moral of the parable is seen in the following. All who sow the seed-word of the gospel of the kingdom have to recognize that there will be different responses in the hearts of the hearers. The fault is not in the seed-word, but the fault is in the ground of the hearers hearts and the results depend on their attitude to the seed-word. That is the major truth of the parable and there are many other supplemental truths which contribute to this, as will be seen in the exposition of this first and foundational parable in Matthew 13.

D. The Key to all Parables

There can be little misunderstanding of this parable, for Jesus Himself interpreted it for us. Each of the Synoptics confirm this. Before we consider the parts of the parable and the additional truths that support the central truth therein, we need to see that this first parable seems to be the key to all parables.

Mark's gospel implies that this parable is like a key to all the parables. The disciples alone with Jesus asked Him about the parable of the sower and the seed. Jesus said to them, "Do you not discern and understand this parable? How then is it possible for you to discern and understand all the parables? (Amp.N.T. Mark 4:13). If they understood not this first parable, how then will they understand any of the other parables?

Understanding the way Jesus interpreted this first parable and its parts provides the expositor with clues on how to interpret other parables of Jesus. For those expositors who maintain that there is ever only one major truth in any parable, and the parts of the parable are only parts of the story and not to be pressed for any additional, supportive or supplemental truths, Jesus certainly does not follow that line of thinking.

Jesus Himself takes most of the parts of the parable, and interprets such as having some symbolic significance and truth. Although there may be a central truth in the parable, the parts of the parable supply supplemental truths. This fact cannot be ignored or the expositor will miss much that Jesus taught in the parables. He Himself is the perfect hermeneutician and the example of parabolic explanation and interpretation (Luke 24:25-27).

E. The Exposition of the Parable

1. The Sower

In each of the Synoptic gospels it simply says, "A sower went forth to sow..." Jesus does not interpret who the sower is in any of the gospels in this parable. However, within the context of the whole of Scripture, one may safely interpret the sower in the parable in the following manner.

(a) The Lord Jesus Himself

Without doubt, Jesus Himself is THE sower of all sowers. Matthew 13:3 with verse 37 would point to the fact that Jesus, the Son of Man, is the sower. He came and sowed the seed-word of the kingdom. He came preaching and teaching the word of the kingdom.

Although the words of Psalm 126:5-6 are applicable to any earthly sower of seed, surely they can also be applied to Jesus as the heavenly sower. "They that sow in tears shall reap in joy. He that goeth forth and weepeth, bearing precious seed, shall doubtless come again, with rejoicing, bringing his sheaves with him."

Jesus came the first time, weeping over Jerusalem and His people. He sowed the precious seed of the kingdom. He has returned to the Father. But He will doubtless come again the second time, with rejoicing, bringing the harvest sheaves with Him (Luke 19:41; John 14:3; Acts 1:11). This parable speaks of the time of sowing, not reaping as yet.

(b) The Holy Spirit

Another application of "the sower of seed" could be the ministry of the Holy Spirit. Jesus is "the Word, the Divine Seed", and the Holy Spirit sows that Seed of the Word in the hearts of people. The Holy Spirit was sent forth to plant the Seed of the Divine Word in the hearts of mankind. So the Holy Spirit can be seen as the sower of the Seed-Word of the Kingdom. In this sense, we would see the Sower as the Spirit, and the Seed as THE WORD! (John 14:26;15:26).

(c) All Believers

The truth would also be applicable to any and all believers, any and all ministers of the gospel. Untold thousands of believers, preachers and teachers and ministers of the gospel have been sowing the seed of the kingdom over generations of church history. Paul says that one sows and another reaps (1Corinthians 3:6-9). It is God who gives the increase. The seed of the word in the believers was scattered in the persecution in Acts (Acts8:4).

Proverbs 11:18 speaks of those who sow righteousness. Jesus speaks of the sower and the reaper rejoicing together in the time of harvest (John 4:35-38). The prophets and righteous men of Old Testament times sowed seed. The apostles of New Testament times were going out to reap the harvest.

Psalm 126:5-6 is also applicable to all who have sowed the gospel word. Many have sown with tears and with their tears have they watered that seed. There will be a time of rejoicing in the final harvest. Sowers and reapers will rejoice together with Jesus in that day. There can be no reaping without sowing. The sower and the reaper need each other, and neither can rejoice without the other. Both will rejoice together in the end of the age. Sowing is the beginning. Reaping is the end.

2. The Seed

There is no mistaking the interpretation of the symbol of the seed. Jesus clearly interprets this part of the parable. The seed is THE WORD!

In Mark 4:14, the sower sows THE WORD (Mark 4:15,16,17,18,19,20).

In Matthew 13:19 is the Word of THE KINGDOM (Matthew 13:20,21,22,23).

In Luke 8:11, the seed is the Word of GOD (Luke 8:12,13,15).

The whole emphasis in this parable is on "the word" (Grk. "Logos"). We speak of Christ, the Living Word, the Bible as the Written Word. The Samaritan believers received "the word" (Acts 8:16).

Peter speaks of "being born again, not of corruptible seed, but of incorruptible seed, by the word of God, which lives and abides for ever" (1Peter 1:23). John confirms the truth of being born again of the seed (the Divine sperm) of God (1John 3:9; John 1:12-13). The sower goes forth bearing the precious seed of the word (Psalm 126:5-6).

It should be seen that there is nothing wrong with the seed of the word of the kingdom.Through this seed one can be born of God, born again into the kingdom of God (John 3:1-12). It is the word of the kingdom (The Student is referred to the Chapter on "The Church & The Kingdom").

The seed of the word has all the Divine potential in it. It is an incorruptible seed, a sinless seed, an immortal seed, a perfect seed, a Divine seed. There is no fault in the seed. It is the word of God. The sower sows THE SEED, THE WORD of the living God, the Word of the Kingdom!

3. The Soil

The Lord Jesus interprets this part of the parable also. The ground symbolizes the human heart. Each of the Gospels confirm this truth (Matthew 13:19; Mark 4:15; Luke 8:12,15). It is a heart condition which determines the response to the word of the kingdom. It is the heart condition about which the prophet Isaiah spoke (Isaiah 6:9-10 with Matthew 13:14-15).

There is no fault with the seed of the word. The problem is with the soil, the heart of the hearer. Each of the four kinds of soil had the same seed fall upon them. Matthew uses the expression, "...he that received the seed..." at least four times (Matthew 13:19,20,20,22,23). The seed of the kingdom fell on each kind of soil, but in each there was a different response. Jesus mentions four types of soil, or four types of heart conditions, representing four kinds of response. Jesus Himself also interprets these parts of the parable; the four conditions of the ground in human hearts. There can be no mistaken interpretation here. Here we see the four classes of hearers: the receptivity, the response, the reaction and the results!

(a) The Wayside Hearer – Matthew 13:4 with verse 19

Each of the Synoptics speak of the wayside hearer (Mark 4:15; Luke 8:12). In every proclamation of the Gospel of the Kingdom, in every congregation of listeners, there are the wayside hearers. The Gospels show some of the characteristics of the wayside hearers.

* They **hear** the word of the kingdom. It is only a surface hearing. The word does not sink down into their ears (Luke 9:44-45). The word goes in one ear and out the other, so to speak. They had ears to hear physically but never really heard spiritually.
* They do not **understand** the word. The word "understand" is used several times in Matthew 13:13,14,15,19,23. There is no comprehension of the word. Instead of the understanding being enlightened, their understanding is darkened (Ephesians 1:18; 4:18).
* The seed is **trodden down,** or, trodden underfoot.
* The **wicked one** (Matthew), Satan (Mark), the devil (Luke), or the fowls of the air devour the seed, catching away the seed that was sown in the heart. Unclean birds are symbolic of evil spirits (Revelation 18:2; Genesis 15:11; Leviticus 11). Satan and evil spirits are always there to make sure the word does not get into the hearts of men. Birds of doubt, unbelief, criticism, pride and prejudice and other 'unclean birds' take away the seed of God's word sown in the heart by preaching, testimony or teaching. These same birds are also seen in Parable three, the Parable of the Mustard Seed Tree.
* The seed is **taken away immediately.** There is no chance or time to produce some result in the heart. It is immediately taken away. They hear it. They lose it.
* The word is taken out of their hearts lest they should be believe and be **saved.** They never are converted to Christ. They never really believe on the Lord Jesus Christ and they are never saved (Acts 15:11; 16:31; Romans 10:9-10). The heart is hard, unbroken, unresponsive, unreceptive and therefore there are no results. The sower still must sow the seed, the word regardless of the results.

This is the wayside hearer. This is the condition of the heart. There is absolutely nothing wrong with the seed but the fault is entirely with the soil. It is open to Satan and demonic activity, snatching the seed out of the heart as it is sown. The wayside hearers do not come to saving faith in Christ.

(b) The Stony Ground Hearer

Each of the Synoptics speak of the stony or rocky places, the stony ground. A visit to the Middle East certainly confirms the truth of "stony ground." The ground in many, many places is indeed very stony. The hearers would certainly understand and interpret what Christ said here.

Jesus, once again, interprets this part of the parable, so there can be no mistaken interpretation here. The Synoptics show the characteristics of the stony ground hearers.

* They **hear** the word and immediately receive it with joy. Simon was an example of this kind of hearer (Acts 8:9-20).
* The stony places do not have much earth. **Shallowness** is their characteristic.
* The stony places allow the seed to spring up quickly. They immediately receive the word with joy and gladness. Immediate response. Too quick to really last.

* The stony places have **no depth.** Surface experience, emotional response is their lot.

* The stony places are **scorched by the sun.** This is interpreted as tribulation or persecution which comes on the stony ground hearer. Aflliction or temptation comes upon them. The heat is applied.

* The seed in the stony places had **no root** and soon withered away (Ephesians 3:17; Colossians 2:7). The root speaks of foundation. They have no root in themselves.

* They endure only for a **short time.** They only believe for a while.

* They are finally **offended** and stumbled and they do not last as a believer for very long. The Psalmist speaks of those who love God's law, and nothing shall offend them (Psalm 119:165). They do not have enough love to overcome being offended because of the word (Note also Matthew 11:6; 13:57; 24:10; Mark 4:17; Luke 7:23). Offences or scandals come over serving Christ. Deep love for the word will overcome any and every offence of the cross.

* They **fall away.**

* They lack **moisture,** according to Luke 8:6. Moisture is what makes the seed grow and take further root.

This is the stony ground hearer. This kind of hearer is different from the wayside hearer. The stony ground hearer hears and receives the word, is excited about it, responds to it and even believes it. There is, however, no real depth in his experience. There is no deep root in his experience and relationship with the Lord. He is a shallow believer. In time, the pressure, trials and persecution for being a Christian arises. He does not last long as a believer. He becomes easily offended and falls away, all through a lack of deep love for the Lord and for the word of the kingdom.

(c) The Thorny Ground Hearer

Each of the Gospels also speak of the thorny ground hearer. Jesus also interprets this symbolic part of the parable. Once again there is no mistaking the interpretation. The Synoptics show the characteristics of the thorny ground hearers, each of the Gospels supplying a particular aspect of the truth about the thorns or the thorny ground hearers.

* They also heard the word (Luke 8:14; Hebrews 6:8).

* They not only heard the word, they also **received** the word.

* They allowed the word to be **choked by thorns** that entered in and sprung up in their hearts. The symbolism of the thorns are defined very clearly for us in the Gospels. The reader is encouraged to read the Scripture references in connection with the various thorns the Gospels mention. The word is choked in their lives.

(1) The thorns of the cares of this age – Mark 8:36; Romans 12:1-2; Colossians 1:4; Ephesians 2:2; 2Timothy 4:10; 1John 2:15-17.

(2) The thorns of the deceitfulness of riches – Mark 10:23-25; Proverbs 11:28; 23:5; 1Timothy 6:9,10,17; Matthew 19:21-22. Although riches in themselves are not evil, when they possess the owner they become

evil. It is the love of money that is the root of all evils. There are numerous warnings against deception in the Bible.

(3) The thorns of the lusts of other things – 1Corinthians 10:6; Galatians 5:16,24; Romans 6:12; 13:14; Ephesians 2:3; 2Timothy 2:22; 1John 2:16-17; 1Peter4:3. The word "lust" speaks of unlawful desires, desires contrary to the word of God.

(4) The thorns of the pleasures of this life – 2Timothy 3:4; Titus 3:3; Hebrews 11:25. The pleasures of sin, the pleasures of this world and other lusts and pleasures take the place of those pleasures which are at the right hand of God (Psalm 16:11; 36:6).

* These become **unfruitful**. They yield no fruit; they bring no fruit unto maturity in the Lord. They are unfruitful believers. Jesus wants His own to become fruitful, as the teaching of the vine and branches show (John 15:1-16).

The thorny ground hearers are like the stony ground hearers. They receive the word of the kingdom, but the thorns (the result of the entrance of sin and the curse – Genesis 3:18; Jeremiah 4:3; 12:13) of worldly cares, deceitful riches, life's pleasure and the lusts of other things, enter in and choke the word. The end result is unfruitfulness in this persons life; or, at the most, fruit that is immature.

This believer becomes slothful and allows the thorns to come in and destroy the word and work of God in his life, even as the slothful man of the vineyard in the Book of Proverbs does (Proverbs 24:30-34; 15:19 with Hebrews 6:7,8,12).

(d) The Good Ground Hearers

Again, each of the Synoptics speak of the good ground hearers. Jesus interprets for us the truth hidden in the symbolic good ground. Each of the Gospels provide characteristics of the good ground hearers.

* They **hear** the word of the kingdom.
* They **understand** the word of the kingdom.
* They **receive** the word of the kingdom. The word is accepted in the heart.
* They **keep** the word of the kingdom.
* They have **good and honest** hearts. Various translations say they have a noble, virtuous, worthy, good and honest heart (KJV; NKJV; NIV). The ground of their heart has been broken open and is ready to receive the seed of the word of God (Hosea 10:12). Proverbs tells us to guard our heart, for out of it comes the issues of life (Proverbs 4:23).

Taking the general meaning of 'honesty' would mean that these hearers are (1) honest with God: (2) honest with themselves, and: (3) honest with others.

* They bring **fruit.** In contrast to the thorny ground hearer who is unfruitful, bringing no fruit to maturity, the good ground hearer brings forth fruit in varying degress. They bring forth fruit in their Christian life – fruit unto the glory of God. Jesus speaks of degrees of fruitfulness in this company of hearers.

(1) Some one hundredfold. Isaac reaped one hundredfold in one year as the Lord blessed his harvest (Genesis 26:12).

(2) Some sixtyfold. A lesser degree of fruitfulness.

(3) Some thirtyfold. Still a lesser degree of fruitfulness.

These speak of degrees of fruitfulness in peoples lives. Jesus spoke of "fruit" (thirtyfold), "more fruit" (sixtyfold), and "much fruit" (one hundredfold) in the fruitfulness of the believer abiding in Him (John 15:1-16). Undoubtedly degrees of fruitfulness in ones life is determined by the degree of commitment to the Lord. Often believers measure of commitment to the Lord is thirtyfold, sixtyfold, more or less, and there are those who are one hundredfold in their commitment to Christ. These bring forth fruit one hundredfold unto the Lord.

* They bring forth fruit with **patience**, that is, endurance. Fruit is not produced in one night or day. It takes time for the fruit to form and to come to maturity. Fruit has to receive the blessings of the seasons; the sun, the rains, the winds, both before and after harvest times.

The good ground hearers have these characteristics. In the analogy and symbolism of this parable, Jesus is not so much speaking of fruit as on fruit trees, but the fruit of grain, probably wheat grain. Jesus spoke of the seed of the kingdom; first the blade, then the ear (head), and then the full corn in the ear (full grain in the head). Read Mark 4:26,27 (KJV with NKJV).

The grain has to ripen for the harvest. The "fruit" here more likely points to "the fruit of the Spirit" (Galatians 5:22-23), and "the fruit of righteousness" (Ephesians 5:9; Hebrews 12:11; James 3:18).

The corn of wheat reproduces itself in fruit "after his kind." So the one who receives the seed of the word of the kingdom will manifest the life of the kingdom. Fruit reveals the inner nature and character of the grain. The word of the kingdom (the seed) will produce righteousness, peace and joy in the Holy Spirit (the fruit of the kingdom – Romans 14:17).

F. The Application of the Parable

Jesus gives both the parable and the interpretation of the parable, working from part to whole and whole to part. By using the column format, it can be seen how Jesus interprets the parable by interpreting the symbolic parts of the parable.

The Parable Symbols	Interpretation of the Parable
1. The sower	The Son of Man (or believers)
2. The seed	The word of the kingdom
3. The soil	The human heart
Wayside ground	Hearers who are not saved
Stony ground	Hearers, respond, but fall away
Thorny ground	Hearers, respond, no mature fruit
Good ground	Hearers, respond, degrees of fruit
4. The birds	Satan and evil spirits
5. The sun	Persecution, pressure, trials
6. The thorns	Worldly cares, riches, pleasures, lusts
7. The fruit, 30, 60, 100 fold	Degrees of fruitfulness in believers

In each case, all **heard the word,** all **received the seed,** but there were **different responses** to what they heard and what they received. The reader is reminded of what has been referred to in previous chapters concerning necessity of having "ears to hear."

1. What the Prophets said

The prophet Isaiah was sent to a people who had ears to hear, eyes to see, and a heart to perceive, but they failed to hear, see and understand (Isaiah 6:9-10).

The prophet Jeremiah lamented that he also had to speak to a people who did not spiritually see or hear (Jeremiah 5:21).

The prophet Ezekiel also laments the same spiritual condition of the people to which he ministered (Ezekiel 12:2).

The prophet Amos spoke of the time when there would be a famine of hearing the word of the Lord. The famine was not in the word, but the famine was in the **hearing** of the word (Amos 8:11-13).

2. What the Gospels and Acts said

On six occasions in the Gospels, Jesus Himself (THE WORD made flesh – John 1:1-3,14-18) spoke about the necessity of hearing. "He that has ears to hear, let him hear" (Matthew 11:15; 13:9,43; Mark 4:9,23; 7:16; Luke 8:8,35). He also took up the prophetic word of Isaiah concerning the people having ears to hear and hearing not, and eyes to see and seeing not, and a heart to perceive but understanding not ((Matthew 13:9-17).

The Book of Acts closes with Paul's word to the unbelieving Jews. He also uses the same quotation from the prophet Isaiah concerning their spiritual state of deafness and blindess (Acts 28:25-27).

3. What Revelation says

Eight times in the Book of Revelation it speaks of "having an ear to hear", with the additional phrases, "what the Spirit says", "unto the churches." There is also this difference. The word "ear" is always in the singular in Revelation, while it is used in the plural in the Gospels.

In the Gospels is it THE WORD made flesh speaking. He is with them in person. In the Revelation it is THE SPIRIT speaking and this demands a more sensitive listening. The word is to the churches of which Christ speaks in Matthew's Gospel, when He said, "I will build My Church" (Matthew 16:15-19).

To the seven churches He says: "He that has an ear to hear, let him hear what the Spirit says to the churches "(Revelation 2:7,11,17,29; 3:6,13,22). The final mention of this exhortation is found in Revelation 13:9. "The Spirit" and "the churches", however, are not mentioned in this particular occasion and surely this is significant in this period of time and trouble in the earth.

It is all a matter of truly **hearing** the word. Biblical hearing is obedience to the word. It is never the fault of the seed of the word. The fault is in the heart condition of the hearer. There is need for "ear inspection" and "heart examination" by the Great Physician, the Lord Jesus Christ Himself.

The Bible speaks of:
1. Dull ears (Acts 28:26,27; Hebrews 5:11)
2. Uncircumcised ears (Acts 7:51)
3. Itching ears (2Timothy 4:3-4)
5. Forgetful ears (James 1:22-25)
6. Hearing ears (Proverbs 20:12)
7. Opened ears (Psalm 40:5-9)
8. Obedient ears (Proverbs 25:12).

It is no wonder that Jesus says to "take heed WHAT we hear" (Luke 8:18), as well as "take heed HOW we hear" (Mark 4:23-25). To the hearing ear, more will be given.

The Bible speak of:
1. A rebellious and revolting heart (Jeremiah 5:23)
2 An uncircumcised heart (Jeremiah 4:4; 9:26)
3. A heart that is deceitful and desperately wicked (Jeremiah 17:5,9,10)
4. A clean heart and broken and contrite spirit (Psalm 51:10,17)
5. A new heart (Ezekiel 36:26)
6. A heart that knows God (Jeremiah,24:7).

For other Scriptures on the heart, read also the words of Jesus in Matthew 12:34-35; 15:18-19; 13:15,19; Mark 7:17-21. The Lord wants to writes His laws in our heart and mind under the New Covenant (Jeremiah 31:31-34).

Because the hearing and the heart are connected relative to the reception and response to the word of the kingdom, the heart needs to be guarded, for out of it are indeed the issues of life (Proverbs 4:23).

Conclusion:

Such are the great lessons to be learned from this first parable of Jesus in Matthew 13: the parable of the sower, the seed and the soil. The primary lesson is the varying response to the word of the kingdom. It shows the absolute necessity of keeping the heart with all diligence in order to come to any or a full measure of fruitfulness in the word of the kingdom.

It will be seen that, beside the central truth, there are a number of supplemental or supportive truths which together make the complete truth in this parable. For those expositors who say that the parts of the parable are only periphial, and not to be made much of, Jesus' interpretation of the parts of the parable refute that theory. Jesus works from part to whole and whole to part. In doing this, He provides interpretative keys to other uninterpreted parables. The interpretation of the parable is within the context of Scripture and sound theology.

In summary:

The word of the kingdom is preached under all circumstances. The hearts of the hearers have various conditions and therefore the responses vary. Some hear and never understand and are never saved. Others hear, respond and fall away. Others hear, respond but never bring forth mature fruit. Others are more noble, respond, and bring forth degrees of fruitfulness according to their degree of commitment to Christ. So the fourfold kinds of hearers are in all the world, and will be unto the coming of Christ. Any one who sows the word of the kingdom must recognize the truth of this parable and not be discouraged. "He who has ears to hear, let him hear."

CHAPTER NINE
THE PARABLE OF THE WHEAT AND TARES

A. The Scriptures on the Parable
1. Matthew 13:24-30

Another parable put he forth unto them, saying, The kingdom of heaven is likened unto a man which sowed good seed in his field:

But while men slept, his enemy came and sowed tares among the wheat, and went his way.

But when the blade was sprung up, and brought forth fruit, then appeared the tares also.

So the servants of the householder came and said unto him, Sir, didst not thou sow good seed in thy field? from whence then hath it tares?

He said unto them, An enemy hath done this. The servants said unto him, Wilt thou then that we go and gather them up?

But he said, Nay; lest while ye gather up the tares, ye root up also the wheat with them.

Let both grow together until the harvest: and in the time of harvest I will say to the reapers, Gather ye together first the tares, and bind them in bundles to burn them: but gather the wheat into my barn.

2. Matthew 13:36-43

Then Jesus sent the multitude away, and went into the house: and his disciples came unto him, saying, Declare unto us the parable of the tares of the field.

He answered and said unto them, He that soweth the good seed is the Son of man;

The field is the world; the good seed are the children of the kingdom; but the tares are the children of the wicked one;

The enemy that sowed them is the devil; the harvest is the end of the world; and the reapers are the angels.

As therefore the tares are gathered and burned in the fire; so shall it be in the end of this world.

The Son of man shall send forth his angels, and they shall gather out of his kingdom all things that offend, and them which do iniquity;

And shall cast them into a furnace of fire: there shall be wailing and gnashing of teeth.

Then shall the righteous shine forth as the sun in the kingdom of their Father. Who hath ears to hear, let him hear.

B. The Setting of the Parable

The setting of the parable is the same as for the parable of the sower and the seed. Jesus is sitting in the boat and the multitude is standing on the seashore (Matthew 13:1-2). The parable, however, is given to the multitude but the interpretation of the parable is given to the disciples in the house, privately by Jesus, and not to the multitude on the seashore (vs 36-43). The interpretation is given to the disciples in response to their question to Jesus about this parable.

C. The Moral of the Parable

The central truth or moral of the parable is seen in the following. The kingdom of heaven in its present state has mixture in it, mixture of good and evil. This condition will prevail unto the end of the age and the coming of Christ. At this time the great separation will take place; the separation of the wicked and the righteous, and the eternal destinies of both are settled for ever. Other supportive truths will also be seen in the interpretation of this amazing parable.

D. The Exposition of the Parable

This parable is only to be found in the Gospel of Matthew, the Gospel of the Kingdom. Again, there can be little misunderstanding or misinterpretation of this parable. Jesus Himself provides an extended analogy and interpretation of this parable even as He did of the first parable. As in a puzzle, Jesus takes the parts of the parable and each of the parts of the parable supply complementary or supplemental truths to the central truth of the parable. Without doubt, the interpretation of the parable of the sower and the seed, and the parable of the wheat and the tares by Jesus Himself, provide guidelines for the interpretation of the parables that Jesus left uninterpreted.

We consider the parts of the parable, working from part to whole and whole to part, and see the supportive truths in these parts as they pertain to the central truth of the parable. As in the first parable, the symbolic elements of the parable have to be interpreted to gain access to the full truth and significance of the whole parable.

When Jesus says, "The kingdom of heaven is **like**...", He is saying that the kingdom of heaven resembles, corresponds to or represents the things that make up the whole parable. There are a number of points of reference in the parable of the wheat and tares to be considered here. The first parable emphasized the **beginning of the kingdom.** This second parable emphasizes the **mixture in the kingdom.**

1. The Sower

There is no mistaking who the sower is in this parable, even though in the first parable the sower was not specifically identified. The man sows seed in the field. The sower is the Son of Man as verses 24 and 37 clearly show. In verse 27 He is spoken of as the householder, or the owner of the field. "Son of Man" is a Messianic name and refers to His humanity, His human nature (Matthew 8:20; 9:6; 10:25; 11:19,27; 12:18). "Son of David" refers to His Messianic line, as the Root and Offspring of David, David's Son and yet David's Lord, as His humanity and deity (Revelation 5:5; 22:16). Note also "the man" in parables two, three, five and six. Undoubtedly it points to the Son of Man Himself who Stephen saw in His glorified state (Acts 7:56).

In Old Testament times God sowed Israel and Judah among the nations of the earth (Jeremiah 31:27). In New Testament times, Jesus sows the church among the nations of the earth.

2. The Wheat Seed

The Son of Man sowed good seed, called wheat in His field. The good seed are clearly defined as "the children of the kingdom" (verses 24,38). The children of the kingdom are called "wheat" (verses 25,29). Sowing time is always the beginning. Harvest time is the end. This parable begins with sowing season and ends with harvest season. It is worthy to see that "the seed" in the fist parable is "the Word of the kingdom". "The seed" in this second parable is "the children of the kingdom." In the first parable we **receive** the seed. In the second parable we **become** the seed! The emphasis in the first parable is "receiving the seed". Here it "becoming the seed" of the kingdom. Believers cannot become the seed of the kingdom until we receive the word of the kingdom!

3. The Field

The sower sowed good seed in his field. A comparison of verses 24 and 38 show that it is "His field", and "the field is the world." Psalm 24:1 tells us that the earth is the Lord's and the fulness thereof; the world, and they that dwell therein. The Son of Man really owns the field. It is His field. It is His world.

4. The Sleeping Watchman

"While men slept", an enemy came in and sowed other seed. It is night time. Although Jesus does not specifically interpret this part of the parable, the context of Scripture as well as cultural custom helps us to understand the matter of night time danger. In Bible times, the owner of the field sometimes had men employed as watchmen over his field, so that no enemy would come by night and seek to corrupt his field by sowing other or evil seed.

In this case, the watchmen slept, and while they slept the enemy came and did his evil work. The field was not left only to good seed. While sleep is a healthy thing, there are Scriptures which indicate the sleep of laziness, indifference, unwatchfulness, and from which God calls us to awake as these references show.

"Watchman, what of the night?" (Isaiah 21:11-12). Peter, James and John fell asleep in the mount of transfiguration and Jesus had to wake them in order to see Moses and Elijah and His glory (Luke 9:28-36). Peter, James and John fell asleep in the garden of Gethsemane and Jesus had to awaken them again (Luke 22:39-46).

Paul says, "It is high time to awake out of sleep..." (Romans 13:11-12). Believers are not to sleep as others do in the night time (1Thessalonians 5:1-10). The wise and foolish virgins all slumbered and slept and had to be awakened at the midnight hour (Matthew 25:1-13).

Church History shows that the ministers of the Gospel over the centuries fell into a state of spiritual lethargy, slumber, indifference, prayerlessness and lack of watchfulness and the enemy of Christ came and sowed evil seed in "His field." The enemy's tactics have always been infiltration and seduction. The old saying is true:" If you cannot beat them, join them; if you cannot destroy them, then corrupt them!" The ministries and leaders in the church are to be God's watchman. History also shows the time of awakening of the Lord's leaders and ministers.

5. The Enemy Sower

There is no mistaking "the enemy" here. "While men slept, His enemy came..." The enemy of Christ and the church is none other than the devil. The devil came and sowed evil seed among the good seed (verses 25,28,39). The devil is Christ's enemy. The devil was at work in parable one, catching away the seed of the word of the kingdom out of peoples hearts. The same devil is at work in parable two, but this time, sowing evil seed among the good seed.

6. The Tares Seed

The devil sowed tares among the wheat; evil seed among the good seed. He did not try here to root up the wheat seed. He tried to mix the seed with evil seed. The tares as the evil seed are defined by Jesus as "the children of the wicked one" (verses 25,26,27,30 with 38, 40).

Various translations say "darnel," or "weed," or "thistles," or simply "black wheat." Strongs Concordance (SC2215) says "of uncertain origin; the darnel or false grain, and is translated as tares. The Jews referred to tares as "bastard wheat" or "degenerate wheat." The Amplified New Testament says "the darnel, or black, wild wheat." It was a counterfeit or illegitimate kind of wheat. The farmer could hardly distinguish one from the other in its early growing stages. The wheat and the tares looked somewhat alike in the early growth stage. They are indistinguishable at their beginning.

(a) Nature of Wheat

Wheat is a wholesome grain. When crushed to flour it is used for bread and for other kinds of food. In its growing stage, it needs chaff to protect it. It has a milk like substance in its early formation. Wheat ripens by absorbing light. Once it comes out of the milk stage, and becomes mature, wheat bows its full head and is then ready for reaping. It is called "golden grain." Satan wanted to sift Peter as wheat but Jesus prayed for him that his faith fail not (Luke 22:31).

(b) Nature of Tares

Tares, as a degenerate kind of wheat, is a black seed. It is really a poisonous grain. If eaten, it is bitter, and causes dizziness to the eater. Within it is this black poison. When tares are fully ripe, they stand stiffly erect in contrast to the bowing heads of the wheat. Only when tares and wheat are full ripe is the inner nature and character of both seen. Tares are useless for food and only fit for burning.

The commandment of the Lord was not to sow ones field with mixture of seed (Leviticus 19:19; Deuteronomy 22:9-11). Israel had mixed marriages and the holy seed was mingled with wrong seed (Ezra 9:2). It was the mixed multitude in Israel that fell to lusting after flesh and despised the heaven-sent manna (Numbers 11:4-6). God hates mixture. Here in the field there is mixture; two seeds, good seed and evil seed, wheat and tares; sons of the Lord and sons of Belial.

The two seed lines are seen in Genesis 3:15: the seed of the woman and the seed of the serpent. The godly line of faith was the good seed. The ungodly line of unbelief was the evil seed. John the Baptist and Jesus Himself spoke of the tares as "the generation of vipers" (Matthew 3:7; 12:34; 23:33). The Pharisees, the Sadducees, the Scribes, and the religious hypocrites of Christ's time – and all times- speak of the tares. The false cults in Christendom are also tares; counterfeit Christians; wolves in sheep's clothing; like angels of light; apostate in nature and falling stars (2Corinthians 11:13-15; Matthew 7:15; Acts 20:28-29. Jude's Epistles has been called "The Acts of the Apostates" and certainly illustrates the religious nature of tares; apostate wheat in the kingdom of God in its present mystery form. If the enemy cannot attack from without, he will seek to destroy and corrupt from within (Revelation 2:13; 2Timothy 3:8).

7. The Enemy Went His Way

The devil knew that the evil seed of the kingdom he had sown would follow the course of nature. The tares would spring up with the wheat and grow amongst the wheat. The enemy's tactic was mixture. The devil knew time would bring results and the manifestation of what he had sown secretly would be revealed. He had confidence in the evil seed he had sown (verses 25,26).

8. The Awakened Servants

When the blade sprung up, and brought forth, then appeared the tares also. In verses 27-29, the servants of the householder came to see that someone had sown tares among the wheat, while they had slept. The invisible became visible. There is an awakening among the servants to see what the enemy had done. The servants of the householder told the master. "You sowed good seed, where do these tares come from?" They were told that an enemy had done this. The servants wanted to pull up the tares, but the owner of the field told them they would ruin the wheat if they tried to separate the tares in this stage.

9. Growing Together

The word of wisdom from the householder was to let both grow together until the time of harvest. The meaning is clear. There is mixture in the kingdom in its present stage. Two seeds grow together in this present age. The good seed, who are the children of the kingdom, and the evil seed, who are the children of the wicked one, these, as wheat and tares grow together in the kingdom until the end of the age. The tares will not die out in this present age. The church of Jesus Christ, and the church of Satan are both developing unto harvest. The mystery of godliness and the mystery of iniquity both are seen together in this era of time and will continue till harvest time (1Timothy 3:16; 2Thessalonians 2:7). The mingled or mixed seed is here until Christ comes the second time (Leviticus 19:19). Sometimes the Lord does not deal with things as soon as ministers would like, but lets things remain as they are until the wheat is mature enough to handle the separation.

10. The Harvest Time

The wheat and tares grow together until the harvest time. Jesus told His disciples that the harvest was the end of the age (verses 30 with 39,40). This means that, during the whole of the church age, there will be good and evil, wheat and tares, children of God's kingdom and children of Satan's kingdom in the same kingdom. It will be a mixture that continues until the coming of Christ. The inner nature and character of the wheat and tares will be fully exposed then in the time of harvest. The same sun and rain that ripens the one will ripen the other. The Lord makes His rain and sunshine to fall on the just and the unjust, the wheat and the tares. Revelation 14 provides visions of the harvest time in the end of the age. The Son of Man is seen there on the cloud and He is given the sickle for reaping the harvest of the earth.

11. The Angel Reapers

Jesus told His disciples that the reapers are the angels (verses 30, 39). The Greek word for "angel" is "angelos" and simply means "messenger." In time of harvest, the Son of Man says to the angel-messengers to go and reap the harvest. Angel-messengers are seen with the Son of Man in the harvest judgments in Revelation 14. The Son of Man shall come again in all His glory, and all the holy angels will come with Him (Matthew 25:31).

12. The Bundled Tares

The reapers are told to **first** bind the tares into bundles; not take the wheat into the garner first! "Gather **first** the tares into bundles... bind them into bundles..." The tares are to be gathered into bundles first and to be burnt in the fire. The interpretation of the tares is found in the expressions, "those that offend, those that are scandals, those who are workers of ininquity." Like is gathered to like here (verses 30,4-42).

The "bundles" can speak of false cults, Satanist churches, apostate Roman, Protestant and Pentecostal/Charismatic Churches and other denominations who have apostatized from "the faith" once delivered to the saints (Jude 3). In our generation we see homosexual churches, false ecumenicism and the rise of the great harlot church of Revelation 17. Many cults call themselves "Christian", but, like the tares, they are degenerate wheat and apostates from the true faith. They appear as Christians, use the Christian Bible, and the language of the Christian faith, but there is that inner twist and corruption that only time exposes. Such will be the "one-world-church" in the final days. The bundles are being gathered in this time of the end – the ecumenical bundles of false religions!

13. The Furnace Of Fire

The fire of verse 40 is interpreted by Jesus in verse 42 to be the furnace of fire and points ultimately to the lake of fire and brimstone where the devil, his angels, and all unredeemed mankind who served the devil will be cast for all eternity (Revelation 19:20; 20:10).

The king of Babylon roasted Zedekiah and Ahab in the fire. He threw the Hebrew youths into the furnace of fire. The latter God delivered from the fire. The previous wicked kings God allowed the king of Babylon to roast in the fire (Jeremiah 29:22; Daniel 3:6; Malachi 4:1-2). So God will cast the devil and all those in his kingdom into the lake of fire from which there is no deliverance (Revelation 14:18-20; 20:11-15).

14. Wailing And Gnashing Of Teeth

In verse 42 Jesus fills out further the interpretation even beyond the details in the parable. Here He speaks of the wailing and gnashing of teeth of those who are cast into the furnace of fire. This expression, "weeping, wailing and gnashing of teeth" is spoken of in Matthew 8:12; 13:42,50; 22:13; 24:51; 25:30 and Luke 13:28. It is used to express the terrible grief, sorrow and regret of eternal punishment for rejection of the kingdom. It also speaks of the sorrow of hypocrisy in the kingdom in its present state.

A careful reading of the Scriptures show that it refers to both unrepentant unbelievers and also apostate believers; those who have apostatized from the truth faith. Whatever the full significance of the expression, the furnace of fire and the weeping, wailing and gnashing of teeth is to be dreaded and shunned whatever the cost may be! The wailing speaks of rage, the gnashing speaks of impatience, and extreme sorrow and torment. The religious leaders gnashed on Stephen with their teeth as they stoned him to death (Acts 7:54).

15. The Gathered Wheat

"Gather the wheat into My barn" is the word to the reapers. The good seed, the children of the kingdom are likened to wheat. The wheat-believers will be gathered into the Lord's barn (verse 30). So the Lord speaks: "Gather My saints together unto Me, those that have made a covenant with Me by sacrifice" (Psalm 50:5). Jacob said also: "Unto Him shall the gathering of the people be..." (Genesis 49:10).

16. The Lord's Barn

Heaven is ultimately God's barn where all the redeemed of earth shall be gathered to worship and serve God and the Lamb eternally. In verse 43 it is spoken of as being the kingdom of the Father. There the righteous shine forth as the sun, in the glory of imputed and outworked righteousness and holiness (Revelation 12:1; 1Corinthians 15:41-42).

17. The Final Separation

In verses 41-43 we have very important truth given by the Lord Jesus. They help us to understand the two aspects of the kingdom as to its present and future form.

(a) Present Mixture

The word of Jesus in verse 41, along with the details of the parable, show that the kingdom of heaven, in this present age, has mixture in it. There is wheat and tares, good seed and bad seed, children of God and children of the Satan. As will be seen, the seventh parable of the dragnet and fish teaches the same truth. The net brings in the good and bad fish. The mixture of the wicked and the righteous will continue to the end of this age. Most of the parables of the kingdom reveal this mixture to be so.

(b) Future Separation

The words of Jesus in verses 41-43 also show that the mixture will end at the close of this age. The Son of Man will send forth His messengers. They will gather out of His kingdom, in its present state (1) all things that offend, and (2) all those who do iniquity or practise lawlessness. The wicked are cast into the furnace of fire and experience weeping, wailing and gnashing of teeth. The righteous are gathered into God's barn and shine forth as the sun in the kingdom of the Father. The present mixture ends. Future separation takes place at His coming. The kingdom present has mixture. The kingdom future (Millennial or Eternal Kingdom) has absolutely no mixture in it. The tares are separated from the wheat, the wicked are separated from the righteous – eternally!

It is possible that the fulness of Christ's interpretation actually finds its ultimate in the eternal states as seen by John in Revelation chapters 20,21 and 22. There we see the wicked cast into the lake of fire, and there we see the righteous in the city of God – the ultimate of Divine destiny for the unsaved and the saved of earth!

E   The Practical Application of the Parable

Jesus in this second parable of the kingdom has given both the parable and its interpretation, even as He did with the first parable. He inteprets most all of the symbols and parts of the parable here as He did in the first, working from part to whole and whole to part. To focus this more sharply we set out the parable symbols and the interpretation that Jesus provided for us.

The Parable Symbols (Matthew 13:24-30)	The Interpretation of the Symbols (Matthew 13:36-43)
1. The Kingdom of heaven is like	The kingdom of heaven resembles
2. A man sowing	The Son of Man
3. Good seed	Children of the kingdom
4. In his field	The field is the world
5. While men slept	Ministries asleep, night time
6. The enemy came	The devil
7. Sowed tares among the wheat	Children of the wicked one
8. Went his way	Done his evil work
9. Blade unto the fruit	Sowing unto harvesting
10. Tares appeared	Mixture in the field
11. Servants of householder	Lord's ministers
12. Saw the tares among the wheat	Saw the mixture of good and bad
13. Gather up the tares or not	Leave them grow together
14. Let both grow together to harvest	Good and evil growing side by side
15. Until the harvest	The end of the age
16. The reapers will be sent forth	The angel-messengers
17. Tares gathered into bundles first	False ecumenicalism of groups
18. To burn them	Furnace of fire, gnashing of teeth
19. Gather the wheat	Gather the righteous
20. Into the barn	Into the Father's kingdom
21. Shine as the sun	The glory of God on His saints

For those expositors who say we are not to make anything, or too much of the parts of the parable, and that there is only one truth in any parable, Christ's own interpretation of this parable (as well as parable one) certainly refutes that. One cannot charge Jesus Himself with allegorization!

Although the central truth of the parable is mixture in the kingdom of God in its present form unto the final separation at His coming, there are certainly a lot of supportive truths in the parts of the parable, as has been seen. Undoubtedly Christ's interpretation of the parts of parables one and two in Matthew 13 certainly provide for us interpretative keys for uninterpreted parables.

The significance of the number "two" is seen in the parable. In the significance of numbers, one with one equals the number of testimony, the number of two, the number of witness. It is positive. When it is one against one, it is negative and equals division or separation.

In the first parable, the sower could be the Lord, the Holy Spirit or any believer or minister of the gospel, sowing the seed of the kingdom. In the second parable, the sower is the Son of Man, sowing the children of the kingdom. In the first parable we receive the word of the kingdom; in the second parable we become the seed of the kingdom. One cannot become seed until we receive the seed.

It is worthy of study to follow "the seed of the woman" through the godly line unto Messiah and the Church. It is also worthy to study "the seed of the serpent" through the ungodly line unto the Antichrist (Genesis 3:15). The godly speak of the wheat, the ungodly and apostates speak of the tares. In the first parable, the seed is God's Word. In the second parable, the seed is God's people!

The final lesson to be learnt here from this parable is that at the end of this age, the wicked and the righteous will be separated unto their eternal destines. The unrighteous shall not inherit the kingdom of God (Romans 14:17; 1Corinthians 15:24,59; John 18:36; Luke 19:2-12; 2Thessalonians 1:7-10; Matthew 7:21-23; Luke 13:24-29; Galatians 5:19-21; Ephesians 5:5; 1Corinthians 6:9-10; Revelation 22:15).

The believer has to recognize this as the age of mixture. This will continue until Jesus comes again. Then the great separation will take place, and the wicked and the righteous will receive their just punishment and reward according to the justice of the Divine Judge, Jesus Christ.

This chapter is concluded with an alternative outline:

1. One field – the whole world (verse 38)
2. Two sowers – The Son of Man and the devil (verses 37,39)
3. Two seeds – The wheat and the tares; children of God and children of Satan
4. Two servants – The servants of the householder and the reapers
5. Two seasons – Sowing time and harvest time
6. Two natures – The character of the righteous, the character of the wicked
7. Two destinies – Tares into the furnace of fire; wheat into His barn.

Thus we have (1) A time of sowing, (2) A time of growth, (3) A time of mixture, (4) A time of exposure, (5) A time of classification, (6) A time of separation, and (7) A time of judgment!

Jesus closes this parable also with the exhortation: "He who has ears to hear, let him hear" (Matthew 13:43), even as He did the first parable (Matthew 13:9).

CHAPTER TEN
THE PARABLE OF THE MUSTARD SEED

A. The Scriptures On The Parable

1. Matthew 13:31-32

Another parable put he forth unto them, saying, The kingdom of heaven is like to a grain of mustard seed, which a man took, and sowed in his field:

Which indeed is the least of all seeds: but when it is grown, it is the greatest among herbs, and becometh a tree, so that the birds of the air come and lodge in the branches thereof.

2. Mark 4:30-32

And he said, Whereunto shall we liken the kingdom of God? or with what comparison shall we compare it?

It is like a grain of mustard seed, which, when it is sown in the earth, is less than all the seeds that be in the earth:

But when it is sown, it groweth up, and becometh greater than all herbs, and shooteth out great branches; so that the fowls of the air may lodge under the shadow of it.

3. Luke 13:18,19

Then said he, Unto what is the kingdom of God like? and whereunto shall I resemble it?

It is like a grain of mustard seed, which a man took, and cast into his garden; and it grew, and waxed a great tree; and the fowls of the air lodged in the branches of it.

B. The Setting Of The Parable

In Matthew and Mark the setting is still by the seaside. Jesus is sitting in the boat and the multitude is standing on the seashore (Matthew 13:1-2; Mark 4:1-2). In Luke, the setting seems to be on a sabbath day, when Jesus was teaching in a synagogue (Luke 13:10,18-19). It is evident that Jesus repeated His teachings on various occasions and in different settings.

C. The Moral Of The Parable

The central truth of the parable of the mustard seed is: The kingdom of heaven in its present state has but a small beginning but an unnatural growth, which attracts all sorts of creature birds (peoples) into it. There are other subservient truths relative to this main truth. Parables three and four reveal the development of the kingdom of heaven in its mystery form, outwardly and inwardly. The mustard seed parable speaks of the external development of the kingdom while the parable of the leaven speaks of the internal development of the kingdom in its present mystery form.

D. The Exposition Of The Parable

This third parable is a parable left uninterpreted by king Jesus. How shall we interpret that which He left uninterpreted? Some expositors believe that we cannot interpret what Jesus Himself did not interpret. The Lord Jesus, however, has already given some hermeneutical keys (principles and keys of interpretation) in the use of the Parabolic and Symbolic principles of interpretation, as well as the Moral principle. Jesus gave to His disciples (and to us) enough interpretative clues in the way He interpreted the first two parables of the kingdom as in Matthew 13.

As already seen, the Scriptures are one whole, and as we work from whole to part and part to whole, within the context of sound Biblical theology and sound Biblical hermeneutics, the expositor will be able to arrive at a sound meaning and understanding of the uninterpreted parables of Jesus.

The expositor should use the Word to interpret the Word. Scripture interprets Scripture. The best interpreter of Scripture is Scripture. The expositor must work from part to whole and whole to part.

The expositor should use the Comparative Mention principle. By comparing spiritual things with spiritual things, and Scripture with Scripture, the expositor will discover more fully what the Bible says about the passage under consideration (1Corinthians 2:13). The human mind or imagination cannot interpret the word of God; otherwise one can fall into the dangers of false teaching or heresy.

The expositor should interpret the symbols in the parable. The spiritual truth is hidden in the symbolic form (Romans 2:20; 1Corinthians 10:1-11). Discover the major truth in the parable and then the other supportive and subservient truths will also be seen.

The parable of the mustard seed is a short and simple parable. As we consider the symbolic parts of the parable, the meaning of the parable can be discovered.

1. **The Kingdom of Heaven**

    The kingdom of heaven is like: that is, it resembles, corresponds to, and represents the things used in symbolic form. It is similar to these things. At least six of the eight parables in Matthew 13 begin with the phrase: "The kingdom of heaven is like..." In other words, the kingdom of heaven resembles all that is in the parable; not just one of the parts but all of the parts that make up the parable as a whole. Mark's Gospel speaks of it being "a comparison" (Mark 4:30).

2. **A Grain Of Mustard Seed**

    The grain of mustard seed is mentioned in each of the Synoptics. The student will see that these first three parables in Matthew 13 are all "seed parables."

    The first parable concerns the sower and the seed, which is the word of the kingdom. Jesus interprets this parable.

    The second parable concerns the sower and two seeds – the children of the kingdom and the children of the wicked one. Jesus also interprets this parable.

    The third parable concerns the grain of mustard seed, here in an unnatural growth and development into a tree. Jesus does not interpret this parable.

    Everything in nature and life comes from the seed as seen in Genesis 1:11-12. The seed is in the fruit and the fruit is in the seed.

    Speaking of the mustard seed, Peloubet's Bible Dictionary says" "It is generally agreed that the mustard seed of Scripture is the black mustard. It is not the smallest of all seeds, but it is the smallest of all garden seeds. The mustard seed is used proverbially to denote anything very minute, hence it is the least of all seeds. The birds lodging in the branches simply means that the birds settled upon it for the sake of the seed of which they were very fond. Some of the wild mustard plants on the rich plains grew as tall as the horse and the rider. If this was so, then it could grow taller if cultivated in a garden."

    A.E. Post, in Hasting's Bible Dictionary says: "The cultivated mustard is 'sinapis nigra'. The seed is well known for its minuteness. The mustards are annuals, reproduced with extraordinary rapidity. In fat soil they often attain a height of ten or twelve feet, and have branches which attract passing birds."

It is evident that there is a development of **"the seed of the kingdom"**, but viewed from different aspects, each setting forth its distinct portion of truth. It is indeed the kingdom seed. In the parable of the sower and seed, the seed is the word of the kingdom. In the parable of the wheat and tares, the good seed represents the children of God while the evil seed represents the children of the wicked one.

In the parable of the mustard seed, the seed takes on another aspect of truth. The seed here is **the kingdom of heaven** in its present manifestation. This will be confirmed further as we consider the other parts of the parable.

There are only several references to the mustard seed in the New Testament. Each are worthy of consideration, especially as to how Jesus used the mustard seed in symbolic sense.

* The **kingdom of heaven** is likened to a mustard seed.

* **Faith** is likened to a mustard seed (Luke 17:6; Matthew 17:20).

The mustard seed is the smallest of all garden seeds. It is the purest of all garden seeds. It has the potential within itself to grow into a tree. So we say, the mustard seed represents the kingdom of heaven in seed form.

3. The Man, The Sower

The man who is the sower (to be consistant with the previous parables) points once again to the Son of the Man, the Lord Jesus Himself (verses 37). In parables two, three, five and six, "the man" points to Jesus, as the Son of Man, iun His humanity.

In parable one, the sower sowed the seed-word of the kingdom. Jesus came preaching and teaching the gospel of the kingdom (Matthew 4:17; 9:35). In parable two, the Son of Man sowed the children of the kingdom as wheat in His field, to bring forth a harvest of other grains of wheat (John12:24). In parable three, the sower sowed the mustard seed of the kingdom. It is the same thought throughout. It pertains to the kingdom (verse 31).

4. The Field

The word "field" is used seven times in this chapter (verses 24,27,31,36,38,44,44). It is the same field as in the parable of the wheat and tares, as also the other parables. It is His field (verses 31,38). In Mark it is "the earth" (Mark 4:31), while in Luke it is "his garden" (Luke 13:19). The field is the world.

5. The Least Of All Seeds

The mustard seed is one of the smallest garden seeds. Least in the garden, yet it can grow greatly. The seed always speaks of the beginning. All begins in seed form. The kingdom of heaven was planted in seed form in the gospels under the ministry of Christ and His apostles. The law and the prophets were until John, since that time the kingdom of God is preached (Luke 16:16).

6. Unnatural Growth

The mustard seed germinated generally grows into a small bush, but in this case, there is unnatural or abnormal growth and development. It speaks of the external development of the kingdom.

7. Became A Tree .

Luke says it grew and became a large tree (Luke 13:19.NKJV). From a small seed it became a great tree. The mustard seed of the kingdom became a great kingdom. A tree in Scripture is either likened to people or to a kingdom, as the following Scriptures show.

In the context of the Bible, the kingdoms of this world, as well as individuals, are likened to trees. All of these Scriptures here confrm the truth that the mustard seed tree symbolizes the development of the kingdom of God from its smallest beginning to an unnatural development during church history.

(a) Symbolic of a Person

* The righteous are likened to a tree planted by the rivers of water who bring forth fruit in their season. They are likened to olive trees also (Psalm 1:1-3; 52:8; 92:12-14; 128:3). Read also Jeremiah 17:5-8.

* The first parable in the Bible speaks of people likened to the olive, the fig and the vine tree as the trees sought for a king to rule over them (Judges 9:8-15).

* The wicked are likened to spreading trees (Psalm 37:35).

* Joseph's branches ran over the wall and people enjoyed his fruit (Genesis 49:22-26).

(b) Symbolic of a Kingdom

* Israel was likened to a vine (Psalm 80; Ezekiel 15), an olive tree (Romans 11), and also the fig tree (Hosea 9:10;14:6; Matthew 21:18-19).

* The kingdom of Assyria was likened to a cedar tree also (Ezekiel 3;1:1-8).

* Jesus likened Himself and the believers to the fruitful vine tree (John 15:1-16).

* Nebuchadnezzar, the king of Babylon, was likened to a great tree, cut down, and then restored after a period of seven years (Daniel 4).The birds of the air lodged in its branches, and the beasts of the field lived under the shade thereof. All the kingdoms of the world trusted in the shadow of Babylon's kingdom.

There is no doubt that the mustard seed tree represents the growth of the kingdom of God in the earth, in "His field." The disciples undoubtedly were familiar with the language of the "tree-kingdoms", and did not ask Jesus for an interpretation of this short parable.

8. The Birds

Consistency of interpretation would see the birds of the parable one (Matthew 13:4) to be the same birds in parable three (Matthew 13:32). In several of the passages above, we see how the birds and fowls of the air (as well as animals) came and lodged in the branches of these world kingdoms. Read Ezekiel 17:23; 31:6; Daniel 2:38; 4:12-14). The birds come to enjoy the seed of the mustard tree as well as make their nests in the branches.

* Abraham drove away the birds that would have defiled his sacrifice (Genesis 15:10-11).

* In Leviticus 11, the Lord defined which birds of the air were an abomination to Him. The Lord gave the distinction between clean and unclean birds of the air and earth (Deuteronomy 14:20; Leviticus 11:13-19; 14:6-7,51-53). Only clean birds were fit for the altar of God's sacrifice.

* Babylon became the habitation of every unclean spirit and hateful bird (Revelation 18:1-2). Evil persons, unclean spirits all point to "the birds" that are spoken of here. The birds also could speak of clean and unclean birds – mixture in the kingdom again! Read also Jeremiah 5:27; 12:9.

* In Peter's vision, the gospel sheet gathered all creeping things and fowls of the air, all of which pointed to the coming in of the Gentiles into the kingdom and the church of God (Acts 10:12; 11:6).

The "clean birds" represent true believers, true converts in the kingdom of God, those who feed on the seed of God's Word. The "unclean birds" represent those birds who feed on seed and flesh. One may think of the raven (unclean) and the dove (clean). The clean speaks of those who have come into the church/kingdom and have been regenerated by the Spirit of God; the unclean speak of those who are unregenerate "church members."

9. The Branches

The birds of the air lodged in the branches. They made their nests there. The birds found refuge and protection in the branches of the tree. The birds liked the seeds in the mustard seed branches and fed on them as food. It is said that the mustard seeds are pleasant, strongly aromantic and good for food for birds.

The unclean birds would not only feed on the seeds of the mustard tree, they would also make their nestings for their young to be hatched. They would also pollute the branches of the tree. Matthew and Luke both speak of the birds in the branches while Mark mentions neither.

Remembering that the kingdom of God is manifested in the church, one may look at the development of the kingdom in the early church from its small beginnings in the Gospels, and the Acts. Over the early centuries, there was unnatural, phenomenal growth, and about the third and fourth centuries onwards, even to our day, we see the great **"branches of Christendom."**

The tree has many branches. The tree shot out great branches, the Scripture says.. There are great denominations that have grown as great branches of the church universal. All sorts of birds (people) are indeed making their nests in these branches and feeding on the seed of the preaching and teaching given therein!

Jesus said He was the vine and the believers were the branches who drew their life from Him and He was the source of their fruitfulness (John 15:1-16).

Paul spoke of the Gentiles being grafted into the good faith-olive tree as branches, drawing their life and anointing from the olive tree, along with the believing Jews (Romans 11).

Many denominations speak of **"branch churches"**. The various denominations in the church universal are represented in these **"branches."** The Catholic,

Anglican, Methodist, Presbyterian, Baptist, Churches of Christ, Pentcostal, Charismatic and all the thousands of denominations and Independant churches – all may be likened to "the branches" of the mustard seed tree!

It is possible also to see the various cults that use the name "Christian" to draw people into their "branch churches."

E. The Practical Application Of The Parable

Although Jesus Himself did not interpret this parable for us, there are enough clues in the context of the Bible to help us interpret the symbols of the parable..

The Parable Symbols	The Interpretation of the Parable
1. The mustard seed	The kingdom of heaven
2. The man who sows the seed	The Lord Jesus Himself
3. The field	The world
4. The great tree	The kingdom/church
5. The branches	The denominations of Christendom
6. The birds	All nationalities who nest in the church

The kingdom of God has grown from its small beginning as a seed, and has spread its branches around the world. Out of every kindred, tongue, tribe and nation, people are nesting in the tree, both good and bad, genuine and counterfeit.

Over the centuries of church history, the church has become a great tree. The growth has been unnatural, abnormal, supernatural. The birds of all kinds, however, have flocked into her denominational branches, bringing their defilements and corrupting philosophies, as well as feeding on the seed that the mustard tree produces. In this end-time generation we see the condition of the "kingdom/church". This is the mystery of the parable of the kingdom seed.

In Summary:

1. The kingdom of God begins as a small seed

2. It has unnatural growth, abnormal growth

3. It becomes a great tree through the years of church history

4. Great denominational branches grow out from it

5. The birds, both clean and unclean, nest in it; people of all nations

6. The birds feed on the seed that the church/kingdom produces

7. This is the mystery of the kingdom parable of the mustard seed which the scribe of the kingdom will recognize as it consummates at Christ's coming.

CHAPTER ELEVEN

THE PARABLE OF THE WOMAN AND THE LEAVEN

A. The Scriptures On The Parable

1. Matthew 13:33

Another parable spake he unto them; The kingdom of heaven is like unto leaven, which a woman took, and hid in three measures of meal, till the whole was leavened.

2. Luke 13:20-21

And again he said, Whereunto shall I liken the kingdom of God? It is like leaven, which a woman took and hid in three measures of meal, till the whole was leavened.

B. The Setting Of The Parable

The setting of the parable is a continuation of the teaching of Jesus by the seaside. Jesus is sitting in the boat and the multitude is standing on the shore. Luke's gospel seems to point to this parable being given by Jesus teaching in one of the synagogues (Luke 13:10,20,21).

C. The Moral Of The Parable

The central truth or moral of the parable is seen as follows. The pure meal of the kingdom of heaven in its present mystery form has been entirely influenced and permeated by teaching given by the false church. The truth of this will be seen in the course of our study of the parable with its attendant parts.

D. The Exposition Of The Parable

The parable of the woman and the leaven is another one of those uninterpreted parables of Jesus. It is one of the more difficult parables to interpret, and more controversial. The exposition therefore, will be dealt with more fully. It is significant that the disciples did not specifically ask Jesus for the interpretation of this parable. It is implied that, when He was alone, He explained the meaning of the parables to them (Matthew 13:10-17,34-36; Mark 4:33-34).

It may be asked, however, Did the disciples have enough clues as to the interpretation of the parable from within the Old Testament context, along with the warnings that Jesus gave to them about leaven? It certainly seems so as our study unfolds.

For those expositors who say that the parts of the parable are only given to make up the parable story, and such have no significant meaning in them, we would ask the questions:

1. Is the kingdom of heaven like **leaven**?
2. Or, is it like leaven which a **woman** took?
3. Or, is it like leaven which a woman took and **hid**?
4. Or, it is like leaven which a woman took and hid in **three measures of meal?**
5. Or, is it like leaven which a woman took and hid in three measures of meal until the **whole was leavened**?

Which part of the parable can be left out? Which part of the parable is the kingdom of heaven really like? The leaven? The woman? The three measures of meal? The whole of the leavened meal? The answer is, as in previous parables, the whole of the parable. No one part can be left out of the Divine puzzle. The whole incident resembles the kingdom in its mystery form in the present age, as in the other parables. One must work from part to whole and whole to part to obtain the full truth hidden in the parable.

Even though Jesus left the parable uninterpreted, within the context of the whole of Scripture, and within the bounds of Biblical theology, the interpretation of the parable can be discovered by a consideration of its parts. It is the central parable of the major seven, before the closing parable (the eighth) about the scribe. It should be remembered that this parable is also "a mystery of the kingdom of heaven", and also a "dark saying" of the Lord Jesus. It is a knot, a hidden and secret saying that needs to be unravelled, as seen in the definition of the meaning of a parable.

False cults teach "the woman" is the church; and "the three measures of meal" represent the three divisions of the human race, from the three sons of Noah; "the leaven" is the gospel and kingdom of God, and "the whole being leavened" signifies the salvation and reconciliation of the whole human race. This, however, is contrary to sound theology and Biblical teaching. The Bible nowhere teaches the ultimate reconciliation of all unrepentant mankind to God. This is heresy. It is unsound theology and unsound hermeneutics, and brings people into deception. What then does the parable really teach?

1. The Kingdom of Heaven

The kingdom of heaven resembles the things contained in this parable. It may be compared to leaven which a woman took and hid in three measures of meal until the whole was leavened. There are three major symbols in the parable which need to be interpreted in order to arrive at the meaning of the parable. These three symbols are: The Leaven, the Woman and the Three Measures of Meal. For the purpose of our study we will take them in the following order: The Woman, the Meal and the Leaven.

2. The Woman

Most all expositors recognize the fact that a woman in Scripture is a type of a church, whether true or false. The Scriptures confirm this truth.

* Zion in Israel was likened to a delicate woman (Jeremiah 6:2)

* The Lord God was married to Israel and Judah under the Old Covenant times. Both houses of Israel are likened to two women who played the harlot. Israel was given a bill of divorce (Jeremiah 3:6-11,20; Ezekiel 16; Ezekiel 23).

* The false church is called, Mystery Babylon the Great, the Mother of Harlots and abominations of the earth (Revelation 17).

* The true church, and the marriage of Christ to His church is likened also to a great mystery (Ephesians 5:23-32).

* Christ gave a parable about the woman who lost the coin and, when she found it after much searching, there was great rejoicing (Luke 15:8-10).

Undoubtedly the woman who hides the leaven in the meal symbolizes or typifies a church. The question to be answered is: If she a picture of the true church or the false church? As the parable unfolds in its interpretation, the answer will be discovered.

3. The Meal

In this parable, the symbol changes. The three previous parables were all "seed" parables, and each brought out a different aspect of truth about the seed of the kingdom. In this parable, it is **meal** which comes from seed, probably wheat flour. Jesus likened Himself to a corn of wheat (John12:24).

Meal in Scripture always speaks of good, wholesome and healthy food, generally being either barley or wheat flour. It does not represent evil in Scripture, as these Scripture references show.

* Barley meal was used in offerings to the Lord (Numbers 5:15; Judges13:23).

* The widow woman made cakes from meal (1Kings 17:12-16).

* The prophet Elisha used meal to purify the pot of poison (2Kings 4:38-41).

* The meal offering was made of fine flour and offered as the morning and evening sacrifice on the altar of the Lord, along with blood sacrifices (Leviticus 2:1-15; 5:13; 6:14,15,20,21,23; Exodus 29:41; 30:9; 40:29; Leviticus 7:9,10,37).

* The prophets and priests lamented when there was no meal offering and drink offering to present to the Lord (Joel 1:9,13; 2:14).

The meal needed no explanation to the disciples for, as Jews, they knew the importance of the meal offering before the Lord. The meal offering points to Christ as the "corn of wheat" who fell into the ground and died. It points to Christ as God's "fine flour", perfect in His nature and being. Christ is the bread of life. Christ is the meal offering accepted by God the Father (John 12:24; John6). The church is also spoken of as bread and called to be unleavened bread also (1Corinthians 10:17; 5:6). The meal in the parable points to the bread or food of God, the Divine meal. The student is encouraged to study the full details of the **Meal Offering** in Leviticus Chapter 2. It is the Lord's offering, His portion, the food of His altar.

4. Three Measures Of Meal

The significance of the number three is found in the number being the number of God, the number of the Godhead; Father, Son and Holy Spirit. Three is the number of a perfect and complete testimony, a perfect and full witness.

Two or three witnesses must provide a complete testimony in all cases of trial. This is confirmed in both Old and New Testaments (Deuteronomy 17:6; 19:15; Matthew 18:16; 2Corinthians 13:1; 1Timothy 5:19; Hebrews 10:28; 1John 5:8).

God Himself is three yet one; the Father, the Son and the Holy Spirit. The number of the Godhead and the testimony of the Father, Son and Holy Spirit make a unified and complete witness to mankind. "There are three that bear record in heaven: the Father, the Word and the Holy Spirit, and these three are one "(1John 5:7-8). The number three therefore, is the number of God in all His fulness. It speaks of the triune Godhead.

The first specific mention of **"three measures of meal"** in the Bible is significant. In Genesis 18 we have the account of the visit of three angels to Abraham, the father of all who believe. Most expositors see that one of the angels (at least) represented the Lord God. Other expositors see the triunity of God in the visit of the angels. Abraham, however, asked his wife, Sarah, to made ready three measures of fine meal and make cakes for the angelic trio (Genesis 18:6).

Saul met some men going up to Bethel carrying three loaves of bread, along with other food supplies (1Samuel 10:3).

The friend in the parable of Jesus came to his friend at the midnight hour and asked him for a loan of three loaves of bread for his journeying friend (Luke 11:5-6).

In some of the meal offerings there had to be **three-tenths** of fine flour (Numbers 15:0; 28:12,20,28; 29:3,4). **Three measures** equalled one ephah; the offerings had a third part of an ephah.

Gideon offered a meal offering before the Lord (Judges5:18-19). Hannah offered a meal offering before the Lord (1Samuel 1:24). The meal offering had a very important place in the offerings on the altar (Leviticus 2:11).

Here in this parable, Jesus speaks of the **three measures of meal** that are leavened by the woman (Matthew 13:33; Luke 13:20,21).

In the light of these Scriptures pertaining to the number three and the measures of meal, the three measures of meal can be understood as the meal of God's Word, the truth that pertains to God, as Father, Son and Holy Spirit. In other words, the three measures of meal may speak of the fulness of the Godhead, the fulness of Divine revelation as in the Word of God. **Three speaks of God! Meal speaks of the Word of God!**

(Note: There is an interesting custom among some of the Orthodox Jews which takes place at the Passover celebration. In brief, and with some variations, this is what takes place.

The house is cleansed of all leaven by the woman of the house. The man, as head of the house declares before God that he has cleansed his house of all leaven and may now keep the Passover with his family. Three pieces of unleavened bread are taken and placed between paper dividers. During the course of the Feast, the middle or central piece is broken and then hidden in another place. They have four cups of wine on the table, one of these for Elijah the prophet. The door is left open in case Elijah should come and announce the coming of Messiah. After the Feast is over, the middle piece of the three unleavened wafers is then eaten. The time is closed with prayer. These three pieces of unleavened wafers are called the Afirkromen! The custom has variations but the basic order is as above.

The believer in Christ should see some of the significance here. The three unleavened wafers speak of the Godhead; Father, Son and Holy Spirit. The middle piece broken and hidden would speak of the central person in the Godhead, the Son, the Lord Jesus Christ, broken for us, and hidden from view since His ascension. The end of the Feast would bring us to the end of the age. Surely this Jewish custom throws light on this present parable).

5. **The Leaven**

For many expositors, interpreting the leaven presents the most difficult symbol in the parable to interpret. Is the leaven here symbolic of good or evil? A surface reading of the parable would imply it is the symbol of that which is good. "The kingdom is heaven is like leaven..."

Because most expositors immediately think of the kingdom of heaven as being good, then it is assumed that the kingdom of heaven being like leaven is good. They interpret the leaven of the kingdom as having influence for good in the whole world until the kingdom is known in all the world.

As already seen, false interpreters take the woman to be the true church, the three measures of meal to be the three divisions of the human race by the three sons of Noah, and the leaven of the gospel of the kingdom ultimately influencing the whole world for God and for good. This interpretation is contrary to sound Biblical theology and sound Biblical hermeneutics.

Let us, therefore, see what the Scriptures say about "leaven" and see if the teaching of the Bible will help us in interpreting this uninterpreted parable of Jesus. We will use the hermeneutical principles of First Mention, Progressive Mention, Comparative Mention and Complete Mention of leaven in the Scriptures. The student is encouraged to read the Scripture references as they are simply quoted in brief here only.

(a) Leaven In The Old Testament

* Lot made unleavened bread for the visiting angels (Genesis 19:3).

* In the Feast of Passover, all leaven was to be put away out of their houses. Any who ate leavened bread would be cut off from Israel (Exodus 12:15-20,34-39).

* In the Feast of Unleavened Bread, all leaven was forbidden. Israel ate unleavened bread for seven days (Exodus 12:15-20;13:1-7; 23:15; 34:18; Deuteronomy 16:3-8).

* In the consecration of the priests to office, unleavened cakes were to be offered to the Lord (Exodus 29:2,23; Leviticus 8:2,26).

* The meal offering was to be of fine flour, mingled with oil and frankincense. No honey or leaven was permitted in the meal offering (Leviticus 2:1-5,11; 6:16,17).

* In the Feast of Pentecost, the two wave-loaves of fine flour, however, were to be baken with leaven, but could only be accepted of the Lord as these were offered with unleavened bread and blood sacrifices (Leviticus 23:15-21; Numbers 28:26-31).

* No blood sacrifice was to be offered to the Lord with leaven (Exodus 23:18; 34:25).

* When an Israelite offered a sacrifice of thanksgiving to the Lord, he could offer leavened bread, but again, this was only accepted by the Lord as it was offered with unleavened cakes and wafers mingled and anointed with oil (Leviticus 7:13; Amos 4:5).

The words "leaven" (ed,eth) are used at least thirty-eight times in the total Bible. The word "unleavened" is used some sixty times in the total Bible.

It will be seen by a proper reading of these Old Testament references to leaven that, (a) Leaven is forbidden in the Feast of Passover and

Unleavened Bread, in the Meal Offerings, and in Blood sacrifices, while leaven is (b) permitted in the Feast of Pentecost and with the Sacrifice of Thanksgiving. These leavened offerings were only acceptable to God in and through the unleavened offerings and blood sacrifices. Otherwise, any who offered leavened bread to God would be "cut off" from Israel.

The nation of Israel understood that leaven, as a whole, had some evil significance to God. It seems also that Israel never could fully understand why God permitted leaven at Pentecost or in the sacrifice of thanksgiving! This, however, will be considered further on in this chapter.

(b) Leaven In The New Testament

With all the references to leaven in the Old Testament, not one verse interprets the symbolic truth of the leaven. The nation of Israel knew that leaven had some evil signficiance in the eyes of the Lord. The very fact that anyone who ate leavened bread at Passover or the Feast of Unleavened Bread would be cut off shows that leaven had evil connotation in the mind of God.

The New Testament, however, clearly defines and interprets the truth in the symbol of leaven, and this, specifically by Jesus and confirmed by Paul.

Jesus said, "Beware of the leaven of the Pharisees." He was not talking about the leaven of bread (Matthew 16:5-12). Jesus was saying to beware of the doctrine of the Pharisees and also of the doctrine of the Sadducees. Luke's gospel defines the leaven of the Pharisees as hypocrisy (Luke 12:1).

The Lord Jesus also warned against the leaven of Herod (Mark 8:15), and Herod's evil lifestyle.

The apostle Paul exhorted the Corinthian church to purge out the leaven of carnality so that they could keep the Feast of Passover and Unleavened Bread. He spoke of the leaven of malice and wickedness. He spoke of the unleavened bread of sincerity and truth (1Corinthians 5:1-8).

In writing to the Galatian churches, Paul warned against the leaven of Judaistic teaching of legalism and ceremonialism.

Between Jesus and Paul we have five major references to leaven, none of them used in good sense. It should be remembered that the Old Testament nowhere specifically interprets the symbol of leaven. The New Testament does so, and this first by Jesus, and then by Paul. Consider the list of these specific Scriptures:

1. **The Leaven of the Pharisees** was hypocrisy and the doctrine of externalism (Luke 12:1). Pharisaical righteousness was external, not internal. Christ's warnings to the scribes and Pharisees was strong in Matthew 23 because of their hypocrisy.

2. **The Leaven of the Sadducees** was denial of the supernatural; the bodily resurrection, angels and spirit (Acts 23:8).

3. **The Leaven of Herod** which was the lusts of worldliness (Mark 8:15).

4. **The Leaven of Corinth** was sensuality and carnality in its numerous forms (1Corinthians 5: 1-13).

5. **The Leaven of Galatia** was legalism, ceremonialism and fleshly licence (Galatians 5:9).

The disciples certainly came to understand the evil meaning of leaven as Jesus used it. Perhaps this was the main reason they did not ask Jesus for the interpretation of the parable of the woman and the leaven. They understood that leaven was evil in the light of these Scriptures, both from the Old Testament and then the New Testament.

It can be asked: Why then would leaven be "good" in this parable in the light of the total revelation of leaven in Scripture? Of the ninetyeight references to "leaven" or "unleavened" in the Scriptures, only on two occasions did the Lord permit leavened bread. One occasion was in the two wave loaves in the Feast of Pentecost (Leveiticus 23:17). The other was in the giving of the sacrifice of thanksgiving (Leviticus 7:13). On neither occasions, however, were these acceptable to the Lord unless offered with unleavened bread and blood sacrifice, as seen previously.

What then is the spiritual meaning and significance of these things?

The definition of leaven is: That which swells up; a yeast-cake, as swelling by fermentation; that which is pungent, tastes sour, or causes fermentation (Refer Strong's Numbers 7603, 7604).

Leaven (or yeast) works silently, secretly, steadily, gradually spreading its influence and power through the whole lump of dough until all is affected. Leaven (or yeast) is that which "puffs up", "makes sour", or "ferments."

Leaven in Scripture is symbolic of evil, of sin, of human fallenness, of false doctrine, of hypocrisy, of unbelief in the supernatural, of carnality, of Judaistic legalism. Paul refers to the action of leaven in the Corinthian epistle when he speaks of Christ our Passover and keeping the feast of Unleavened Bread. He speaks of those in the Corinthian church who are **"puffed up."** The effect in the church at Corinth is that others are **"puffed up"** about the sin of fornication in the church as yet undealt with. Paul urges the Corinthians to **purge out the leaven of immorality in this unrepentant member** lest the whole lump of believers at Corinth become affected by this leaven (1Corinthians 4:6,18,19; 5:2, 6-13; 8:1; 13:4; 2Corinthians 12:20-21). The Corinthians had to discipline the fornicator. As long as he was inside the church, God could not discipline him. "Them that are within ", the church must discipline. "Them that are without", God judges. Only when the fornicator was "purged out" could God deal with him, bring him to repentance and restored fellowship. "Unleavened bread" is sincerity and truth. "Leavened bread" is malice and wickedness in its various forms. The principle is true today!

What then was the reason God permitted leaven in the Feast of Pentecost in the **"NEW MEAL OFFERING?"** – "New" because the regular meal offering had no leaven in it! The reason God permitted leaven in the Feast of Pentecost was His recognition of sin and imperfections in His people, in the Church born at Pentecost, in the Spirit-filled believer, or, in the "Pentecostal Church". This is seen in the church at Corinth, and the churches of Galatia, as in every church on the face of the earth. No born-again, or Spirit-filled believer is sinlessly perfect, even though the Holy Spirit dwells within. Leaven in the wave-loaves speaks of this imperfection. But the "two leavened wave loaves "(believing, yet imperfect Jews and Gentiles) are **accepted in Christ,** who is our "unleavened bread" (the sinless one), and our "blood sacrifice" (for cleansing our sin). The leavened is accepted in the unleavened. The imperfect is accepted in the Perfect One- Christ!

Jesus is our Passover Lamb. Jesus is our Unleavened Bread. Jesus is our Meal Offering. In all things He is sinlessly perfect. There was no leaven of sin or false doctrine in Him. There was no hypocrisy, nothing that caused corruption, fermentation, or puffing up of pride. There was nothing sour in Him because of who He was!

The same is true of the sacrifice of thanksgiving. All our praise, worship and thanksgiving is tainted with our imperfection ("leaven"), but all is accepted through Christ's perfections ("unleavened") and His precious blood of redemption. The Father has made us **"accepted in the beloved"** (Leviticus 23:11 with Ephesians 1:6).

These two occasions, however, were the only occasions in which God permitted leaven, but such were only acceptable to Him through the unleavened bread and the sacrificial blood. Every other reference to leaven in Scripture is clearly seen in evil manner. The leaven which the woman took and hid is evil, evil doctrine that was put into the pure meal of the Word of God.

6. **Hidden Leaven**

   The woman took the leaven and **hid** it in the three measures of meal. Paul says that we do not **hide** the gospel from those who are perishing (2Corinthians 4:3-4). The gospel of the kingdom is not hidden leaven. The woman is doing something that is forbidden by practically all the Scriptures on leaven. She is corrupting the pure meal with leaven. She is doing something contrary to Passover, contrary to the Feast of Unleavened Bread and contrary to the laws of the Meal Offering. She is **hiding the leaven in the meal!** The very word "hid" means "to conceal in, to incorporate with." The root of the English word "cryptic" is "to conceal by covering." The gospel is not hidden, otherwise it is hidden from those who are lost.

7. **The Whole Meal Leavened**

   As seen already, leaven is yeast, which means, "swelling by fermentation." It causes the dough to swell up, to puff up. It works silently and secretly, gradually influencing the whole lump of dough. Only fire can arrest the action of leaven. The three measures of meal finally became totally influenced by the action of the hidden leaven by the woman. "A little leaven leavens the whole lump" is the principle by which the woman worked.

E. **The Practical Application Of The Parable**

   Although Jesus left the parable uninterpreted, within the context of the whole of Scripture, we believe the truth is discovered by interpreting the symbols used in the parable.

The Parable Symbols	The Interpretation of the Parable
1. The kingdom of heaven is like	Kingdom represents, is compared to
2. Leaven	False teaching and lifestyle, evil
3. A woman took	The false or harlot church
4. And hid	Secret and subversive action
5. In three measures of meal	The Word of the Eternal Godhead
6. Until the whole was leavened	The whole truth influenced by the false

Whereas the parable of the mustard seed spoke of the external or outward development of the kingdom in mystery form, and its pollution by the birds of the air; the parable of the leaven and the woman speaks of the internal corruption, and inward permeation of the pure meal of the kingdom.

The believer must recognize the fact that, over the history of the church, a false church has risen and the subtil leaven of false doctrine has influenced the whole of the pure Word of God. The woman points to the Harlot Church. She corresponds with Jezebel of Revelation 2:20 and the Great Harlot who rules over many peoples in Revelation 17:5. She is the one who has something to hide. It is the leaven of false teachings and corrupt practices. The true church, the Bride of Christ, has nothing to hide.

An extended list could be given but this chapter is already complete enough. Sufficient to give some clues as the "leaven" hidden in "the pure meal of God's Word." We think of all the great doctrines of the Bible and can see how the false church has corrupted these doctrines. The authority of the Bible has become leavened with the authority of man; the Biblical traditions with the traditions of the church; repentance with penance; justification by faith with justification by works; water baptism by immersion with sprinkling; the priesthood of all believers with clergy/laity; the gifts of the Spirit by human talents; the fruit of the Spirit with personality of educated men, and many, many other things could be listed.

The Reformers endeavoured to "purge out the leaven" from "the pure meal of God's Word" over the years, but there is still much to be purged in order to get back to the pure Word of God. The true church, the bride of Christ, will have a pure Word and not be corrupted by the leavening influences of false teachings and false practices!

In Conclusion:

The fact that "the kingdom of heaven" may be compared with all the parts of the parable continues the truth that the kingdom in its present form has both good and evil in it – in other words, mixture!

In parable one, the various soils are seen and the evil birds. Good soil and poor soil.

In parable two, the wheat and the tares are seen. Two seeds are seen, good and evil.

In parable three, the mustard seed tree and the birds are seen. Mixture is here.

In parable four, the leaven hidden in the meal by the woman is seen. Corruption is here.

It is because "the kingdom of heaven is like leaven," and the belief that the kingdom is a perfect kingdom, that expositors take "leaven" to represent the good influence of the kingdom. The kingdom works like leaven in mankind. Once, however, a complete study of the word about leaven in Scripture is considered, then the truth of leaven as evil should be understood. It speaks of evil influences and mixture.

The mixture of good and evil will continue in the kingdom in its present mystery form unto the second coming of Christ. The major lesson of this parable is the corruption of the Word of God by the evil influences of the leaven of wrong doctrine and practice. The parable reveals once more the mixture of good and evil. The meal is good. The leaven is evil. Both are blended together.

Jesus told His disciples to "beware of the leaven" of the Pharisees, the Sadducees and Herod. Paul told the Corinthian and Galatian Churches to "purge out the leaven" of malice and wickedness and keep the Passover (Christ) and Unleavend Bread with sincerity and truth. The Lord will have a church with a pure word and all leaven will be purged out in the time of the end!

CHAPTER TWELVE
THE PARABLE OF HIDDEN TREASURE

A. The Scripture on the Parable
1. Matt 13:44

Again, the kingdom of heaven is like unto treasure hid in a field; the which when a man hath found, he hideth, and for joy thereof goeth and selleth all that he hath, and buyeth that field.

B. The Setting of the Parable

The first four parables in Matthew 13 have been given to the multtitude standing on the seashore. In Matthew 13:36 Jesus sent the multitudes away and went into the house. These last four parables are given exclusively to the disciples.

C. The Moral of the Parable

The central truth of the parable of the treasure hidden in the field is this. There is a price to be paid to obtain God's kingdom-treasure. It will cost all. This parable speaks of the price of the kingdom.

D. The Exposition of the Parable

The fifth and sixth parables in the kingdom series in Matthew 13 both have a similar message. The kingdom costs one's all.

Again, this simple and short parable is left uninterpreted by Jesus. The disciples did not ask Jesus to interpret this parable, as far as can be gathered. So the expositor has to seek within the context of the whole of Scripture, and within the bounds of sound theology to find the interpretation of the parable and its parts. The parts of the parable are arranged in the order set out here to help in the exposition of the parable.

Matthew's Gospel is the only Gospel which gives account of this parable of the hidden treasure. Like other parables, this parable has also been misunderstood and misinterpreted.

1. The Kingdom Of Heaven Is Like

The kingdom of heaven is like, it resembles, corresponds to and can be compared to a treasure hidden in the field. When the man finds it, he hides it again and sells all that he has to buy the field. Obtaining the field, the treasure is also obtained. All the parts of the parable make up the parable. The kingdom of heaven in not like one part of the parable; it involves all the parts in its comparison.

2. The Treasure

It seems that interpreters of this parable have taken the treasure to be several different things. Several ideas are seen here before endeavouring to really understand what the treasure is.

Some interpreters say that the treasure is **Christ,** and once the believer finds Christ, it will cost the believer his all. These interpreters use Scripture like Luke 14:25-33 to confirm this view. They say that it will cost all to find and follow Christ. It is true that it costs one all to follow Christ, but Christ is "not for sale." We do not "buy Christ" as He "buys us." Therefore, although Christ is indeed the treasure of all treasures, the writer does not believe that the treasure in this parable refers to Christ.

Some interpreters say that the treasure is the chosen nation of **Israel,** using Psalm 135:4, Exodus 19:4-6 and Deuteronomy 14:2 to confirm this. In those Scriptures it does speak of Israel as being God's treasure, and the Lord has chosen Jacob for Himself. Israel was His peculiar (special) treasure. These interpreters speak of the Lord's cost in purchasing Israel as a nation for Himself. The writer believes that Israel was indeed God's peculiar treasure in Old Testament times, Since the cross, however, and the coming in of the New Covenant era, this has changed. This will be seen as the parable is expounded more fully.

Other expositors say that the treasure is the New Testament **Church,** and it is Christ who paid the price – His all- to buy the church. The writer of this text holds to this third view for reasons that will be seen as the exposition of the parable unfolds.

The word **"treasure"** has to do with **"a deposit"** and **"wealth"**, and this word is used in a number of different ways. But it is within the context of the parable itself that we can discover what the "treasure" of which the Lord is speaking.

* The Bible speaks of treasure cities (Exodus 1:11; Hebrews 11:26), where all the wealth of the Pharoah's of Egypt was stored.

* Babylon had its treasure house where the wealth of Babylon from the spoils of war was stored (Ezra 5:17; 6:1; 7:20; Daniel 1:2).

* The temple of the Lord at Jerusalem also had chambers or rooms which were used as a treasure house for the tithes and offerings of the people (1Chronicles 29:8; 9:26; 28:11-12; Nehemiah 10:38; 13:13).

* Solomon gathered all kinds of treasures from the nations and the kings about him (Ecclesiastes 2:8).

* The eunuch of Ethiopia had charge of all the treasure of Candace, queen of the Ethiopians (Acts 8:27).

* The righteous have much treasure in their house (Proverbns 15:6; 21:20).

* Jesus spoke of treasure in the heart of man (Matthew 6:21; 12:35; Luke 6:45). He also spoke of having treasure in heaven (Matthew 19:21; Mark 10:21; Luke 12:33-34). Where the treasure is, that is where the heart is.

* Paul speaks of having "this treasure" in earthern vessels (2Corinthians 4:7). Other Scriptures speaking of "treasure" in different aspects are Psalm 119:161; Proverbs 15:6; 21:20; Colossians 2:3; Isaiah 33:5-6;; 45:3).

But WHAT is "the treasure" in this parable? It certainly is not material things. The treasure here symbolizes **people.** The "peculiar treasure" is people. In Old Testament times, Israel was "a kingdom of priests" and God's "peculiar treasure" (Exodus 19:5; Psalm 135:4). When we come to the New Testament, however, the Gospel of Matthew clearly shows, along with the Epistle of Peter, that it is the New Testament **Church** that is now God's treasure, since the cross.

In Matthew 21:43, Jesus said, "the kingdom shall be taken from you (Jewry) and given to a nation that will bring forth the fruits thereof." The apostle Peter takes the truth on further, and writing to the believers told them that they are "a royal priesthood, a holy nation, a peculiar people (1Peter 2:5-10). The kingdom was taken from Jewry and given to the church. The church is now a kingdom of priests unto God and His Christ. The church is now God's holy nation. The church is now God's peculiar **treasure,** His peculiar people.

The language of 1 Peter 2:5-9 is taken directly from Exodus 19:1-6, and what was then given to and applied to Israel as a holy nation is now given and applied to the church, God's holy nation. In the Old Testament, before the cross, Israel was God's treasure. In the New Testament, since the cross, the church is now God's treasure. The treasure therefore, in the parable represents the church. This is confirmed further by a consideration of the other parts of the parable. Paul speaks of God's people being His peculiar people also in Titus 2:14.

3. The Field

The treasure was hidden in the field. Consistency of interpretation would accept the fact that the field here is the same field as in the other parables in Matthew 13. The field is the world (verse 38).

The seed of the kingdom was down in differing soils of the earth (verses3-8). The wheat and the tares were sown in His field (verses 24-30). The mustard seed was sown in His field (verses 31-32). The treasure is found hidden in the field (verse 44).

The Psalmist tells that the earth is the Lord's and the fulness thereof, the world and they that dwell therein (Psalm 24:1-2). It is HIS field. The field belongs to God and to His Christ. The field does not belong to the devil.

In Leviticus 25:16-25, the laws for estimating the value of a field were given, and the priest valued it according to the produce of seed. The earth is God's field!

4. The Man

Consistency of interpretation in this series of parables, as well as other parables, confirm the fact that "the man" is none other than "the Man Christ Jesus" (1Timothy 2:5-6).

In parable one the sower man is the sower of the seed of the kingdom (verse 3). In parable two the sower man is the Son of Man (verse 37). In parable three the man sows the mustard seed (verse 31). In parable five the man finds the treasure hidden in the field (verse 44). Undoubtedly it is the same man – THE MAN, Christ Jesus.

In the incarnation, the eternal WORD, became flesh, and took upon Himself the form of man in order to die for sinful man (Philippians 2:5-11; Hebrews 10:12). When the WORD was made flesh, He was called Jesus. Jesus is the name of the Son in His humanity. The Son of God became the Son of Man. He is the Man Christ Jesus (1Timothy 2:5-6; Zechariah 6:12). He is the Man whose name is the Branch!

5. Hidden, Found, Hidden

There is an interesting sequence of events pertaining to the treasure. The treasure is **hidden** in the field. The treasure is **found** in the field. The treasure is **hidden again** in the field.

(a) Treasure Hidden

It was a custom sometimes to hide treasures in a field for protection from enemies or from thieves (Compare Jeremiah 41:8; Deuteronomy 33:19; Job 3:21; Proverbs 2:4; Psalm 17:14; Matthew 6:19-20).

Israel, as a nation in Old Testament times was spoken of as God's "hidden ones" (Psalm 83:3). Jeremiah and Baruch could not be found at one time for the Lord hid them (Jeremiah 36:26). The New Testament church is spoken of as a mystery hid in God and also hidden from previous ages and generations (Ephesians 3:9; 1:4; Colossians 1:26; 2Timothy 1:9-10; 1Peter 1:20; Titus 2:14; Romans 16:25-26).

The New Testament church is indeed God's treasure hidden in the world of mankind but known by the Father God. It is a mystery even as this is a mystery parable of the kingdom.

(b) Treasure Found

The treasure is found by the man. The whole ministry of the Man Christ Jesus was to "seek and find" that which was lost.

We are not told how the treasure came to be hidden in the field, but the church has been in the mind of the Father from eternity. The Lord Jesus found this treasure. "For the Son of Man is come to seek and to save that which was lost" (Luke 19:10).

The man found the treasure in the field – the world. In the next parable, the man found the pearl of great price (Matthew 13:46). The shepherd found the lost sheep (Luke 15:5-6). The woman found the lost coin (Luke 15:9). The father said his prodigal had been lost but now he was found (Luke 15:24,32).

The church as God's treasure is made up of people, people who once were lost but have now been found, even as in Old Testament, Israel was lost but found and became God's peculiar treasure, so it is for the church in New Testament times.

(c) Treasure Hidden Again

The true church, as God's treasure, was hidden in the field of the world by the Father. The Son found this treasure and now, in His absence, the church is hidden again. The church is hidden from the eyes of the world. The world sees the structual and organized religious institutions, but it cannot see the true church as God's treasure, the special people of God.

John said "The world knows us not, because it knew Him not", and, "As He is, so are we in this world" (1John 3:1; 1John 4:17). The same thing is spoken of the church as of Christ. Here in the field of the world, the kingdom-church is not recognized as God's peculiar treasure. Jesus said that His own were in the world and the world does not know them. Truly the true church is hidden from the eyes of the carnal world.

6. His Joy

The man, after finding the treasure, and hiding it again, for the joy thereof, goes and sells all he had to buy the field. He knows if he buys the field, the treasure is also his by right of purchase.

This points to the joy of Jesus over the church, His treasure. Hebrews 12:2 speaks of Jesus, "who, for the joy that was set before Him endured the cross..." We see how often Jesus spoken of **"His joy"** to the disciples in order that their joy might be full (John 15:11; 16:20-24; 17:13).

There is joy in heaven and in the presence of the Father and the angels over one sinner that repents (Luke 15:7,10). To the faithful servant, He says, "Well done, good and faithful servant, enter into the joy of your Lord" (Matthew 25:21). The prophet Zephaniah tells us also how the Lord rejoices over us with joy, and will joy over His people with singing (Zephaniah 3:17).

John the Baptist said that Jesus, as the bridegroom, had the bride (even as Adam had Eve within him, yet to be manifested), and the friend of the bridegroom rejoiced to hear the bridegroom's voice. John was "the friend of the bridegroom", and John said his joy was complete (John 3:29-30). Christ indeed finds joy in His church, His peculiar treasure.

7. Sold His All

To obtain the treasure in the field, it cost all that the man had. From being in the Father's glory, in the Father's house, and coming to earth in the humility of the virgin birth, laying aside His reputation, and becoming a man, a servant, and being obedient unto death, even the death of the cross – it cost Jesus His all!

Theologically speaking, it is spoken of as the "kenosis theory", or "the self-emptying of Christ" in the incarnation (Philippians 2:6-11). From being in the form of God, and taking upon Himself the form of man, it cost Jesus His all. For all eternity He is now the God-Man, having taken humanity with Him in His deity. Who can understand what it cost Jesus in the incarnation and in His humiliation as a Man unto the death of the cross?

For the joy that was set before He endured **the cross** (Hebrews 12:2). It cost Him His all, His life-blood for the church, His treasured people, His peculiar people (Deuteronomy 14:2; 26:18; Titus 2:14; 1Peter 2:5-10). Calvary was the cost. There we were bought with such a price (1Corinthians 6:20; 1Peter 1:18-20).

8. Bought The Field

The man buys the field. He could not obtain the treasure without buying the field. Whoever owned the field owned the treasure in the field. If he got the field, he gets the treasure by right of ownership. The treasure is found, hidden and purchased.

There is great significance in the buying of the field. The Greek word for **"buy"** is **"agorazo"** (SC 59), and means, "to go to market, ie., (by implic.) to purchase; specially to redeem." It is translated by the words "buy, bought, redeem."

The believer certainly does not buy the world (the field) to obtain Christ as his treasure! It is the Man Christ Jesus who bought or redeemed the world (the earth, the field) to obtain the church!

We are redeemed with the precious blood of Christ the lamb of God (John 1:29,36; 1Peter 2:5-9; 1:18-21; Acts 20:20). We are redeemed to God by His blood out of every kindred, tongue, tribe and nation (Revelation 5:9-10; 1:6). We are bought with a price (1Corinthians 6:20). Jesus, by the incarnation became our Kinsman Redeemer. He has obtained eternal redemption for us by His blood to be His peculiar treasure and people (Hebrews 9:11-15; Titus 2:14). He bought us. He redeemed us. Calvary was the price of redemption. His blood was the ransom price. None can count the cost of the cross. Jesus gave Himself for the church. The church has been redeemed out of the market place of Satan.

The field is His. The church-the treasure- is also His, and this by right of redemption!

E. Practical Application Of The Parable

As already seen, Jesus left this parable uninterpreted and the disciples did not ask for the interpretation of it. It is possible that Jesus explained this short and simple parable to them, or else the disciples, as Jews, were familiar enough with their Old Testament Scriptures to understand the truths in the symbolism of the parable.

In concluding our exposition of the parable, there are two particular Old Testament real life situations which illustrate and confirm the truths set forth in the parable of the treasure in the field.

1. The Kinsman Redeemer – Boaz

In the Book of Ruth we have the beautiful account of the role of a kinsman redeemer. Naomi, after ten years in Moab, came back to the land of Bethlehem-Judah with Ruth her Gentile daughter-in-law. She has lost her land, her inheritance. The only way it could be restored to her was by a kinsman redeemer.

The laws of redemption of a lost inheritance, or the redemption of a field are given in Leviticus 25:16-25. A kinsman redeemer must have the qualifications, as seen here.

* He must be a near kinsman
* He must be able to pay the price of redemption
* He must be willing to pay the redemption price to obtain the inheritance.
* The evidence of this was written in a book and sealed before witnesses. Only the kinsman redeemer could break the seals of the book and redeem the inheritance.

In the final chapter of Ruth, we see Boaz, the kinsman redeemer marrying the Gentile bride, Ruth. Not only was he to take Ruth to be his bride, he was also obligated as the kinsman redeemer to **buy the field** that belonged to Ruth's mother-in-law, Naomi (Ruth 4). He could not have the bride without buying the field. He redeemed both the bride (Ruth) and the field (the forfeited inheritance)!

This points to Christ, our kinsman redeemer. The consummation of this is seen in Revelation 4-5 and Revelation 10:1-7. Christ, as the kinsman redeemer, has bought "the field" – the world. The devil, the ursurper, took claim over it when Adam fell and forfeited his inheritance and the inheritance of unborn generations to the devil in the Fall (Luke 4:5-6).

Christ purchased the field at Calvary. We have the earnest of our inheritance but still await "the redemption of the purchased possession" (Ephesians 1:14). The seven-sealed book is the title-deed, the evidence of the purchased possession. Jesus, as the kinsman redeemer, became our near kinsman in the incarnation. He was able to pay the price of redemption. He was willing to pay the price of redemption. All fall down and worship the lamb, the kinsman redeemer, who purchased us (the treasure) and the field (the earth) by His priceless blood "out of every kindred, tongue, tribe and nation." Jesus has bought the bride (the treasure) and the field (the earth) with His own blood. He alone, as the kinsman redeemer, can break the seals of the book, the Divine title-deed, and claim the forfeited inheritance as His own and for His own.

This is the truth of the parable of the treasure hidden in the field. The Man, Christ Jesus, has redeemed both the field and the treasure; the earth and the church!

2. The Kinsman Redeemer – Jeremiah

In the Book of Jeremiah we have the account of Judah going into Babylonian Captivity. The Jews were losing their land, their God-given inheritances. Jeremiah's first cousin was told to sell his field to him. He must sell it to a relative. It would remain his until the year of jubilee when all forfeited inheritances would go back to the lawful owner (Leviticus 25:25).

A study of Jeremiah 32 provides these insights. Jeremiah, the prophet, is a kinsman redeemer. The right of redemption of his. Jeremiah bought **the field** for seventeen shekels of silver. The evidence of this purchase was written in books, one a sealed book and the other an open book. Evidence of the purchase price was written in the book of purchase, the book of redemption. At the close of the seventy years captivity to Babylon, the Jews would be released and they would have their lost inheritances – their fields – restored to them. The land belonged to Judah. Jeremiah's enactment shadowed the truth that he, as the kinsman redeemer, had paid the price of redemption. The sealed book contained the evidence. In due time, the sealed book would be opened and the fields returned to the rightful inheritors.

Revelation chapters 4-5 confirm, once again, the same truth as in the Book of Ruth. Jesus, our sacrifice, our lamb, our kinsman redeemer, has bought the earth with the blood of redemption. He alone is qualified to break the seals of the book and claim the forfeited inheritance for His bride, the church. He is THE Prophet, THE Word of God.

The same central truth is seen in the parable of the treasure hidden in the field. Boaz redeemed the bride, Ruth, and the lost inheritance, the field of Naomi. Jeremiah, as the kinsman redeemer, purchased the fields that were taken by the Babylonians, and the evidence of the purchase price was written in a book. Jesus, the kinsman redeemer, by reason of His incarnation, has redeemed **the field** (the earth) and purchased **the treasure** (the church) and both are His by right of redemption.

Undoubtedly the disciples were familiar with the accounts in Ruth and Jeremiah and would have some understanding of the symbols in the parable of the hidden treasure, whether Jesus interpreted it for them or not. The context of the Scriptures provides clues to the interpretation of its symbols.

The Parable Symbols	The Parable Interpretation
1. The Kingdom of heaven	Resembles, comparable to
2. A Treasure	The Church
3. Hidden	The Church hidden in the mind of God
4. In a Field	The world
5. Which a Man found	The Man, Christ Jesus
6. Hides it again	Church hidden in the world
7. For joy thereof	The joy set before Jesus
8. Goes and sells all he has	Cost Christ all He had-the price paid
9. Buys the field to obtain the treasure	Redeemed the earth and the church

There are no negative parts in the parable of the treasure, as there is in the previous four parables. There are no unclean birds, or enemy, or counterfeit work, or evil in this beautiful parable.

The kingdom of heaven has within it the church as the treasure which Christ bought with His blood. He endured the cross for the joy set before Him of obtaining His bride and the forfeited inheritance. This is the truth symbolized in this short but simple kingdom parable!

CHAPTER THIRTEEN
THE PARABLE OF THE MERCHANT AND THE PEARL

A. The Scripture on the Parable
Matthew 13:45-46

Again, the kingdom of heaven is like unto a merchant man, seeking goodly pearls: Who, when he had found one pearl of great price, went and sold all that he had, and bought it.

B. The Setting of the Parable

The setting remains the same as for the last four parables. Except that, Jesus is in the house and the parable, and maybe its meaning, is given to His disciples.

C. The Moral of the Parable

The fifth and sixth parables are actually twin parables, both teaching the same central truth. The lesson of the parable of the pearl is: There is a price to be paid for the kingdom pearl and the one who sees its value will pay all that it costs him to obtain it. The moral is the priceless value and the cost of the kingdom pearl.

D. The Exposition of the Parable

Once again we have an uninterpreted parable of the kingdom, unless of course, Jesus explained it His disciples and they did not record its interpretation. It is a simple but beautiful short parable. In seeking to understand and interpret this parable, the expositor must seek to do so within the boundaries of sound theology and sound heremenutics. All the parts of the parable need to be considered as, once again, we work from part to whole and whole to part: the merchant man, the pearls and the pearl of great price.

The most general interpretation of this parable is that Christ is the pearl of great price and it will cost the believer all he has to have Christ in our possession. Old Gospel songs sing: "I've found the pearl of greatest price, My heart doth sing for joy; And sing I must, for Christ I have, Oh what a Christ have I!"

The same mistaken interpretation, however, is seen in this parable as in the previous parable. Christ is not "the hidden treasure", nor is Christ "the pearl of great price." A consideration of the parts of the parable show that this interpretation is not theologically or Scripturally correct. It does, indeed, cost the disciple his all to follow Christ, but Christ is "not for sale." He cannot be bought for a price, as the parable teaches. Christ cannot be purchased with any human price. The sinner has nothing with which to buy Christ. Salvation cost Jesus His all, but salvation is a free gift which we "buy without money or without price" (Isaiah 55:1). What then is the teaching and truth of this short parable?

1. The Kingdom of Heaven

The kingdom of heaven again, in this parable, is likened to, or represents, corresponds to and may be compared to the merchant man who seeks goodly pearls. After finding one special pearl, he sells all he has and buys that pearl. All the parts of the parable is what the kingdom of heaven is like, not just one of the parts. All the parts of a puzzle are part of the whole and no one part is the whole. So it is with the parables of the kingdom.

2. The Merchant Man

Consistency of interpretation of the kingdom of heaven parables once again points to the fact that the merchant man is the Man Christ Jesus.

The sower in the parable one points to Christ. The sower of good seed in parable two points to Christ. The sower in parable three who sows the mustard seed points to Christ. The man who found the treasure hidden in the field points to Christ. And here again, the merchant man points to Christ.

Jesus became "the Man" by His incarnation. He is the one who brought the gospel of the kingdom. He is the king of the kingdom. He is the kingdom personified. What ever the king is, so is His kingdom (Romans 14:17).

3. The Seeking

The merchant man was **seeking** goodly pearls. In the parable of the hid treasure, the man **found** the treasure hidden in the field. In the parable of the pearl, he is **seeking** goodly pearls. Christ Jesus came seeking for man. He came to seek and to save that which was lost (Luke 19:10). The shepherd sought the lost sheep; the woman sought the lost coin, and the father rejoiced when the lost son came home (Luke 15:1-32). Here the merchant man is seeking for pearls. Christ's ministry was a seeking ministry!

4. The Finding

The merchant man, after seeking, **found** one pearl of great price. That man found the treasure in the field. The shepherd found his sheep that was lost (Luke 15:5-7). The woman found the piece of coin of was lost (Luke 15:8-10). The father rejoiced when his prodigal son was lost but found (Luke 15:11-32). The merchant man found this great pearl. So Jesus' whole ministry was involved in "the lost and found" people!

5. The Selling

The merchant man, after seeking and finding, went and sold all he had. Jesus told the rich young ruler to "sell all" he had. But he was not willing to sell all the wealth of his material life for Jesus to gain the gift of eternal life (Luke 18:22-23). The man who wanted the treasure in the field, and the man who wanted the goodly pearl of great price, sold all they had to gain. So Jesus paid the supreme price. It cost Him His all, as in the parable of the treasure and the parable of the pearl.

6. The Buying

The merchant man then bought the pearl at a great price. The same truth as seen in the buying of the field and treasure is seen in the buying of the pearl. The same Greek word **"agorazo"** is used here, meaning to go to the market place and redeem at a price. So Jesus has been to the market, and He has redeemed this pearl. It was indeed bought with a price (1Corinthians 6:19; 1Peter 1:18-20). It cost Him His all at Calvary. The price was the blood of atonement. Jesus has bought the church – His pearl of great price (Ephesians 5:23-32). The Church does not buy Christ as Christ is not for sale! Christ buys the Church with His own blood; the ransom price for our redemption!

7. The Pearl of Great Price

Apart from those expositors who believe that the pearl of great price is Christ, most others see the pearl as a symbol of the New Testament Church.

The word "pearl" is used about nine times in Scripture as the following references show.

* The one pearl of great price (Matthew 13:45-46).

* The twelve gates of the city of God were each of one pearl as the redeemed enter the bride city (Revelation 21:21).

* Jesus told His disciples not to cast their pearls before swine lest they trample them under foot and turn on the owner (Matthew 7:6).

* Women are not to be overly adorned with pearls and costly garments (1Timothy 2:9).

* The great harlot church was arrayed in gorgeous clothing and decked with precious stones and pearls (Revelation 17:4). In the harlot city, pearls were precious gems also (Revelation 18:12,16).

What are the lessons and truths that are to be gleaned from a study of the pearl in Scripture? The Bible does not provide information regarding the formation of the pearl or its significance. Therefore, the student must refer to those textbooks that deal with gem-stones or other precious stones and pearls. The following information has been gleaned from these kind of textbooks, and will help us to see some of the great spiritual truths in the "goodly pearl" that Jesus referred to in this parable.

E. A Study of Pearls

1. Pearls in Scripture

A consideration of the references to pearls in Scripture will give us some insight to the truths hidden in the symbol of the pearl.

(a) A pearl represents precious truths in God's Word

Jesus said, "Cast not your pearls before swine lest they trample them under feet." As pearls are formed, so Scripture themes and truths are like the formation of pearls. The valuable things of God are not to be cast before those persons of swine nature (the unclean), who have no sense of value for Divine things, and thus trample them under foot (Matthew 7:6).

Jesus and Peter both speak of "dogs" and "swine" – both unclean animals who have no real sense of value. The student should note these Scriptures (Matthew 7:6; Philippians 3:2; Revelation 22:15; Luke 8:33; Prov 11:22; 2Peter 2:22). The Lord gives His people Scripture gems. Believers may receive a verse which acts like a "sand-grain" in his heart, and then "line upon line, precept upon precept", a pearl of Divine truth is formed, which, when surfaced, reflects the glory of God. These are the valuable pearls of truth that are not to be cast before unclean, or religious hypocrites, or backsliders, who would trample them under foot and even turn against us.

(b) A pearl represents glory through suffering

In Revelation 21 John is given a vision of the bride city. The twelve gates of the city of God are each of one pearl. All the redeemed of all ages enter through these gates, symbolic of the suffering and the glory that comes through suffering. Every pearl in nature is produced through suffering. So the redeemed are brought to birth through the sufferings of Jesus and Calvary's redemptive price.

2. The Church – The Pearl

The writer believes that "the pearl of great price" in this parable is a symbol and picture of the glorious church, the bride of Christ. There are many spiritual lessons to be drawn from the formation of the pearl, as found in those textbooks that deal with such. The following lessons from the natural pearl are applied to the spiritual pearl – the Church of the Lord Jesus Christ.

(a) The pearl was 'unclean' to Israel

The word "pearl" is not mentioned in the Old Testament. The pearl, coming from the oyster, was an unclean stone to the orthodox Israelite or othodox Jew. The laws of food from the waters included those creatures that had fins and scales (Leviticus 11:9-12). Probably this is why the pearl is not mentioned in the Old Testament (Note: "pearls" in Job 28:18 is translated "quartz" in NKJV). Pearls are not mentioned among the twelve stones on the breastplate of the high priest (Exodus 28:15-21).

The Church was 'unclean' in the eyes of Jewry because of the coming in to the kingdom of the 'unclean Gentiles'.

(b) The pearl is a most valuable gem

The Church is God's most valuable gem; it is the bride of Christ, bought at such a price, the blood of Jesus.

(c) The pearl is formed through suffering

The pearl is a unique gem. The pearl is the product of a living creature. It is the only gem like this. The formation of the pearl is like this. A foreign substance, like a grain of sand, enters the shell and pierces the side of the oyster. It causes suffering. The oyster makes a special substance called 'nacre' which lines the inside of its shell. This smooth lining is called 'the pearly layer', formed by certain cells in the body of the animal. When the grain enters the side of the oyster, these 'nacre' forming cells begin to work. They cover the invading substance with thin sheets or layers of this 'nacre', gradually building circular successive layers of 'nacre' until the foreign body is completely enclosed in the shell-like substance, thus forming the pearl.

Concentric layers form the pearl. Thus 'layer upon layer' this fluid enfolds until the formation of the pearl is completed. This flows out of the wound in the side of the oyster shell. In other words, the pearl is formed out of suffering, life and death.

So the Church is formed out of the sufferings of Jesus, from His wounded side. The Church is a foreign substance, in the natural, but Jesus accepts such and generation after generation, the church is being formed in the wounded side of Jesus. Isaiah 53 speaks of the sufferings of Christ. His death brings the church to birth. Out of His suffering, life and death comes our life (Philippians 2:5-12; Galatians 2:20; Hebrews 12:2). As the pearl is manifested through the death of the oyster, so the church is manifested through the death of Christ. She, as the pearl, owes her existence to another.

The themes of Peter's two Epistles are "the suffering" and "the glory". So Christ experienced first the suffering, then the glory, and the same is true of the church (1Peter 1:10-12).

In the Book of Acts the Lord "added to the church daily those were being saved" (Acts 2:41-47; 5:14; 11:24).

(d) The pearl formation is a mystery
The church is a mystery also, hidden in the mind of God and then revealed to His holy apostles and prophets by the Spirit (Ephesians 3:1-12; 5:23-32). The church is the great mystery. Its formation is in secret (Psalm 139:7-17), like the formation of the human body is in secret.

(e) The pearl is formed unseen in the sea
Parables five and six concern the sea, while the previous parables concern the earth. In Revelation 10:1-2 we see the Jehovah Angel with His feet on the earth and the sea, for all things are under His feet. The pearl is from the sea. The good and bad fish are from the sea. The sea represents the restless masses of humanity; the Gentiles nations more especially (Isaiah 57:20-21; Daniel 7:1-3; Revelation 13:1; Isaiah 17:12-13; Revelation 17:1,15). The sea speaks of the restlessness of the nations, the cross-currents, the under-currents of humanity, yet deep down beneath a pearl is being formed. Out of every kindred, tongue, tribe and nation, and out of the Gentiles, the Lord is taking a people for His name (Acts 15:14-18). He is forming the pearl of His church.

Joseph received a Gentile bride. Moses received a Gentile bride. Jesus receives a bride of both Jew and Gentile out of the sea of humanity.

(f) The pearl best formed in salt waters
Fresh water pearls do not have the same value as those formed in sea water. Salt is necessary, otherwise the pearl lacks something in its very fibre. The church needs the "salt of God's word" (Colossians 4:6; Mark 9:50; Mathew 5:13).

(g) The pearl is a taken-out gem
Diamonds and other stones are formed under pressure. The pearl is formed in a living creature, and then 'taken out' of the oysters side. The church is the 'ekklesia', or the 'called and taken out company' for the Lord Jesus Christ.

(h) The pearl and its light
Though pearls are formed in the depths of the sea, in the darkness of the oyster shell, yet when it is brought to the surface, it has all the colours of rainbow light in it. The colours of grey, pink, orange, gold, or white may be seen in the beauty of the pearl. Other pearls have the rainbow colours. Mineral stones reflect light. Pearls absorb light as well as reflect light (Matthew 5:14; Revelation 12:1). The church, though formed in the darkness of this world, and the sea of the nations, yet when brought to full

manifestation will reflect the light of God which she has absorbed in the time of her formation (Matthew 5:14). The world does not see the beauty in the church's formation but God does. She is all-glorious within (Psalm 45:9-13).

(i) A perfect pearl is without blemish

Perfect pearls have no blemish. Pearls that have only one blemish can have this blemish removed, if the flaw is not too deep. Carefully trained men called 'peelers' carefully scrape away the blemished layers. When the flaw is removed, the pearl is smaller, but perfect, and worth great value, even sometimes more than the larger and blemished pearl. Jesus is going to have a church "without spot, or wrinkle, or blemish, or any such thing" (Ephesians 5:23-32).

(j) A pearl has a unique unity

A diamond, or gold, or other gem stones can be cut, but one cannot cut a pearl without destroying its unity. Only gem like it is the genuine pearl. The merchant man found this one pearl of great price. Though made of many layers, it is still one pearl. It is a compound unity. So is the unity of the true church in answer to the prayer of Christ (John 17). Though many members, there is one body (1Corinthians 12). Though many stones, there is one temple (Ephesians 2:19-22; 1Peter 2:5-8). This church is the undefiled one, the choice one in the Song of Solomon (Song 6:8-10). Read also Acts 20:28; Revelation 12:1; 19:6-8.

(k) A pearl has varying glory

The pearl has the same lustre and colour as the lining of the oyster shell. When the pearl is brought to the surface, each pearl has its distinctive light and glory. The outward beauty of the pearl is exactly that of the inner beauty. So is the resurection of the saints. The saints will have the glory of the sun, the glory of the moon, or the glory of the stars in resurrection glories (1Corinthians 15:41-42). There will be the same beauty outwardly as there is inwardly.

(l) A pearl has to be cared for

Pearls need caring for. They have to be washed, graded and polished to be be all that they were made to be. So believers in the church need to be washed and polished by the Word and Spirit of God to be all that the Lord made them to be.

(m) A pearl has various 'sea enemies'

The pearl has various sea enemies that seek to destroy its very life and existence. Certain fish, like the black porky fish, or the star-fish will seek to destroy the oyster and in doing so destroy the pearl. Other sea creatures like the eel, or the octopus will cut the oyster shell or suffocate it and then eat the shell-fish, thus destroying the pearl. Other enemies could be listed. So the church has 'sea enemies' who seek to suffocate her life, and destroy her formation. These have to be guarded against in the formation of the church in the sea of the nations. Satan and his demonic forces seek to destroy the church.

There are many other lessons which may be learned from a study of the natural pearl and its formation. Sufficient lessons are seen here as spiritually applicable to the church.

F. The Practical Application Of The Parable

As already seen, parables five and six are twin parables, both teaching the same truth: the priceless value of the kingdom, as a treasure and a pearl. A comparison of both these parables confirm this truth.

The Parable Of The Treasure	The Parable Of The Pearl
1. The Man	The Merchant Man
2. Found	Seeking
3. Hidden treasure	Goodly pearls
4. Sold all he had	Sold all he had
5. Bought the field	Bought the pearl
6. The field and treasure his	The pearl from the sea is his

There is no thought of 'evil' or 'mixture' in this mystery parable of the kingdom, even as there is none in the parable of the treasure in the field. Both teach the same truth basically under different symbols. Both had a man in them. Both find something valuable. Both sold all they had. Both bought the valuable. One was a treasure, one was a pearl. One was hid in the field, the other hid in the sea. The cost for one was all, the cost for the other was all.

The Church is the pearl of great price. It is formed in the wounded side of Jesus, in the sea of the nations of earth. It is formed in the darkness of this world, formed through suffering, as member upon member is 'added to the church' (Acts 2:41-47).

The various pearls can represent the different groupings of God's people formed over the centuries of church history, each shining in their glory. In Revelation 21:12,21 we see the various tribes of Israel on the names of the twelve gates of pearl. Each of the tribes of spiritual Israel will have their various glories in their formation through suffering.

The "one pearl" speaks of "the glorious church", without spot, or wrinkle, or blemish or any such thing for which Jesus paid the supreme price at Calvary (Ephesians 5:23-32; Galatians 3:13; 4:5; Revelation 5:9-10). What a glorious privilege and honour to be part of the "pearl of great price". Christ is the merchant man who sought us, bought us at such a price. He has the church as His treasure and now He has the pearl as His glory!

Such is the wonderful truth in the parable of the merchant man and the goodly pearls!

CHAPTER FOURTEEN
THE PARABLE OF THE NET AND FISH

A. The Scripture on the Parable
Matthew 13:47-50

Again, the kingdom of heaven is like unto a net, that was cast into the sea, and gathered of every kind:

Which, when it was full, they drew to shore, and sat down, and gathered the good into vessels, but cast the bad away.

So shall it be at the end of the world: the angels shall come forth, and sever the wicked from among the just,

And shall cast them into the furnace of fire: there shall be wailing and gnashing of teeth.

B. The Setting of the Parable

The setting is the same as in the last two parables, parables five and six. Jesus is in the house with His disciples teaching further truths by means of parables.

C. The Moral of the Parable

This is the seventh parable in this series. This seventh parable actually has enough interpretation given by Jesus Himself and the moral of the parable is basically the same as seen in the parable of the wheat and tares. Parable two and parable seven are twin parables. The central truth, along with other supportive truths is: The gospel net brings into the kingdom in its present mystery form both good and bad. This mixture in the kingdom will continue until the end of the age when the final separation takes place and eternal destinies are settled for ever. This parable is only to be found in Matthew's Gospel. It reveals the fact that there is mixture in the kingdom is its present mystery form and manifestation.

D. The Exposition of the Parable

As already seen, this is a twin parable and corresponds in truth to the parable of the wheat and tares. The truth is the same although the symbols are different. Present mixture, future separation is taught in the second and the seventh parables. Here Jesus gives a reasonable extended analogy of the parts of the parable, so there is not too much left for human imagination. Jesus interprets parables one, two and seven enough to provide interpretative clues and keys for other uninterpreted parables.

The parables of the mustard seed, the woman and the leaven, the hidden treasure and the pearl of great price were left uninterpreted for us. Or else, Jesus interpreted them to His disciples in the house. Alternatively, the expositor would interpret the uninterpreted within the bounds of Biblical theology and Biblical hermeneutics. This is what the writer has sought to do in this text.

However, this present parable has enough interpretative clues given by Jesus for us in order to work from part to whole and whole to the part.

1. The Kingdom of Heaven

Once again, the kingdom is heaven is likened to, it resembles, or may be compared to a net cast into the sea, gathering good and bad fish. When it is full, it is brought to the land and the fish are separated; the good being placed in vessels and the bad being thrown away and cast into a furnace of fire.

2. The Net

The net here is the "gospel net". The Greek word has the meaning of a "drag-net", not an ordinary fishing net. As the gospels show, there were several ways of catching fish, as seen here.

* There was the fishing line cast from the shore, catching one fish at a time. This Peter did when the Lord told him to catch a fish with the temple tax money in its mouth and pay the tax for both Peter and Himself (Matthew 17:24-27). The fishing line needs a hook, a sinker and bait to catch the fish.

* There was the casting net from the shore, catching a small shoal of fish.

* There was the larger casting net thrown from the boat out in the ocean. This is seen in Luke 5:1-11 and John 21.

* Here in this parable it is a **drag-net.** It is different from the fishing-nets. The drag-net is that kind of a net which actually drags the bottom of the sea and brings in anything and everything in its pathway. The word is only used here in this parable. The other word used in the Gospels is a large fishing-net, and is spoken of mainly in the other Scriptures concerning nets. That is, the drag-net (Gk. **'sagene'**), is different from the fishing-net (Gk. **'diktuon'**) and a large fishing-net (Gk. **'amphiblestron'**).

For regular fishing-nets see Matthew 4:20,21; Mark 1:18-19; Luke 5:1-6; John 21:1-12; Matthew 4:18.

For casting-nets see Ezekiel 26:5,14; 47:10.

For the drag-net see Psalm 41:10; Isaiah 19:8 and Matthew 13:47-50.

A net is a mesh of strong cords used to catch things, or a means of catching birds, beasts, fish or otherwise. The drag-net is especially used for drawing all kinds of fish from the bottom of the sea where one is fishing. The drag-net is the gospel net and speaks of the ministry of Christ's disciples when He called them to be "fishers of men" and do the great work of evangelization of the world.

The drag-net speaks of a great ingathering of fish, not the catching of one fish at a time. It is a great catch of fish, like at the beginning and end of Christ's ministry where the disciples threw their nets in for a miraculous catch of fish (Luke 5:1-11; John 21:1-12).

In the gospels we see the disciples (a) **Casting** their nets (Matthew 4:18), and (b) **Mending** their nets (Matthew 4:21), and (c) **Washing** their nets (Luke 5:2)! The net is very important and must be kept in good condition and order to catch fish for the Master!

3. The Sea

It is significant to see that the first five parables in Matthew 13 have to do with the earth, while the last two have to do with the **sea,** the ocean. The first five parables concern the product of the field or the earth. Seed, birds, mustard tree, meal, leaven are of the earth. Pearls and fish have to do with the sea. The parables moves from the land to the sea. In Revelation 10:2 John sees the Jehovah-Angel who has one foot on the land and the other on the sea. It signifies all things are under His feet (See also Revelation 13:1,11).

The Scriptures interpret the sea and the waters for us when used in symbolic sense. "The wicked are like the troubled sea whose waters cannot rest, tossing up mire and dirt" (Isaiah 57:20-21). The waters speak of nations, kindreds, tongues and peoples (Revelation 17:1,15). The sea speaks of the restlessness, cross-currents and under-currents of sinful and restless humanity. Read also these Scriptures: Isaiah 17:12-13; Daniel 7:1-3; Revelation 13:1; Jeremiah 50:42; Habakukk 1:14.

4. The Ingathering

The drag-net gathered fish of every kind, the good fish and the bad fish. It was a mixed catch indeed. It gathered of every kind. It is the seventh parable and speaks of the end-time ingathering of good and bad into the kingdom in its present mystery form.

The laws of the Lord given to Israel were the laws by which they could discern the good fish from the bad fish, the unclean from the clean fish. The two signs of clean fish were fins and scales, whether in the waters of the sea, or the rivers of the land. Anything else was an abomination to them. They were unclean and forbidden to eat these kind of fish (Leviticus 11:9-12; Deuteronomy 14:9-10). So the Lord knows the signs of the good fish and the bad fish in the same net!

5. The Mixture in the Net

Again, as in previous parables, we see there is mixture in the kingdom. There are both wheat and tares, meal and leaven, mustard seed tree and birds, good and bad fish. The wedding feast gathered in "good and bad guests" (Matthew 22:10). Five out of these seven parables have **mixture** in them and this mixture will remain in the kingdom in its present state unto the end and the second coming of Christ. Mixture has to be recognized in this age relative to the kingdom of God as manifested in the church.

6. The Full Net

When the net was full, it was brought to shore. The "full net" speaks of the "fulness of time", the end of the age. It brings one to the second advent of Christ. God will bring all to account, the righteous and the wicked, the wheat and the tares, the good and the bad fish.

In the parable of the wheat and the tares, the harvest is "the end of the age" (verses 39,40). In the parable of the good and bad fish, the full net is "the end of the age" (verse 49). It is the fulness of time (Ephesians 1:10).

7. The Great Separation

Once the drag-net is full, it is drawn to shore. The fishermen sit down and separate the good fish from the bad fish. They know which is the clean and the unclean by the two signs of "fins" and "scales". Nobody knows what is in the net until it is emptied out. In spiritual sense, the clean fish are those having "fins" (which speaks of movement), and "scales" (which speaks of separation)! The clean fish must have spiritual and onward movement in the sea of humanity, and be separated by holiness from the pollution of the sea of humanity.

Jesus supplies an additional interpretative word to this parable in verses 49-50. He says the angels (messengers) are the ones who come forth and separate the wicked from among the just, as they also separated the tares from among the wheat (verses 41 with 49). The present mixture is headed for separation at the end of this age and the time of judgment. Angel-messengers are involved in the judgments of God both throughout history and the end of the age (Matthew 24:31; 25:31 and Revelation 14:18-19). In this age there is association, in the end it is separation!

8. The Judgment

Separation comes before judgment. The judgment of the bad fish, the wicked, is the same as that of the tares, the children of the wicked one (verse 42 with 50). Both tares and bad fish, the wicked and the children of the wicked one, are cast into the furnace of fire. There is wailing and gnashing of teeth (Revelation 19:20; 20:10; Matthew 8:12; 22:13; 24:51). Grief and sorrow and eternal torment are their portion.

The wheat is taken into God's barn. The good fish are gathered into vessels. Both these symbols point to the Father's kingdom (verses 30,40,48).

The same truth will be seen in the separation of the sheep and the goats. The sheep inherit the Father's kingdom and eternal life. The goats are cursed into everlasting punishment, and everlasting fire prepared for the devil and his angels (Matthew 25:31-46). The reader is referred to read the parable of the wheat and tares once more.

E. The Practical Application of the Parable

Because a number of the disciples were fishermen by trade, Jesus taught them many lessons by means of their fishing skills. Following the Scriptures through provides an excellent study and much truth that has a bearing on this seventh parable of the drag-net and the fish. All believers are called to "fishers of men" for Christ. But Jesus, though a carpenter by trade, is still the Master Fishermen and He knows how to "catch men" far better than we do. Following, in outline form, is a study of the major Scriptures pertaining to the role of the fishermen in Christ's time, and has its spiritual and practical lessons for our times.

1. Jesus called His disciples to follow Him and He would make them to become "fishers of men" (Mark 1:16-20; Matthew 4:18-22). Simon, Andrew, Peter and John were called to follow Christ. They would "catch men" for Christ even as they had caught fish in their trade.

2. Ezekiel, in vision, saw the fishermen spreading their nets that gathered in all kinds of fish from the river. The fish were according to their kinds, as fish of the great sea, and exceeding many (Ezekiel 47:1-12). There was a great multitude of fish. Fish are symbolic of souls being brought into the kingdom of God by the gospel net.

3. The Lord prophesied through Jeremiah that He would send for many fishers and hunters and they would fish and hunt for His people, from every nation, hill and even the holes of the earth (Jeremiah 16:16).

4. At the beginning of Christ's ministry, the disciples had toiled all night and caught nothing. At the word of Jesus they let down the nets and enclosed a multitude of fishes. The nets were broken and they called other partners to help them with such a haul. Peter realized that the Lord Jesus had drawn those fish

into the net and confessed his sinful unbelief at the Lord's word to "let down the nets." Christ's word to Peter was, "Fear not, from this time forth you will catch men!" (Luke 5:1-11; Matthew 4:18).

5. Jesus fed the five thousand people with a miracle of multiplied bread and fish (Luke 9:12-17).

6. Jesus also fed about four thousand people with a miracle of multiplied bread and fish (Matthew 15:32-39).

7. Jesus told Peter to catch a fish and in its mouth would be sufficient money to pay for them both in the temple tax. The one fish catch was a miracle (Matthew 17:24-27). In obedience to the word of Jesus, Peter experienced this miracle catch to meet a financial need.

8. At the close of Christ's earthly ministry, the disciples had toiled all night and caught nothing. At the word of Jesus, they let down the nets and caught a great number of fish, one hundred and fifty fish in all. The net was not broken this time. In the meaning of numbers, one hundred and fifty three is the number of revival, the number of ingathering.

The disciples learnt many lessons over this three and one half years of Christ's ministry. Peter, as well as the other fishermen, knew all the tricks to catch fish, they knew the right bait and moments, but, with all their wisdom and 'know-how', they toiled all night and caught nothing.

At the word of Jesus, they let down the nets and experienced a miraculous catch of fish. How did it all happen? They knew that He had moved upon those fish, and drew them into the net. There was something of Divine sovereignty in it all, along with human responsibility. They did the possible ("let down the nets"), and Jesus did the impossible (drew the fish into the nets)! The Lord has power over all men, and power in heaven and in earth (John 17:2; Matthew 11:27; John 6:44,45,65; Song of Solomon 1:4).

The disciples had natural skills but they would need spiritual skills to catch men. Jesus had to teach them reliance on His word, obedience to His word and His ways. Then they would become fishers of men, not by their might or power, or their skills, but by the Holy Spirit's power. The parable of the drag-net and the fish would have its significance in the light of their time with Jesus.

The Parable Symbols	The Interpretation of the Parable
1. The kingdom of heaven is like	His kingdom represents, is comparable
2. The drag-net	The gospel net
3. Cast into sea	The sea of humanity in the nations
4. Gathered of all kinds	The ingathering of souls
5. Good and bad fish in the net	Mixture in the kingdom and church
6. The net became full	The fulness of this dispensation
7. The bad fish cast away	Judgment, fire,wailing, gnashing
8. The good fish into vessels	The righteous into the kingdom

The disciples of Jesus, both then and now, must recognize that the gospel net will draw in both good and bad. This has existed through out church history. This age is an age of mixture, and this mixture will continue until the end of this present age, unto the coming of Christ. At the time, the judgment and separation will take place and eternal destinies will be settled.

It is fitting to conclude this chapter with a brief comparison of two parables; the parable of the wheat and tares and the parable of the net and fish.

Parable of Wheat and Tares	Parable of Drag-Net and Fish
1. Wheat and tares	Good and bad fish
2. In the field	In the net
3. Mixture of seed in the field	Mixture of fish in the net
4. Gathered the tares and wheat	Gathered the good and bad fish
5. The harvest time	The full net
6. The end of the age	The end of the age
7. The great separation	The great separation
8. By the angel messengers	By the angel messengers
9. Wheat into the barn	Good fish into vessels
10. Tares into bundles	Bad fish thrown away
11. The furnace of fire	The furnace of fire
12. Wailing and gnashing of teeth	Wailing and gnashing of teeth

Both parables teach the same central truth as well as other supportive truths. It is an age of present mixture in the kingdom but future eternal separation. The believer can expect the greatest ingathering of souls in this end of the age, the time of the seventh parable, but must recognize that there will be mixture unto the second coming of Christ and the final separation of the wicked from the righteous – for ever!

CHAPTER FIFTEEN
THE PARABLE OF THE HOUSEHOLDER

A. The Scripture on the Parable
Matthew 13:51-52

Jesus saith unto them, Have ye understood all these things? They say unto him, Yea, Lord.

Then said he unto them, Therefore every scribe which is instructed unto the kingdom of heaven is like unto a man that is an householder, which bringeth forth out of his treasure things new and old.

B. The Setting of the Parable

The setting is still in the house with His disciples. This is the conclusion of this special series of kingdom of heaven parables. It is only to be found in Matthew's Gospel.

C. The Moral of the Parable

The major lesson of the parable is: Christ's disciples are to be like scribes, and as every disciple has received instruction in the things of the kingdom, he must also instruct others in the same way. He must teach others what he himself has been taught.

D. The Exposition of the Parable

Some expositors accept this as the eighth parable in this series, others only accept the seven distinct or more particularly designated parables. However, the first parable, and this eighth parable, though not strictly designated as "parables" have the instruction about the kingdom of heaven in them. It would seem that the eight parable actually tells the disciples what to do with the seven parables they have been given.

The writer accepts this as a short and simple parable or simile. It presents its challenge to the disciples in the light of all that Jesus had taught them in this parabolic grouping. Jesus closes off this teaching of parables by asking the disciples, "Have you understood all these things taken together? They said, Yes, Lord" (Amplified N.T. verse 51). By their answer, they must have understood even the parables that are left uninterpreted, as far as we are concerned. Or else, they understood them in the context of Old Testament Scripture and Jewish culture.

As seen in the first parable, many in the multitude "heard and understood not" (Matthew 13:13,14,15; 15:10,17; 16:9,11; Mark 8:21; Luke 8:10). Philip asked the Ethiopian, as he was reading the prophet Isaiah, "Do you understand what you are reading?" He replied, "How can I, except someone guide me?" (Acts 8:29-31). After the resurrection of Jesus, He opened the understanding of the disciples that they might understand the Scriptures (Luke 24:45). The issue is: Do we understand what Jesus taught in these parables? This leads us to the parts of the parable needing interpretation and explanation.

1. The Scribe and Householder

Jesus said that every scribe was like an householder, providing two significant thoughts here which need to be understood: the scribe and the householder.

(a) The Scribe

The scribes, also called, lawyers, were the theologican of Christ's day. They were the official interpreters of the Word of God. The Greek word for scribe in Strong's Concordance is **"grammateus"** (SC 1122), meaning, a writer, ie., (professionally) scribe or secretary. The scribes guarded the Scriptures and the sacred writings.

Over the years, however, they became, along with the Pharisees, the Sadducees and the priests, some of the greatest enemies of Christ. Through faulty theology and faulty hermeneutics, they had "taken away the key of knowledge" (Luke 11:52). The priests were to be the spiritual rulers; the elders were to be the rulers in the synagogues, but the scribes were to be the moral rulers, sound in theology and sound in principles of interpreting the sacred writings. It seems that history points to Ezra, the priest and scribe, as being "the father of hermeneutics" who read and explained the law to the people of Judah when they came out from the Babylonian Captivity (Nehemiah 8 with Ezra 7:6,11).

In the wisdom of God, He would raise up apostles, prophets, evangelists, shepherds and teachers. To these would be given "the key of knowledge", and they would become the theologians and hermeneuticians of the Scriptures in the stead of the Old Testament ministries who crucified Christ. The New Testament ministers, like the apostles of Jesus, would become the teachers of New Covenant truths (Luke 11:49,52; Matthew 23:34; Ephesians 4:9-16). The kingdom and the keys would be taken from Jewry and given to the church, God's holy new nation (Matthew 21:43; 1Peter 2:5-9). The disciples and believers today are likened therefore, to "scribes" – teachers, instructors of the sacred writings, the Scriptures!

(b) The Householder

Jesus said the kingdom of heaven is like unto a man who is an householder. The kingdom of heaven represents, resembles or may be compared a man who is an householder. This is the thought here.

The Greek word **"oikodespotes"** (SC 3617), translated "householder" comes from **"oikos"** (SC 3624), meaning "a dwelling", by implication, "a family", and also from SC 1203, meaning "a husband, an absolute ruler." The householder was head of the family, the master of the house (Matthew 13:17,52; 20:1; 21:33; Luke 14:21).

A related word is **"oiknomos"** (SC 3623 coming from SC 3624 and the base of SC 3551), that is, "a steward". This word speaks of a house distributor, a manager, or overseer, or an employer in that capacity, or a fixed agent in the charge of a treasure. It is translated by the words chamberlain, governor and steward (Luke 12:42; 16:1-8; 1Peter 4:10).

Paul, as a preacher of the gospel, knew he was a steward of the mysteries of God (1Corinthians 4:1-2). Paul knew that a dispensation of the gospel of the grace of God had been committed to him and was faithful in the dispensing of the same to the people of God (1Corinthians 9:16-17; Ephesians 3:1-2; Colossians 1:25; Romans 2:16; 16:25).

The husband, as head of the family, or the steward of a household was responsible to provide the right and proper food to the family. They were to be **faithful and wise** stewards.

So Jesus shows the apostles in this parable that they, along with all ministers of the gospel are called to be householders, stewards of the mysteries of God and feed God's people according. Stewards are called to be faithful, responsible and accountable in their stewardship. The steward is the one to whom things have been committed. He is a house manager (Matthew 25:14-30; Luke 12:41-48).He is in charge of Divine treasure. These are the thoughts of a disciple being a scribe and householder. He is a teacher and dispenser of Divine truths.

2. The Instruction
The scribe or the man who is a householder has received instruction in the kingdom of heaven, the kingdom of heaven parables in the context of Matthew Chapter 13.

Through the series of the parables here, and the whole of the Gospel of Matthew, Jesus has instructed His disciples about the kingdom of God. The Gospel of Matthew is especially "the Gospel of the kingdom." The kingdom would be taken from Jewry and given to the church, the new and holy nation (Matthew 21:43; 1Peter 2:5-9). In the forty days of post-resurrection ministry, Jesus instructed His disciples about the things pertaining to the kingdom of God (Acts 1:3).

The Book of Proverbs has much to say about a wise man who receives instruction and he will be much wiser (Proverbs 1:2,3,7,8; 8:33; 9:9; 12:1; 15:33; 21:11; Luke 1:4; Acts 18:25). One who instructs others must also be willing to receive instruction himself. One can only teach others if one himself is teachable. The Scriptures are profitable for doctrine, for reproof, for correction, for **instruction in righteousness,** that the man of God may be perfect, throughly furnished unto all good works "(2Timothy 3:16-17).

3. The Treasure
As seen in the parable of the treasure hid in the field, the Scriptures speak of various kinds of treasure; treasure houses, treasure places and treasures of all kinds of things. The student is referred back to the number of Scriptures on "treasure" in that parable.

Undoubtedly, the most appropriate Scripture on "the treasure" in this short parable is Matthew 12:35. Here Jesus said: "A good man out of the **good treasure of his heart** brings forth **good things,** and an evil man out of the **evil treasure** brings forth **evil things**" (See also Luke 6:45; Matthew 12:34; 6:21; 2Corinthians 4:7). Although the Word is a treasure, and we have a treasure in earthern vessels, in the context and understanding of this parable, "the treasure" would speak of **the heart** of the scribe or householder. It is out of the abundance of the heart that the mouth speaks (Matthew 12:34-35). The New Testament scribe and householder will bring forth good things that Jesus entrusted to him out of the good treasure of his heart.

4. Things Old and New

Jesus said the scribe or householder will bring forth out of his treasure "things NEW and OLD" (verse 52).

The expression "old and new" would be familiar to the disciples, both from their Old Testament Scriptures and the teachings of Jesus, as well as Jewish culture. The Lord promised Israel that He would bless them in the land He gave them, and He would establish His covenant with them. The promise was given: "And you shall eat the **old** store and bring forth the **old** because of the **new"** (Leviticus 26:7-10). As the new harvest store came in, they would eat of the old in the transition from the old to the new. The Lord promised them that, if they kept the sabbaths of the land (every seventh year), He would bless them in their fruits. He would command His blessing on them in the sixth year to bring forth fruit for three years, even to the ninth year. They would eat of the **old** unto the ninth year (Leviticus 25:19-22). They ate of the old until they could eat of the new.

When Israel entered Canaan land, the manna ceased (the old wilderness food), and they ate of the "old corn" of the land, and then in due time the fruit of the land (Joshua 5:12). From the old store to the new fruit was the Lord's way.

The bride in the Song of Solomon spoke of "all manner of pleasant fruits, **new and old,** which I have laid up for you, O my beloved "(Song 7:10-13).

Jesus spoke of the **old and the new** in the parables of the new wine and old wineskins, and the new garment and the old garment (Matthew 9:17; Mark 2:21-22; Luke 5:36-39).

The whole truth of the "old and the new" is found in Hebrews 8 with Jeremiah 31:31-34. There the Lord spoke of the OLD Covenant and the NEW Covenant (Hebrews 8:13).

It is in this sense that an application may be made to this parable. The householder or steward of the mysteries of God, the mysteries of the kingdom of heaven, can bring forth treasures both new and old. That is, truths coming from the New Testament that were in seed form in the Old Testament. Because the Old Covenant pointed to the New Covenant, one cannot understand the New without the Old!

It has been said, concerning the Testaments:

"The New is in the Old contained, The Old is in the New explained,

The New is in the Old concealed, The Old is in the New revealed,

The New is in the Old enfolded, The Old is in the New unfolded,

The New is in the Old replete, The Old is in the New complete."

The teacher instructed in the kingdom of heaven will be able to bring forth truths out of the Old Covenant, bring them to and through the cross, and teach New Covenant realities. The Old Covenant was to bring in the New Covenant through the cross of Jesus. The Old Covenant was fulfilled and abolished at the cross. We are now New Covenant believers. The teacher only goes back to the Old Covenant to bring his hearers to the New Covenant. Things are taught from the Old (Law) and from the New (Grace). The Law was given by Moses, but Grace and Truth came by Jesus Christ (John 1:17). He can instruct others as he has been instructed. One cannot understand the New Testament without the Old Testament and the Old cannot be understood without the New. It is here that the steward brings forth "things both new and old!" In Christ are stored all the treasures of wisdom and knowledge (Colossians 2:3), and knowing Christ, the instructor can receive things new and old. He will use the Old Testament to illustrate the truths in the New Testament, for, there is no New Testament truth or doctrine that cannot be illustrated from the Old Testament shadows. Whether it be justification, salvation, redemption, sacrifice, priesthood, approach to God, worship, and numerous other truths, all doctrines in the New are shadowed forth in the Old!

E. The Practical Application of the Parable

Woven throughout the exposition and interpretation of the parable there has been much practical application to believers and ministers of the gospel. The symbols in the parable have been interpreted, as seen in column form here.

The Parable Symbols	The Interpretation of the Parable
1. The Scribe	The teacher or minister
2. The man, the householder	Believers and stewards of the Word
3. The instruction	The kingdom of heaven parables
4. The treasure	The heart of the steward
5. Things new and old	Truths of God in Old and New Covenants

The Christian teacher is a scribe, a householder, a steward of the mysteries of God, and as such he is responsible to instruct others in the kingdom of heaven.

In concluding this chapter, as well as the mystery parables of the kingdom, it is fitting to see how the Lord Jesus gave His apostles, as His stewards, the mysteries pertaining to His purposes. As seen, Paul said he was **a steward of the mysteries of God,** and it is necessary for a steward to be faithful in the handling of these mysteries (1Corinthians 4:1-2). Jesus, Paul and John are the three major teachers of these mysteries. These are listed here for the consideration of the diligent student.

1. The Lord Jesus

The mysteries of the kingdom of heaven parables (Matthew 13). A mystery is "that which is known to the initiated "(Matthew 13:11; Mark 4:11; Luke 8:10). Heathen cults had initiation ceremonies in the cultic mysteries. It is the Holy Spirit who initiates the believer-steward into the mysteries of the kingdom of heaven parables (Matthew 13).

2. The Apostle Paul

The mystery of Israel's blindness (Romans 11:25).

The mystery of the Gospel (Romans 16:25; Ephesians 6:19).

The mystery of the resurrected and immortalized saints (1Corinthians 15:51-55; 1Thessalonians 4:16-17).

The mystery of God's will (Ephesians 1:9-11).

The mystery of Jews and Gentiles in one body (Ephesians 3:3-9).

The great mystery of the marriage of Christ and His Church (Ephesians 5:22-32).

The mystery of Christ in you (Colossians 1:26-27).

The mystery of God the Father and Christ (Colossians 2:2-3).

The mystery of Christ (Colossians 4:3).

The mystery of iniquity (2Thessalonians 2:7).

The mystery of the faith (1Timothy 3:9).

The mystery of godliness (1Timothy 3:16).

The mystery of widom of God (1Corinthians 2:7-10).

The mysteries spoken in unknown tongues (1Corinthians 14:2).

3. The Apostle John

The mystery of the seven stars and seven lampstands (Revelation 1:20).

The finished mystery of God (Revelation 10:7).

The great mystery, Mystery Babylon, Mother of Harlots (Revelation 17:5,7).

Believers are scribes, instructors, and stewards of the mysteries of the kingdom of heaven and the other mysteries laid out in the Word of God. As householders, feeding the house of God – the church – with the food of the kingdom, all must speak the truth in love. Paul said, "... though I understand all mysteries and have not love, I am nothing..." (1Corinthians 13:2).

Conclusion:

A cursory glance over the eight parables expounded show that there is Divine pattern in their order. This pattern is summarized here as a suitable conclusion to Matthew Chapter 13 and the eight "kingdom of heaven" parables.

Grouping One	**Grouping Two**
To the multitude	To the disciples
Outside the house	Inside the house
Parables given	Parables given
1. The Word of the Kingdom	8. The Scribe of the Kingdom
2. Wheat and Tares – Mixture	7. Good and Bad Fish – Mixture
3. Mustard Seed Tree and Birds	6. Pearl of Great Price
4. Leaven in the Meal	5. Treasure in the Field

There is much instruction for every believer in the mystery parables of the kingdom!

CHAPTER SIXTEEN
THE PARABLE OF THE KING AND HIS SERVANTS

A. The Scripture on the Parable
Matthew 18:23-35

Therefore is the kingdom of heaven likened unto a certain king, which would take account of his servants.

And when he had begun to reckon, one was brought unto him, which owed him ten thousand talents.

But forasmuch as he had not to pay, his lord commanded him to be sold, and his wife, and children, and all that he had, and payment to be made.

The servant therefore fell down, and worshipped him, saying, Lord, have patience with me, and I will pay thee all.

Then the lord of that servant was moved with compassion, and loosed him, and forgave him the debt.

But the same servant went out, and found one of his fellowservants, which owed him an hundred pence: and he laid hands on him, and took him by the throat, saying, Pay me that thou owest.

And his fellowservant fell down at his feet, and besought him, saying, Have patience with me, and I will pay thee all.

And he would not: but went and cast him into prison, till he should pay the debt.

So when his fellowservants saw what was done, they were very sorry, and came and told unto their lord all that was done.

Then his lord, after that he had called him, said unto him, O thou wicked servant, I forgave thee all that debt, because thou desiredst me:

Shouldest not thou also have had compassion on thy fellowservant, even as I had pity on thee?

And his lord was wroth, and delivered him to the tormentors, till he should pay all that was due unto him.

So likewise shall my heavenly Father do also unto you, if ye from your hearts forgive not every one his brother their trespasses.

B. The Setting of the Parable

The place seems to be at Capernaum, Jesus home town (Compare Matthew 4:13; 17:24; 18:1). The setting has to do with Peter's question about forgiveness. Jesus had spoken about trespasses between brothers in the church and the procedure of reconciliation. In the whole chapter context (Matthew 18), the theme has to do with offences and forgiveness, as seen in brief here:

Verses 1-10 speaks of offences against little ones in the kingdom.

Verses 15-20 speaks of trespasses and faults between brothers, even unto excommunication, if there is no reconciliation. Jesus teaches that the first step in reconciliation should be between individuals – one on one – between each other alone. Failing that, two or three witnesses should be brought together in order to effect reconciliation. If, however, the person refuses reconciliation, then the case should be brought before the church. If the person refuses to hear the church, then the end result is disfellowship from the church.

It is in the light of this that Peter comes to Jesus and asks Him how often should forgiveness be given to an offending or sinning brother. Should forgiveness be granted seven times, more or less?

Jesus told Peter that forgiveness should go beyond seven times to seventy times seven (verses 21-22). Did Jesus mean that a brother (or sister) should be forgiven 490 times and then no more forgiveness? (Read also Luke 17:1-4).

Verses 23-25 have to do with the parable Jesus gave in answer to Peter's question about forgiveness. The whole of Matthew Chapter 18 has to do with this theme.

C. The Moral of the Parable

Although there are other supportive truths on the parable, the central truth is really given by Jesus Himself in verse 35. If forgiveness for trespass is not forgiven to fellow brothers or sisters. and this from the heart, then the heavenly Father will not forgive our trespasses. An unforgiving attitude is punished by torments in prison.

D. The Exposition of the Parable

This parable of Jesus is far easier to interpret than some of the uninterpreted parables of Jesus. Its language is less symbolic and has to do with **persons** more than **symbols** as in the series of parables in Matthew 13. This is a more **personal** and **relational** kind of parable also than Matthew 13 which, as has been seen, are far more of a symbolic nature.

Matthew's Gospel is the only Gospel which specifically records this parable. The exposition follows this outline.

1. The Kingdom of Heaven

This is another parable opening with the key expression, "The kingdom of heaven is like..." The kingdom resembles or may be likened to all of the parts of the parable, working once more from part to whole and whole to part.

2. The Certain King

The certain king points to the heavenly Father. In verse 23 He is spoken of as "a certain king", and in verses 26,27,31,34 as "Lord", while in verse 35 He is spoken of as "the heavenly Father."

The Father God is indeed THE KING, THE Lord, although in a secondary sense Jesus is King of Kings and Lord of Lords, one with the Father (Revelation 19:16).

3. The Servants

In verses 23,26,27,28,29,31,32,33 the words "servant" or "fellow-servants" are used about nine times. Without question, the servants or fellowservants are believers, fellow members in the Body of Christ, or fellow citizens in the kingdom of God. Believers are spoken of as:

* Fellow-citizens (Ephesians 2:19)
* Fellow-disciples (John 11:16)
* Fellow-heirs (Ephesians 3:6)
* Fellow-workers (2Corinthians 8:23; Philippians 4:3)
* Fellow-labourers (1Thessalonians 3:2; Philemon 1:1).

4. The Accounting

In verses 23,24 we see the king taking account of his servants. The truth is that all believers have to realize that there is a day of reckoning to come. Every one must given an account of himself in that day (Romans 14:12).

We have to give account of our **words** (Matthew 12:36-37), and an account of **souls** (Hebrews 13:17) as well as an account of our **stewardship** (Luke 16:1; 1Corinthians 4:1).

5. **The Forgiven and Unforgiving**

Two particular servants are singled out in the parable; one who is forgiven and one who is unforgiving.

(a) **The Forgiven**

In verses 24-27 one the king's servants was brought before him. In the reckoning he was found to owe 10,000 talents (some say approximately $20 million dollars), a phenomenal sum of money to be in debt to the king. It was an impossible debt for him to ever pay. The lord of that servant commanded him to be sold, his wife, his children and anything he had to make payment.

A similar situation is found in 2Kings 4:1 where the creditors came to take the two sons of a widow as bondmen to pay the debt of the widow's dead husband in the school of the prophets.

The servant in the parable fell down before the king, in utter prostration, begging for time to pay all, begging the king's patience. The king was moved with compassion, loosed him (released) him and forgave the whole debt. The servant experienced the **compassion** of the king. He was **loosed (released)** from being sold. The impossible debt was freely and completely **forgiven!** What a tremendous picture of the grace of God in every believer's life. Compassion, release, forgiveness because he had absolutely nothing to pay. Such compassion and forgiveness provides eternal ground upon which every servant of God, every believer, can worship.

There was absolutely no way the servant could pay this impossible debt even though he asked for time to pay it. The forgiveness was entirely based on the king's grace. So every forgiven sinner must depend on the grace of God, for none have anything to pay of debt to God.

(b) **The Unforgiving**

In verses 28-30 the forgiven servant goes out and finds one of his fellow-servants who owes him a mere one hundred pence (about $20.00). The forgiven servant mercilessly takes his fellow-servant by the throat endeavouring to force him to pay all.

The fellow-servant fell down at his feet, begging for the very thing the fellow-servant had asked of the king – patience to pay all.

In spite of mercy shown to him by the king, he showed no mercy to this fellow-servant. He threw him into prison until the debt should be paid. How was he to pay the debt while in prison, who knows? Though himself forgiven, he was unforgiving.

6. **Delivered to the Tormentors**

In verses 31-34 we are told how the other fellow-servants, when they saw what was done by one fellow-servant to another fellow-servant, came to their lord and told him all that was done.

The Lord called that servant and said,, "You **wicked servant!** I forgave you all that debt because you begged me. Should you not have had compassion on your fellow-servant just as I had **pity** on you?"

The result was, the king was **angry** and delivered him to the **tormentors** (NKJV. "the torturers") until he should pay all that was due to him, which was really impossible.

(a) A Wicked Servant

The king called him – a believer – "You wicked servant." Unforgiving servants are wicked servants. Wicked and slothful servants are those who do not use their talents the Lord has given them (Matthew 25:26). Wicked servants fail to use what they have been entrusted with (Luke 19:22).

Believers, servants, yet wicked servants will have to be dealt with by the Lord. "He shall have judgment without mercy that showed no mercy" is certainly true and applicable to this unforgiving, wicked servant (James 2:13).

(b) An Angry King

The king was angry. Not only did the king show **compassion;** he also showed anger. God shows compassion and pities His people, but He also can be angry. Both are in perfect balance in the Lord. The fellow-servant experienced both the compassion and the anger of the king.

There are many Scriptures which speak of God's compassion (Deuteronomy 13:17; Psalm 78:38; 86:15; 112:4; Matthew 9:36; 14:14; 15:32; 20:34; Lamentations 3:22). He expects us to have compassion one towards another also (Matthew 18:27,33; Hebrews 5:2; 1Peter 3:8; 1John 3:17; Jude 22; Acts 5:31; 13:38; Colossians 1:14).

There are, on the other hand, many Scriptures which also speak of God's anger, even in dealing with His people (Exodus 4:14; Numbers 11:1,10; 12:9; 25:3,4; 32:10-14; Deuteronomy 32:16; Joshua 7:1,26; 1Kings 15:30; Nehemiah 9:17).

The Lord becomes angry with His people for their sins (1Kings 11:9; 2Kings 17:18). His anger is never a sinful anger, but a righteous anger (Mark 3:5). God is angry with the wicked every day (Psalm 7:11).This is an aspect in the nature of God that is often overlooked. But the qualities of compassion and anger are both perfect in their action in God, the king, the lord, and our heavenly Father.

(c) The Tormentors

The tormentors or torturers are not specifically interpreted in the parable for us. Other Scriptures give indications of what these tormentors might be.

The unforgiving servant is cast into prison, as hard as that is, but there was added sorrow for he was given into the hands of the torturers of the prison. The Scriptures which speak of "torment" are the same Greek word used in this parable.

* Demons knew they would be tormented in due time (Matthew 8:29; Mark 5:7; Luke 8:28).

* The rich man in hades was in a place of torments (Luke 16:23,24,25,28).
* Fear has torment (1John 4:18).
* Demons torment people also (Revelation 9:5).
* Hell is a torment also for all who go there (Revelation 14:10-11; 20:10).
* Sickness and disease are torments (Matthew 8:6; 4:24).

Many Christians are spiritually in prison, and tormented mentally, emotionally, physically and spiritually, as well as other ways, because of unforgiveness. The believer, brother or sister, who, having received the pity and compassionate forgiveness of the Lord, and refuses to give the same to fellow believers, leave themselves open to prison and the tormentors. Only the Lord knows what will bring them to their spiritual senses.

The believer in Corinth, who was a fornicator, was delivered over to Satan for the destruction of the flesh in order that his spirit might be saved (1Corinthians 5). In due time, however, he came to repentance and a restored relationship in the church (2Corinthians 2:5-8).

Numerous "case histories" could be provided through out the church universal of believers suffering under the hands of the tormentors. Fear, guilt, depression, oppression, sickness, demonic spirits, etc., often (not always) come because of an unforgiving spirit and attitude.

E. The Practical Application of the Parable

The practical application of the parable is given by Jesus Himself in verse 35. The heavenly Father will do to His servants all that was done to the unforgiving servant. This is part of the Divine chastening and scourging of the Father to His sons and daughters (Hebrews 12:5-13).

The reason? Unforgiven sin! If we do not forgive others, and this must not be lip-service, but **"from the heart"**, which only God sees, then our own sins are not forgiven. Numerous Christians have unforgiven sin in their lives because of an unforgiving spirit, and therefore they are open to the tormentors! Forgiveness has to do with "loosing" a person, and not "binding" them (Matthew 16:19; 18:18)

We pray, "Forgive us our debts as we forgive our debtors" (Matthew 6:12). The servant was not willing to forgive a small debt of $20.00 when his phenomenal debt of $20,000 million dollars had been forgiven. And again, "If we forgive men their trespasses, your heavenly Father will also forgive your trespasses; but, if you forgive not men their trespasses, neither will your Father forgive your trespasses! (Matthew 6:14-15; Ephesians 4:32). The major points of the parable are seen in outline form here.

The Parable Parts	The Interpretation of the Parable
1. The kingdom of heaven	Resembles, is like, comparable to
2. The king and lord	The rule of the heavenly Father
3. The fellow-servants	Fellow believers
4. The forgiven servant	All believers have been forgiven
5. The debt	Impossible to pay
6. Yet unforgiving to another	The sin of an unforgiving spirit
7. Experienced compassion	The Father's compassion
8. The anger of the king	Divine anger and chastening
9. Delivered to prison and torment	Divine punishment by various means

There are many Scriptures on forgiveness. "If You, O Lord, should mark (keep account) and treat us according to our iniquities, O Lord, who could stand? But there is forgiveness with the Lord that He may be feared" Psalm 130:3-4).

"Bless the Lord, O my soul, and all that is within, bless His holy name. Who forgives all our iniquities and heals all our diseases..." (Psalm 103:1-4; Jeremiah 31:31-34). With the merciful God Himself shows Himself merciful (Psalm 18:25-26; Matthew 5:7; Luke 6:36; James 5:9).

Without dealing with the theology of forgiveness, the Bible does teach that repentance precedes forgiveness and the remission of sins (Luke 24:47; Acts 5:31). Jesus said, If a brother trespass against you seven times in one day, and he **repents,** then you are to forgive him (Luke 17:1-4).

In conclusion, we return to Peter's question to the Lord: How often shall my brother trespass against me and I forgive him? Until seven times? (Matthew 18:21; Luke 17:1-4). Apparently the Jews would forgive three or at the most four times because of the word of the Lord through the prophet Amos (Amos 1:3; 2:6; Job 33:14-30).

The Lord's response was: Not until seven times but until seventy times seven! This surely does not mean literally to forgive someones trespass 490 times, and then retaliate and withhold forgiveness! Beneath the surface reading of Christ's answer is a deeper and fuller meaning. It has to do with "prophetic time periods" known as "The Seven Times Prophecy" and "The Seventy Times Prophecy."

Without dealing with an exposition of these significant "time periods", the student is encouraged to read the following Scriptures and meditate on them. Sufficient to say that the "Seven Times" has to do with the end of this age, while the "Seventy Times" brings one right to the second coming of Christ.

Seven Times – Genesis 33:3; Leviticus 4:6,17; 8:11; 26:24,28; Numbers 19:4; Joshua 6:15; 2Kings 4:3;5; 5:10,14; Daniel 3:19; 4:16; Luke 17:4.

Seventy Times Seven – Genesis 4:24; Matthew 18:22.

The matter of forgiveness has to do with God's forgiveness of us as believers and the believer's forgiveness of other believers. This forgiveness should extend right through to the second coming of Christ. The Father God has a spirit of compassion and love and forgiveness available for all who will come to Him, through Christ, and in genuine repentance. This same attitude and spirit of forgiveness must be in all believers. Believers who have unforgiveness, bitterness, resentment and wrong attitudes to others, especially to fellow believers, destroy themselves. Bitterness generally does not hurt the one you are bitter against, whether right or wrong, but it destroys the person who has it. The key word in this whole passage is "forgiveness" (Matthew 18:15,21,22,32,35).

May the Lord give us grace, as His servants, to forgive others, from the heart, with the same pity and compassion which the Father has forgiven us lest we be put in a prison and delivered to the hands of the tormentors! Forgive and we shall be forgiven!" Whosoever sins your remit (forgive, release, let go), they are remitted; but whosever sins you retain (hold back, keep in account), they are retained "(John 20:21-23). This is the Lord's word to His people!

CHAPTER SEVENTEEN
THE PARABLE OF THE VINEYARD LABOURERS

A. The Scriptures on the Parable
Matthew 20:1-16

For the kingdom of heaven is like unto a man that is an householder, which went out early in the morning to hire labourers into his vineyard.

And when he had agreed with the labourers for a penny a day, he sent them into his vineyard.

And he went out about the third hour, and saw others standing idle in the marketplace,

And said unto them; Go ye also into the vineyard, and whatsoever is right I will give you. And they went their way.

Again he went out about the sixth and ninth hour, and did likewise.

And about the eleventh hour he went out, and found others standing idle, and saith unto them, Why stand ye here all the day idle?

They say unto him, Because no man hath hired us. He saith unto them, Go ye also into the vineyard; and whatsoever is right, that shall ye receive.

So when even was come, the lord of the vineyard saith unto his steward, Call the labourers, and give them their hire, beginning from the last unto the first.

And when they came that were hired about the eleventh hour, they received every man a penny.

But when the first came, they supposed that they should have received more; and they likewise received every man a penny.

And when they had received it, they murmured against the goodman of the house, Saying, These last have wrought but one hour, and thou hast made them equal unto us, which have borne the burden and heat of the day.

But he answered one of them, and said, Friend, I do thee no wrong: didst not thou agree with me for a penny?

Take that thine is, and go thy way: I will give unto this last, even as unto thee.

Is it not lawful for me to do what I will with mine own? Is thine eye evil, because I am good?

So the last shall be first, and the first last: for many be called, but few chosen.

B. The Setting of the Parable

The setting of the parable is found in Matthew 19:16-22 and 19:23-30. In the first passage, the rich young ruler came to Jesus asking Him what he could do to obtain eternal life. After the Lord's test to him about keeping the commandments, which the young ruler felt he had kept, Jesus went to the heart of the matter. The young man kept the commands Jesus had quoted, but the test was to "love his neighbour as himself." Jesus told him to sell all he had, give it to the poor, take up his cross and follow Him (Mark 10:17-22; Luke 18:18-23). The rich young ruler went away sorrowful for he had great possessions.

Jesus then turned to His disciples and told them how hard it was for the rich to enter the kingdom of heaven. The disciples were astonished, wondering who could ever be saved. With men, Jesus said, it is impossible. Only with God all things are possible.

It is Peter again who raises the question on behlaf of the rest of the apostles. Peter reminds Jesus that they have left all to follow Him. What are they going to get out of it all? Jesus promises them that they will sit with Him on thrones in the regeneration. Anyone who has left family and material possessions will be rewarded and will inherit that which the young ruler wanted, and walked away from, that is, eternal life.

Then comes the enigmatic saying, "But many that are first shall be last, and the last shall be first "(Matthew 19:30). It is out of this setting that the parable arises. At the conclusion of the parable, the same words are repeated with the added final words, "So the last shall be first, and the first shall be last: for many be called, but few are chosen."

C. The Moral of the Parable

The central truth of the parable is a warning of the Lord against having a hireling spirit in the service of the Lord. In the Lord's saying: "The first shall be last, and the last shall be first, for many are called, but few are chosen", preceding and concluding this parable, there is an enigmatic rebuke. It has to deal with wrong motives, wrong attitudes, and wrong expectations in a believer's labouring for the Lord. Other supplemental and supportive truths in the parable confirm this central truth. Those that be first in their own eyes shall be last in the eyes of others. There are those who are last in their own eyes but shall be first in the eyes of the Lord. This is because their motives, attitudes and expectations were right in the eyes of the Lord of the vineyard.

D. The Exposition of the Parable

This parable is only to be found in Matthew's Gospel. This extended parable is easy to understand in some of its parts, while others parts are more difficult to understand. Once again, sound theology and sound hermeneutics should help to provide a sound understanding of the truths of the parable, as we work from part to whole and whole to part.

1. The Kingdom of Heaven

The parabolic formula is used once again even though it is not specially defined as a parable. The kingdom of heaven is like; that is, it resembles, may be compared to, or corresponds to the various parts that make up the parable. That is, all the parts, not just one or two parts.

2. The Man, the Householder

In verses 1, 11, there is "the man", "the householder", or "the goodman of the house", or "the landowner" (NKJV). In verse 8 he is called "the lord of the vineyard." As in most of the parables in Matthew's Gospel, "the man" seems always to point to, either the Man Christ Jesus, or else to God the Father.

This parable of the vineyard labourers (Matthew 20:1-16), and the parable of the vineyard and winepress (Matthew 22:33-46), both speak of "a householder" (Matthew 20:1; with 22:33). In the context of the parable, the householder (or landowner) both point to God the Father as the owner and possessor of all things (Psalm 24:1-2). Because the Father and the Son are one in the plan of redemption, sometimes this facet of truth is applicable to either.

3. The Vineyard

The picture of the vineyard was very common in the minds of the Jews in Christ's time and in Bible times as a whole. The vineyard speaks of God's world, His field of labour for His people to labour in. It is **His vineyard.**

Israel was God's vineyard in Old Testament times (Psalm 80:15-19; Isaiah 27:2-3; Jeremiah 12:10). Isaiah sang a song of "the well beloved" about His vineyard (Isaiah 5:1-7).

Jesus told several vineyard parables as recorded in the Gospel of Matthew

*   The vineyard and the labourers (Matthew 20:1-16),
*   The vineyard and the two sons (Matthew 21:28-32),
*   The vineyard and the husbandman (Matthew 22:33-36; Mark 12:1-12; Luke 20:9-19),
*   The vineyard and the fig tree (Luke 13:6-9).

The Old Testament Israel, and the Jews in Christ's time were familiar with the whole concept of the vineyard and labourers in the vineyard for the owner. In the New Testament, the vineyard is God's field of service into which He calls His people to labour for Him. It corresponds to "the field is the world" in the parables of Matthew Chapter 13.

4. The Labourers

There should be no mistake in understanding who the labourers are in the parable. The labourers represents all those who are called by the Father and the Son to labour in His vineyard. Jesus spoke of the harvest being great but the labourers were few. He told His disciples to pray the Lord of the harvest to send forth labourers into the harvest (Matthew 9:37-38; Luke 10:2).

Paul tells us that believers are labourers together with God in God's husbandry or field (1Corinthians 3:9; 2Timothy 2:6). Every believer is saved to become a labourer for the Lord in His vineyard, in His field – the world! Old Testament believers (Israel), and New Testament believers (Church) are labourers in God's vineyard.

5. The Hiring Hours

The vineyard harvest is ready. All that is needed is labourers. The lord of the vineyard now goes out to hire laboures to send into his vineyard. The hiring or call to the vineyard labour has several special time-periods that deserve attention, especially when it comes to the fifth and final call. Jesus did not just give these details to be skimmed over and miss supplemental truths therein. There were twelve hours in the day when a person could work, Jesus said (John 11:4,9,10).

(a) The Early Morning Hire – Verses 1-2

The first labourers hired agreed with the householder for a penny for the days labour in the vineyard. The first ones agreed to the set salary. The time probably was about 6 AM in the morning, as the Jewish day was from 6AM to 6PM, sunrise to sunset approximately.

(b) The Third Hour Hire – Verses 3-4

At this hour (possibly 9AM), the vineyard lord found people standing idle in the marketplace. The lord did not like to see people idling away their – or His – time.He told them to go into his vineyard and he would pay them for their service. Though these were hired later than the early morning labourers, they went into the vineyard trusting the integrity of the lord of the vineyard.

(c) The Sixth Hour Hire – Verse 5

Those hired at this hour (possibly 12 Noon) knew the same call as those of the third hour. These also responded to the call and went into the vineyard trusting the integrity of the lord of the vineyard.

(d) The Ninth Hour Hire – Verse 5

The same call at the ninth hour (possibly 3PM) and response is seen in the labourers hired at this time.

(e) The Eleventh Hour Hire – Verses 6,7,9

In this fifth and final call, there is something unusual. So far it has been the early morning, the third, the sixth, the ninth hour calls. One would expect this final call to be the twelfth hour call. But it is an eleventh hour call (possibly 5 PM). That shows there is something unusual about the call of this hour.

At this call, the lord of the vineyard goes out yet again, and finds others just standing idle. After asking why they were idle, they replied that no one had hired them. The vineyard owner told them to go into his vineyard and, as said to the others, he gave his word that he would pay them what was right. They also trusted the honesty and integrity of the landowners word.

This call was the fifth and final call. It was the last call to bring in the vineyard harvest, and these labourers responded to the call and sending of the lord of the vineyard.

The **first labourers** agreed with the lord of the vineyard for a penny. Their expectation was to receive the penny for the days service. The other labourers **trusted the integrity** of the lord of the vineyard. They trusted his word. They did not have set expectations, just confidence in the word given when hired. The **last labourers** also trusted the word and integrity of the lord who had hired them. These also had no set expectations, just confidence in the word given them when hired for service in the vineyard.

(d) The Even Time

In verse 8, the harvest of the vineyard is finished. From the early morning call, the third hour call, the sixth hour call, the ninth and eleventh hour calls, the labourers have worked in the vineyard. The evening here is the close of the day, harvest time is ended, and now it is time to receive payment from the lord of the vineyard.

The "evening time", for us, speaks of "the end of the age", the harvest is over and the Lord of the vineyard comes to reward His own for their service in His vineyard.

6. The Steward

In verse 8 we are told that the lord of the vineyard called his steward at eventide and told him to pay the labourers, but this was in an unusual order: "beginning from the **last** to the **first**."

Depending on whether the householder or lord of the vineyard speaks of the Father or the Son would determine whether "His steward" speaks of the Son or the Holy Spirit.

In the notable account of father Abraham looking for a bride for his only begotten son, Isaac, we see Eliezer, the steward of the house, sent into a far country to obtain that bride (Genesis 15:2; Genesis 24). Many expositors see Abraham as a type of the Father God, Isaac as a type of the only begotten Son of God, Jesus, and Eliezer, the steward, as a type of the Holy Spirit.

Most households had a steward over the distribution of food and goods (Genesis 43:19; 44:1,4; 1Chronicles 28:1; Luke 8:3; 12:42; 16:1). Elders are to be good stewards over the house of God (Titus 1:7; 1Peter 4:10). Paul counted himself as a steward of the mysteries of God (1Corinthians 4:1-2).

Because we have applied "the householder" to the Father God, we could apply "the steward" to represent the Lord Jesus, as the Bishop, Elder and Steward over the Church, the House of God. Regardless, the fact is, the steward was told by the lord of the vineyard to give the labourers their hire for the days service.

7. The Motive

In verses 8-13 we see the steward beginning with the **last** and these are paid **first.** Those who were hired **first** were paid **last.** Not only that, those hired last were paid the penny – a days wages – and those that were hired first were paid the penny. All received the same penny, whether hired first or last or in between! Many that are first shall be last, and the last shall be first was fulfilled here (Mark 10:31). What did this do? It exposed what was the **motive** and what was in the **heart** of those who had been employed first.

As they stood waiting for their pay, they undoubtedly questionsed why the **last** were paid **first.** Then when they saw that the **last** were paid what they as the **first** had been promised, that is, a penny, they supposed that they would receive several times more than that. The thoughts and motives of their hearts are revealed in their words of murmurming and complaint against the lord of the vineyard. They complained that the **last** had been made equal to the **first.** They, as the **first,** had borne the heat and burden of the day, while the **last** had come in at the close of the day. Their eye was evil because of the goodness of the lord of the vineyard. After all, the goodman of the house could choose to give more or less to the last as he had agreed with them at the first. It was lawful for him as the employer to be generous. After all, these last labourers had responded to an urgent and last minute harvest call without question, "What shall we have?" They trusted the word and integrity of the vineyard owner as they laboured with pure motives.

In our time, many employers will give the same bonus to all their employers whether there for three, six or twelve months. The issue for the vineyard owner was that part of the harvest could have been lost at the last of the day. So why were their reactions evil when all were paid the same penny? It showed that the motives of the heart were not pure in serving in the lord's vineyard. It is the same exposure of the heart as seen in the parable of the unforgiving servant forgiven, but unforgiving. The motives of his heart were manifest in his cruel treatment of his fellow servant.

Such are some of the lessons we learn from the different attitudes of the labourers in the Lord's vineyard.

8. The Penny

In verses 2,9,10,13 we see the penny (or denari) that was paid for a days labour.

In interpreting the parts of the parable, this part has been a difficult part to understand, especially as it relates to eternal matters.

What is to be understood by "the penny"? What is to be understood by all the labourers receiving the same pay whether first or last or in between? If believers are labourers together in God's vineyard, does the Lord pay believers for working in His vineyard? What is to be understood by "the penny"?

Perhaps a brief consideration of **what the penny is not** may help us to understand **what the penny is!**

9. Not Rewards for use of Talents

The penny is not the rewards given to the saints at the coming of Christ. The saints receive different rewards according to faithfulness in the use of their talents. The parable of the talents in Matthew 25:14-30 and the parable of the pounds in Luke 19:11-27 confirm this fact. One servant was commended with: "Well done, good and faithful servant...", while the other was reproved with: "You wicked and slothful servant..." (See also Revelation 11:18-19). In these parables, they receive different rewards. Luke's parable teaches that believers will have different positions and responsibilities in the kingdom. In the present parable of the vineyard, all receive the **same penny**, regardless of attitude or length of service because all laboured in the vineyard of the lord.

(a) Not Rewards for Works

The penny is not rewards or loss of rewards for works done in the Lord's service. Some believers works are like gold, silver and precious stones and will stand the test of fire. They will be rewarded. Some believers works are like wood, hay or stubble. All will be reduced to ashes. They wll be saved as by fire, but will receive no reward (1Corinthians 3:5-17). The present parable shows that all labourers receive the **same penny.**

(b) Not Resurrection Glories

The penny cannot represent the varying glories of the saints as in the resurrection. The differing glories of the saints are symbolized by the varying glories of the sun, the moon, and the stars. So is the resurrection of the saints (1Corinthians 15:41-42). The present parable shows all receive the **same penny.**

(c) But Eternal Life

What then may the penny point to in spiritual reality? Of the various expositions of the parables this writer has read, the best application of "the penny" is that it speaks of "eternal life!"

All believers, or labourers in God's vineyard, regardless of time spent in the service of the Lord, are rewarded with eternal life. All, regardless even of attitude in service, receive the **same eternal life!** Whether they come into God's vineyard first or last, or in between, one thing all believers receive in common is eternal life.

A study of the above passages of Scripture do show that all do not receive the **same commendation,** or the same rewards, or even the **same resurrection glory.** All, however, do receive the **same penny** – or ETERNAL LIFE!

But, it may be asked, Does a believer **work** for eternal life? Is eternal life payment for hire for labourers? Or is eternal life entirely a free gift regardless of what a believer does? A study of the Scriptures show that all believers are saved by grace through faith, not of works, lest any should boast (Ephesians 2:8-10).

This parable, however, is not to do with a believer's **salvation,** but it has to do with a believer's **service!** The parable is not dealing with sinners, or a person before they are saved, but with believers after they are saved! The labourers in the Lord's vineyard are not the unconverted but the converted. They are believers. We are saved to serve. We are called to be labourers in God's great vineyard, not to be idle believers in the marketplace.

Satan pays wages to those in his service. "The wages of sin is death" (Romans 6:23). Balaam, the mysterious prophet, received the wages of unrighteousness (2Peter 2:15).

The Lord pays wages to those in His service. "He that reaps receives wages, and gathers fruit unto eternal life" (John 4:36).

Although eternal life is a gift from God, we are exhorted to "fight the good fight of faith, lay hold of eternal life, whereunto you are called..." (1Timothy 6:12,19). Jude exhorts us to "keep yourselves in the love of God, looking for the mercy of our Lord Jesus Christ unto eternal life" (Jude 21). John exhorts us also, "Look to yourselves, that you lose not those things that you have wrought, but that we receive a full reward" (2John 1:8).

One of the dangers in the early church was that of the believing Jews (who had served the Lord over many years), complaining that the believing Gentiles were receiving the same salvation and same Spirit as they had, and were baptized into the same body (Acts 11:18). Jews or Gentiles, regardless of time in serving the Lord, would receive the same reward of the Lord – the reward of eternal life.

In 1Samuel 30:18-31 we have an interesting story from the life of David and his men. In it we find a principle that David established for all times. David was pursuing the enemy from Ziklag when he and his men lost everything. As they continued in the battle, some of his men, about four hundred, became faint and had to stay behind. The rest of the men continued in the chase and they recovered all that was lost; the women, the children and the spoils. David brought them back. But some of the men that were with David did not want to share the spoils with those who had been faint and stayed by the stuff. David said that everyone, those who went to the battle, and those who stayed by the stuff, were to get **the same rewards.** This became a lasting principle in Israel from this time on. David established this as an ordinance from this day onwards.

The Son of David, and David's Lord, follows the same principle in this parable. Those that work for a while, half a day, the whole day, or those who come in to labour in the vineyard of the Lord, will receive the **same penny** at the close of the day.

Whatever may be the full spiritual significance of all receiving the same penny, the greatest "pay" the Lord can give those who have laboured in His vineyard is eternal life!

E. The Practical Application of the Parable

This parable could be superimposed on a "time line" of Church History in order to bring the practical application of the parable to our time.

The early morning call to labour in the vineyard could speak of the Gospels and the Book of Acts. Other calls could speak of the calls of the Lord to the various generations over church history. But the final call, the unusual, the unexpected call, came at the end of the day, the end of this generation, the final part of the harvest period. The harvest is the end of the age.

The Holy Spirit sends the call throughout the nations of the earth. There is a sense of urgency in the final decade of harvest. This is like the "eleventh hour call." In the parable of the virgins, it is the "midnight hour call", but in this parable it is the final and unusual call of the eleventh hour. This is day-time; the other is night-time!

The Lord of the vineyard does not want any idle Christians in the marketplace. He wants all to be labourers in His vineyard so the final part of the harvest is not lost.

The parable teaches us to guard the motives and attitudes of our heart in our service to the Lord, as seen in our final lessons from this parable.

The workers who started first had their attitudes exposed:

1. They exposed a mercenary spirit and attitude. In other words, What are we going to get out of it? They served for what they could get.

2. They had a critical and murmuring attitude towards the Lord of the vineyard. "Why should he give us only a penny and they get the same as us. We should get more than that!"

3. They had a false concept of the Lord of the vineyard and felt he was unjust, that he was not fair!

4. They had wrong attitudes to the other vineyard labourers who came in at the last part of the harvest and laboured for the Lord. They were upset that they received the same as they did for less time of labouring.

The workers who came in at the last also had their attitudes exposed:

1. They had an attitude of trust in the Lord of the vineyard.

2. They had a responsive attitude. When called, as idle, they were happy to work.

3. They did not have a mercenary spirit, a bargaining spirit or murmuring attitude. They trusted the integrity of the Lord of the vineyard.

The truth is: It does not matter **where** we serve the Lord, or **how long** we serve the Lord. The place and the time matters not, so long as we **do serve** the Lord with a pure motive and a good heart. In this end of the age, millions come to the Lord in His vineyard and will receive eternal life. Those of us who have served the Lord for many years, and in many places, and have suffered the burden and heat of the day, need to rejoice with the final-call labourers, for the Lord's harvest is in. Those who sow, and those who reap will rejoice together when the harvest is finally in (Psalm 126)!

CHAPTER EIGHTEEN
THE PARABLE OF THE TWO SONS AND VINEYARD

A. The Scripture on the Parable
Matthew 21:28-32

But what think ye? A certain man had two sons; and he came to the first, and said, Son, go work to day in my vineyard.

He answered and said, I will not: but afterward he repented, and went.

And he came to the second, and said likewise. And he answered and said, I go, sir: and went not.

Whether of them twain did the will of his father? They say unto him, The first. Jesus saith unto them, Verily I say unto you, That the publicans and the harlots go into the kingdom of God before you.

For John came unto you in the way of righteousness, and ye believed him not: but the publicans and the harlots believed him: and ye, when ye had seen it, repented not afterward, that ye might believe him.

B. The Setting of the Parable

A comparison of Matthew 21:23 and Mark 11:30 shows that Jesus was teaching in the temple precincts. The chief priests and the elders of Jewry came questioning His authority. They wanted to know by **what** authority He did the things He did, and **who** gave Him that authority. Jesus, as He often did, asked them a question, which, if they would or could answer, He would then answer their question.

The question concerned the baptism of John. Was John's baptism of heaven or of earth? Was it of God or of man? They were caught. They reasoned among themselves. If they said it was "of heaven" Jesus would ask them why then they did not believe John and receive baptism of him. If they said it was "of men" they feared the people, because the people believed John was a prophet sent from God.

They answered Jesus by saying that they could not tell. Because they could not or would not tell, Jesus did not have to tell them the source of His authority. It is out of this setting that the parable of the two sons in the vineyard arose. It illustrated the difference between the religious leaders and the common people in Jewry and their attitude towards God and obedience to His will and word.

C. The Moral of the Parable

The central truth of the parable is: It is better to do the will of God when you said you would not than say you would do the will of God and fail to do it. Other suportive truths are seen in the exposition of the parable.

D. The Exposition of the Parable

It has already been seen that there are three particular parables concerning the vineyard of the Lord.

The first has been considered in the previous chapter in our exposition of Matthew 20:1-16. The second is considered in this present chapter and is found in Matthew 21:28-32. The third follows in the next chapter and is an exposition of Matthew 21:33-44.

1. The Certain Man

Undoubtedly the "certain man" points to the Father God here because this "certain man" had two sons.

2. The Vineyard

The work in the vineyard points once again to work in the kingdom of God and the bringing in of the fruits to the Father and Husbandman's glory and praise.

3. The Two Sons

There is no mistaking who the "two sons" represented. Jesus Himself interprets the parable as He applies it to His hearers. The two sons represent the religious and the irreligious, the irresponsive and the responsive, the self-righteous and the unrighteous.

This parable is very similar to the parable of the two sons in the parable of the father and his sons, the prodigal son and his self-righteous elder brother.

(a) The First Son

The father came to his first son and said, "Go and work today in my vineyard." His immediate response was, "I will not!" But afterwards, this son repented – he changed his mind – and went to work in the vineyard. There was the call, the self-will, then repentance followed by obedience to the father's will.

(b) The Second Son

The father came to the second son and gave him the same command and call to work in his vineyard. His immediate response was, "I go!" But he changed his mind and word and he simply did not go to work in the father's vineyard. Here we have the call, the consent of the mind and will but followed by disobedience.

4. The Father's Will

After this simple illustration, Jesus asked the chief priests and elders, "Which of these two sons did the will of the father?" They fall into the trap and are forced to acknowledge that it was the first son only that did the father's will.

E. The Practical Application of the Parable

In verses 31b-32 Jesus Himself interprets the parabolic illustration and He Himself applies it practically to the chief priests and elders.

The **"second son"** pointed to the company of religious leaders of Christ's time; the priests, the scribes, the Pharisees, the Sadducees, the elders and the religious Jews as a whole.

John came to them in the way of righteousness, a man sent from God (John 1:6-8). But the religious leaders did not believe John nor accept his baptism of repentance unto faith in the coming Messiah. Though they assented mentally and verbally to the will of God, they were disobedient to the will of God, and refused John's baptism. They felt they had nothing for repentance, so there was no need for John's baptism of "sinners unto repentance."

They rejected the counsel of God against themselves and did not submit to John's baptism of repentance (Luke 7:29-30; Acts 19:3-4).

The **"first son"** pointed to the great company of the common people in Christ's time. The publicans and harlots responded to John's ministry, as well as to Christ's ministry. They came to the baptism of sinners unto repentance and faith in the kingdom of God and the long-promised Messiah. They heard the call, "Repent, for the kingdom of heaven is at hand" (Matthew 4:1-2,17; Mark 1:4). These did the will of God.

The tragic thing is that, even when the religious leaders saw the response of the common people, they still did not repent and come to faith and accept the message of the kingdom.

The whole issue is **doing the will of God!** Religious people, self-righteous and religious leaders, so often know the will of the Father and assent to it mentally and verbally, but do not do it. Repentance, faith and obedience are the fruits that the Father wants. Disobedience to the Father's will is the evidence of an unrepentant and therefore, unbelieving heart. These are shut out of the kingdom. They actually shut themselves out of the kingdom.

The irreligious, the unrighteous and the prodigal people more often respond to the Gospel of the kingdom and come to repentance, faith and obedience to the Father's will. Truly, as Jesus said, the publicans and the harlots go into the kingdom of God before the self-righteous, religious leaders. It is not every one who calls Jesus 'Lord' that enters the kingdom, but he that does the will of the Father in heaven. These are the true and spiritual relatives of Jesus (Matthew 12:50).

Every person will either do God's good, perfect and acceptable will (Romans 12:1-2), or do their own self-will, following in the steps of the five "I will's" of Lucifer in his fall (Isaiah 14:12-14).

As one comes to genuine repenance, and faith, and obedience, then they will work joyfully in the Father's vineyard, pleasing the Father's heart. Every person decides which kind of a "son" they will be!

CHAPTER NINETEEN
THE PARABLE OF THE VINEYARD AND HUSBANDMEN

A. The Scriptures on the Parable

1. Matthew 21:33-46

Hear another parable: There was a certain householder, which planted a vineyard, and hedged it round about, and digged a winepress in it, and built a tower, and let it out to husbandmen, and went into a far country:

And when the time of the fruit drew near, he sent his servants to the husbandmen, that they might receive the fruits of it.

And the husbandmen took his servants, and beat one, and killed another, and stoned another.

Again, he sent other servants more than the first: and they did unto them likewise.

But last of all he sent unto them his son, saying, They will reverence my son.

But when the husbandmen saw the son, they said among themselves, This is the heir; come, let us kill him, and let us seize on his inheritance.

And they caught him, and cast him out of the vineyard, and slew him.

When the lord therefore of the vineyard cometh, what will he do unto those husbandmen?

They say unto him, He will miserably destroy those wicked men, and will let out his vineyard unto other husbandmen, which shall render him the fruits in their seasons.

Jesus saith unto them, Did ye never read in the scriptures, The stone which the builders rejected, the same is become the head of the corner: this is the Lord's doing, and it is marvellous in our eyes?

Therefore say I unto you, The kingdom of God shall be taken from you, and given to a nation bringing forth the fruits thereof.

And whosoever shall fall on this stone shall be broken: but on whomsoever it shall fall, it will grind him to powder.

And when the chief priests and Pharisees had heard his parables, they perceived that he spake of them.

But when they sought to lay hands on him, they feared the multitude, because they took him for a prophet.

2. Mark 12:1-12

And he began to speak unto them by parables. A certain man planted a vineyard, and set an hedge about it, and digged a place for the winefat, and built a tower, and let it out to husbandmen, and went into a far country.

And at the season he sent to the husbandmen a servant, that he might receive from the husbandmen of the fruit of the vineyard.

And they caught him, and beat him, and sent him away empty.

And again he sent unto them another servant; and at him they cast stones, and wounded him in the head, and sent him away shamefully handled.

And again he sent another; and him they killed, and many others; beating some, and killing some.

Having yet therefore one son, his wellbeloved, he sent him also last unto them, saying, They will reverence my son.

But those husbandmen said among themselves, This is the heir; come, let us kill him, and the inheritance shall be ours.

And they took him, and killed him, and cast him out of the vineyard.

What shall therefore the lord of the vineyard do? he will come and destroy the husbandmen, and will give the vineyard unto others.

And have ye not read this scripture; The stone which the builders rejected is become the head of the corner:

This was the Lord's doing, and it is marvellous in our eyes?

And they sought to lay hold on him, but feared the people: for they knew that he had spoken the parable against them: and they left him, and went their way.

3. Luke 20:9-19

Then began he to speak to the people this parable; A certain man planted a vineyard, and let it forth to husbandmen, and went into a far country for a long time.

And at the season he sent a servant to the husbandmen, that they should give him of the fruit of the vineyard: but the husbandmen beat him, and sent him away empty.

And again he sent another servant: and they beat him also, and entreated him shamefully, and sent him away empty.

And again he sent a third: and they wounded him also, and cast him out.

Then said the lord of the vineyard, What shall I do? I will send my beloved son: it may be they will reverence him when they see him.

But when the husbandmen saw him, they reasoned among themselves, saying, This is the heir: come, let us kill him, that the inheritance may be ours.

So they cast him out of the vineyard, and killed him. What therefore shall the lord of the vineyard do unto them?

He shall come and destroy these husbandmen, and shall give the vineyard to others. And when they heard it, they said, God forbid.

And he beheld them, and said, What is this then that is written, The stone which the builders rejected, the same is become the head of the corner?

Whosoever shall fall upon that stone shall be broken; but on whomsoever it shall fall, it will grind him to powder.

And the chief priests and the scribes the same hour sought to lay hands on him; and they feared the people: for they perceived that he had spoken this parable against them.

B. The Setting of the Parable

By comparing Matthew 21:23, 24:1 along with Mark 11:27; 13:1 and Luke 20:1, it would seem that this group of parables:

The Parable of the Two Sons and the Vineyard,

The Parable of the Vineyard and Husbandman, and

The Parable of the Wedding Feast, along with other teachings, were all given by Jesus on one of the days of teaching within the precincts of the temple of Jerusalem.

These are the last parables that Jesus gave within the temple area. The final parables in the Gospel of Matthew are given after Jesus departs from the temple, and as He sits on Mt Olivet with His disciples. This parable of the vineyard and husbandman is distinctly aimed at the religious leaders of Jewry in Christ's time.

C. The Moral of the Parable

There are a number of lessons in this parable but the major lesson is really given by Jesus Himself in Matthew 21:43. "The kingdom of God will be taken from you, and given to a nation bringing forth the fruits thereof."

In other words: Those in spiritual leadership over the people of God will forfeit what He has entrusted to them, and it will be taken from them and given to other leadership who will produce fruit unto God. In this case, the kingdom of God would be taken from Jewry and given to the New Testament Church! Other supportive truths will be seen in the exposition of the parable.

D. The Exposition of the Parable

As a preliminary to an exposition of this parable, it should be seen that this is one of those **historical-prophetical** parables. It reaches over a good period of time, from the founding of Israel as a nation, under theocratic rule, right through to the first coming of Christ and on to the destruction of Jerusalem in AD.70, under Prince Titus and the Roman armies and the birth of the New Testament Church.

It will be helpful to remember the puzzle approach as our exposition unfolds, for it works from part to whole and whole to part.

To interpret this designated parable, the parallel accounts of Mark and Luke have been compared. Here in our exposition, the Comparative Mention Principle, along with the Symbolic Principle of interpretation are used as we interpret this extended parable.

It is worthy of consideration that the hearers – the chief priests and the Pharisees – got the message of the parable through understanding its parts. They perceived that Jesus spoke this parable of them. They knew the parable had been spoken against them (Matthew 21:45-46; Mark 12:12; Luke 20:19). We proceed to the interpretation and explanation of the parts of the parable.

1. A Certain Householder

The certain householder or certain man here represents none other than the Father God. God often used men to represent Himself or His Son. Abraham, the father of the only begotten son, Isaac, represented the Father God and Isaac represented Jesus, God's only begotten Son.

2. Planted a Vineyard

The vineyard represents the kingdom of God in the nation of Israel, the Old Testament people of God. Isaiah clearly says, "The vineyard of the Lord of hosts is the house of Israel" (Isaiah 5:1-7 should be read along with these Scriptures. Isaiah 27:1-7; Jeremiah 2:21; Psalm 80:8; Genesis 49:11; Song of Solomon 8:11). These Scriptures may be compared with John 15:1, where Christ speaks of Himself and His followers as the "True vine and the branches."

3. Hedged the Vineyard

The hedge speaks of Divine protection (Isaiah 5:5). Israel, as God's vineyard, was hedged in by God's laws. As God placed a hedge around Job and his family, (Job 1:10), so God placed a hedge around the chosen nation of Israel.

4. Dug a Winepress

The winepress or winevat would be for the wine of the fruit of the vineyard that would come from good grapes (Isaiah 5:2; Judges 9:27; Isaiah 65:3).

5. **Built a Tower**

The tower in the vineyard would be a watchtower where the watchman could watch for enemy attacks on the vineyard. They could warn the vinedressers or the husbandman.

6. **Let out to Husbandmen**

The vineyard was leased out to vinedressers. The husbandmen represented the leaders of the nation of Israel; the kings, the priests, the Levites, the elders and rulers of the people of Israel (Jeremiah 32:33; Ezekiel 34:2; Malachi 2:7).

7. **Went into a Far Country**

The far country speaks of the heavenly country (Hebrews 11:10-16). After God established the nation as His vineyard at Mt Sinai, He spoke to them in the cloud, and through Moses, and His desire was to rule over the nation as a theocratic kingdom, a kingdom in earth ruled from heaven.

8. **For a Long Time**

The long time speaks of the centuries in which God allowed Israel to occupy the land of Canaan, becoming established as a nation. The Books of Joshua, Judges and Samuel well cover this period of Israel's history.

9. **The Time of the Fruit**

Fruit bearing season was the whole purpose of God in planting Israel as His vineyard. Fruit takes time to produce. The centuries of God's dealings in His vineyard should have been time enough for fruit to come.

10. **He Sent His Servants**

Various servants are sent over the centuries of time, by the Lord, to His vineyard, the nation of Israel. The parable shows how the vinedressers and husbandmen treated the various servants God sent.

(a) **A Servant**

Mark and Luke speak of a servant sent to receive the fruit of the vineyard. The husbandmen caught him, beat him and sent him away empty handed.

(b) **Another Servant**

Mark and Luke speak of another servant being sent. The husbandmen cast stones at him, wounded him in the head, and sent him away shamefully treated, and sent him away empty handed.

(c) **Another Servant, a Third**

Mark and Luke speak of the third servant being sent. He was wounded, cast out and killed by the husbandmen responsible for the vineyard under God.

(d) **Many Other Servants Sent**

More servants were sent than the first. The husbandmen did to them as they had to the previous servants. They beat some. They killed some.

While each of these servants may not be exactly identified, there is no doubt about who the servants represent. The servants represent the prophets of God. The Major and Minor Prophets were sent of God to receive fruit for God from the nation of Israel.

Hebrews 1:1 tells how God spoke in time past unto the fathers by the prophets.The prophet Jeremiah laments the grief of the Lord: "Also, I have sent to you My servants the prophets." He called His people to produce the fruits of repentance, and the fruits of righteousness. He sent them again and again. The student should read these Scriptures (Jeremiah 7:25-26; 35:15; 25:4-7; 26:5; 29:19; 32:32-33; 35:15; 37:15; 2Kings 17:13-15).

King Asa put Hanani the seer into prison in his anger against the word of the Lord (2Chronicles 16:7-14).

Zechariah the prophet was stoned after the Spirit of God spoke the word of the Lord through him (2Chronicles 24:19-21).

The people of God mocked the messengers of God, and despised His words and scoffed at His prophets (2Chronicles 36:14-16).

Jesus lamented over the fact that Jerusalem killed the prophets and stoned those who were sent to them (Matthew 23:29-37 with Acts7:52 and Hebrews 11:36-38).

Tradition says that Isaiah was the prophet "sawn asunder "spoken of in Hebrews 11:36-40.

How many of the prophets suffered rejection, stoning, mocking, abuse and even death at the hands of the religious leaders and husbandmen of God's vineyard, Israel.

11. Last of all – He Sent His Only Son

"Last of all, He sent His Son saying, They will reverence (or respect) My Son" (Matthew).

"Having yet therefore, one Son, His well-beloved, He sent Him also last unto them, saying, They will reverence (respect) My Son "(Mark).

"The Lord of the vineyard said, What shall I do? I will send My beloved Son; it may be they will reverence (respect) Him when they see Him" (Luke).

There is no mistaking who the well-beloved Son is. It is none other than the Lord Jesus Christ. The "time element" brings us historically to His birth and ministry to the Jewish nation (John 3:16; Hebrews 1:1-2; 3:5-6; Luke 16:16; Song of Solomon 2:3,8,9,10,16,17; Isaiah 5:1; Matthew 3:17; 12:18; 17:5; Ephesians 1:6).

Just as Jacob, the father, sent his beloved son, Joseph, to his brethren, and they sold him for silver (Genesis 37), so God the Father sent His beloved Son to the Jews who sold Him out for crucifixion (John 11:47-53; Matthew 17).

12. Reverence My Son

The Father hoped that the husbandmen would at least reverence or respect His Son when they saw Him. But, the Gospels show how they sought to stone Him also at various times when He spoke in the Father's name (John 10:31-33; 11:8).

13. The Husbandmen Kill the Son

The religious leaders recognized the Son. They knew He was God's Son, the Father's heir (Psalm 2:8; Hebrews 1:2). As the parable shows, they caught Him in Gethesame, slew Him by crucifixion and cast Him outside the city of Jerusalem (Read Matthew 26, 27 with John 19:7; Hebrews 13:11-13 and Acts 10:39-43).

These references show that it was not a sin of ignorance on behalf of the religious leaders when they crucified Jesus. They reasoned among themselves and came to this conclusion that Jesus was God's Son and heir. Although they heard the prophet read every Sabbath day, they fulfilled the prophet's writings in condemning Jesus, the Son of God (Acts 13:27).

14. The Husbandmen Destroyed

When the Lord of the vineyard saw what the husbandmen had done to His Son, He asked what should be done to the wicked husbandmen. The answer? Destroy those wicked men and give the vineyard to other husbandmen who would give the seasonal fruits to the owner of the vineyard. Some of the listeners cried, God forbid!

The fulfilment of this judgment was seen historically in AD 70 when God allowed the Roman armies under Prince Titus to destroy the city of Jerusalem and the leaders of the Jewish nation. The temple, the city, the people and the land were desolated under the Roman seige (Matthew 24:1-2; Luke 19:41-44). This fulfilled this point of the parable.

15. The Vineyard given to Church Ministries

The "other husbandmen" represent the various leaders and ministers of the New Testament Church. The "nation bringing forth the fruits" represents the church. The church is God's "holy nation" to bring forth fruit unto God (1Peter 2:5-9). God has set in the church apostles, prophets, evangelists, shepherds and teachers to equip the saints and bring them to maturity in the Lord, and to bring forth the fruit of the Spirit (Ephesians 4:9-16).

16. The Fruit of the Kingdom

The whole purpose of a vineyard is to bring forth "fruit." The people of God are God's vineyard. The Old Testament Church (Acts 7:38) failed to bring forth fruit unto God. The New Testament Church must bring forth fruit. The Old Testament leaders were to encourage this fruit to be brought forth to God by response to the ministry of the prophets. The New Testament ministries are to see the saints bring forth fruit in their lives to the Father God as people respond to the ministry of the Word and the Spirit.

There must be:

1. Fruits of repentance (Matthew 3:8; Luke 3:8),
2. Fruits of righteousness (Philippians 1:11; Amos 6:12),
3. Fruit of the Spirit (Galatians 5:22; John 15:1-16),
4. Fruit of the Divine nature (Matthew 7:16-20; 12:33), and
5. Fruit unto holiness (Romans 6:22).

The parts of the parable are clear in their interpretation and explanation. Undoubtedlly the religious leaders saw the connection and comparison between the prophecy of Isaiah and the parable of Jesus, as the comparison is outlined here.

Isaiah 5:1-7	Parable of Jesus
1. The vineyard-Israel	Jewish nation
2. The pleasant choice vine	The House of Judah

3. The well-beloved	The Lord Jesus
4. The fence, hedge and wall	Divine protection
5. The stones taken out	Clearing hindrances
6. The fruitful hill	Promised land
7. The tower	Watchfulness
8. The winepress	For fruitfulness
9. The wild grapes	Fruit unto himself (Hosea10:1)
10. The judgment-no hedge	Jerusalem and Jewry destroyed
11. No rain, no clouds	No blessing
12. Trodden down	Trodden down of Gentiles-AD70

There is no mistaking the link up with Old Testament prophecies in the historical and prophetical parable of Jesus.

E. The Practical Application of the Parable

There are a number of practical lessons seen already in the exposition of the parable. Jesus has given the key to its interpretation. The kingdom of God would be taken from Jewry and given to the church, God's new ethnic, God's new nation, composed of believing Jews and believing Gentiles. The true church would preach and teach the Gospel of the kingdom and bring forth fruit unto the Father God (Matthew 3:1; 4:17; 24:14).

In the Book of Acts we see the ministries of the church preaching and teaching the Gospel of the kingdom and good fruit resulting therefrom (Acts 1:3; 8:1;2; 14:22; 19:8; 20:25; 28:23,31; Romans 14:17; Colossians 1:13).

Because truth is applicable in every generation, it is evident that, if an individual or a church fails to bring forth fruit unto God, then they also can forfeit the kingdom, even as Israel and Judah did (1Corinthians 6:9-10; Galatians 5:19-21; Ephesians 5:5-6). Without fruit unto holiness, such shall not inherit the kingdom of God, as these Scriptures clearly show.

The chief priests, the scribes, the elders, and the Pharisees perceived the message of the parable (Matthew 21:42-46; Mark 12:10-12; Luke 20:17-19). The Messianic Stone Kingdom would fall on them and they would be crushed, because they would not fall on the Stone and be broken (Isaiah 8:14,15; 28:9-13; Psalm 118:22-24; Daniel 2).

We close this chapter off with a basic overview of the parable and its various parts as interpreted within the realm of Scriptural revelation.

The Parable	The Interpretation
1. A certain householder	God the Father
2. Planted vineyard, hedged it	Israel as a nation
3. Digged winepress, built tower	Winepress for fruit
4. Let out to husbandmen	Rulers, kings, priests, elders of Israel
5. Went to far country	Heavenly country
6. Time of fruit drew near	Purpose of vineyard
7. Sent His servants	Prophets sent
8. Husbandmen cruelly treated them	Rejected, killed the prophets
9. More servants sent	More prophets-Major and Minor
10. Treated them likewise	Ill treated as previous
11. Last of all sent His Son	The Son of God, Jesus
12. Husbandmen killed the Heir	Heir of all things, Jesus

13. They caught Him	In Gethsemane
14. Cast Him out of the vineyard	Outside the city of Jerusalem
15. Slew Him	Slew, hanged on a tree
16. The Lord of husbandmen to destroy those husbandmen	Jerusalem destroyed, AD 70
17. Let out vineyard to other husbandmen to receive the fruits	Kingdom taken from Jewry, given to the Church, the holy nation, who will render to Him the fruits.

Such are the great lessons to be learned from the parable of the vineyard and the husbandman; lessons for all people of all ages!

If the parable were super-imposed on a "time-line", then the historical part of the parable would be seen before and up to the cross of Jesus, and the prophetical part would be seen since the death, burial, resurrection and ascension of the Lord and His continued ministry in the New Testament Church!

CHAPTER TWENTY
THE PARABLE OF THE MARRIAGE OF THE KING'S SON

A. The Scripture On The Parable
Matthew 22:1-14

And Jesus answered and spake unto them again by parables, and said,

The kingdom of heaven is like unto a certain king, which made a marriage for his son,

And sent forth his servants to call them that were bidden to the wedding: and they would not come.

Again, he sent forth other servants, saying, Tell them which are bidden, Behold, I have prepared my dinner: my oxen and my fatlings are killed, and all things are ready: come unto the marriage.

But they made light of it, and went their ways, one to his farm, another to his merchandise:

And the remnant took his servants, and entreated them spitefully, and slew them.

But when the king heard thereof, he was wroth: and he sent forth his armies, and destroyed those murderers, and burned up their city.

Then saith he to his servants, The wedding is ready, but they which were bidden were not worthy.

Go ye therefore into the highways, and as many as ye shall find, bid to the marriage.

So those servants went out into the highways, and gathered together all as many as they found, both bad and good: and the wedding was furnished with guests.

And when the king came in to see the guests, he saw there a man which had not on a wedding garment:

And he saith unto him, Friend, how camest thou in hither not having a wedding garment? And he was speechless.

Then said the king to the servants, Bind him hand and foot, and take him away, and cast him into outer darkness; there shall be weeping and gnashing of teeth.

For many are called, but few are chosen.

B. The Setting of the Parable

The setting of the parable is the same as the parable of the vineyard and the wicked husbandman. It was given on one of the days of Christ's teaching in the temple precincts.

C. The Moral of the Parable

As in the previous parable, so it is in this parable. There are a number of lessons to be learnt along with the major moral of the parable. A cursory glance over both of these parables (Chapters 19 and 20), show several similarities. The moral of the parable teaches us that, in the rejection of the Divine invitation, there comes Divine judgment on those who rejected, while there is Divine blessing on those who respond.

D. The Exposition of the Parable

Some expositors make this passage in Matthew's Gospel about the marriage of the king's son to be the same parable as that of the parable of the great supper in Luke 14:15-24. Even though, however, there are some similarities between the parables (as in the "twin parables" of Matthew 13), there does seem to be a major difference.

The parable in Matthew centers more around the marriage of the king's son. The parable in Luke centers more around a great supper. Perhaps the supper could be the marriage supper for the king's son. However, enough expositors do see enough differences to interpret them as two distinct parables. Here the parable is dealt with as a separate and distinct parable.

This parable is also one of those **historical-prophetical** parables. It covers a certain period of time when the invitations are sent out to the marriage of the king's son, and then on to the destruction of the city of those who reject the call.

In other words, the "time-element" covers at least, the period of Israel's history to the first coming of Christ in the gospels and His rejection of Jewry. Then it continues to the desolation of the city of Jerusalem in AD70 by the Roman armies under Prince Titus and the going forth of the gospel to the Gentile nations of the world.

The setting is an ancient Eastern wedding – not a Western wedding! It represents that which takes place on earth, not in heaven. Here there is mixture of good and bad, the bad being cast out into darkness, not entering heaven and being cast out of heaven. This will be seen as the parable unfolds and we work once again, from part to whole and whole to part.

1. **The Kingdom of Heaven**

    This is distinctly a kingdom of heaven parable. Once again, Jesus shows that the kingdom of heaven is like, or resembles or can be compared to the various parts of the parable which make up the story.

2. **The Certain King**

    The certain king here represents once more the Father God.

3. **The King's Son**

    The son in the parable is "His Son!" There is no mistaking who the Son is. It is the son and heir of the vineyard parable, the well beloved Son of God (Matthew 21:37-38; 3:16; John 3:16). Jesus is the Son of Man as to His humanity, the Son of God as to His Divinity (Matthew 16:13-17; Proverbs 30:4; Psalm 2; Isaiah 6:14; 9:6-9). He is the virgin born son of Mary.

4. **The Marriage**

    The marriage points ultimately to the marriage of the Lamb (Revelation 19:6-9). The parable of the wise and unwise virgins also speaks of the marriage of the bridegroom (Matthew 25:1-13). Because of the king's son, this is to be a royal wedding. In Psalm 45 we have a description of what a royal wedding would be like. There the glory of the king and the bride-to-be and the attendants is set forth in the royal palace. In Genesis 24 we have the picture of father Abraham arranging for the marriage of his only begotten son, Isaac. All such shadows for the Father God making a marriage for His only begotten Son, Jesus.

5. **The Servants Sent Forth**

    Just as in the parable of the vineyard, servants were sent forth to receive the fruits of the vineyard (Matthew 21:34-36), so here His servants are sent forth to call the invited to the wedding.

    Though the "time-element" of the parable may possibly extend over Israel's history (as in the vineyard parable, Matthew 21:39), it could be more aptly applied to the time of Christ in the Gospels and the ministry of the Church in Acts. This is the application used here though not excluding the Old Testament prophets as "servants" also. The picture, however, in the Old Testament, is that of Jehovah married to Israel, as the chosen nation. This parables pictures the marriage for the Son.

(a) First Invitation and Refusal

The Father God sent forth His servants to call those who had been invited to the wedding. These servants may represent John the Baptist and the twelve apostles of Christ Jesus, the King's Son. John the Baptist said that Jesus was the bridegroom who had the bride, and he rejoiced, as the friend of the bridegroom, to hear the bridegroom's voice (John 3:27-30).

The ones invited would not come. They were not willing to come. They actually refused to come. This refusal to accept an invitation of a king to His Son's wedding – a royal wedding – was counted as the greatest insult possible to Father and the Son, the King and His Son!

This invitation and refusal could well apply to the period of time in the Gospels, and the ministry of the servants there. "He came unto His own, and His own received Him not..." (John 1:11-12).

(b) Second Invitation and Refusal

The Father God, the King, once again sent out other servants and these give the same call to those who had received the invitation. He reminds them that the banquet dinner is ready. The oxen and fatted cattle have been killed. Everything is ready. Come to the marriage! It is very much like those who refuse the invitation to the great supper in Luke 14:15-24.

What was their response? They made light of the invitation and the call. It was such a breach of etiquette not to accept. Every one went their own ways, one to the farm, and another to his business. As if this was not insulting enough, the rest of them seized the king's servants, treated them spitefully and killed them, just as in the parable of the vineyard and husbandmen.

This second invitation and call to the same people would bring us to the ministry of the Holy Spirit in the Acts of the Apostles, and through the believers in this time.

Having rejected John the Baptist, and the apostles in the Gospels, they now reject the apostles and ministry of the Church in the Acts. Hostility, spite, persecution and even stoning are seen in Acts and this by the religious leaders and the Jewish nation (Matthew 23:34). The apostles were beaten after being imprisoned (Acts 4:3; 5:18,40). Stephen is stoned to death after his testimony to the Sanhedrin (Acts 7:51-53). The church is scattered abroad everywhere by violence, persecution, prison and even death (Acts 8:1; 9:1-2).

Even Saul, after his conversion, experiences stoning and continuous persecution by the Jews (Acts 12:1-3; 13:42-52; 14:19-20; 17:5; 21:30; 22:21-22; 23:2 with 1Thessalonians 2:14-16).

As John wrote, "He came unto His own, and His own received Him not.." (John 1:11-12). It was basically a national rejection of the King (God the Father) and His Son (Jesus).

6. Destruction of Jerusalem

That the first and second invitations belong more in the "time-element" of the Gospels and Acts is confirmed by the clear reference to the destruction of "their city." If one drew a "time-line" setting this out, it would focus the whole parable more sharply.

When the king heard of the rejection and treatment of his servants, he was furious. He sent for his armies, destroyed those murderers, and burnt their city.

All this was indeed in fulfilment of the prophetic word of Jesus, the King's Son. In AD70, God the Father allowed the Roman armies under Prince Titus to destroy the temple, the city – Jerusalem – the people of Judah and desolate the land. Jewry was scattered until the times ·of the Gentiles would be fulfilled (Matthew 24:1-2,15; Luke 21:20-24; Mark 13:14-23). Note Stephen's use of the word "murderers" in his word to the Sanhedrin, the highest Jewish court in the land (Acts 7:51-53). The word was not used lightly, for the law made distinction between manslaughter and murder. There was a city of refuge for any who were guilty of manslaughter, killing someone ignorantly and not out of hate. There was no city of refuge for those who wilfully murdered another, and this out of hatred (Numbers 35).

7. The Gospel to the Gentiles

.This is actually the third invitation, the third call. After the rejection of the invitations to the wedding or marriage by Jewry, the King now sends His servants out further abroad. He said to His servant, The wedding is ready, but those who were invited are not worthy. Go into the highways and as many as you can find, invite to the wedding. Who can fail to see here the Gospel going now to the Gentile world. The invitation is intensified after the destruction of Jerusalem and the scattering of Jewry to the four winds of heaven.

The Roman Empire was noted for the **"highways"** it built for faster and smoother transport of its armies through out the Empire.

Acts Chapters 1-12 show Peter's apostolic ministry to the Jews and to the Samaritans. Acts Chapters 13-28 show Paul's apostolic ministry to the Gentiles, from Antioch to Rome and further.

The Gospel had indeed gone **"to the Jew first".** but as a nation they had spurned it. The 3000, the 5000 and multitudes of men and women had accepted it and became the beginning and foundation members of the New Testament Church. The nation, as a whole, however, rejected it. After Paul himself went always **"to the Jew first",** he was ultimately forced to go to the Gentiles who accepted it (Read carefully Acts 3:26; 13:46; 26:20,23; Romans 1:16; 2:9-10 with 1Thessalonians 2:14-16).

As John said, "He came unto His own (the Jews), and His own received Him not, but to as many as received Him (Jews and Gentiles), to them He gave the power to become the sons of God..." (John 1:11-12).

The apostles and the early believers went everywhere preaching the Gospel to every creature, Jews and Gentiles, gathering as many as they could to respond to the Word (Matthew 28:15-20; Mark 16:15-20; Luke 24:47-49). The invitation went to Jerusalem, Judea, Samaria and then the uttermost parts of the earth (Matthew 8:10-12; Acts 1:8).

8. The Mixture of Wedding Guests

As a result of the wedding invitations, the wedding was furnished with guests, both good and bad. This fact of mixture in the kingdom of God in its present state has been seen in our exposition of the parables of Matthew 13.

* The mixture was seen in the parable of the wheat and tares (Matthew 13:24-43).

* The mixture was seen in the net of good and bad fish (Mathew 13:47-52).

* The mixture is seen in the parable of the king's son. Both good and bad come in as guests, responding to the invitation to the wedding.

It is important to understand that the kingdom of God in its present state has mixture in it. This mixture will continue right through to the second coming of Christ when the great separation takes place.

* Israel had a mixed multitude that fell to lusting after the miraculous exodus from Egypt (Exodus 12:38; Numbers 11:4).

* Nehemiah separated Israel from the mixed multitude after the Babylonian Captivity (Nehemiah 13:3).

* The final kingdoms of the Antichristal Empire have mixture of iron and clay seen in the ten toes, the feet of the great image of world kingdoms (Daniel 2).

The kingdom of God in its present manifestation has both good and bad, religious and irreligious, moral and immoral, the genuine and the counterfeit, sincerity and hypocrisy, wheat and tares, good and bad fish, and good and bad guests – all will take their place in the kingdom!

9. The Man without a Wedding Garment

The time came when the king came into see the guests. As he looked around, he saw a man there without a wedding garment. He said, "Friend, how did you come in here without a wedding garment?" The man stood there speechless. He had nothing to say.

In order to understand the symbolism of the wedding garment, it is necessary to bridge the cultural gap between ourselves and the Biblical writers. This is Eastern! It is not a Western wedding!

R.C.Trench, in "Notes on the Parables of Our Lord" (pps 80-81) has this to say about the wedding garment.

"It was part of the state of wealthy persons in the East, to have great store of costly dresses laid up (Isaiah 3:6; 2Kings 10:22). Chardin says, "The expenditure of the king of Persia for presents cannot be credited. The number of dresses which he gives is infinite. His wardrobes are always full of them; they are kept in assorted warehouse." We know, moreover, that costly dresses were often given as honourable presents, marks of especial favour (Genesis 45:22; 2Kings 5:5); that they were then, as now, the most customary gifts; and that upon marriage festivals (Esther 2:18) gifts were distributed with the largest hand. If the gift was one of costly raiment, it would reasonably be expected that it should be worn at once, to add to the splendor and glory of the festal time – not to say that the rejection of a gift, or the appearance of a slight upon it, is ever esteemed as a contempt of the giver.

But this guest was guilty of a further affront in appearing at the festival in mean and sordid apparel. He did not feel that he had anything to say for himself; **he was speechless,** literally, his mouth was stopped; he stood self-condemned" (End quote).

This guest was plainly guilty in coming into the wedding festival in his own clothes. He had refused the provided garment. This was an insult to the King and His Son, to be at the marriage and not be attired for the occasion.

G.Campbell Morgan in **"The Parables and Metaphors of Our Lord"** (p.133) shows that the man had found his way in but he lacked the true insignia of relationship. He was violating the true order of that kingdom. The man showed indifference, carelessness and objection.

G.Campbell Morgan goes on to explain that there are two different Greek words translated **"not"** in verses 11-12. In verse 11, the man did not have a wedding garment. It simply states a fact. He did not have the provided garment on. In verse 12, when the king asks why he did **not** have on the wedding garment, it was because he did **not** intend to have one on. He had definately, of his own thought and will intended not to accept the wedding garment. He was determined **not** to have it on! That was his decision!

The garment was provided, but not accepted. It was a deliberate choice. He knew it. It was his own fault. Undoubtedly he felt that the garment he had on ·was suitable for the wedding. He did not and was not willing to accept the garment provided by the king.

He was not willing to be dressed for the ocassion – a royal wedding. The marriage of a king's son! He had refused to accept the garment freely provided by the king for the marriage. This was indeed an insult to the king and his son, even though he – unlike others – had accepted the invitation. No wonder he was speechless! He had no valid excuse. His mouth was stopped. He stood self-condemned (Romans 3:19).

What is the "wedding garment?" Without doubt, the only garment that God the Father provides for acceptance in the marriage of His Son, Jesus, is the garment of salvation, the garment of faith-righteousness. The Bible speaks of:

*   The garments of salvation (Isaiah 61:10; 52:1; Psalm 132:9,16)
*   The garment of praise (Isaiah 61:3)
*   The garment of righteousness (Revelation 19:7-9).

The bride makes herself ready for the marriage of the Lamb by being clothed in the pure, fine and white linen of faith-righteousness. We are called to "put on Christ", and this garment is provided freely for us from God the Father, the King (Romans 13:14; Galatians 3:27). No one can attend this marriage in sloppy clothes of self-righteousness! It is salvation internally, and righteousness manifested externally.

It pictures the Jew who hung on to their old garments, dirty old robes of self-righteousness, and refused the garment God provided through faith. There will be those who accept God's invitation, but are still clothed in their own garments of self- righteousness, or, righteousness by the works of the law. They have refused to accept the faith-righteousness that is of God, the only thing that makes them acceptable in God's sight (Romans 9:30-33; 10:1-4; Philippians

3:1-11). This man had not put on Christ. He was self-satisfied, self-righteous, making and trusting his own garments to be acceptable to the King and His Son. He refused and rejected the freely offered robe of faith-righteousness! He was speechless. There was nothing to say. There was no excuse!

10. Bound and Taken Away

The man was bound and taken away, taken out of the wedding. The truth is certainly inapplicable to heaven. No one gets into heaven without the Divinely provided wedding garment, and then is cast out of heaven. This is a parable that applies more to this end of the age and the final separation of the good and bad, as in the parables of the wheat and tares, and the good and bad fish.

Jesus said, "Whatsoever is bound on earth shall be bound in heaven..." (Matthew 16:19 with Matthew 18:18). Heaven works with earth in the final judgments. The man is bound and taken away from the wedding joys.

11. The Outer Darkness Judgment

He is bound, taken away from the feast and then cast into "outer darkness." This is the judgment and Divine punishment on the one without the wedding garment. The guest is thrown into outer darkness – "in the darkness outside" – more literally. The king told his servants to bind him hand and feet, take him away and put him into the outer darkness of the court. There would be weeping and gnashing of teeth. This was a terrible sentence. It is the oriental language expressing the deepest grief, sorrow and mourning.

Again the cultural gap must be bridged. In that time, within the banquet hall or palace of the king, there was brilliant light, joy and festivity, in the presence of the King and the marriage of His Son. Outside the palace there was darkness and coldness in the outer court. Under the sense of shame and guilt, the unworthy guest was cast out and experienced the weeping and gnashing of teeth in regret for having accepted the King's invitation, but refusing the freely given wedding garment. This was the "outer darkness" which the guest experienced!

Expositors differ as to the full significance and interpretation of "the outer darkness" and "weeping and gnashing of teeth." Some expositors believe this speaks of the final and eternal judgment, where those who were but professors of Christ and religion will be cast into outer darkness, the lake of fire and brimstone, and suffer eternal weeping, wailing and gnashing of teeth (Revelation 14:9-11; 18:15,19; 20:11-15). Both Jude and Peter speak of angels in chains of darkness, bound for judgment on that day (Jude 6; 2Peter 2:4).

A few expositors believe this speaks of judgment in and through this age, or the final judgment period before the second coming of Christ. The picture cannot apply to heaven as no one enters heaven and then is cast out.

There are a number of occasions where the truth of "outer darkness" and "weeping, wailing and gnashing of teeth" are seen. Undoubtedly they point to the same thing. There are three occasions of it in Matthew's Gospel as well as similar language in other parables. They are listed here for the student's consideration.

(a) The Kingdom

The children of the kingdom will be cast out into outer darkness, where there is weeping and gnashing of teeth, because they lack that faith in Christ that the Gentiles have as they sit down in the kingdom with Abraham, Isaac and Jacob (Matthew 8:5-13; Luke 13:28-29).

(b) The Talents
The unprofitable servant who failed to use his Divinely given talents was cast into outer darkness where there was weeping and gnashing of teeth, while the profitable servant entered into the joy of his Lord (Matthew 25:14-30).

(c) The Wedding Garment
The guest without the wedding garment was cast into outer darkness and experienced weeping and gnashing of teeth, while those who accepted the garment enjoyed the royal wedding (Matthew 22:1-14).

For other references that are similar to these, there is the portion for the evil servants and hypocrites (Matthew 24:42-51; Luke 12:41-48), and the foolish virgins are shut outside (Matthew 25:1-13), and outer court of the temple is cast out and trodden under foot for three and one-half years period (Revelation 11:1-2). Even the salt that has lost its savour and effectiveness is cast out and trodden under foot of men (Matthew 5:13).

·The three major occasions in Matthew's Gospel have to do with believers, or those who profess faith in Christ.

It is possible that the judgment pertains to the period of tribulation prior to the coming of Christ. The believer does not forfeit his salvation but forfeits the reward and joy of the Lord and His kingdom glory.

Without doubt, which ever school of interpretation may be followed, there is Divine discipline on the ones involved in the parables. Jesus said that the Church's ministry and discipline would involve "binding and loosing". "Whatever you **bind** on earth shall have been bound in heaven, and whatever you **loose** on earth shall have been already loosed in heaven "(Matthew 16:15-18; 18:15-20. AmpNT).

What regret and sorrow the guest who refused the wedding garment suffered, as he wept and ground his teeth over missing the royal banquet, bound and in darkness!

The parable closes with the same words as that of the parable of the vineyard labourers. "For many are called, but few are chosen" Matthew 20:16). Those that are with Christ are called, chosen and faithful (Revelation17:14).

E. The Practical Application of the Parable
As already seen, there are many lessons interwoven throughout the parts of the parable. God the Father has sent out His servants over the centuries with invitations to the marriage of His Son, Jesus Christ.

The chosen nation, as a whole, rejected the invitation. The servants of God were treated evilly and cruelly and at times, they were killed. God the Father, after allowing the city of Jerusalem to be destroyed, sent similar servants and the same invitation to the Gentile world. The kingdom of God gathers all kinds into it. There is mixture in the kingdom in its present state.

The time will come, however, when the separation will take place. All who do not have on the Divinely provided garment of faith-righteousness will suffer the Divine discipline, whether in this life or the life to come. The guest is not just an individual but represents all those individuals who refuse to accept God's faith-righteous garment. They will be speechless in "that day." Those who are clothed in the wedding garment will enjoy the blessedness of the marriage of the Lamb (Revelation 19:7-9). Such are the great lessons learned from the parable of the marriage of the king's son!

(**Note:** Because the parable is a **historical-prophetical** kind of parable, it is recommended that the student draw a "time-line" and superimpose upon it the major points of "time", as to the Gospels, the Acts, the destruction of Jerusalem in AD70, and then the going forth of the Gospel to the Gentiles, and then the final separation at the coming of Christ of the good and the bad! The particular verses of the parable find their place in these "time" indicators!).

CHAPTER TWENTY-ONE
THE PARABLE OF THE WISE AND FOOLISH VIRGINS

A. The Scripture on the Parable
Matthew 25:1-13

Then shall the kingdom of heaven be likened unto ten virgins, which took their lamps, and went forth to meet the bridegroom.

And five of them were wise, and five were foolish.

They that were foolish took their lamps, and took no oil with them:

But the wise took oil in their vessels with their lamps.

While the bridegroom tarried, they all slumbered and slept.

And at midnight there was a cry made, Behold, the bridegroom cometh; go ye out to meet him.

Then all those virgins arose, and trimmed their lamps.

And the foolish said unto the wise, Give us of your oil; for our lamps are gone out.

But the wise answered, saying, Not so; lest there be not enough for us and you: but go ye rather to them that sell, and buy for yourselves.

And while they went to buy, the bridegroom came; and they that were ready went in with him to the marriage: and the door was shut.

Afterward came also the other virgins, saying, Lord, Lord, open to us.

But he answered and said, Verily I say unto you, I know you not.

Watch therefore, for ye know neither the day nor the hour wherein the Son of man cometh.

B. The Setting of the Parable

The setting of the parable is on Mt Olivet and it is part of the Olivet Discourse. In Matthew 23:37-39 and 24:1-2 we see Jesus had departed from the temple, calling it "your house" – desolate! He ascended Mt Olivet and as He sat there, He gave, first of all, a panoramic view of events from the destruction of the temple, under Prince Titus and the Roman armies, through to His second coming. The theme of Matthew Chapter 24 is the coming of Christ.

Some expositors see the events of this chapter fulfilled in AD70 and in the destruction of Jerusalem. Others see the ultimate fulfilment of this chapter at Christ's return. Both schools do agree that the finalle of the chapter is Christ's actual second coming.

At the conclusion of Matthew 23:45-51, Jesus asked the question: "Who then is a **faithful** and **wise** servant whom his lord has made ruler over his household, to give them meat in due season?"

The two parables following seem to be a definate expansion in parabolic form of these two words, **"faithful"** and **"wise"**. The order is Matthew 25 is like this.

1. Matthew 25:1-13 is the parable of the **wise and foolish** virgins.
2. Matthew 25:14-30 is the parable of the **faithful and slothful** servants.

Both parables are "end-time" parables and bring us to the coming of the Lord. Matthew Chapters 24-25 are given to cover things pertaining to Christ's return. This is the setting of these last recorded parables of Christ, only to be found in Matthew's Gospel.

C. The Exposition of the Parable

The parable of the wise and foolish virgins is only to be found in the Gospel of Matthew. As the parable of the marriage of the king's son (Matthew 22:1-14), so is the parable of the wise and foolish virgins. Both have to do with a marriage. In this parable it is the marriage of the bridegroom to his bride.

The wedding is Eastern – not Western! A general custom in an Eastern wedding is that the bridegroom is attended by his friends, "the children of the bridegroom" (Matthew 9:15). The bridegroom goes to the home of the bride and with gladness brings the bride to his own home. The bride is accompanied from her father's house by her young companions (Psalm 45:15), while others, the virgin bridesmaids of the parable meet the procession at some convenient place, and enter with the bridal company into the hall of feasting. Most marriages in the East took place at night time. The virgin bridesmaids accompanied the bride with torches (or lamps), amidst much rejoicing.

D. The Moral of the Parable

There is no mistaking the major moral of the parable. Jesus Himself gives the lesson in verse 13. "Watch therefore, for you know neither the day nor the hour wherein the Son of Man comes."

The moral of the parable is that believers need to be ready always, waiting and watching for the coming of the Lord in that unknown day and hour, lest they find themselves excluded. The message is, "Coming, ready or not!" Note these Scriptures exhorting believers to watch and be ready for the coming of the Lord (Matthew 24:42-44; 25:13; Mark 13:33-37; Luke 12:37-39; 21:36; 1Thessalonians 5:1-8).

E. The Exposition of the Parable

As in all the parables, all the parts of the parable make up the parable. It is not one part without the other. One must constantly work from part to whole and whole to part and gather up the fragmentary truths that make up the central truth of the parable, as seen in the unfolding and exposition of the parable.

1. The Kingdom of Heaven

The kingdom of heaven is like, it resembles, it may be compared to the various parts of the parable of the wise and foolish virgins. The parable is especially in the context of the days of the second coming. The "time-element" is "THEN shall the kingdom of heaven be likened to..." The rule and reign of heaven resembles or is represented to the details of the wise and foolish virgins parable.

2. The Virgins

Virgins in Scripture represent purity, those who have kept themselves from immoral defilements and corruptions. The church is likened to a pure, chaste virgin being presented to Christ.

Isaac married the virgin Rebekah (Genesis 24:16,43).

The high priest had to marry a virgin of his own people. He was forbidden to marry a widow, a divorced woman, a profane person or an harlot (Leviticus 21:14-15).

There are 144,000 virgins seen with the Lamb on Mt Zion (Revelation 14:1-5). Paul desired to present the Corinthian believers as "a chaste virgin to Christ" (2Corinthians 11:2).

The virgins here speak of Christians. They do not represent unbelievers who are defiled by sin. They do not represent non-Christians, or professors of Christ. Virgins represent those who are cleansed by the blood of Christ and are walking with the Lamb, without deceit or fault. An unconverted sinner is never likened to a virgin. Whether wise or foolish, they were all likened to virgins.

Some expositors see the virgins here as representing the church, the bride of Christ. Others see the virgins here as the bridesmaids attending to the bride (Psalm 45:9-15; Song 1:3; 6:8-9). James Moffatt's translation writes: "Then shall the Realm of heaven be compared to ten maidens who took their lamps and went out to meet the **bridegroom and the bride**" (Matthew 25:1). In Moffatt's footnote he states that the Latin and Syriac versions have this rendering. He says "the omission of these words may have been due to the feeling of the later church that Jesus as the Bridegroom ought alone to be mentioned."

3. Ten Virgins

The number ten is used in symbolic sense. Ten in the Scripture is the number of responsibility and accountability. Ten is made up of two fives. One may think of the ten toes on the Image (Daniel 2), or the ten horns (Daniel 7), or ten talents, ten pounds or ten virgins, as in the parables of Jesus (Luke 19:13). Five fingers on each hand, five toes on each foot, all were responsible for working and walking.

Ten is also the number of law and order as well as the number of testing and trial (Exodus 20; Numbers 14:22). For any ten Jews living in one place, this was counted as a congregation, enough to build a synagogue.

These ten virgins would be held responsible before the bridegroom to be watching and waiting with their lamps burning brightly! Believers, as pure and chaste virgins before the Lord are responsible for watching for Jesus to come again the second time.

4. The Lamps

The lamp in Scripture is used to represent either the Holy Spirit, or the Word of God or man's spirit, as these Scriptures confirm.

The seven lamps on the golden lampstand symbolized the light of the seven Spirits of God (Exodus 27:20; 25:37 with Revelation 4:5).

The Word of God is likened to a lamp-light (Psalm 119:105; Proverbs 6:23).

The spirit of man is the candle (literally, the lamp) of the Lord (Proverbs 20:27; 24:20).

In the context of this parable, the lamp represents the spirit of man. However, a lamp needs oil in order to give light. Man's spirit, in the Fall, went into darkness. It is the Holy Spirit coming into man's spirit by new birth that re-lights man's spirit (John 3:1-5; Romans 8:16-17). The lamp is man's spirit. The oil in the lamp is the Holy Spirit.

5. The Bridegroom

There is no mistaking who the bridegroom is here. It is none other than the Lord Jesus Christ Himself, who is also (as in the previous parable), the King's Son.

John the Baptist referred to Jesus as the bridegroom. "He that has the bride is the bridegroom but the friend of the bridegroom, which stands and hears him, rejoices greatly because of the bridegroom's voice: this my joy is fulfilled" (John 3:29). Read also Isaiah 61:10; 62:5. In this present time, the bridegroom is away (Luke 5:34-35; Matthew 9:15; Mark 2:19-20).

6. **Five Wise and Five Foolish**

Of the ten virgins, five are wise and five are foolish. The Book of Proverbs is a book that shows the wisdom of the wise and the folly of the foolish. In Matthew 7:24-27, Jesus told the undesignated parable of the **wise and foolish** builders. There it had to do with the foundation of obedience. Here it is the parable of the **wise and foolish** virgins. Here it has to do with oil enough in readiness for the bridegroom's coming. If the five wise and the five foolish were taken numerically, it means that, percentage-wise, it is fifty-fifty that are wise and foolish.

7. **The Lamps and Oil-Vessels**

In verses 4-5 we have the distinct difference between the wise and the foolish virgins. The foolish had lamps and oil in their lamps only, but took no extra vessel with them. The wise had lamps and oil in their lamps, but also took extra oil in the oil-vessels. It was this extra vessel of oil that made all the difference. They had an extra supply of oil.

The lamp has been seen to represent the human, regenerated spirit, the spirit of the believer. The oil in Scripture symbolizes the Holy Spirit. What is the lamp without the oil? No oil in the lamp means no light shining from the lamp (John 5:35). The human spirit needs the oil of the Holy Spirit. The Holy Spirit is the oil in the lamp of man's redeemed spirit (1Samuel 10:1,6; 16:13; Leviticus 8:10-12; 21:12).

The seven lamps on the golden lampstand had to have oil supplied to the lamps morning and eveing. There were vessels of extra oil for this in the tabernale of the Lord (Exodus 25:31-40; Numbers 8:1-4; Exodus 30:7-8).

The seven lamps of the golden lampstand had to be supplied from the golden oil in the golden bowl in the vision God gave to Zechariah (Zechariah 4:1-14).

The Jewish mind would be familiar with the symbolism of the lamps, the vessels and the need of a continual supply of oil to cause the lamps to shine.

So the believer needs a constant "supply of the Spirit" in his spirit. The believer needs not only to be born of the Spirit but to be constantly filled with the Spirit (Acts 2:1-4; Philippians 1:19; Ephesians 5:18).

8. **The Bridegroom Delayed**

During the course of time, the bridegroom was delayed. In Matthew 24:45-51, the evil servant said in his heart, "My Lord is delaying His coming." So here in the parable of the virgins. The bridegroom delayed His coming. He did not come back at the time the virgins (the church) thought He would (Luke 12:45).

Many in the early church, especially the Thessalonians, expected the Lord to return in their time. Paul's epistles to the Thessalonians were written to adjust their thinking on the Lord's coming.

A time of dclayal is a time of testing. The Lord Jesus, as the heavenly bridegroom, will come right at the appointed time. For many believers, it seems that the Lord is delaying His coming. The test is: What will we do in this apparent delayal?

9. The Virgins Slumbered and Slept

In this waiting period, the spirit of slumber and sleep fell on all the virgins. They all – wise and foolish – fell into sleep. This was not the sleep of rest, but the sleep of lethargy, the sleep and slumber of spiritual drowsiness and unwatchfulness. The Scriptures give plenty of warning against this kind of sleep, as seen in these passages.

In the vision of the golden lampstand, with the golden bowl, the golden oil and the seven lamps, Zechariah had to be awakened out of his sleep (Zechariah 4:1-2).

The disciples had to be wakened out of sleep on the Mt of Transfiguration in order to see the glory of the Lord and Moses and Elijah there with Jesus (Luke 9:32).

These same disciples, Peter, James and John, had to be awakened in Gethsemane when they should have been praying with the Master (Matthew 26:4).

Paul told the Roman believers that it was high time to wake out of sleep because their salvation was nearer than when they believed (Romans 13:11-12).

To the Thessalonian believers, Paul writes, "Therefore, let us not sleep as do others, but let us watch and be sober" (Read 1Thessalonians 5:1-8). The point of the parable is that all slumbered and slept, the wise and the foolish. All needed to be awakened!

10. The Midnight Cry

Midnight – the darkest hour of the night, when one is in the deepest kind of sleep, is significant of the end of the age.

The theme of the midnight hour runs through the Word of God, both Old and New Testaments. Following we see some of the important events that took place at the midnight hour.

There was a great cry at the midnight hour in Egypt at the time of Passover deliverance (Exodus 11:4; 12:29). Those that did not have the blood on the house suffered Divine judgment.

Samson took the gates of the city at the midnight hour (Judges 16:3).

Ruth the bride-to-be was found at the feet of Boaz, the kinsman-redeemer, at the midnight hour (Ruth 3:8).

Midnight can be a time of trouble (Psalm 119:62), or it can be a time of praise (Job 34:20). Christ could come at the midnight hour (Mark 13:35).

Here there is the midnight cry of the bridegroom, Jesus. The call and cry is, "Behold, the bridegroom comes, go out to meet Him." Undoubtedly there has been an awakening in a great portion of the church that Christ is coming soon.Where a great percentage of believers have been spiritually asleep, wise and foolish, there is a response to the cry of the Spirit to awake – the Lord is coming soon!

11. Trimming the Lamps

With the great awakening of the virgins, there came a time of lamp-trimming. The language would be familiar to the hearers, the disciples.

Aaron, the high priest, had to trim the seven lamps on the golden lampstand and supply oil, morning and evening, in the tabernacle of Moses. The same was true for the lampstands in the temple of Solomon (Exodus 25:37; 30:7-8; 35:14; 40:25; Leviticus 24:1-4; Numbers 8:1-3; 1Kings 7:49-50; Zechariah 4:1-2).

Jewish customs varied, but often the bridesmaids would go out to meet the bridegroom, as he was leaving his house for his waiting bride. Whatever the custom, the truth is, the lamps had to be trimmed and fresh oil had to be supplied in order for the lamps to be burning brightly.

The church in Revelation Chapter 1-2-3 is likened to the golden lampstand. The local churches needed to have their lamps trimmed, and they needed the supply of the oil of the Holy Spirit.

Trimming the lamps is significant of believers preparing for the coming of Christ. We are to shine forth as lights in the midst of a crooked and perverse generation (Matthew 5:14-16; Philippians 2:15). Jesus said, "Let your loins be girded about you and your lamps burning" (Luke 12:35).

12. Lamps Going Out

With the midnight cry, and the great awakening from sleep, all the virgins began to trim their lamps in readiness for the bridegroom.

The foolish suddenly realized that their lamps were "going out" (not "gone out"). The foolish came to the wise asking for some of their oil from their extra vessels. The wise replied that they could not give their oil lest there be not enough for their own readiness to meet the bridegroom. They exhort them to go to those who sold oil and buy for themselves.

Proverbs 21:20 says: "There is treasure to be desired and oil in the dwelling of the **wise,** but a **foolish** man spends it up." The wise virgins had oil in their lamps and the extra vessel. The foolish had spent their oil up and their lamps were going out. They had no extra supply of the Spirit, the holy oil of God.

The lesson here should be clear. Each believer, every Christian, must seek the Lord for themselves. Each must pay the price for the holy oil in their lives; a life of total surrender to do the will of God. There must be daily prayer, daily meditation on God's Word, daily relationship with the Lord, a daily filling with the Holy Spirit. No other believer can do this for another believer. By daily walking in the Spirit, there will be that supply of the Spirit. This is wisdom. Otherwise the believer becomes like a foolish virgin and squanders the oil until they find their lamps going out. No one can borrow or live on another's experience. It is a personal relationship with God by the Holy Spirit.

13. The Bridegroom Came

While the foolish virgins are on their way to buy oil for themselves, the bridegroom came. It speaks of the coming of Jesus, the heavenly bridegroom.

The central theme of Matthew Chapters 24-25 is the coming of the Lord, the coming of the bridegroom. Distinct references to His coming are seen in Matthew 24:3,27,30,37,39,42,43,48,50 and 25:27,31). Jesus said, "If I go away, I will come again and receive you unto Myself..." (John14:1-3;Acts 1:9-11). Over three hundred references to Christ's second coming are to be found in the New Testament. The bridegroom will surely come!

14. The Ready Ones enter The Marriage

Verse 10 simply says that those who were ready went in with Him to the marriage. The great multitude rejoice when the marriage of the Lamb comes for the bride has made herself ready (Revelation 19:7-9; Matthew 22:2,4,9). The church as the bride of Christ is to make herself ready for the marriage to the bridegroom.

It was "the ready ones", the wise virgins, the wise believers, who went into the marriage. Marriage speaks of unity, oneness and the closest relationship with the Lord.

Paul tells us in Ephesians 5:23-32 that the marriage of Christ to His church is a great mystery.

15. The Shut Door

The wise went into the marriage, and the door was shut. A door was shut from the inside. Once the door was shut to wedding guests, none could enter or force the door. The foolish came later on, knocking on the shut door, pleading with the Lord to open the door to them. There is no reference to them obtaining the extra oil.

Whatever may be the full significance of "the shut door", it speaks of exclusion, being left outside of the marriage.

In the days of Noah, God shut the door (Genesis 6:16; 7:16). In the days of Lot, the angels shut the door (Genesis 19:6-11). In the days of Christ's coming, the door will be shut. It will be too late once the door is shut. In the light of this, all are exhorted to be on the right side of the door. The short song puts it this way: "One door and only one, And yet the sides are two, Inside and outside, Which side are you?" The foolish virgins were shut out from the marriage.

16. I Know You Not

The foolish virgins came crying, "Lord, Lord, open to us!" The Lord says from within, I know you not."

Although not exactly the same, the language is very similar to that of Matthew 7:21-23 and Luke 13:25-27. In both cases, the cry is, "Lord, Lord, open to us." They reply that they have prophesied in His name, cast out devils in His name and have done many wonderful works in His name. They remind the Lord that they had communion in His presence and He had taught in their streets. In each passage, the Lord says: "I know you not; I do not know where you are from; depart from Me you workers of iniquity." The door is shut!

Some expositors make the group in each passage of the Scripture one and the same. They teach that the foolish virgins, along with the miracle-workers, and so-forth, are but professors of Christ. They are not genuine believers. If that is the proper interpretation, then the solution is easier to discover.

It is difficult, however, to apply these passages to unbelievers, or the unregenerate, for the following reasons:

* Sinners are not spoken of as virgins; all were virgins in the parable.

* Sinners are not looking for the coming of the bridegroom, as these virgins, wise and foolish, were.

* Sinners do not have the lamp of light or the oil of the Holy Spirit in them, as all had lamps and oil. The unregenerate spiritually are in darkness.
* Sinners do not go out to meet the bridegroom, as here the wise and foolish heard the midnight cry and rose to meet the coming bridegroom.

And again:

* Sinners do not believe in the name of the Lord.
* Sinners do no prophesy in His name.
* Sinners do not cast out devils in His name.
* Sinners do not work miracles in His name.
* Sinners do not eat and drink in His presence.
* Sinners do not follow the teachings of Christ.

The weight of the Scripture is, that in each passage, the persons are believers, genuine believers or believers who had become apostates from the faith. When the Lord says to the foolish virgins, "I know you not", He is saying that He never had that intimate, spiritual relationship with them as with the wise.

When the Lord says to the miracle-workers; "I never knew you, depart from Me you workers of iniquity", He is talking to those who have fallen from the faith into apostasy. They have turned from their righteousness and died in their iniquity and this is what the Lord remembers. A careful study of Ezekiel Chapters 3,18, and 33 confirm these things.

Whichever School of Interpretation one follows, the Scriptures teach that there is some form of Divine discipline that some believers experience in the end of the age.

The evil servant of the Lord who said in his heart that the Lord was delaying His coming, and then began to beat his fellow-servants, and eat and drink with the drunken, came under Divine discipline. "The Lord of that servant shall come in a day when he looks not for Him, and in a hour that he is not aware, and shall cut him asunder, and appoint him his portion with the hypocrites; there shall be weeping and gnashing of teeth" (Matthew 24:45-51).

This passage is in the context of the **faithful and wise** servants, which prepares the way for the parable of the **wise and foolish** virgins and the parable of the **faithful and slothful** servants!

F. The Practical Application of the Parable

As in all extended parables, there are a number of spiritual lessons to be learnt from the parts of the parable. The major lesson is in the words of Jesus. "Watch therefore, for you know neither the day nor the hour when the Son of Man comes." It is the lesson of vigilence.

Christians, as virgins in the sight of the Lord, must constantly keep filled with the Spirit, and be ever ready for the coming of the Lord. All will be either wise or foolish. The decision is theirs.

Whatever may be the full significance of the parable, there is enough there to warn all believers to be awake, to keep their lives constantly filled with the Holy Spirit, and be ready for His advent. It would be terrible to be "shut out" in that day!

CHAPTER TWENTY-TWO
THE PARABLE OF THE USED AND UNUSED TALENTS

A. The Scripture on the Parable
Matthew 25:14-30

And this gospel of the kingdom shall be preached in all the world for a witness unto all nations; and then shall the end come.

When ye therefore shall see the abomination of desolation, spoken of by Daniel the prophet, stand in the holy place, (whoso readeth, let him understand:)

Then let them which be in Judaea flee into the mountains:

Let him which is on the housetop not come down to take any thing out of his house:

Neither let him which is in the field return back to take his clothes.

And woe unto them that are with child, and to them that give suck in those days!

But pray ye that your flight be not in the winter, neither on the sabbath day:

For then shall be great tribulation, such as was not since the beginning of the world to this time, no, nor ever shall be.

And except those days should be shortened, there should no flesh be saved: but for the elect's sake those days shall be shortened.

Then if any man shall say unto you, Lo, here is Christ, or there; believe it not.

For there shall arise false Christs, and false prophets, and shall shew great signs and wonders; insomuch that, if it were possible, they shall deceive the very elect.

Behold, I have told you before.

Wherefore if they shall say unto you, Behold, he is in the desert; go not forth: behold, he is in the secret chambers; believe it not.

For as the lightning cometh out of the east, and shineth even unto the west; so shall also the coming of the Son of man be.

For wheresoever the carcase is, there will the eagles be gathered together.

Immediately after the tribulation of those days shall the sun be darkened, and the moon shall not give her light, and the stars shall fall from heaven, and the powers of the heavens shall be shaken:

And then shall appear the sign of the Son of man in heaven: and then shall all the tribes of the earth mourn, and they shall see the Son of man coming in the clouds of heaven with power and great glory.

B. The Setting of the Parable

The setting of the parable is the same setting as that of the wise and foolish virgins. It is part of the Olivet Discourse of the Lord to His disciples pertaining to events of His second coming at the close of the age.

C. The Moral of the Parable

There are a number of lessons in this extended parable but Jesus, once again, provides the major moral of the parable in verse 29. "For unto everyone that has, more shall be given, and he shall have abundance: but from him that has not shall be taken away even that which he seems to have." Or, in other words: To every one who has used what he was given, more shall be given, but to every one who has not used what he was given, what he was given shall be taken away. The moral is: You gain what you use, you lose what you do not use!

D. The Exposition of the Parable

The parable of the talents in Matthew's Gospel is similar to the parable of the pounds in Luke's Gospel (Luke 19:11-27). There are, however, some differences and both need to be considered separately. These three parables each teach responsibility and accountability.

1. The Parable of the Wise and Foolish Virgins (Matthew 25:1-13
2. The Parable of the Talents, Used and Unused (Matthew 25:14-30)
3. The Parable of the Pounds (Luke 19:11-27).

As the parable of the **wise and foolish** virgins dealt with the **"wise"** servants of Matthew 24:45, now the parable of the **"faithful and slothful"** servants deals with the **"faithful"** servants of the same passage (Matthew 24:45-51). This parable is also one of those **historical-prophetical** parables, reaching over time unto the second coming of Christ. The parable of the virgins speaks of watchfulness or watchlessness. The parable of the talents speaks of faithfulness or slothfulness.

1. The Kingdom of Heaven

Once again, the formula, "the kingdom of heaven is like" is used. The kingdom of heaven represents or may be compared to or likened the details found in the parable of the talents. The reader is reminded that the parable works from part to whole and whole to part in the exposition of the parable.

2. The Man

The man in this parable represents the Son of Man, the Lord Jesus Christ. In other parts of the parable He is spoken of as Lord and Master.

3. The Far Country

The Son of man travelled into a far country. This speaks of the heavenly country (Hebrews 11:10-16). In the "time-element" of the parable, the travelling into the far country would point to Christ's ascension into heaven until the time of His second coming (Acts 1:9-11).

4. Called His Own Servants

The calling of the Lord is to His own people. those who are called out of darkness into the light of His kingdom, those who are serving, those who are true believers.

5. Delivered His Goods

The "goods" delivered to them were **His** goods, not theirs, but the Master entrusting His goods to His servants. This makes the servants responsible and accountable for what the Master entrusts to them.

6. The Talents Given

To each of the servants the Lord gave talents. It is to be seen that the talents given were according to each person's **ability**.

One servant received five talents. Another received two talents. The other received one talent. The Lord did not give talents beyond their ability. He knew the different abilities of each of His servants. He knew what they could handle and did not give them goods beyond their ability to handle, so there could be no excuse.

The Lord never gives Christians things beyond their ability. All can serve the Lord according to their measure; no less and no more. To serve the Lord to the best of our ability is all that He requires (Ezra 2:69; Nehemiah 5:8; Daniel 1:4; Acts 11:29; 1Peter 4:11).

In Bible times, a talent varied according to the Romans, Greeks and Hebrews. It could be silver or gold. According to James P. Boyd's Bible Dictionary, "a talent was a Hebrew weight and denomination for money, equal to three thousand shekels, and about 94 pounds of silver and varying in value from $1500 to $2000. The fact is, the Lord entrusted talents to His servants, expecting them to do business for Him.

So the Lord gives to all believers "His goods" to be used for His glory and the extension of His kingdom.

After giving His goods, His talents, to the different servants, He immediately went on His journey. As already noted, this speaks of the Lord's journey back to heaven, back to His Father (John 16:27-28).

7. Trading With The Talents

The different servants went out with the talents and traded with them; that is, two of the one mentioned, while the third servant failed.

The servant who received five talents traded with these and gained five other talents; that is one hundred percent. He used what he was given. The servant who received two talents did likewise. He traded with his two talents and gained two other talents; that is one hundred percent increase. He used what he had been given. The servant who received one talent went and dug a hole in the earth, and then hid his Lord's money. He did not use what he was given. He gained nothing for His Lord. There was no investment or gain, even if he had deposited this one talent for some interest.

In the parable of the virgins, they were waiting for their Lord. In the parable of the talents, the servants are working for their Lord.

8. After A Long Time

The "long time" speaks of the church age. No one knows how long that time is, between the Lord's departure for the heavenly country and His return again. While the Lord, however, is in the heavenly country, He expects His servants to be doing business for Him with His goods! He expects us to "redeem the time" and buy up every opportunity (Ephesians 5:16; Psalm 92:12).

9. The Lord Comes

As already seen, Matthew Chapters 24-25 and the associated parables especially deal with the Lord's second coming (Read Matthew 24:3,217,30,37,39,42,43,48,50; 25:27,31). "This same Jesus shall come again... as you have seen Him go into heaven" (Acts 1:9-11).

10. The Time Of Reckoning

When the Lord returned, He called His servants to reckon with them. It is a time of settling the accounts, a time of reckoning. All His servants have to give an account to Him of what they have done with what He gave them, what they have done with His goods.

Ability equals responsibilty and both equal accountability. There is never responsibility without accountability. The Scriptures speak of the day when all shall give account to the Lord. Saints will give account at the judgment seat of Christ (Romans 14:12; Hebrews 13:17; Matthew 12:36; 18:23; Luke 16:2;

1Peter 4:5). Sinners will give account of themselves at the great white throne judgement (Revelation 20:11-15).

11. Reward For Faithfulness

The two who used their talents were rewarded for their faithfulness. God who is faithful expects His servants to be faithful (Deuteronomy 7:9; Psalm 101:6). The five-talent servant was able to tell the Lord how he had used his talents – His Master's good – to gain more talents. The two-talent servant was also able to tell the Lord how he had used his talents – His Master's goods – to gain two more talents.

Both received the same reward of approval from the Lord. "Well done, **good and faithful** servant; you have been faithful over a few things, I will make you ruler over **many** things: enter into the joy of the Lord."

The issue is **faithfulness!** "It is required of steward that a man be found **faithful.**" (1Corinthians 4:1-2; Luke 12:42). These servants were not only **good** servants but **faithful!** That is, they were reliable, trustworthy servants.

Moses was a faithful servant in his house (Numbers 12:7; Hebrews 3:1-6).

A faithful man abounds with blessings (Proverbs 23:20).

He that is faithful in that which is least is faithful also in much (Luke 16:10-12).

If one cannot be trusted with another's man's goods, how could he be trusted with his own goods. If one does not look after that which belongs to another, will he look after his own goods?

Paul was counted faithful (1Timothy 1:12).

The word of truth is to be committed to faithful men (2Timothy 2:1-2).

Faithfulness in using their God-given talents qualified them to be trusted with more from the Lord. They could be rulers over many things. Their reward was the Lord's, "Well done", and entering into the "joy of their Lord" (Hebrews12:1-2; John 15:11; 16:24; 17:13; Romans 14:17; 15:13).

12. Judgment For Unfaithfulness

The one-talent servant came before the Lord and simply revealed what was in his heart. His whole attitude and thoughts about his Lord shows the reason for his unfaithfulness, his not trading with what the Lord had given him.

Proverbs 25:19 says: "Confidence in an **unfaithful** man in time of trouble is like a broken tooth and a foot out of joint." One cannot depend on a broken tooth for eating and chewing one's food. One cannot depend on a foot out of joint or put his weight on it for walking. Both are unreliable. So this one-talent man servant showed how unreliable, unfaithful and untrustworthy he was. He could not be depended upon.

Note the confessions of his lips which expose the inner attitude of his heart to the Lord, for, "out of the abundance of the heart, the mouth speaks" (Matthew 12:33-37). He called Jesus his Lord, and no man can truly say Jesus is LORD but by the Holy Spirit (1Corinthians 12:1-3). He is a believer, not an unregenerate person!

* Lord, you are a **hard** (austere) man, reaping You have not sown, and gathering where You have not scattered seed. Lord, you expected too much from me, beyond my ability. He felt he could never please him no matter what he did.

* Lord, I was **afraid;** fearful to do anything with the talent you gave me. I was not going to take any risks. Fear bound this servant from doing anything with his talent. John tells that us: "There is no fear in love, but perfect love casts out fear: because fear has torment. He that fears is not made perfect in love" (1John 4:18). Love for His Lord would have overcome his fears.

* Lord, I went and **hid** Your talent in the earth, and here it is, just as You gave it to me, unused and untraded.

These confessions of his lips reveal a totally wrong attitude of the heart to the Lord. He felt his Lord was hard. He was fearful he might lose the talent if he used it. So he hides it. He did not understand that you lose what you do not use, naturally and spiritually speaking.

The Lord's word of discipline is severe. The Lord called him a **wicked** and **slothful** (lazy) servant. It is the very opposite to being a **good** and **faithful** servant. The Lord reminded him that he knew his Lord would expect results from where He did not sow because He expected His servant to sow and reap by trading with his talent. The servant could have, at least, put the money to the bankers and earned some interest on it. Instead, he hides the Lord's talent and gains absolutely nothing on it. A little interest from the money-lenders would have been better than nothing.

The end result is seen in the fact that the talent was taken from him and given to the ten-talent servant, the servant who had gained ten more talents by his trading.

The Lord Himself provides the lesson, as paraphrased here. "For to everyone who has used what he was given, more shall be given him, and he will have abundance. But from him that has not used what he was given, it shall be taken away and he shall have nothing!" The message is clear! Believers, as the Lord's servants, lose what they do not use. To those who use what the Lord has given, more shall be given.

13. The Outer Darkness Judgment

As has been seen in the previous parable, the outer darkness and weeping and gnashing of teeth speaks of Divine discipline on those believers who were unfaithful with the Lord's goods. Rather than repeat the comments here again, the reader is referred back to the previous chapter and the various accounts of "outer darkness" and "weeping and gnashing of teeth" – the great sorrow and remorse of those who fail the Lord in their calling and responsibility. The three major accounts in Matthew's Gospel are found in Matthew 8:5-13; 22:1-14 with 25:14-30).

The Master's discipline was evidenced in:-

* The Master's words, calling him a **wicked** and **slothful** (lazy) servant (Note Matthew 24:48 and 25:26).

* There is **no reward** for unfaithfulness.
* The **losing** of the one talent he did not use.
* Being called an **unprofitable** servant.
* The casting into **outer darkness.**
* The **weeping** and **gnashing of teeth.**

What a sad end to a Lord's servant who failed to use what the Lord had entrusted him.

E. The Practical Application Of The Parable

In this extended parable, there are many lessons to be learned. Every believer in Christ is given talents by the Lord. These are according to each believers ability. In Bible times, the "talents" have to do with weights, money, and investment. In spiritual sense and application the believer's "talents" may be represented in the following ways:

1. Natural "talents", seen in tradesmen skills, leadership giftings, music ministry, singing, youth ministry, children ministries, men and women's ministries and numerous other areas, where Christians may use the "talents" the Lord has given them.

2. Spiritual "talents", seen in the nine gifts of the Holy Spirit in 1Corinthians 12. Words of wisdom, words of knowledge, prophecy, faith, miracles, healings, discerning of spirits, and tongues and interpretetaion – all are gifts of the Spirit given severally as He wills. These are to be used for the extension of the kingdom and the building of the Church.

3. Spiritual "talents" seen in the five-fold ascension-gift ministries of apostles, prophets, evangelists, shepherds and teachers (Ephesians 4:9-16). All are to be used in the kingdom of God and in His Church.

4. Spiritual and natural "talents" of serving, helps, giving, exhortation, shewing mercy and administration, handling finance as well as numerous others that the Lord gives to His servants (Romans 12:1-8).

All the talents, gifts, ministries and graces in the members of the Body of Christ may be likened to the "talents" the Lord entrusts us with. He does not give beyond our ability to handle. Each believer must use what the Lord gives and reproduce what the Lord has given. Teachers reproduce teachers; evangelists reproduce evangelists; musicians reproduce musicians, mercy-showers and lovers of hospitality reproduce themselves, and so on through the various giftings, grace, ministries and talents that are in the Body of Christ. This is what is represented as "trading" with what the Lord gives us of "His goods." Everything is of Him, from Him and back to Him! All are to minister according to the grace and ability He has given us – no more, no less (1Peter 4:10-11).

And to whom much is given, more shall be required (Luke 12:48). Believers must not neglect the gift that is in them, through fear, timidity or other things that hinder the use of the Lord's goods (1Timothy 4:14; 2Timothy 1:6).

No one need be jealous of the "talents" given to another, for, the more one has been given, the greater the responsibility and accountability. There is no need to hide the one talent the Lord may have given us in the "earth" of our hearts, where no one can see it, or find it, or enjoy it or take it away. It remains locked in one's selfish heart, unused for the Master and the benefit of others.

The greatest reward that the believer can received from the Lord is this, "Well done good and faithful servant, You have been faithful over a few things, I will make you ruler over many things: enter into the joy of your Lord."

The greatest discipline (or punishment) is to hear the Master's word, "You wicked and lazy servant. You are unprofiable. Take the talent from him. Cast him into outer darkness and he shall experience weeping, wailing and gnashing of teeth."

Expositors may differ as to the full significance of the rewards and punishments. All believers should be challenged to use what the Lord has given them or lose what they do not use, rather than find out in reality what the punishments mean!

Because this is another of those **"historical/prophetical"** parables, the student could draw a "time-line" which covers from the Lord's ascension (the "far country journey"), on through to His second coming ("the time of reckoning"), and in between, place the truths of ability, responsibility and finally, accountability.

In conclusion: The measure of a person's **ability** is the measure of a person's **responsibility** and the measure of a person's ability and responsibility is the measure of a person's **accountability!**

CHAPTER TWENTY-THREE
THE PARABLE OF THE SHEEP AND GOATS

A. The Scripture On The Parable
Matthew 25:31-46

When the Son of man shall come in his glory, and all the holy angels with him, then shall he sit upon the throne of his glory:

And before him shall be gathered all nations: and he shall separate them one from another, as a shepherd divideth his sheep from the goats:

And he shall set the sheep on his right hand, but the goats on the left.

Then shall the King say unto them on his right hand, Come, ye blessed of my Father, inherit the kingdom prepared for you from the foundation of the world:

For I was an hungred, and ye gave me meat: I was thirsty, and ye gave me drink: I was a stranger, and ye took me in:

Naked, and ye clothed me: I was sick, and ye visited me: I was in prison, and ye came unto me.

Then shall the righteous answer him, saying, Lord, when saw we thee an hungred, and fed thee? or thirsty, and gave thee drink?

When saw we thee a stranger, and took thee in? or naked, and clothed thee?

Or when saw we thee sick, or in prison, and came unto thee?

And the King shall answer and say unto them, Verily I say unto you, Inasmuch as ye have done it unto one of the least of these my brethren, ye have done it unto me.

Then shall he say also unto them on the left hand, Depart from me, ye cursed, into everlasting fire, prepared for the devil and his angels:

For I was an hungred, and ye gave me no meat: I was thirsty, and ye gave me no drink:

I was a stranger, and ye took me not in: naked, and ye clothed me not: sick, and in prison, and ye visited me not.

Then shall they also answer him, saying, Lord, when saw we thee an hungred, or athirst, or a stranger, or naked, or sick, or in prison, and did not minister unto thee?

Then shall he answer them, saying, Verily I say unto you, Inasmuch as ye did it not to one of the least of these, ye did it not to me.

And these shall go away into everlasting punishment: but the righteous into life eternal.

B. The Setting Of The Parable

The setting is still of Mt Olivet and is the final part of the Olivet Discourse. Though not specifically defined as a parable, a number of expositors list this among the number of undesignated parables, peculiar to Matthew's Gospel. There are parabolic and symbolic elements in the passage, such as, the shepherd separating the sheep from the goats, the everlasting fire, and so on.

C. The Moral Of The Parable

As other extended parables, this has a major moral as well as a number of other supportive lessons. The major lesson of the parable is given by Jesus Himself and is woven throughout the details of the passage. The moral is: What ever ministry is given to the members of the Body of Christ is done as unto Him and will be rewarded in due time. And, whatever evil is done to the members of Christ's Body – the Church – is also done as unto Him and will be punished in the day of the Lord's judgment.

D. The Exposition Of The Parable

Many expositors speak of this undesignated parable as the judgment of "the sheep and goat nations" which takes place at the second coming of Christ.

It is taught, generally by the Dispensational School of expositors that the "sheep nations" are those nations who have treated Christ's brethren after the flesh (the natural Jews), kindly, especially in the period called "The Great Tribulation" at the end of this age. The "goat nations "are those nations who have been guilty of Jewish persecution (anti-Semitism) and for this, those nations will be sent into hell fire and eternal damnation. The "sheep nations" will be taken into the Millenniel Kingdom as a reward for their kindness to the Jews, or Israel, Christ's brethren after the flesh.

There are other expositors who do not hold to this view. These believe that the truth pertains to Christ and His Church.

Questions arise over these schools of opinion. Which view is correct? Are either of these views sound Scripturally and theologically? Our exposition hopefully will answer these questions.

This writer believes that this is another of those **historical-prophetical** parables, reaching over a certain span of time. Most of the language of the passage is clear and not characterized by much symbolic language, the major symbols being "shepherd" and "sheep and goats."

1. The Son Of Man Comes In Glory

There is no doubt about the "time element" is this first part of the parable. It is the time when the Son of Man comes in His glory, or, the actual second coming of Christ.

As mentioned in an earlier parable, there are over three hundred references to the second coming of Christ in the New Testament. The present chapters on the Olivet Discourse have to do with His coming. The three parables of "The Ten Virgins", "The Talents" and "The Sheep and Goat Nations" are all second coming parables. The student is encouraged to read again Matthew 24:3,27,30,37,39,42,43,48,50 and 25:27,31).

In His first coming it was "the sufferings", but in His second coming it is "the glory" (1Peter 1:10-12; Matthew 16:27; 19:28; Mark 8:38; Revelation 1:7; 19:11-21). It is first the cross, then the crown. John saw heaven opened, and the King of Kings and Lord of Lords coming, riding on a white horse. This speaks of the Lord's actual, literal, visible coming again.

Jesus said He would come again (John14:1-3). The messengers dressed in white said He would come in like manner as He went away. He left Olivet. He will return to Olivet. It is significant that Jesus is giving this Discourse on Mt Olivet (Acts 1:9-11; Zechariah14:4).

2. The Holy Angels

He comes the second time with holy angels. Various Scriptures pertaining to His second coming take place at this time and should be brought together for this one and the same event.

* He will come in **glory,** majesty and brightness (Matthew 16:27).

* He will come in the **glory of His Father** (Matthew 26:64; Mark 8:38; Luke 9:26).

* He will come in the **clouds of heaven** (Matthew 26:64).
* He will come with the **holy angels** (1Thessalonians 4:13-18).
* He will come with His **saints** (Jude 14-15).
* He will come in **flaming fire** (2Thessalonians 1:7-10).

The Book of Revelation abounds with references to the ministry of angels in the last days and on to the second coming of Jesus. The Lord will come with His holy angels, those angels who are elect (1Timothy 5:21) and did not follow Satan and his angels in the great, heavenly apostasy (Revelation 12:7-10). Daniel, John and other writers all speak of the Lord coming with the angels (Daniel 7:9-10; Psalm 68:17; Matthew 13:39-41,49).

3. The Throne Of His Glory

"WHEN the Son of Man comes...THEN He shall sit upon the throne of His glory..." There is much in the Scripture that speaks about the throne of God and the Lamb.

* The Father's throne is a heavenly throne (Psalm 103:19; 11:4).
* It is an eternal throne (Psalm 45:6).
* It is a throne of holiness (Psalm 47:8).
* It is a throne of grace (Hebrews 4:16)
* The Son of God sits as a king-priest in the throne (Zechariah 6:13; Hebrews 1:8; 12:2; Revelation 3:21). The Son sits in the Father's throne.
* It is finally seen as the throne of God and the Lamb (Revelation 22:1-2).
* The twelve apostles of the Lamb will sits upon thrones in the regeneration (Matthew 19:28). The twenty-four elders sit upon thrones around the throne of God (Revelation 4:4). The saints also sit upon thrones (1Samuel 2:8).
* The great white throne judgment is the final judgment of all created beings, angelic or human, and there eternal destinies are finally settled (Revelation 20:11-15).

This "throne of glory" is now a throne of judgment (Psalm 9:4,7). Justice and judgment are the habitation of God's throne (Psalm 89:14; Proverbs 25:5). The Book of Proverbs also says: "A king that sits in the throne of judgment scatters away all evil with his eyes" (Proverbs 20:8).

The second coming of Christ is a time of judgment upon all human beings, upon all mankind. Jesus sits as King, Priest, Shepherd and Judge at His second advent. The throne of glory here is no longer a throne of grace but a throne of judgment! The time of grace has come to an end. It is now the time of judgment!

4. The Shepherd-King

In this passage, Jesus is seen as (a) The Son of Man (verse 31), (b) The Shepherd (verse 32), and (c) The King (verse 34). He is the Shepherd-King!

Moses was a shepherd-king. David was a shepherd-king. Jesus is THE shepherd-king. In each case, it was first a shepherd, then a king. First, the suffering shepherd, then the reigning and glorious king.

5. **All Nations Gathered Before Him**

It is important to understand the conditions that prevail on earth immediately prior to the coming of Christ, and who these "nations" are gathered before the throne of His glory. Some of the things which need to be considered are:

* Untold millions of people on earth are destroyed under the various judgments manifest under the seven seals, trumpets and vials of wrath in the Book of Revelation. Famine, war, pestilence and death are evident in the nations of the earth. The judgments of God are in the earth (Revelation Chapters 6-18 provide the details).

* At Christ's advent, "all nations" have gathered together at Jerusalem for the battle of Armageddon, which takes place at the coming of Christ (Zechariah 14:1-9; Revelation 16:12-16).

* Antichrist and his armies war against Christ and His armies at His coming, as the Scriptures show (Revelation 19:11-21).

* At the second coming of Christ there is the "first resurrection" of the righteous, for they are rewarded as they enter the thousand year kingdom of Christ (Revelation 20:1-10).

* According to John, the wicked dead live not until the end of the thousand year period and then all come up in the "second resurrection" for the great white throne judgment (Revelation 20:11-15).

These are some of the things which have to be harmonized with this teaching of Jesus on the judgment of the sheep and goats. The "time setting" for the judgment here seems to be at or after the battle of Armageddon is over. The writer believes that this judgment is not to be confused with the great white throne judgment at the end of the thousand year kingdom era. It would seem that this judgment has to do with the "living nations" who are alive at Christ's coming, while the great white throne judgment has to do with the judgment of all the wicked resurrected dead, as well as the judgment of all fallen angelic hosts under Satan.

The nations are angry at this time, for it is the time of judgment and wrath. The nations will be cast into the winepress of God's wrath. The nations will be judged (Revelation 11:2,9,15; 19:15; Psalm 9:17).

Whatever may be the exact details, only His second coming will fully clarify. At His coming, however, "all nations" – all ethnic groupings – will stand before Him for the judgment from His throne of glory.

6. **The Sheep And The Goats**

These "all nations" are gathered together as a shepherd gathers his sheep and goats. The traditional and general (or Dispensational) teaching on the sheep and goats speaks of these as being "sheep nations" and "goat nations". The "sheep nations" are those nations that were kind to Christ's brethren after the flesh; that is, the Jewish nation or the nation of Israel. The "goat nations" are those nations who cruelly treated the Jewish nation, Christ's brethren after the flesh. The question needs to be asked: Is this what Jesus is really teaching?

A closer study of the present "parable-symbols", along with other teachings of Jesus, and other Scriptures, show that this interpretation does not harmonize theologically. What then do the "sheep" and the "goats" represent? The answers to be these questions should be governed by Scripture and sound theology, which the writer endeavours to do here.

(a) Firstly

First of the all, the Scriptures show that, although God deals with and judges nations as a whole for their treatment of other nations, the final judgment is a judgment of **individuals** in each nation. "Every one shall give an account of himself to God" (Romans 14:12; Matthew 12:36; 18:23; Luke 16:2).

So then, though the nations are gathered before the Lord for judgment, it is the **individual in each nation** who is judged. The Lord is not going to cast whole nations into everlasting fire, or take into the kingdom of God, whole nations, for their treatment of the Jewish nation, or any other nations. History shows the evil treatment of all nations by other nations in the conflicts and possession of their lands. So these cannot be rightly called **"sheep and goat nations"** but there are **"sheep and goats"** individuals in every nation!

(b) Secondly

The **"sheep"** are interpreted here by Jesus Himself as **"the righteous"**, and they are set on His right hand and blessed. The **"goats"** are interpreted, by implication as **"the unrighteous"**, and they are set on His left hand and cursed. What makes a person a "sheep" or a "goat?" What makes a person "righteous" or "unrighteous?"

The answer is given by Paul in his writings. The only righteousness that God accepts this side of the cross is **faith-righteousness!**

* Self-righteousness is as filthy rages (Isaiah 64:6).

* Works-righteousness is law-righteousness (Philippians 3:9).

* Faith-righteousness is the only righteousness God accepts (Romans 10:1-12).

If nations are saved or counted as "sheep nations" on the basis of their treatment of the Jewish nation (or other nations), then it becomes a matter of salvation by works, not a faith-righteousness! If people thought they could be saved and enter the kingdom of God, and receive eternal life, on the basis of caring for Jewish or any other ethnic grouping, then many people would do it. But this is contrary to New Testament theology. The New Testament teaches we are saved by **grace,** through **faith,** not of **works,** lest any one should boast (Ephesians 2:8-10). However, though we are not saved **by good works,** we are saved to **do good works!** "Let your light shine before men, that they may see your good works and glorify your Father which is in heaven" (Matthew 5:14-16). Works before the cross and salvation are **"dead works"** and need to be repented of, for, a person "dead in trespasses and sins" can only produce dead works, even if they are good works (Hebrews 6:1-2; 9:14-15; Ephesians 2:1-3).

7. The Separation And Division

The language of the verse is clear. As a shepherd gathers the sheep and goats together, so the Lord gathers the ethnic groupings of the earth. "He shall separate them one from another, as a shepherd divides his sheep from the goats." The nations are (a) Gathered, (b) Separated and (c) Divided! It is a division of the nations. They are not divided into nations, as nations, but into two classes of nations. That is, those of the nations who are **sheep,** and those of the nations who are **goats!** Regardless of national distinctions of this present time, they are either sheep or goats in the eyes of the Lord, the Sheperd-King, and go either to the right hand or the left hand of Jesus.

In this present age, the sheep and the goats are together. There is the mixture of animals. Saints and sinners are together in this life. At His coming, saints and sinners are separated from one another. There comes the great gathering, the separation and the division. This is the same truth as seen in previous parables of mixture and separation.

* The wheat and the tares grow together. Then at His coming there is the gathering, the separation and division. The tares are bundled together and burnt in the fire. The wheat is gathered into His barn.

* The good and the bad fish are gathered together in the same gospel net but are separated at the end of this age. The good fish are placed into vessels, and the bad are cast into the furnace of fire.

* The sheep and the goats graize together in this present life, but at His coming, they are gathered together, separated and divided. The sheep enter the kingdom. The goats go into the everlasting fire.

The same truth is constant through these parables. Mixture is seen in the present age, separation and division at Christ's coming. All the world are either sheep or goats. There are but two groupings, two classes of people on earth, two companies of mankind. All are either sheep or goats. Two is the number of division and separation, in the setting here.

8. The Sheep And The Goats

The interpretation of the sheep and the goats was evidently clear to the disciples as they heard these things. The Jewish nation was a pastural nation, and constantly had to handle sheep and goats and the shepherd's life.

* **The Sheep** speak of God's people, the true believers, the redeemed. Numerous Scriptures speak of God's people as sheep, who had once gone astray but now have returned to the shepherd and bishop of their souls. The student is encouraged to read these references. The truth is familiar and the Scriptures are too many to quote (Numbers 27:17; Matthew 9:36; Psalm 95:7; 110:3; Isaiah 53:6; John 10:2; 21:16; 1Peter 2:25).

In the passage under consideration, the sheep are called "blessed of the Father", and "the righteous" and they call the king "Lord", and they receive eternal life and enter the kingdom prepared for them (verses 34,37,46). These sheep are the redeemed out of every kindred, tongue, tribe and nation. They are the true Christians – the Lord's sheep! Jesus said to the religious Jews of His day, "You believe not, because you are **not of My sheep**" (John 10:26-27). These were Christ's brethren after the flesh, but they did not believe on Him, therefore they were not His sheep, He said. The "other sheep" that were not of the fold were the Gentiles who would come to faith in Christ, and there would be one shepherd and one fold, as believing Jews and Gentiles came into the New Testament Church as the flock of God (Acts 20:28-30).

The great Shepherd chapters in the Bible are Psalm 23, Jeremiah 23, Ezekiel 34, John 10, Acts 20, and 1Peter 5. Jesus is seen there as (a) The Good Shepherd, (b) The Great Shepherd and (c) The Chief Shepherd.

* **The Goats** speak of the unredeemed, the unbelievers, the ungodly, the sinner and the hypocrites of every kindred, tongue, tribe and nation.

The goat in Scripture is often associated with sin. The goat was especially used in the sin-offering on the Day of Atonement in Israel (Leviticus 16). Jesus was offered as the Lamb of God for our redemption, but He was also presented as the Goat for our Sin-offering. If mankind rejects Christ as the Sin-offering, then they remain in their sin. They remain as the Devil's goats, and do not become "new creatures" – God's sheep. That is the symbolic picture being dealt with here. The reader is referred to several Scriptures which speak of "goats" as the Sin-offering or other negative conotations (Numbers 29:22-38; Ezra 8:35; Zechariah 10:3; Ezekiel 34:17; Hebrews 9:13-14; 10:4; Daniel 8:5,8,21).

The goats in Christ's teaching here refer, without doubt, to the unsaved, the sinners, the unbelievers, the unredeemed. The goats are called "the cursed", and sent away into everlasting fire, the place prepared for the Devil and his angels. They experience everlasting punishment (verses 41,46). There can be no mistake here. All peoples of all ethnic groupings are either the Lord's sheep or the Devil's goats! The inner nature and character of all are open to Him who is the perfect Judge.

9. The Right Hand Or Left Hand

The righteous sheep are set on the right hand. The goats, the sinners, are set on the left hand. Not all, but a number of Scriptures show that the right hand is the hand of blessing, and the left hand is the hand of judgment.

* In Genesis 48 Jacob blessed the sons of Joseph; Ephraim and Manasseh, his right hand being on Ephraim, who receives the blessings of the firstborn, and his left hand being on Manasseh who receives the lesser blessing (Jeremiah 30:9).

* In Deuteronomy Chapter 27, along with Joshua 8, we have the account of Israel's entering into the promised land. Six tribes stood on the Mount of Blessing, Mt Gerizim, and six tribes stood on the Mount of Cursing, Mt Ebal. The ark of the covenant was in the valley between, and the Levites read the blessings and cursings of the law before the twelve tribes; six on the right hand, and six on the left hand.

* Jesus sits on the right hand of the Father in power, glory and blessing (Psalm 110:1; Mark 16:15-20; Hebrews 8:1-2).

In the judgment of Christ here, as He "judges between cattle and cattle, between the rams and the he-goats" (Ezekiel 34:17-22), it is clearly seen that the right hand is the hand of blessing and the left hand is the hand of cursing.

10. The Kingdom Or The Fire

The two destinies are seen to be "the kingdom" or "the everlasting fire." The kingdom is for the righteous, the everlasting fire for the wicked.

(a) The Kingdom

To those on the right hand, the righteous, the Son of Man, the Shepherd-King says: "Come, you blessed of My Father, inherit the kingdom prepared for you from the foundation of the world."

The righteous (the sheep) inherit the kingdom. For some interpreters, this speaks of the eternal kingdom. For this writer, it speaks, first of all, the Millenniel Kingdom and includes the kingdom everlasting.

Paul is clear on the fact that the unrighteous "shall not inherit the kingdom of God" (1Corinthians 6:9-11; Ephesians 5:19-21).

"Blessed are the meek, for they shall inherit the earth" (Matthew 5:5; Psalm 37:9-11). David says, "For such as be blessed of Him shall inherit the earth, and they that be cursed of Him shall be cut off" (Psalm 37:22). The goats do not inherit the kingdom when the king establishes His kingdom in earth.

Daniel speaks of the time when the Son of Man receives the kingdom from the Father, and the saints, with Him, possess (inherit) the kingdom (Read fully Daniel Chapters 2 and 7 with Luke 19:11-28). It is the Son of Man Kingdom. It is the Stone Kingdom. It destroys the kingdoms of this world (Revelation 11:19).

In the parable of the wheat and tares, when the angels reap the harvest of earth, they gather out the kingdom in its present mystery form, all that offend, and do iniquity. When the wicked, as tares, are taken out, then the righteous, as wheat, shine forth in the kingdom of the Father (Matthew 13:40-43).

It is the same thought here as for the sheep who inherit the kingdom prepared of the Father and when the goats are judged by fire.

For other Scriptures which speak of the saints inheriting the kingdom, read 1Corinthians 15:50; Galatians 5:21; Isaiah 57:13; 60:21; 65:9; Psalm 82:8; Proverbs 3:35; Acts 26:18; Colossians 1:12; Romans 4:13. No sinner-goat will enter that kingdom.

(b) The Everlasting Fire

To those on the left hand – the goats – the Shepherd-King says: "Depart from Me, you cursed, into everlasting fire, prepared for the Devil and his angels." Just as the kingdom was prepared of the Father for the righteous, so the everlasting fire was prepared – not for man – but for the Devil and his angels. If mankind serves the Devil in time, then they will live with the Devil and his angels for all eternity in gehenna, the lake of fire. The sheep are blessed. The goats are cursed.

"Everlasting fire" is spoken of in these Scriptures and always points to eternal judgment in the lake of fire (Matthew 18:8; 25:41; Jude 7).

It is unquenchable fire (Matthew 3:12; Mark 9:43-48).

It is hell fire, or Gehenna fire (Matthew 5:22; 18:9).

It is the furnace of fire (Matthew 13:40-41,50).

It is fire and brimstone (Revelation 14:10; 19:20; 20:10,14,15; 21:8).

Jesus Himself comes in "flaming fire" of judgment at this time (2Thessalonians 1:8).

In verse 46, Jesus speaks of the wicked going away into everlasting punishment, and the righteous into everlasting life. It shows that eternal destinies are at stake here. The kingdom for the righteous involves eternal life. The everlasting fire for the wicked involves everlasting punishment.

Paul speaks of the Lord's coming with mighty angels, and in flaming fire, taking vengeance on them that know not God, and that obey not the gospel of the Lord Jesus Christ. These shall be punished with everlasting destruction from the presence of the Lord and from the glory of His power, when He comes to be glorified in His saints and all those who believe (2Thessalonians 1:4-10). Matthew and Paul have certain correspondences here worthy of consideration.

Matthew	Paul
Christ's second coming	Christ's second coming
Comes in glory	The glory of His presence, power
With holy angels	With mighty angels
Wicked to everlasting fire	Flaming fire
Wicked to everlasting punishment	Banished, everlasting destruction
Righteous into kingdom	Glorified in saints and believers
Inherit eternal life	The kingdom of God

There is only **one second coming,** so a comparison of Matthew and Paul shows that this judgment is at Christ's second advent.

11. Ministry To Christ's Brethren

The issue of the judgment matter here is "what ever is done to the least of Christ's brethren is done as unto Him." This is applicable to the righteous or the wicked, the sheep or the goats.

Who then are Christ's **brethren** here? Is it the natural Jew after the flesh, or is it the spiritual, after the spirit? The traditional teaching says it is the treatment of natural Israel, the Jew, Christ's brethren after the flesh.

The New Testament, however, reveals that there are Jews "after the flesh", as well as Jews "after the spirit" (Romans 9:1-5; 10:1; 2:28-29; Revelation 2:9; 3:9). Paul had great heaviness and burden of spirit for his natural brethren. This passage, however, is not dealing with Christ's brethren after the flesh, but those who are after the Spirit. How is this so? By reason of the following two major reasons.

The **first reason** is found in Matthew 12:46-50. Jesus' mother and brethren came to Him while He was teaching and were desirous of speaking with Him. On the surface, Jesus seemed to be rude about their request. He told the people, saying, "Who is My mother? And who are My brethren?" And then answering His own questions, He stretched forth His hand towards His own disciples, and said, "Behold My mother and My brethren. For whosoever shall do the will of My Father which is in heaven, the same is My brother, and sister and mother" (See also Mark 3:31-35).

In the natural, this was an affront to His natural mother, Mary, and to His brethren after the flesh. The truth, however, is clear. Christ's brothers and sisters and mothers are those after the spirit – that is, those members of His body, the body of Christ. The unbelieving Jews who do not the will of the Father, are not

His brethren. Paul says, he is not Jew which is one outwardly, but one inwardly (Romans 2:28-29). This is the new relationship that exists in the Church, the body of Christ, made up of believing Jews and believing Gentiles.

The **second reason** is found in Pauline theology. The next reason that proves that these "brethren" are not Christ's brethren after the flesh is the eternal destinies of the sheep and goats, and the reason why.

No one is going to receive eternal life or everlasting punishment only on the basis of their treatment of Christ's brethren after the flesh – the Jewish nation (or, for that matter, any other nation)! The qualification for eternal life is repentance and faith in the Lord Jesus Christ. The qualification for eternal fire is the rejection of the Lord Jesus Christ. Otherwise, all one needs to do to gain eternal life is to look after the Jews physically, materially, financially or socially! This would be salvation **by works, not of grace and faith** (Ephesians 2:8-10). They would have something to boast about!

The only way into the kingdom of God, both now and then, is by being born again, being born from above (John 3:1-5). Corruptible flesh and blood will not inherit the kingdom of God once Jesus returns (1Corinthians 15:50).

When the great white throne judgment takes place, and all are judged out of the book of their works, those whose names are not written in the Lamb's book of life will be cast into the lake of fire (Revelation 20:11-15). This is the theology of the New Testament Scriptures. Sound theology must interpret this parabolic and symbolic teaching.

12. Done To My Brethren – Done to Me

Jesus says to the sheep and to the goats: As much as you did these things to My brethren, you did it to Me! What are these things?

(a) To the Sheep

1. I was hungry – you gave Me meat.

2. I was thirsty – you gave Me drink.

3. I was a stranger – you took Me in.

4. I was naked – you clothed Me.

5. I was sick – you visited Me.

6. I was in prison – you came to Me.

The sheep, the righteous, ask: "When?" to these statements of the Lord. The Shepherd-King replies, "As much as you did it to the least of these My brethren, you did it as unto Me." Their reward is to be blessed and to enter the kingdom of the Father and into eternal life.

(b) To the Goats

The same words are said to the goats, the unrighteous.

1. I was hungry – you gave Me no meat.

2. I was thirsty – you gave Me no drink.

3. I was a stranger – you did not take Me in.

4. I was naked – you did not clothe Me.

5. I was sick – you did not visit Me.

6. I was in prison – you did not visit Me

The goats, the unrighteous, also answered: "When?" When did we see You in any of these conditions? The Shepherd-King replies, "As much as you did it not to the least of these My brethren, you did it not to Me." Their punishment is to be cursed and sent away into everlasting fire and everlasting punishment.

Although Christians are to be kind to all men, and bless any who are needy, Christians are especially to be careful to minister to those in the household of faith (Romans 12:18-21; 1Timothy 5:8; Matthew 10:40).

Numerous denominations and church workers and government workers are involved in much "social work"; caring for the poor, the sick, the needy, the orphans, the homeless, the prisoners, and untold millions of people in hospitals, and so forth. None of this is at all despised. Most of the "social work" of the church has been done over the centuries based on the understanding of this passage, all of which will be rewarded of the Lord.

However, no "social work" on its own merits eternal life, or entrance into the kingdom of God. Every one must be born again to see and enter the kingdom. The truth of this passage especially concerns the church, the members of Christ's body in earth.

When Saul persecuted the Christians, the Lord Jesus asked him on the Damascus Road, through the blaze of heavenly glory, "Saul, Saul, why are you persecuting Me?" (Acts 9:1-9). Who was Saul persecuting? Christ's members. As much as he did it to the least of them, he was persecuting Christ Jesus.

In 1Corinthians 8:12, Paul challenges the Corinthian believers not to allow their liberty on non-essentials to offend members of the body of Christ. He says "When you **sin against the brethen,** and wound their weak conscience, **you sin against Christ.**" Why? Because Christ is in His body. The members of Christ's body are His brethren.

It is the body of Christ in action, members caring for one another (1Corinthians 12). It is Christ's sheep caring for the lambs. Any service of need and love is done as unto Christ Himself and will be rewarded in that day. These things are done out of faith in Christ, not on the basis of works to earn salvation and eternal life.

On the morning of the resurrection, Jesus speaks of "My Father and your Father, My brethren and your brethren" (John 20:17 with Romans 8:29; Hebrews 2:11; Psalm 22:22).

The opposite is also true. For those who reject Christ and who oppose His Church, there is judgment and eternal punishment. One may think of the governments and dictatorships in various nations over the years, who have persecuted the church, have slaughtered Christians by the millions. For the name of Christ, millions of believers have become martyrs, even from the time of the Roman Emporers to the modern day dictatorships in various nations. Truly, "Inasmuch as it was done to Christ's brethren, it was done as unto Christ." It is the rejection of Christ in His members. Jesus said, You will be hated of all nations for My name's sake (Matthew 24:9).

E. The Practical Aplication Of The Parable

As has been seen, no one parable contains the whole of God's truth, and no one parable can be used to violate Biblical theology.

All the world is divided into two camps; the saved and the lost; the blessed and the cursed. In the teaching of Jesus in this final parable on Mt Olivet we have:

1. Two symbols – sheep and goats
2. Two classes – righteous and unrighteous
3. Two positions – right hand and left hand
4. Two judgments – blessed and cursed
5. Two destinations – the kingdom or everlasting fire
6. Two reasons – treatment of Christ's brethren, good or bad
7. Two announcements – come or depart
8. Two destinies – eternal life or eternal punishment.

All mankind will be judged by Christ at His coming. The sheep are the faith-righteous, whose faith is seen in Christ and confirmed by their ministry in and to the body of Christ. The goats are those who know not Christ and have rejected and ill-treated Christ in His body. The saints will inherit the kingdom both in the Millenniel Age and the Eternal Ages to come. The sinners will be banished from His presence with everlasting destruction into the lake of fire. To every person is given the choice – become God's sheep or the Devil's goat! It is your decision!

False cults who do not accept the Biblical revelation of "everlasting fire", or "everlasting punishment" seek to distort the Greek word to mean only "age-lasting", or lasting for an age. The same Greek word **"aionios"** is used for "eternal life" or "everlasting fire."

For Scriptures on "eternal life", see Matthew 19:29; Luke 16:9; 18:30; John 3:16,36; 4:14; 5:24; 6:27,40,47; 12:40; Acts 13:46; Romans 6:22; Galatians 6:8; 1Timothy 1:16. Eternal life is the life of God. It is timelessness.

For Scriptures on "eternal punishment", and relative words, see Mark 3:29; Matthew 18:18; Matthew 25:41,46; 2Thessalonians 1:9; Daniel 12:2; Jude 6,7. Everlasting chains, everlasting fire, everlasting punishment and torment – all are the same duration as everlasting life! Everlasting punishment is everlasting restraint placed on the wicked of the universe.

In conclusion, it has been mentioned that this teaching is one of those historical and prophetical kind of teaching. Once again, this may be super-imposed on a "time-line" to sharpen the teaching with sharper focus, especially in the light of these concluding comments.

Though there are Scriptures that seem to link the resurrections of the righteous and the wicked together, as one resurrection event (John 5:29; Acts 24:15; Daniel 12:2; Luke 14:14), it is the apostle John who sets one thousand years between the resurrection of the righteous and unrighteous. It is spoken of as the first and the second resurrection. The first resurrection is for the holy and righteous and these are blessed. The second resurrection is for the unholy and unrighteous and these are cursed. There is a thousand years between these two resurrections (Revelation 20:1-10). This thousand years is spoken of as the Millenniel Kingdom.

The writer believes that the sheep who inherit the kingdom enter the Millenniel Kingdom and continue on into the eternal kingdom. The goats who are cursed into everlasting fire, prepared for the Devil and his angels, are cast there after the great white throne judgment at the close of the thousand years Millenniel Kingdom. This takes place before the inauguration of the new heavens and new earth and eternal realities are provided for the redeemed of all ages.

If this is so, then it is the nations that are alive at the coming of Christ who are judged according to Matthew 25:31-46. And the rest of the wicked dead (nations) are judged at the second resurrection, and these, altogether are cast into the lake of fire. The second coming of Christ, with relevance to the saints inheriting the kingdom, would be "those who are alive to the coming of the Lord, and the dead in Christ being raised "in the first resurrection" (1Thessalonians 4:13-18). These would be those who "inherit the kingdom"- both Millenniel and at the close of that period, the Eternal Kingdom!

The "time-line" could then be:

The Throne of His Glory

The Sheep	The Thousand Years	The Goats
The Righteous	Millenniel Kingdom	Unrighteous
Right Hand		Left Hand
Blessed		Cursed
Living Believers		Living Nations
First Resurrection		Second Resurrection
Inherit the Kingdom		Everlasting Fire
Eternal Life		Eternal Punishment
Prepared by the Father		Prepared for Devil

The coming of Christ will indeed arrange in chronological order what may be (or is) uncertain to the believers at this time. Nothing, however, of the writings of Matthew, Mark, Luke, John, Daniel, and the prophets, and Paul, pertaining to Christ's coming will contradict the other. Christ's coming will settle it all. The writer believes that, what has been presented in this chapter, is in reasonable harmony with the various prophecies and events of Christ's coming.

This chapter brings us to the close of the kingdom of heaven parables in the Gospel of Matthew. They provide a panoramic view of events from Christ's ascension right through this church era and on to the second coming of Christ, and into the kingdom future.

The kingdom in its present mystery form has the dual aspect of good and evil – mixture – but in the finale of all things, at His coming, all evil shall be cleansed, and sin and sinners and Satan will be cast out of the earth, and the kingdom shall be the Lord's. His saints shall rule and reign with Him for a thousand years in the glory of that kingdom (Revelation 20:1-10).

PART THREE

Parables

in the

Gospel of Mark

CHAPTERS 24 – 26

CHAPTER TWENTY-FOUR
THE PARABLE OF THE LIGHTED LAMP AND CITY

A. The Scriptures on the Parable

1. Mark 4:21-22

And he said unto them, Is a candle brought to be put under a bushel, or under a bed? and not to be set on a candlestick?

For there is nothing hid, which shall not be manifested; neither was any thing kept secret, but that it should come abroad.

2. Luke 8:16-17

No man, when he hath lighted a candle, covereth it with a vessel, or putteth it under a bed; but setteth it on a candlestick, that they which enter in may see the light. For nothing is secret, that shall not be made manifest; neither any thing hid, that shall not be known and come abroad.

3. Matthew 5:14-16

Ye are the light of the world. A city that is set on an hill cannot be hid.

Neither do men light a candle, and put it under a bushel, but on a candlestick; and it giveth light unto all that are in the house.

Let your light so shine before men, that they may see your good works, and glorify your Father which is in heaven.

B. The Setting of the Parable

It is evident from the Synoptics that Jesus repeated various parables and teachings in different towns and villages of Judea. The above Scriptures on the short parable of the lighted lamp is found in different settings.

In Mark's Gospel (apparently the first Gospel written), we are told that Jesus was teaching by the seaside, sitting in a boat while the multitude was standing on the shore. It was after the giving of the parable of the sower and the seed that this parable of the lighted lamp was given (Read Mark 4:1-20).

In Luke's Gospel we are told that Jesus went throughout the various cities and villages preaching the good news of the kingdom of God. In Luke's account, the parable of the lighted lamp follows the giving of the parable of sower and seed, similiar to that in Mark's Gospel (Read Luke 8:1-15).

In Matthew's Gospel, we are told that Jesus went up into a mounain and gave what has been called "The Sermon on the Mount" (Matthew 5:1-2). The parable of the lighted lamp was given after the Beatitudes (Read Matthew 5:1-12).

Corresponding the gospels confirms that fact that Jesus repeated His teachings in different places and to different congregations. Truth must be repeated to each generation and applied accordingly.

C. The Moral Of The Parable

Although the parable of the lighted lamp is repeated in each of the Synoptics, there are a couple of major morals to be found. The moral of the parable is: The only purpose for the existence of a lampstand is to manifest light. Mark and Luke both show that all things will be exposed by light; nothing can be hidden when light reveals. Matthew shows that believers are called to be the light of the world, and that light can only be manifested through them to others by good and godly works that bring glory to the heavenly Father.

D. The Exposition Of The Parable

In our exposition, we bring together the similar yet varied thoughts seen in this short parable in each of the Gospels. The two major symbolic pictures in these references are those of (1) The Lighted Lampstand, and (2) The Lighted City.

1. The Lighted Lampstand

Each of the Synoptics use the word "candle" (KJV); however, the more suitable word used in other translations is "lampstand." The simple word is that no person takes a lampstand, lights it and then hides it under a bed or any other vessel. The result would be, the light would either be put out, or simply not be seen by others, and therefore fail to serve its purpose. The lampstand was not just meant to be an ornament. The whole purpose of its existence is to provide light. Light must not be hidden.

For the nation of Israel, the lighted lamp was a common daily duty. They were familiar with the ministry of the Temple of the Lord. In the original Tabernacle of Moses, there was the golden lampstand made by the wisdom of the Lord. Upon the lampstand were the seven golden lamps. For the Tabernacle, the golden lampstand was the only light in the Holy Place, which measured ten by ten by twenty cubits. The priests would minister at the table of shewbread, and the golden altar of incense in their daily ministrations. The same truth was true also in the Temple of Solomon, except the Temple had ten golden lampstands, bearing seventy lamps in all. The lighted lampstands were the only light in "the house of the Lord." Otherwise all would be in darkness.

Aaron, the high priest, or the Temple priests, had their daily ministration of trimming the wicks of the lamps, supplying oil, and the daily lighting of the lamps, so they were to shine continually. This ministry took place morning and evening (Exodus 25:31-35; 30:27; 1Kings 7:49; 2Chronicles 4:7; Zechariah 4:2; Revelation 11:4).

For the Jewish household, the lamps were lit morning and evening, and all those in the house enjoyed fellowship in the light. Light scattered the darkness. Light reveals. Light exposes. Light unveils. Light dispels. Light overpowers the darkness.

This is the first picture the Lord provides in this short parable of the lighted lampstand.

In application to believers, comments need to be made about the "lamp". The Scriptures speak of the lamp in several different aspects, as the following reveals.

* **The spirit of man is the lamp of the Lord** (Proverbs 20:27). When man fell, his spirit went into darkness. The coming of the Lord Jesus into a person's life in salvation relights that lamp. Once they are enlightened, and their spirit is relighted, there is life and fellowship restored with God. The spirit of the unregenerate person is in darkness.

* **The Word of God is also a lamp** (Psalm 119:105; Proverbs 6:23).

* **The Holy Spirit is likened to a lamp** (Revelation 4:5). John saw seven lamps of fire burning before the throne of God and likened these to the

seven spirits of God sent forth into all the earth. This speaks of the fulness and perfections of the Holy Spirit at work in the earth.

The issue is, in each case, the lamp needs oil to make light possible. Man's spirit, as the lamp, needs the oil of the Holy Spirit. The Word of God, as a lamp, needs the oil of the Holy Spirit to make it shine. As seen in the parable of the wise and foolish virgins, all had lamps, but all needed the oil in their lamps for light. Light is simply the manifestation of burning oil. John the Baptist was a **burning** and **shining** light (John 5:35). Man's spirit (the lamp) needs the Divine oil (the Holy Spirit) in order to let his light shine before men. This is the truth of the lighted lamp!

2. The Lighted City

The second picture the Lord provides is found in Matthew's Gospel. There Jesus told the disciples they were the light of the world. He then said that a city that is set on a hill cannot be hid. Many of the cities of Judea were placed on the summits or sides of mountains, and therefore, could be seen from afar. This was the case with Jerusalem. These statements by Jesus in Matthew's Gospel preceded Christ's comments on the lighted lampstand, and the good works of the disciples being done to glorify the Father. From the lighted lampstand to the lighted city is the thought here. The simple language was full of meaning to the Jewish mind.

There were several customs that took place in Christ's time which made this short parable full of meaning.

(a) The Feast of Lights

One of the popular and most joyous festival in Jewry was a festival instituted by Judas Maccabees (BC.164), after the recovery of Jewish independance from the Syro-Grecian domination. The temple had been cleansed and the services had been restored at the times of the Maccabees. It was called the Feast of Lights. The feast commenced on December 25th, and lasted for eight days. In this time, there was the grand illumination of the temple, the same as in the Feast of Tabernacles. According to tradition, sacred candelabras were lit in the temple courts. In the Jewish homes, the head of the house would light a candle, either one for all, and one lamp for each member of the family. This seen from afar gave the magnificant appearance of "a city set on a hill" – a lighted city! Traditions varied at times, but this was the basic joy of the Feast of Lights!

(b) The Feast of Tabernacles

In "The Life and Times of Jesus the Messiah" (pages 282-287), Alfred Edersheim has this to say about the Feast of Tabernacles which took place in John's Gospel, Chapters 8,9,10. It was at this time, Jesus opened the eyes of the blind man and declared Himself as the LIGHT of the world (John 8:12; 9:5).

"... after the sacrifice and the outpouring of the water, at the close of the first day of the feast, the worshippers descended to the Court of the Women where great preparations had been made. Four golden candelabras there, each with four golden bowls, and against them four ladders. Four youths of the priestly descent held a pitcher of oil and filled each bowl. The old, worn breeches and girdles of the priests served for wicks to these lamps. There was not a court in Jerusalem that was not lit up by the light... The light shining out of the temple into the darkness around, and lighting up every court in Jerusalem, must have been intended as a symbol, not only of the Shekinah, which once filled the temple, but of that **"great light"** which **"the people that walked in darkness"** were to see, and which was to shine **"upon them that dwell in the land of the shadow of death"** (Isaiah 9:2).

And once again, from pages 149-150: "... at night, the vast temple buildings stood out, illuminated by the great candelabras that burned in the Court of the Woman, and by the glare of the torches, when strange sound of mystic hymns and dances came floating over the intervening darkness... the whole of this night and morning scene was symbolical: the temple illumination, of the light which was to shine out from the temple into the dark night of heathendom."

Thus the temple, the city of Jerusalem, would indeed be likened to "a city set on the hill that cannot be hid."

Whether in the Feast of Lights or the Feast of Tabernacles, the truth was basically the same, and undoubtedly Jesus had these things in mind, and the Jewish hearers were familiar with these things.

The Church is likened to God's **Golden Lampstand,** and the Church is likened to the **City of God** (Revelation 1:11-20; Revelation 21-22). The purpose of her existence is to manifest the light and glory of God.

As the golden lampstands in the Tabernacle of Moses and Temple of Solomon were to give light all "in the house" of the Lord for ministry, so the church is to give light to all in God's house.

As the city of Jerusalem, the city of God, was meant to be a holy and righteous city, and meant to send spiritual light to the Gentile nations of the world, so the Church, as the city of God, is to send light to all the nations of the earth (Matthew 28:18-20; Mark 16:15-20; Acts 1:8). The people and nations of the earth would be drawn to the light in the city of the great King – the Lord Jesus Christ. The reader is encouraged to read these Scriptures on the city of God (Isaiah 26:1-4; 52:1; Psalm 46:4; 48:1; 87:3; Hebrews 11:10-16; 12:22; 13:14; Revelation 3:12).

E. The Practical Application of the Parable

By the law of opposites, if believers in the church are the light of the Lord, then it means that the world is in darkness.

1. Light and Darkness

The very first principle in Genesis 1:1-5,14-19 reveals the two states: light and darkness. Creation is seen there and darkness was upon the face of the deep. The Spirit of God moved. God spoke, saying, "Let there be light, and there was light." The light and the darkness were divided. The light was called day, and the darkness was called light. The apostle Paul takes this very language of creation and makes it the language of redemption in his Epistle to the

Thessalonians (1Thessalonians 5:1-8). Believers are of the day, and of the light; unbelievers are of the night, and of the darkness. It speaks of the kingdom of light and the kingdom of darkness. There is no kingdom between. All are in the kingdom of darkness or the kingdom of light.

The prophets speak of the world covered in gross darkness (Isaiah 60:1-2). Amos speaks of the day of the Lord as darkness and not light (Amos 5:18-20). Joel confirms the same theme of darkness and light running parallel together from the Fall unto the second coming of Christ.

The way of the wicked is as darkness; they know not at what they stumble (Proverbs 4:19).

Jesus confirms that all those who do evil hate the light, and will not come to the light lest their deeds be discovered (John 3:19-20). Those who do the unfruitful works of darkness do not know where they are going (Ephesians 5:11; John 3:19-20).

As the plague of darkness was upon the Egyptians, but light was in the dwellings of the Israelites, so the world is in spiritual darkness and believers are in spiritual light (Exodus 10:21-23). The same cloud of glory was light to God's people, but darkness to the Egyptians (Exodus 14:19-20). It all depends on which side of God's cloud one is found.

2. The Lighted Lamp

Jesus told His disciples, You and you alone are the light of the world. How is the believer light? How does he become light? How does he let his light practically shine forth?

*   God Himself is light and the Father of Lights (1John 1:5; James 1:17).

*   Jesus Himself also was the Light of the world while He was in the world (John 8:1-2; 9:5; 12:35-36,46; 1:1-9). As the Lamb, He is the Light of the eternal city of God (Revelation 21:23; 22:5).

*   The Church – the believer – is now the light of the world, and more especially Christ has returned to the Father (Matthew 5:14-16). When we receive Christ in our hearts as light, then He dispels the darkness of sin, and lightens our lamp. There is no light in or of ourselves. The light of the glorious gospel shines into our hearts, even as light shone in the early creation (2Corinthians 4:3-6 with Genesis 1:1-5 and Colossians 1:13). We are now to walk as children of the light (Ephesians 5:8-14; Colossians 1:14; 1Thessalonians 5:5; 1Peter 2:9; Rmans 15:1-4).

*   Ministers of the Gospel are to be lights (John 1:42; Isaiah 49:6; Revelation 1:12-20).

*   The Church, as the bride of Christ, is clothed with the light of the sun, moon and stars (Revelation 12:1).

There are numerous lessons about light. There are Scriptures too numerous to mention also about believers as light, a few more which are referred to in brief here.

*   Light is pure, transparent, and cannot be contaminated (Revelation 21:11,21).

* The path of the just is light shining more and more to the perfect day (Proverbs 4:18).

* Light is burning. John was a burning (within) and shining (without) light (John 5:35).

* Our life should be the light of men (John 1:4).

* Light that is not walked in eventually becomes darkness; how great is that darkness (Matthew 6:22-23). Satan was Lucifer, the light-bearer but became the angel of darkness when he fell into rebellion against God and His Word (2Corinthians 11:14).

* Believers are to walk in the light as He is in the light (1John 1:5-8).

* In God's light we continually see light (Psalm 36:9).

3. The Light Of Good Works

To bring our exposition and practical application of this short parable to its conclusion, a few comments are needed on the practical outshining of light.

It is written of Jesus: "In Him was life and the life was the light of men "(John 1:4).

The life Christ lived then was the light of the world. A believers **Christian life** should be the **Christian's light** to men! Our life is light! Paul puts it this way when he said to the Philippians believers that they "shone forth **as lights** in the midst of a crooked and perverse generation" (Philippians 2:15-16). It is the believers **good works** that become **light** to those round him. It is the Christian life-style practically lived before others that makes his life light. Who we are, what we say, and what we are is the light of life manifest to a lost world. Whether at home, abroad, work or in scoiety – our life is the light of men! The matter of "works", however, needs some clarification here, for many, many believers confuse the issue of "grace" and "works" relative to salvation.

* **Dead works of the law** can be simply religious works, done by those who are dead in trespasses and sins. A person dead in sin can only produce dead works. (Ephesians 2:8-11; Titus 3:5; 2Timothy 1:9). These have to be repented of, as there is no salvation possible through works of the law, which only produce self-righteousness. Jesus warned His disciples about doing works, even good works, such as almsgiving, prayer, fasting, and so on just to be "seen of men" and to receive "glory of men" (Matthew 6:1-6). Paul the Pharisee knew all about that and counted these as filthiness to gain eternal life in Christ (Philippians 3:9; Romans 10:1-4). Jesus is not talking about these kind of works.

* **Works of the flesh,** which are listed in Galatians 5:22-23 are evil works of the unregenerate man. They that do such things shall not inherit the kingdom of God. These, as religious works from unregenerate religious people, also have to be repented of, for together all these things constitute **"dead works."**

No one is saved by works before salvation. We are all saved by grace, through faith, and not of works. Though we are not saved **by works,** we are saved **unto good works.** Good works, religious works, works of the flesh – before the cross

– done by unregenerate and religious unregenerate people are simply dead works. They must be repented of (Hebrews 6:1-2; 9:14). Good works, after salvation, are done from life, not from death. That is the difference, as these brief references confirm.

* The works Jesus did glorified His Father (John 14:12-15; 15:24; 17:4).

* Dorcas was a believer who did good works (Acts 9:36; 1Peter 2:12).

* Paul says that believers are to be a pattern of good works ((Titus 2:7,14). Believers are to be zealous of good works and to maintain good works (Titus 3:8,14).

* Paul, who was very clear in his teaching about salvation by grace and faith, and not by works in which one could boast, was also very clear in his teaching on goods works after salvation by grace and faith. Paul's teachings in these Scriptures are clear that believers are to maintain good works, once they have been redeemed from "dead works" of the law, or evil "works of the flesh" (1Timothy 2:10; 5:10,25; 6:18; 2Timothy 3:17; 4:14).

* To each of the seven churches in Revelation, Jesus said, "I know your works..." (Revelation 2:2,5,9,13,19,23,26; 3:1,2,8,15; 14:13). The ultimate of all things is that all mankind will be judged out of the books of works at the great white throne judgment (Revelation 20:11-15).

In conclusion:

Whatever good works are done by believers, as unto others, must be done with a **pure motive**, and that is, **to glorify the Father who is in heaven!** Not to gloirify ourselves, or to glorify others, but to glorify the Father in heaven! This is the fulfilment of the parable of the light lamp – in the house and in the city! This is allowing our **life** to be the **light** of men!

CHAPTER TWENTY-FIVE
THE PARABLE OF THE KINGDOM SEED

A. The Scripture On The Parable
Mark 4:26-29

And he said, So is the kingdom of God, as if a man should cast seed into the ground;

And should sleep, and rise night and day, and the seed should spring and grow up, he knoweth not how.

For the earth bringeth forth fruit of herself; first the blade, then the ear, after that the full corn in the ear.

But when the fruit is brought forth, immediately he putteth in the sickle, because the harvest is come.

B. The Setting Of The Parable

Mark 4:1-2 confirms the setting to be very similar to that in the Gospel of Matthew. Jesus is at the seaside. A great multitude gathered to hear Him teach. Jesus entered into a boat as the whole multtitude stood on the seashore, and Jesus taught them many things by parables.

C. The Moral Of The Parable

Again this is one of those short, undesignated parables, but it involves the kingdom of heaven, and is found in the course of Christ's teaching of parables. The lesson is simple: The kingdom of God grows mysteriously, silently, secretly, as a seed once planted, because within in it the principle of Divine life. In due time, the fulness of kingdom life is seen in the harvest of a person's life.

D. The Exposition Of The Parable

This parable is a short and simple parable, and only to be found in Mark's Gospel, as it is. Mark does repeat other parables of the kingdom as found in Matthew and Luke, but this parable, as it stands, is only found in Mark.

Undoubtedly the "seed parables" found in Matthew's Gospel (Chapter 13) provide the interpretative "key" to this "seed parable." Some expositors list this parable in with the seed parables in Matthew, especially with that of the sower and the seed. But, there is a simple completeness about it, as it stands, that makes it a parable on its own, though it is inter-related with the kingdom-seed parables. There are several additional thoughts worthy of consideration in this parable in Mark.

1. The Kingdom of God

This is another kingdom parable. Mark speaks of it as "the kingdom of God" while Matthew emphasizes it as "the kingdom of heaven." The kingdom of God and the kingdom of heaven are synonymous terms, as a comparison of Scriptures show. This matter has been explained fully in Chapter Five, **"Understanding The Church And The Kingdom"**, and does not need to be repeated here.

2. The Sower Man

In the parable, "the man" could be any believer, or any minister of gospel who sows the gospel seed of the kingdom (Matthew 3:1-2; 4:17; 24:14).

In this parable, it does not speak of the Lord Jesus Christ, as in the first, second and third parables of Matthew Chapter 13.

In this parable, the sower-man does not know how the seed grows. Christ Jesus does. The minister of the gospel or the believer does not understand this mystery. The wind blows here and there, and no one can tell where it comes from or where it goes. So is every one who is born of the Spirit and born of the incorruptible seed of the Word of God (John 3:1-8; 1Peter 1:23).

3. The Kingdom Seed

The seed here, undoubtedly, speaks of the seed of THE WORD. It is the gospel seed, the seed of the kingdom, the same seed as seed in the first, second and third parables of Matthew 13. Jesus said, "The SEED is THE WORD" (Luke 8:11). Jesus also said that this gospel of the kingdom would be preached in all the world for a witness unto all nations before the end of the age would come (Matthew 24:14).

Those who receive the seed of the kingdom are born again, born from above, born into the kingdom of God. They are born of the Spirit and born of the incorruptible seed, which is the Word of God which lives and abides for ever. The seed is the Divine sperm (John 3:1-8; 1Peter 1:23-25; John 1:11-13).

There is nothing wrong with the kingdom seed. It has all the potential Divine life, the very life of God in it, if the one who receives it will allow that seed to remain in him (1John 3:9). It is a perfect seed, a sinless seed, an immortal seed, an incorruptible seed – the Divine seed life of the kingdom.

4. The Ground

The ground here would represent the human heart. In Matthew 13 and the seed parables given there, it has been seen that the various types of soil represent the ground of the human heart. The seed fell on to stony ground, hard ground, thorny ground and good ground. It is the same truth here.

However, the ground in this parable seems to point to the "good ground hearer." There is good response to the seed sown here. Undoubtedly this ground, in this parable, is the honest and good heart spoken of in Luke 8:15. One has to make sure the ground of his heart is clear of thorns, thistles, weeds, stones, and any other hindrances to the fruitful potential of the seed of the kingdom.

5. Night And Day

The man, in the normal routine of life, having cast the seed into the ground, can do nothing more. He rests in the night, and rises and works in the day, trusting the potential life that is in the seed to germinate. God would have to cause the rain, the dew, the sun and nature to cause that seed to grow. The sower did the possible, God does the impossible. The sower does his part, God will do his part.

6. The Seed Growth

The man can do nothing of himself to make the seed he has sown to grow. It has life in itself. It is no use digging it up daily to see if it is growing. It springs up, and grows, the man knows not how. He cannot explain the mystery of life in the seed. He trusts the seed sown to God.

No minister of the gospel, no believer, can explain the Divine potential, the mystery of the hidden life of a seed. He plants the seed and trusts God for the rest to make it grow. It grows secretly, silently, and mysteriously because of the life placed in that seed by God Himself. So is every one that is born of the Spirit.

It is the law of creation, the law of reproduction after its kind. As the Book of Genesis shows, it is "... the herb yielding seed, and the fruit tree yielding fruit after his kind, whose seed is in itself...after his kind..."

7. The Tri-unity of Growth

In verse 28 we have the mystery of life in the seed unto fruitfulness in a tri-unity of growth. "First the blade, then the ear, then the full corn in the ear" is the word of Jesus about this kingdom seed.

(a) First the Blade

The blade is the beginning, the source, the foundation, the first evidence of life springing forth from the seed.

(b) Then the Ear

Then comes the ear (or the head). As the mystery of life continues from the blade, then comes the ear, or the head in which the corn seed is developing.

(c) Then The Full Corn

Then we have the full corn in the ear, or the head of corn itself. This is the fruit of the life that was hidden within the kingdom seed. It is the full manifestation.

It is the principle of life out of death, as Jesus said of Himself: "Truly, truly I say to you, Except a corn of wheat fall into the ground and die, it abides alone; but if it die, it brings forth much fruit" (John 12:24).

8. Fruit Unto Harvest

The ground of the heart has received the seed of the kingdom. The seed has gone through the process of death, and out of inward death, life has come forth, in the blade, then the ear and now the full corn in the ear. Fruit is brought forth. The harvest has come and the sickle is thrust in to reap that harvest.

If there is no seed sowing, there can be no harvest. Seed time and harvest time, being the beginning and the end belong together (Genesis 8:22).

The harvest always speaks of the end of this age (Matthew 13:30,39). In Revelation 14:14-16 the harvest of the earth is reaped by the sickle of the Son of Man on the white cloud. The prophet Joel also spoke of the time: "Put in the sickle for the harvest is ripe" (Joel 3:13).

So in the end of this age, the seed of the kingdom that has been sown over the centuries of church history, will bring forth its harvest and the Son of Man, with the angels, shall together reap the final harvest. Such is the teaching of this, and other, seed parables!

E. The Practical Application Of The Parable

As in most of the parables in Matthew's Gospel, we can format in outline the major details of this short but beautiful parable.

The Parable Symbols	The Interpretation of the Parable
1. The Kingdom of God	God's rule, reign and sovereignity
2. The Sower man	Whosoever sows the gospel

3. The Seed	The Seed-word of the kingdom
4. The Ground	The responsive heart of the hearer
5. Night and day	Rest and work
6. Seed growth	The mystery of hidden life
7. The blade	The beginning of evident life
The ear	Evidence of growth
The full corn	Fruit, the purpose of life
8. The Sickle and harvest	The end of the age

In bringing our exposition of this parable of the kingdom seed to its conclusion, there are several final thoughts worthy of consideration and application to this parable.

Herbert Lockyer, in his excellent book, **"All The Parables Of The Bible"** (pages 251-254), has this to say about this parable.

> "The Kingdom of God, in contrast to kingdoms ruled by men, represents His rule, His reign, His triumph over all human affairs.But for the bringing in of His harvest, the seed must first be sown. Because of the eschatological aspect of the parable, its prophetic interpretation which so many seem to miss but which provides the key to the glorious, ultimate purposes of God, is clearly evident. Our Lord was directing His disciples to the three stages of **The Kingdom of God.**
>
> 1. The **Blade,** or the Kingdom in mystery, the Church Age during which the Holy Spirit is active in completing "the mystery hid from ages," namely, the Church of the living God.
>
> 2. The **Ear,** or the Kingdom in manifestation, which will be experienced during the Millennial Reign of Christ, which was the main theme of the Old Testament. "Thy Kingdom come."
>
> 3. The **Full Corn,** suggests the Kingdom in all its majestic perfection, the New Heavens and New Earth when God will be all in all. This will be the "Kingdom Ultimate," The Eternal Ages: the "Dispensation of the fulness of times "about which Paul wrote (Ephesians 1:10)." (End Quote – Emphasis his).

A couple of other illustrations of the "tri-unity" principle of the kingdom-seed may also be seen in the arrangements of the Books of the Bible:

1. The Penteteauch – Five Books = The Blade,

2. The History, The Poets, The Prophets – Thirty Four Books = The Ear

3. The New Testament = Twentyseven Books = The Full Corn in the Ear.

And finally, the revelation of the New Testament Church may be seen unfolding as the kingdom-seed also:

1. The Four Gospels – First the Blade,

2. The Book of Acts – Then the Ear,

3. The Epistles and Revelation – The Full Corn in the Ear.

The parable is simple and short, but it is a kingdom parable, and the seed of the kingdom, once planted in a believers heart will grow, develop and come to full maturity in the eternal kingdom of the Father!

CHAPTER TWENTY-SIX
THE PARABLE OF THE ABSENT HOUSE MASTER

A. The Scripture On The Parable
Mark 13:32-37

But of that day and that hour knoweth no man, no, not the angels which are in heaven, neither the Son, but the Father.

Take ye heed, watch and pray: for ye know not when the time is.

For the Son of man is as a man taking a far journey, who left his house, and gave authority to his servants, and to every man his work, and commanded the porter to watch.

Watch ye therefore: for ye know not when the master of the house cometh, at even, or at midnight, or at the cockcrowing, or in the morning:

Lest coming suddenly he find you sleeping. And what I say unto you I say unto all, Watch.

B. The Setting Of The Parable

The parable is the closing part of Mark's account of the Olivet Discourse. Mark Chapter 13 should be corresponded with Matthew Chapters 24-25 and Luke 21:5-38. Each passage distinctly pertains to the uncertainty of the Lord's second coming and the absolute necessity of watchfulness.

Because of this inter-relatedness, the distinctive passsages in Mark, Matthew and Luke are brought together here for the exposition of the parable in Mark's gospel. The reader should read the three passages together, for, from these three passages we will be able to draw forth the lessons for our exposition of the parable of the absent house-master. Following are the passages from the corresponding gospels.

1. Matthew 24:42-44

Watch therefore: for ye know not what hour your Lord doth come.

But know this, that if the goodman of the house had known in what watch the thief would come, he would have watched, and would not have suffered his house to be broken up.

Therefore be ye also ready: for in such an hour as ye think not the Son of man cometh.

2. Luke 21:34-36

And take heed to yourselves, lest at any time your hearts be overcharged with surfeiting, and drunkenness, and cares of this life, and so that day come upon you unawares. For as a snare shall it come on all them that dwell on the face of the whole earth. Watch ye therefore, and pray always, that ye may be accounted worthy to escape all these things that shall come to pass, and to stand before the Son of man.

C. The Moral Of The Parable

The word is very simple. With regards to the second coming of Christ, the Lord Jesus, the believer is told to take heed, watch and pray. Although there are additional exhortive words in each of the above passages, the key word in each passage is the word **"Watch"**, and it is spoken not only to the disciples of Christ then, but to all disciples of all times. No one knows the day nor the hour of His coming; therefore, be warned against sleeping and other evils that so easily beset the Christian, especially in the days preceding the Lord's coming.

D. The Exposition Of The Parable

It is a short parable in Mark, and as the corresponding Scriptures in the Synoptics show, each point to the importance of watchfulness in the days of the coming of the Lord. Let us consider the most notable points of reference in the parable.

1. The Man

The man is identified by the Lord Jesus Himself as "the Son of Man". He became the Son of Man by the incarnation, in His virgin birth. In His deity, He is the Son of God; in His humanity, He is the Son of Man. He became the Son of Man in order that, through redemption, the sons of men may become sons and daughters of the living God.

2. The Far Journey

The Son of Man was likened to a man taking a far journey. It is the same truth as seen in previous parables. Whether it a man going into a far country or taking a far journey, it points to the ascension of Jesus into the heavenly country, back to His Father where He was before the world began, and before His incarnation (John 16:26-27; Hebrews 11:10-16).

3. He Left His House

The house spoken of here would undoubtedly refer to the church of the Lord Jesus, "whose house are we" (Hebrews 3:1-6). The church is a spiritual house, made up of spiritual and lively stones. It is the pillar and support of the truth. It is God's house that He said He would build in the last days (1Peter 2:5-9; 4:17; 1Timothy 3:5,15; Isaiah 2:1-4). Jesus is the Master of the house! At present He is the absent house-master, absent from earth, but in heaven with the Father.

4. His Servants

As Jesus returned to the Father, leaving His house – His church – here in the earth, He gave authority to His servants. Previous parables have confirmed that all believers are His servants, here to serve Him and to serve one another, as well as serving a lost and dying generation. We are actually His bondmen, His love-slaves, His servants.

Whether apostles, prophets, evangelists, shepherds, teachers, administrators, helps, mercy-showers, giving ministry, and on and on, all believers are His servants in the house of the Lord.

5. He Gave Authority

The word "authority" here is the Greek **"exousia"**, meaning: "ability, privilege, force, capacity, competency, freedom, and delegated influence" (SC. 1849). It also involves privilege and responsibility for what the Master of the house has given to each of His servants.

The Father gave Jesus all power and authority in heaven and in earth (Matthew 29:15-20). Jesus gave His apostles power and authority to preach the gospel, heal the sick, cask out devils and proclaim repentance, forgiveness, baptism and the kingdom of God (Matthew 10:1; Mark 3:15; 6:7; Luke 10:19-20).They were given authority, under His headship, to preach the gospel and make disciples of all nations, seeing all ethnic groupings coming into the house of the Lord. Each had their charge. Each had their particular task. Each had their especial orders from the Master of the house. It is the same message as those in other parables who were given talents "according to their ability."

6. Gave To Each His Work

Every member of God's house has their distinctive work to do, their distinctive grace, calling, gifting, talents and abilities given by the Lord. To each member the Master of the house gave each his work. Each are responsible for this work, not to do some one else's work. Jesus knew the Father had given Him a work to do and He did it (John 4:34; 17:1-4). So each believer has his work to do.

7. Commanded The Porter To Watch

The porter in those days represented the door-keeper. There was always a door-keeper on duty, especially at night time. They could rest in the day time. But someone had to be on duty in the night watches.

Ministers of the gospel are like "watchman", and there must always be someone on duty day and night, watching for any one who would come, or the sudden, unexpected return of the Master of the house.

8. No One Knows The Day or Hour

It is significant to see the emphasis on the fact that no one knows the day nor the hour when the Son of Man – the Master of the house – would return. Someone must always be watching, waiting, expecting His return. Note those who Jesus mentions, as the Son of Man, who do not know the house or day of His coming.

1. No believer knows the day or hour of His return.

2. The angels in heaven do not know the day nor the hour of His return either.

3. The Son of Man does not know the day nor the hour of His return. It should be remembered that, here Jesus is speaking in His humanity. As subject to the Father, He only said and did what the Father showed Him. It is evident that at this time of His speaking the Olivet Discourse, the Father had not showed Him the day or hour of His coming, just the fact that He would come again the second time.

It would seem from Revelation 1:1 that the Father did give the revelation to His Son of the time of His coming once He returned to the Father in heaven. However, the Son of Man **in His humanity** did not know the day nor the hour of His coming. That is very clear in these verses.

4. Only the Father which is in heaven knew the exact day and hour in which He would send His Son the second time to earth. The Father has reserved some things in the secrets of His counsel in the purpose and plan of redemption (Deueteronomy 29:29). Some things He has revealed to us. Some things He has kept secret.

The coming may be: at any of the watches of the night:-

* At even (9pm)
* At midnight (12 midnight)
* At cockcrowing (3am)
* In the morning (6am).

No one knows the day nor the hour, no believer, no angel, not even the Son of Man, but the Father has the exact moment of the Son's return. Therefore, be always ready for the time when the Master of the house comes to take account of His servants.

E. The Practical Application Of The Parable

As the several passages from the Synoptics are compared, there are a number of very practical lessons which can be applied to the believers life, especially as it speaks of the time of the end, and the time of the Lord's second advent. From these passages we list some of these exhortive words, all of which was involved in the key word "Watch!"

1. Take Heed

The Amplified New Testament says, "Be on your guard, constantly alert..." There are many exhortations to "take heed" to oneself in the New Testament writings. At least twentyeight times the expresson "take heed" is used. Believers are to take heed to themselves, take heed that they come not under deception, take heed to the life-style they live, that it is a life of holiness, and take heed to the Word of God and the Spirit of God. Following are some of these "take heed" warnings in Scripture and these provide a profitable list of those things all believers should be on their guard against (Matthew 24:4; Mark 13:5,9,23,33; Luke 8:18; 21:8,34; Acts 20:28; 1Corinthians 10:12; Galatians 5:15; Hebrews 3:12).

2. Watch

The word "watch", as already noted, is the key word in each passage. It is used in the three passages under consideration and in connection with the Markean parable at least eight times.

The opposite to watchfulness is sleepiness. The Lord warned against the time He would come, "lest coming suddenly He finds you sleeping.".

In the parable of the wise and foolish virgins, a number of Scriptures warning against sleeping were provided. Paul warns the Thessalonian believers against sleeping, and not being found awake at His coming (Matthew 25:1-13; 2Thessalonians 5:1-8). The reader is reminded of those comments in that particular parable. To watch is to be alert, awake, to be vigilant, to keep guard, to be attentive.

3. Pray

Mark's account calls the disciples to also pray, as also does Luke's account. The believer is to pray always (Luke 21:36; 2Thessalonians 1:11; Luke 18:1). It is not the bodily position of prayer but the constant spirit and attitude of prayerfulness that Jesus is speaking of here. The believer will have daily prayer, special seasons of prayer, but there will be always be that underlying spirit and attitude or prayer, regardless of time and place and circumstance. One must pray to keep in touch with the Lord who alone can warn the believer of the time of His unexpected return.Though one may not know the day nor the hour, the believer who takes heed, watches and pray will indeed know the "times and seasons" of the Lord's coming, even as Paul said.

4. Be Ready

Matthew's gospel uses the illustration of the coming of a thief in the night, in which, when he comes, he finds the goodman (the porter) of the house asleep, and suffered his house to be broken into. In the light of this sudden "thief-like" coming of the Lord, the porter must always be awake. He must always be ready for that unknown, unexpected hour.

The Lord will come as "a thief in the night" to some unwatching believers, and to the unwatching and godless world. However, the true believer, who is watchful and prayerful will not be caught by the coming of the Lord as a thief in the night. These Scriptures clearly show the truth of these statements (Luke 12:39; 1Thessalonians 5:1-8; 2Peter 3:10; Revelation 3:3;16:15).

5. Watch Your Heart

Luke's gospel adds some thoughts that are not found in Mark or Matthew but certainly belong to the period of time under consideration, the Lord's return. Luke warns:

* Take heed to yourselves ("Self" in one's greatest enemy; Acts 20:28;1Timothy 4:16). Be discreet, attentive and ready, says the Amplified.

* Take heed to your heart that it not be overcharged with surfeiting. The Amplified says: "But take heed to yourselves and be on your guard lest your hearts be overburdened and depressed – weighed down – with the giddiness and headache and nausea of self-indulgence, drunkenness, and worldly worries, and cares pertaining to the business of this life.."

The words should be noted carefully. Overburdened, depression, giddiness, headache, nausea, self-indulgence, drunkenness, worldly worries and cares pertaining to the business of this life.

These are the things that believers are in great danger of being caught up with in the days prior to the Lord's coming.

6. The Snare On The Earth

Jesus said (Luke's Gospel) that His coming will come as a snare upon all those that dwell on the face of the whole earth. None will escape these things. The word "snare" means "a trap" or "a noose".

Just as a bird or an animal is caught suddenly, unexpectedly and when least watching, in a trap or a noose, so the whole earth will be caught unexpectedly, suddenly and when least watching when the Lord comes. For the believer, there is no excuse, for the Lord has given many signs and many warnings and exhortations to be ready for His coming again. If a believer takes heed to these practical exhortations in this section, he will not be caught unawares.

7. Worthy To Escape

Luke's word closes with the exhortation that the believer watch, and pray always, that he may be accounted **worthy to escape** all these things that shall come to pass and be able to **stand before the Son of Man!**

Paul speaks of a time when mankind will say, "Peace and safety, but then sudden destruction shall come on them, as travail upon a woman with child, and **they shall not escape...**" (1 Thessalonians 5:3).

The writer to the Hebrews asks the question: "How shall we escape if we neglect so great salvation...? (Hebrews 2:3). But the epistle concludes with the word to those who refuse to hear Him who speaks from heaven: "They shall **not** escape..." (Hebrews 12:25).

In conclusion, this beautiful, short parable of Mark's gospel has much to teach us, along with the corresponding gospels of Matthew and Luke. The believer needs to take heed to himself, to watch, to pray, to be ready always, to guard his heart against the things of this world (like the thorns in parable of the sower and seed), and pray that he will be reckoned worthy to escape the things coming on the earth at Christ's advent, and to be able to stand before Him in that day. The Master of the house will return. And what He told His disciples, He says unto us all: **Watch!**

PART FOUR

Parables in the Gospel of Luke

CHAPTERS 27 – 50

CHAPTER TWENTY-SEVEN
THE PARABLES OF THE GARMENTS AND WINESKINS

A. The Scriptures On The Parables

1. Luke 5:36-38

And he spake also a parable unto them; No man putteth a piece of a new garment upon an old; if otherwise, then both the new maketh a rent, and the piece that was taken out of the new agreeth not with the old. And no man putteth new wine into old bottles; else the new wine will burst the bottles, and be spilled, and the bottles shall perish. But new wine must be put into new bottles; and both are preserved.

2. Matthew 9:16-17

No man putteth a piece of new cloth unto an old garment, for that which is put in to fill it up taketh from the garment, and the rent is made worse. Neither do men put new wine into old bottles: else the bottles break, and the wine runneth out, and the bottles perish: but they put new wine into new bottles, and both are preserved.

3. Mark 2:21-22

No man also seweth a piece of new cloth on an old garment: else the new piece that filled it up taketh away from the old, and the rent is made worse. And no man putteth new wine into old bottles: else the new wine doth burst the bottles, and the wine is spilled, and the bottles will be marred: but new wine must be put into new bottles.

B. The Setting Of The Parable

By a comparison of the Synoptics, the setting of the parable is preceded with the question concerning the disciples of John and the disciples of the Pharisees (Luke 6:33-35; Matthew 9:14-15; Mark 2:18-20).

The question is asked of Jesus, Why do the disiciples of John the Baptist fast, and the disciples of the Pharisees fast and make prayers, but the disciples of Jesus were eating and drinking instead of fasting?

Jesus replied that, when the bridegroom is with the children of the bridechamber, they do not fast. They eat and drink and rejoice together. However, the days woud come when the bridegroom would be taken away from them. In his absence they would then fast and pray.

What the disciples of John and the Pharisees had to come to realize was that, under the Old Covenant, there were times of mourning, prayers and fastings. But at the present moment, Jesus, the Author of the New Covenant, was with His disciples, and they could rejoice together. Jesus Himself is the bridegroom, as John clearly indicated (John 3:29-30), and while Jesus was with His disciples, they need not fast or mourn. However, the day would come when He would be taken away from them into heaven (Acts 1:9-11).

We are living in those days now when the bridegroom is still away, and it is during this time, His disciples have times of prayer and fasting, waiting for His return. The disciples of Christ, needed to see the distinction between the Old Covenant and the New Covenant.

It is in this setting that the twin parables of the old and new garment, and the old and new wine and wineskins arose.

C. The Moral Of The Parable

The major moral of these twin parables shows that the things of the Old Covenant and the New Covenant will not mix. One cannot take portions of the "Old Covenant garment" and sew it on to the "New Covenant garment". Nor can one take the "new wine of the New Covenant" and put into into the "old wineskin of the Old Covenant", or else both will be lost. The Old Covenant wineskin has become dry, brittle, and inflexible. One must become a new wineskin (" a new creature") in order to be able to receive and contain the New Covenant truths ("the new wine"). Our exposition of these twin parables confirm the truth of these things in a fuller way.

D. The Exposition Of The Parable

As has been seen, each of the Synoptic Gospels give the account of these twin parables of Jesus concerning the new and the new wineskins and the old and the old wineskins as well as that of the new and the old garment. Our approach in the exposition of these twin parables will be by way of (1) Illustration, (2) Interpretation and finally (3) Application.

1. The Illustration

The twin parables were actually illustrations of that which was taking place in the Gospels and on into the Acts and the Epistles. These parables were just common narratives of Jewish life. And as seen, it was one of the Lord's favourite methods of communicating truth, especially after the rising rejection of the religious leaders of His day. We consider first the parable of the garment, and then the parable of the wineskin.

(a) Parable of the Garment

This first parable is simple and clear in its illustration. The interpretation and application would come to those who had an ear to hear, and an eye to see and a heart to perceive.

If one has an old worn out garment, and they take a piece or patch of a new garment and sew it on to the old, it will tear the garment. The strength of the new patch will not match the old weakness of the old garment. The "new patch" here is referring to a piece of material that is unbleached or unshrunk cloth. The rent or tear is made worse. The new and the old do not mix; and the new and the old materials just do not agree.

Jesus is saying that you cannot mix the old and the new or there will be problems. One needs to get rid of the old garment. It is worn out. It is thread-bare. It has served its purpose. It was once new and now it has become old. One needs to have a totally new garment.

(b) Parable of the Wineskin

The second parable, though more extended, is also simple and clear in its illustration and interpretation. Again, the application would come to those who had ears to hear, eyes to see and hearts to perceive.

If one has new wine, then it has to be placed into new wineskins. Otherwise, if the new wine is placed in the old wineskins, then the wineskins will burst, the new wine will be lost, and the old wineskins destroyed. The only way to preserve the new wine is to have such poured into new wineskins, then both will be preserved.

Wine, when fermentation is complete, can be put into any bottle, old or new, without losing the bottles or wineskins and wine. Wine, intended to ferment, would burst any bottles, whether new or old. Unfermented wine must therefore be put into new skins.

(1) The Wineskins

In Bible time, the custom was to make bottles (or wineskins) from the skins of animals, generally goats or kids of goats to contain the new wine. They would retain the figure of the animal (head and feet cut off), as the skin was stripped from the complete body of the animal. Sometimes the neck of the animal was used as the neck of the bottle and the thighs as handles. The skins were treated to hold the wine or water that would be poured into them. When the skin was green (new), or fresh, it had the ability to expand. It was flexible and expandable with any pressure of new wine that may come.

(2) The Wine

The Greek word "oinos" from Strong's (SC 3631) gives the general view that this wine would be given to fermentation. The Gospel writers use "oinos" for new wine, and "angukos", must, for new wine (SC 1098), which is used only once in the New Testament, in Acts 2:13. The usage presupposes intoxication, even though it is defined as must, fresh juice. On the Day of Pentecost, the people charged the Spirit-filled disciples as being drunk on new wine.

Therefore, its use by Jesus in relation to wineskins, new and old, indicate wine in the process of fermentation, producing pressure on the wineskin by the building up of carbon dioxide.

(3) Old Wineskins

Over the year, a wineskin becomes old, seamed, and dry, cracked and brittle. As it cracks, becomes hard, it will not stand any pressure. It loses its flexibility. It just does not have the ability to expand any longer.

Thus Jesus is saying, that new wineskins must be made for new wine. One cannot pour new wine into old bottles. The new wine will burst the old bottles. The wine is spilled. The bottles are rent. One loses both the wine and wineskins. The new wine must be put into new bottles. The result? BOTH wine and wineskins are preserved. The NEW must go to the NEW. The OLD must go to the OLD. The new and the old will not, they cannot mix without the resultant problems and losses.

2. The Interpretation

Having looked quite fully at the illustrations, what then is the interpretation of these twin uninterpreted parables of Jesus?

As will be seen, in each parable we have TWO symbolic elements which need to be interpreted. In the first parable, we have the old garment and the new piece. In the second parable we have the old wineskins and old wine and the new wineskins and the new wine.

In the Gospels we have the parables of Jesus given as the illustrations. In the Book of Acts and the Epistles we see what can truly be the unfolding of the parables and then discover the interpretation. However, one needs an overview of Israel's history first in order to appreciate the interpretation of these twin parables. Both the "old" and the "new" have to do with the OLD and the NEW Covenants.

(a) Israel And The Old Covenant

(1) The Wineskin

God took the nation of Israel from the midst of other nations (Exodus 19:1-6; Deuteronomy 4-5 Chapters). They were the CHURCH in the wilderness (Acts 7:28), and the instrument for the KINGDOM of God in the earth. As such, the nation became God's **new wineskin,** the structure, the bottle, His church in the earth in the midst of the nations. The purpose of any wineskin is to contain wine. It is no use having a wineskin without wine or wine without a wineskin. The wineskin was Israel, the chosen nation, the people of God, His structure.

(2) The Wine

God then proceeded to pour into this nation – this wineskin – Israel, His covenantal truths; the nine great things found in Romans 9:4-5 and 3:2.

* The adoption (Exodus 4:22-24; Hosea 11:1)
* The covenants (The Abrahamic, Mosaic, Palestinian, Davidic Covenants)
* The giving of the Law (Moral, Civil, Health and Ceremonial)
* The service of God (The Tabernacles of Moses, David, and Temple services)
* The promises (The Messianic promises especially)
* The fathers (Abraham, Isaac and Jacob)
* The Messiah (The Lord Jesus Christ, after the flesh)
* The oracles of God (The Sacred Scriptures).

The wine was symbolic of all these things involved in the covenantal truths which God poured into the nation of Israel, His wineskin, His structure.

But what happened over the years of Israel's history? The nation became hard, inflexible, dry, brittle and corrupted and lost the ability to expand in the things of God. They also corrupted the wine of God's truth.

In Christ's time, religion had become the old, stiff, brittle and inflexible wineskin of Judaism. Paul called it "the Jew's religion" (Galatians 1:13-14. Lit. 'Judaism'). Not only that, they had run out of wine, and what they had was corrupted by mixture. The people were thirsty for something fresh from the God of Israel. The religious leaders hung on to the old wineskin, the old structure of Judaism.

Judaism had become an "old garment", torn, ragged, threadbare and worn out, but the religious leaders hung on to the old to try and keep themselves spiritually warm.

(b) The Church And The New Covenant

(1) The New Wine

When Jesus Christ came, He came to bring new wine, a fresh revelation of God from God, His Father. He came to bring new covenantal truths. He came to bring a new garment. They clung to the old garment. He came to bring new covenant wine. They hung on to the old wineskin. The new wine represented the teaching of Jesus in all its freshness, newness, originality and power. The Gospels reveal this. However, the Scribes, the Pharisees, the Priests, the Sadduccees and religious leaders said, "the OLD is better" and did not want or have any desire for that which Jesus was bringing.

(2) The New Wineskin

The old wineskin bottles could not contain or receive the new covenant wine. The old wineskins represent the Pharisees, Scribes, Priests, Sadducees and religious leaders of Judaism, bound to the old interpretation of the law by the Talmudic traditions they taught.

So what was Jesus to do? He had to make a NEW WINESKIN, a new structure, to hold the NEW WINE of the NEW COVENANT. The new wineskin is the New Testament (covenant) Church for new covenant truths (Matthew 16:15-20).

On the Day of Pentecost, Jesus formed "the new wineskin", and He poured in "the new wine" of His Word and His Spirit (New Covenant truths), so much so, that the Jews said the disciples were "drunk with new wine" (Acts 2). From here on, the apostles founded New Covenant churches of believing Jews and Gentiles holding the New Covenant truths.

(c) Judaism And Christianity

What do we see happening in the Book of Acts and the Epistles, and especially in the Book of Galatians? Most of the religious leaders, the Scribes, Priests and Pharisees, totally rejected the new garment Christ came to bring, and hung on to the old garment. Or, in other words, most of the relgious leaders totally rejected the new wine and wineskins that Christ came to give and to make for them.

Some of the religious leaders, however, tried to MIX the old and the new and the result was "rent" or schism, division and mixture. The Judaizers took the **old covenant garment** and sewed **"patches"** of the **new covenant** to it and the garment was torn. They tried to mix Old Covenant truths of Sabbath days, circumcision, clean and unclean meats, and ceremonialisms of the law in with New Covenant truths. The result was a torn garment and covenantal confusion. The rent was made worse.

The law forbids mixture. The wearing of a garment of wool and linen was forbidden (Deuteronoy 21:11; Leviticus 19:19). Wool speaks of sweat; linen speaks of no sweat. Beyond the literal, there is the spiritual truth.

One is Old Covenant, the other is New Covenant. Mixture of the old and the new is forbidden by the Lord. A mixed garment becomes disfigured and eventually destroyed.

The Epistle to the Galatians shows this mixture of Law and Grace; Moses and Jesus; Works of the Law and the Faith of Grace; Old Covenant and New Covenant. The result? Divisions came into the Jewish Synagogues as Acts 10,11,15 and other chapters reveal.

The Judaizers tried to impose Judaism on the Christian Gentiles, thus evidencing confusion of covenants. They tried to put New Covenant wine-truths into the Old Covenant Judaistic wineskins. Both were lost. The wineskins burst, and the new wine was spilled. Judaism and Christianity would and could never mix without creating schisms in the Synagogues of the land.

E. The Practical Application Of The Parable

Having considered the illustrations and interpretation of these twin parables, we conclude with some practical application for our times. The truths considered in the exposition can certainly be applied to Church History; both personally and individually as well as corporately and denominationally.

The early church as a "new wineskin", like Israel, degenerated over the years, and became, as it were "an old wineskin". In what has been called "The Dark Ages", the church as a structure had become hard, dry, stiff, brittle and inflexible, unable to expand, and it had also run out of the wine of God's Spirit and Word. It had become a wineskin without wine.

What does the Lord do? He makes a "new wineskin" to hold the "new wine" truth. Thus movement after movement, denomination after denonomination come and go, rise and fall. They begin with that which is fresh from God and end up becoming an old wineskin, unable to receive the new wine of restored truth. The result? Division, schisms, splits, bursts wineskins, and confusion in so many places around the world. Hardly a denomination in the world has not been affected by fresh awakenings, revivals or outpourings of the Spirit, as well as recovery of fresh truth, that has not brought schism into their movement

What is the problem? It is the parables of a new garment and the need for new pieces on it, and the new wine needing to be poured into new wineskins. Some old wineskin denominations and old garments have taken some of the new wine, and some of the new patches and tried to pour it into the old denominational structure, and sew a new patch on the old garment. This is exactly what the Judaizers tried to do in the early church.

Many also say, "The OLD is better", and do not want the NEW. History keeps on repeating itself in every generation, and in every visitation of the Holy Spirit and in every recovery of Biblical truth.

Numerous churches today also confuse elements of the Old Covenant with the New Covenant. In principle, they are like the Judaizers and become involved in mixture. It is a mix of the Old Covenant and the New Covenant, Moses and Jesus. The point of exchange is at the cross. Jewry would not come to the cross and let go of Old Covenant shadows and symbols and take hold of New Covenant substance and realties.

The issue is: The Lord Jesus wants to make His people continually open to His freshness, and to receive the new wine of heaven, and not become old, stiff, dry, brittle denominational wineskins, inflexible to anything fresh the Lord does in His church, by fresh visitations of the Holy Spirit.

Following is a list of the things that speak of the New Covenant and the things that belong to the new creature, whether believing Jews and Gentiles.

1. The New Birth (John 1:12-13; 3:1-7; 1Peter 1:23)

2. The New Creature (Galatians 6:15; 2Corinthans 5:17)

3. The New Man (Ephesians 4:24; Colossians 3:10)

4. The One New Man composed of Jews and Gentiles in Christ (Ephesians 2:15)

5. The New Garment (Matthew 9:17; Luke 5:37-39; Mark 2:21)

6. The New Wineskin and New Wine (Matthew 9:17; Mark 2:21; Proverbs 3:10)

7. The New Tongues (Mark 16:17; Acts 2:1-4)

8. The New Commandment of Love (John13:34; 1John 2:7,8; 2John 5)

9. The New Doctrine of Christ (Mark 1:27)

10. The New and Living Way (Hebrews 10:20)

11. The New Name (Revelation 2:17; 3:12; Isaiah 62:2)

12. The New Song (Revelation 5:9; 14:3; Psalm 33:3;40:3;96:1;98:1; 144:9;149:1)

13. The New Unleavened Lump of Dough (1Corinthians 5:7)

14. The New Heart (Ezekiel 18:31; 36:26)

15. The New Spirit (Ezekiel 11:19; 18:31; 36:26)

16. The New Covenant (Hebrews 8:8; 12:24; Jeremiah 31:31-34)

17. The New Testament (Matthew 26:28; Mark 14:24; Luke 22:20; 1Corinthians 11:25)

18. The New Mercies of the Lord (Lamentations 3:23)

19. The New Jerusalem (Revelation 3:12; 21:2)

20. The New Heavens – New Earth (2Peter 3:13; Revelation 21:2; Isaiah 65:17; 66:21)

The Lord indeed says, "Behold, I make ALL THINGS NEW "(Revelation 21:2). The believer individually, and the church corporately, must ever keep open, and fresh to the Lord's new wine He brings to the Church, and beware of becoming a stale, stiff, dry, hard and inflexible wineskin. Structure is needed (the wineskin), but truth must be continually fresh (the wine) in order for the Church to be all that the Lord intended it to be!

CHAPTER TWENTY-EIGHT

THE PARABLE OF THE WISE AND FOOLISH BUILDERS

A. The Scriptures On The Parable

1. Luke 6:46-49

And why call ye me, Lord, Lord, and do not the things which I say?

Whosoever cometh to me, and heareth my sayings, and doeth them, I will shew you to whom he is like:

He is like a man which built an house, and digged deep, and laid the foundation on a rock: and when the flood arose, the stream beat vehemently upon that house, and could not shake it: for it was founded upon a rock.

But he that heareth, and doeth not, is like a man that without a foundation built an house upon the earth; against which the stream did beat vehemently, and immediately it fell; and the ruin of that house was great.

2. Matt 7:24-29

Therefore whosoever heareth these sayings of mine, and doeth them, I will liken him unto a wise man, which built his house upon a rock:

And the rain descended, and the floods came, and the winds blew, and beat upon that house; and it fell not: for it was founded upon a rock.

And every one that heareth these sayings of mine, and doeth them not, shall be likened unto a foolish man, which built his house upon the sand:

And the rain descended, and the floods came, and the winds blew, and beat upon that house; and it fell: and great was the fall of it.

And it came to pass, when Jesus had ended these sayings, the people were astonished at his doctrine: For he taught them as one having authority, and not as the scribes.

B. The Setting Of The Parable

Luke's Gospel presents the parable of the wise and foolish builders at the close of "The Sermon on the Plain", while Matthew's Gospel presents the same parable at the close of the commonly known word, "The Sermon on the Mount" (Luke 6:17; Matthew 5:1-2).

There are a number of parables in this repeated "sermon". Matthew's Gospel presents the fuller account of the "Sermon on the Mount" (Matthew Chapters 5,6,7), while Luke's account gives lesser material.

One would have to consider all the laws of the kingdom in these "sermons" of Jesus to see the complete setting. The issue, however, is that Jesus told this parable to illustrate who is a wise and who is a foolish builder. Everybody is building something in their lifetime. The wise man built. The foolish man built. The wise man built his house upon a rock foundation and it stood the storms. The foolish man built his house on the sand and when the storms came, great was its ruin.

The setting for the parable is the sermon in the plain (Luke) or the sermon on the mount (Matthew). It comes as a fitting and practical conclusion to all that Jesus had taught on the laws of the kingdom of God. The people were astonished at His teaching, and His authority, for it was not as the teaching of the scribes, who generally quoted Talmudic writings most often without any Divine authority to support them.

C. The Moral Of The Parable

The moral of the parable is that one must truly hear the words of Jesus. The Biblical concept of "hearing" is "obedience" to the word heard. The wise man heard the word. The foolish man heard the same word, the laws of Christ's kingdom. One heard and obeyed. The other heard and did not obey.

Obedience to the words of Christ determines whether a person is a wise builder or a foolish builder. The wise man is a hearer and doer of the sayings of Jesus. The foolish man is a hearer and not a doer of the sayings of Jesus.

The foundation of a person's life is obedience to the Word of God. Disobedience in a person's life is a house without a foundation. Obedience is the rock on which to build. Disobedience is building on the sand. Though there have been many songs or even hymns composed on this parable, the true moral of the story is:

Obedience to the word of Christ is the only true foundation for being a wise builder!

D. The Exposition Of The Parable

Most every expositor of this parable sees that there are also a number of other lessons that may be learnt along with the major moral of the parable. There are a lot of similarities between the two builders, but there is the one major difference. For the purpose of our exposition, we will contrast the two builders and then consider the three most important things in the building of a house.

These truths could be applicable to the building of a person's life, or building a society, or even the building of a church. There are symbolic realities in the parts of the parable that are worthy of serious consideration.

The Two Builders

The Wise Man	The Foolish Man
Built a house	Built a house
Laid a foundation	Without a foundation
On a rock	On the sand
The rains descended	The rains descended
The floods came	The floods came
The winds blew	The winds blew
It fell not	Great was the fall
House not ruined	Great was the ruin
Wise man heard the Word	Foolish man heard the Word
Obeyed the Word	Obeyed not the Word
A hearer and a doer of Christ's sayings	A hearer and not a doer of Christ's sayings

A comparison shows the correspondences and yet the major contrast between the two builders. These things provide lessons for all people, of all ages, of all generations and for all times.

1. All are Building

Every person is building. They are either building a life, a family, a home, a character, or, even the building may be appplied to building the church, the house of the Lord. Paul uses the symbol of a builder to the Corinthian believers, saying, "Take heed how you build...." (1Corinthians 3:9-12).

2. All are either Wise or Foolish Builders

There are numerous Scriptures on being wise or foolish that could be applied to these two builders. The Book of Proverbs abounds with references that speak of a person either being wise or foolish, and the characteristics of the wise and foolish.

Jesus speaks of wise and foolish builders (Matthew 7:24-27; Luke 6:46-49). The test, as already seen, was over having a foundation or no foundation.

Jesus speaks also of wise and foolish virgins (Matthew 25:1-13). The test was over having sufficient oil when the bridegroom came.

Proverbs 14:1 states: "Every wise woman builds her house, but a foolish woman plucks it down with her hands."

Proverbs 9:1 says: "Wisdom has builded her house, she has hewn out seven pillars."

Proverbs 24:3-4 says: "Through **wisdom** is an house built, and by **understanding** it is established; and by **knowledge** shall the chambers (rooms) be filled with precious and pleasant riches." The three key words in the Book of Proverbs have to do with wisdom, understanding and knowledge. It has been said:

* Knowledge is the acquisition of facts – Observation

* Understanding is the explanation of facts – Interpretation

* Wisdom is the application of facts – Application.

3. All are Building a House

A "house" in Scripture is used actually and symbolically in a number of different ways.

It is used of a person's own life. A person has their 'house' cleansed of evil spirits, swept and garnished, but if there is no occupant in the 'house', then seven more wicked spirits could enter in and dwell here (Matthew 12:43-45). A person's own life is likened to a house here.

It is used of a person's family, a home or household. A leader in the church must be able to take care of his own 'house' (family, household) before he could qualify to take care of the 'house' (the church) of God (1Timothy 3:4,5,12).

The symbol of a 'house' is also used of the New Testament church, the Lord's house, 'whose house are we' (Hebews 3:1-6; 1Timothy 3:5,15; 1Peter 4:17; 2:5-9; Ephesians 2:19-20).

So the truth may be applied in symbolic reality to any of these things. Whether a person is building a life, a character, a family, a society, or a church, one needs to be a wise builder, not a foolish builder. As Paul said, "Take heed how you build..." (1Corinthians 3:9-12). Every person in life is building something, they are building 'a house'.

4. Building Houses

In the building of any house, there are **three major things** involved. There must be proper foundations, proper structure, and proper roof covering. This is true naturally, whether building a material house and it is true spiritually, whether building a spiritual house. Each of these three provide spiritual lessons in this parable.

(a) Proper Foundations

Scripture speaks often about proper foundations. The wise man built his house on a **rock foundation**. Luke brings in another thought that he dug deep, found a rock, and then laid the foundation on the rock. Both thoughts are true and consistent with the Scriptures.

In symbolic sense, Christ is THE Foundation of a Christian life, a Christian family, or the true Christian Church. He said, "Upon this Rock (Himself), I will build My church" (Matthew 16:18).

Paul said to the Corinthian believers, "I have laid the foundation, and other foundation can no man lay than that which is laid, which is Christ..."(1Corinthians 3:9-12). The Psalmist asked the question, "If the foundations be destroyed, what can the righteous do?" (Psalm 11:3).

Abraham, Isaac and Jacob were looking for a city which had foundations, whose builder and maker is God. That city is seen with twelve foundations of the Book of Revelation (Hebrews 11:10-16 with Revelation 21-22).

Another aspect of the "foundation" is seen in Hebrews 6:1-2. There the writer speaks of the first principles of the doctrine of Christ. The foundation of repentance from dead works, faith towards God, baptisms, laying on of hands, resurrection of the dead and eternal judgement. These are foundational principles of the teachings of Christ, and every believer is called to follow in these truths as he follows Christ in obedience to His word. The Church is built upon the foundation laid by the apostles and prophets (Ephesians 2:19-22).

The foolish man built his house on the sand. He built his house without a proper or any foundation at all. Truly a foolish builder. No one ever buys a house without checking the foundations, no matter how beautiful the house may appear.

(b) Proper Structure

A house must also have proper structure, a good framework in order to withstand the winds, hurricanes, tornadoes, and storms that come its way. Structure speaks of framework. A wise person builds their life, their family, their home upon the structure and within the framework of God's Word.

The Ark of Noah illustrates this truth. God gave Noah the instructions how to build the ark of safety; its measurements, its framework, its covering. It had to be built according to the Divine pattern in order to withstand the deluge that would come. Only those within the framework of the ark had that sense of Divine security in the storms that lasted forty days (Genesis 6,7,8).

The Tabernacle of Moses also illustrates the same truth. God gave the pattern for His house. It included silver sockets foundations. It included the framework or structure of the boards and bars for the tabernacle itself. Then the appointed coverings were over head on the Tabernacle of the Lord. The framework held all together amidst the desert winds or storms in the wilderness over the forty years wanderings of Israel (Exodus 25-40 Chapters provide the details). The priests of the Lord ministered unto the Lord in the daily ministrations within the Divine structure.

So the wise man, who builds his life, his character, his family, his home or even the house of the Lord – the church – will do all within the framework of God's government. This is safety and security.

(c) Proper Covering

The third major thing a house needs is to have a proper roof, a proper covering, in order to protect it from the rains and the storms.

The same illustrations as above confirm the truth. The ark of Noah had its foundation, its structure and its covering. All were safe within the ark of Noah when the storms fell. The ark had its covering, even though the material was not specified (Genesis 8:13).

The Tabernacle of Moses had distinctive coverings over its structure to protect those who ministered therein, as well as the furnishings of the Lord's dwelling place. All were protected from the storms and tests of the desert winds. The priests ministered under the shadow of the wings of the cherubims in the linen curtains, as well as under the security of the other coverings of ram's skins dyed red, the goats hair skins and the badgers skins. The student is referred to just several Scriptures on the thought of "covering" (Numbers 9:15-16; Exodus 26:4; Psalom 91:4).

5. The Threefold Test Of A House

In the parable that Jesus gave, one can see that there was a threefold test that came to both houses, the wise man's house and the foolish man's house. There is surely some truth in symbolic form in this threefold test.

(a) The Floods Tested The Foundation

One may think again of the flood in the days of Noah. The foundation was surely tested in the flood (Genesis 6:17; 7:6-10). The occupants of the ark of Noah were surely glad for the solid foundation that bore the ark through the deluge. The Bible speaks of times when the "enemy would come in like a flood", and at that time the Spirit of the Lord would raise a standard up against him (Isaiah 59:19). In Revelation 12:15-16 we see the great old serpent, the devil, sending a flood to seek and destroy the church, the woman in the wilderness.

In today's society, there are "floods" of evil philosophies flooding the world; socialism, atheism, humanism, new-ageism, and numerous other Satanic philosophies which are attacking the very foundations of civilization. "If the foundations be destroyed, what can the righteous do?" (Psalm 11:3).

A wise man will make sure his foundations are right in order to withstand the floods of lies, propaganda, deceit and evil philosophies that would seek to destroy the foundations of a Christian home.

(b) The Winds Tested The Structure

The same winds tested both houses, the wise man's house and the foolish man's house. Paul speaks of "every wind of doctrine" that blows about to shake the Divine structure of the church (Ephesians 4:14). In the natural, Satan sent great winds against Job's house and his sons and daughters were destroyed (Job 1:19).

The winds tested the ark of Noah and the Tabernacle of Moses. The winds test everything any one builds. There are strong winds, contrary winds, hurricanes and tornadoes that bring devastation to anything that is not made of strong structure. The lesson is clear. The wise man will build Biblical structure that will stand the test of the winds, whether in his own character and life, his family, or church life.

(c) The Rains Tested The Covering

The rains tested the covering. The truth is applicable to Noah's ark, and to the Tabernacle of Moses (Genesis 7:12; 8:13; Exodus 26:4; Isaiah 4:5-6).

If these Divinely patterned structures had not a proper covering, then the rains or floods would have poured inside and great would have been the disaster. Covering speaks of protection, preservation, oversight. The Scriptures speak of being under the "covering" of the Lord (Psalm 91:1-4). Under His covering there is safety from rains, torrential rains, and floods. The rains tested the covering for both the wise and foolish man's house.

Paul uses another symbol and says that every person's work will be tested by fire in "that day", to see what sort of work and material has been built into the house. Paul speaks of himself as a "wise master-builder" (1 Corinthians 3:9-16). Whether we speak of the test by rain or by fire, the end result will be the same if there is no proper foundation, proper structure or proper covering!

Both the wise man's house and the foolish man's house experienced these same tests. The floods, the winds and the rains tested the foundation, the structure, the covering. The wise man's house stood the test. The foolish man's failed the test. Though the foolish man probably had some form of structure, and covering, the unseen foundation was missing and great was the ruin thereof.

The people in the wise man's house had that sense of security and safety through the storm. Those in the foolish man's house, without doubt, perished in the storms. The foolish man's house certainly went up the quickest, but lasted the shortest time. The wise man's house took more time to build, but it lasted the longest! The wise man built for the long term; the foolish for the short term!

Whether building a Christian life and character, a Christian family and household or a Christian church, this threefold test will come. All who hear the sayings of Jesus will experience these tests. The question is: Will our **house stand in that day?** Will we be a wise builder or a foolish builder.

These are some of the great lessons that may be learnt from the symbolic elements in this true to life parable. Proper foundation, proper structure and proper covering are the things that build a safe and sure house!

E. The Practical Application Of The Parable

Although there are many lessons in the parable of the two builders, the true and proper interpretation and the real issue and application is **obedience to Christ's words!** It is being a **hearer AND doer** of the sayings of Jesus.

The Bible shows us that there are a number of things relative to the Word of God that believers are called to do, as seen in the following.

Believers are called to:

1. **Read** the Word (Deuteronomy 17:10; 1Timothy 4:3)
2. **Hear** the Word (Revelation 1:3)
3. **Study** the Word (2Timothy 2:15)
4. **Meditate** on the Word (Psalm 1:1-3; 119:15,23,48)
5. **Remember** the Word (Numbers 15:37-41)
6. **Learn** the Word (Psalm 119:71,73)
7. **Preach** the Word (2Timothy 4:1-4).

But the most important thing of all is to:

8. **OBEY** the Word (Ezekiel 33:30-33; Luke 6:46-47; Revelation 1:3; John13:17; Mattthew 23:1-3; 7:24-27).

The apostle James warns the person who is a forgetful hearer of the Word and fails to obey the Word. The one who is a hearer of the Word and not a doer deceives himself. He is like a man who looks into the mirror, and sees himself as he really is, and then forgets what sort of a man he was (James 1:22-25).

So was the foolish man who built on the sand. He heard the Word, obeyed it not and was self-deceived and great was the ruin of his house. The wise man heard the Word and obeyed it and his house stood fast.

Matthew's Gospel closes the "Sermon on the Mount" with this parable. Luke's Gospel closes the "Sermon on the Plain" with the same parable. The moral is the same. **Obedience** to the words of Jesus is the one and only sure **foundation** to building a Biblical Christian life, character, family, household or church!

CHAPTER TWENTY-NINE
THE PARABLE OF THE CREDITOR AND TWO DEBTORS

A. The Scripture On The Parable
Luke 7:41-43.

> There was a certain creditor which had two debtors: the one owed five hundred pence, and the other fifty.
>
> And when they had nothing to pay, he frankly forgave them both. Tell me therefore, which of them will love him most?
>
> Simon answered and said, I suppose that he, to whom he forgave most. And he said unto him, Thou hast rightly judged.

B. The Setting Of The Parable

The setting of the parable of the creditor and two debtors is found in Luke 7:36-40. It is in the house of one of the sect of the Pharisees. This account should not be mistaken for a similar account in Matthew 21:7; Mark 14:3; and John 12:3. Simon was a common name in Jewry. Therefore we have Simon of Bethany, and Simon of Nain (Luke 7:11). Here we have a Pharisee by the name of Simon.

A Pharisee had invited Jesus to come for a meal to his house. Jesus was therefore the invited guest. As Jesus was sitting at the table, and as custom was, probably in a reclining position, a woman of the city slipped into the room and began to minister to Jesus. She entered the house as an uninvited spectator. She was a woman of the city and known to be a great sinner of evil lifestyle. The things recorded of her had great significance in the eyes of Jesus.

1. She stood behind Jesus, as His **feet.**
2. She stood there **weeping** profusely.
3. She **washed** His feet with her **tears.**
4. She wiped His feet with her **hair**
5. She **kissed** His feet.
6. She opened her costly **alabaster** box.
7. She **anointed** His feet with the expensive ointment.

When the Pharisee who had invited Jesus to his house saw what the woman was doing, the thoughts of his heart were exposed to God alone, who knows the hearts and thoughts of all men. He thought and spoke within himself, saying, If Jesus was really a Prophet, He would **know** what sort of the woman this was who was touching Him. The woman was a sinner, notoriously wicked; in other words, a prostitute. The Old Testament law clearly said that no hire or money of a whore (harlot, sodomitess) was to be brought into the house of the Lord. Such kind of people were an abomination to the Lord (Deuteronomy 23:17-18).

The Pharisees, in Christ's time, thanked God every day of their life that they were not born "a dog, a Gentile or a woman." No Pharisee would let a woman of ill-repute and uncleanness touch him lest he became defiled. Jesus, perceiving the thoughts of the heart, said, Simon, I have something to say to you. His response was, Say it, Master! It is out of this setting that this short parable arises.

C. The Moral Of The Parable

It is Jesus Himself, once again, who provides us with the moral of the parable. It is very clear and found in verse 47. "The one who receives forgiveness of little, loves little; the one who receives forgiveness for much loves much." The moral of the parable is any one forgiven by Jesus of any and all sin should have the greatest attitude of gratitude.

D. The Exposition Of The Parable

1. A Certain Creditor

The certain creditor respresents God, or else the Lord Jesus Christ Himself, the forgiver of all sin. He is the Divine creditor. All mankind owes their life and existence to Him; all they are, and have and ever hope to be. The creditor represented the money-lender of that time.

2. The Two Debtors

In this parable there are two debtors. They represent two kinds of persons, as the setting of the parable reveals.

(a) The First Debtor

The one in debt of five hundred pence represents the woman here; or, in general, the irreligious sinner in debt to God; a debt incurred by sin.

(b) The Second Debtor

The one in debt of fifty pence represents Simon here. In general, he represents the religious sinner, the self-righteous or Pharisaical person; religious but unregenerate.

(c) The Debt

One debtor owed the creditor five hundred pence. The other debtor owed fifty pence, or, ten times as much as the first debtor. One owed much. One owed little. A penny in those times was a day's work. Both, however, were in debt to the creditor. The point is, that all mankind, religious or irreligious, are in debt to the Lord, whether little or much, some more, some less. All we have and ever hope to be, we owe to Him. Paul himself said, "I am a debtor..." (Romans 1:14).

4. Unable to Pay

Both the debtors were broke financially. Both had absolutely nothing to pay off their debt. The Pharisee and the woman had nothing by which they could clear themselves before God. The issue is: What could anyone ever pay to God, and who could ever pay enough to pay the debt of sin created by the Fall to a perfect, sinless, holy and righteous God? Mankind has nothing by which he can clear Himself before the Lord, the Divine creditor. In Old Testament times a creditor could take a widow's sons as slaves to pay her late husbands debts (2Kings 4:1-7). But God cannot be characterized by the standards and behaviour of human creditors, for all owe their very existence to Him.

5. Freely Forgiven

The creditor of his own free will and graciousness saw that both debtors had absolutely nothing to pay, and both would have been in debt to him indefinately. He graciously forgave them both. He freed them from their debt. He loosed them from the bondage of debt. Both were in debt. Both were unable to pay. Both were freely forgiven. How often Jesus said to people, "Your sins are forgiven..." (Matthew 9:2,5; 12:31; Mark 2:5; Luke 5:20). Forgiveness means to be released, to be loosed from bondage, to remit, to send away a person's sins.

6. Question, Answer And Marks

Jesus, who the Pharisee thought was not a real, insightful Prophet, did not realize that Jesus not only knew his heart and evil thoughts, but also the heart and thoughts of the woman, the sinner. He did not judge after the sight of His eyes, the hearing of His ears, or His natural senses. He judged by the spirit, and could discern the thoughts, intents and motives of the hearts of men. He knew what was in man (Isaiah 1;1:1-4; John 2:24-25). He was indeed THE Prophet, THE Word of God made flesh.

(a) The Question

Jesus asked Simon, after giving the short parable: "Which one of the debtors would love the creditor who forgave them the most?"

(b) The Answer

Simon answered that he supposed the one who had been forgiven the most would be the one who would undoubtedly love the most.

(c) The Marks

Jesus gave him "full marks" on his answer. He told him he had rightly judged in his hearing and understanding of the parable. The Pharisee had, however, certainly wrongly judged both Jesus and the woman and her actions towards Jesus. He was right theologically and legally,but wrong spiritually and attitudinally!

E. The Practical Application Of The Parable

In Luke 7:44-50 we have the practical application of the parable. There can be no mistaking it for Jesus Himself applied practically the lesson of the parable. The contrast between the self-righteous Pharisee and the harlot sinner is vivid. Jesus turned to face the woman and in front of her gave this stinging reproof to the Pharisee, as only Jesus could.

The contrast in the columns make this more significant.

The Pharisee-What he left undone	The Woman – What she had done
1. Jesus entered his house	The woman entered the house
2. No water to wash His feet	Stood behind Him at His feet
3. Which was custom (Genesis 18:4)	Washed His feet with her tears
4. No towel to dry His feet	Wiped His feet with her hair, woman's glory
5. No kiss given to Jesus	Kissed His feet, fondly, carressed
6. As was custom (Genesis 22:4)	Kiss of peace, friendship, adoration
7. No anointing His head with oil	Anointed His feet with ointment
8. As was custom (Psalms 23:5)	Costliest, aromantic ointment
9. Little sins forgiven	Many sins forgiven
10. Little love – Simon, religious	Loved much – deep love, regenerated

Note how Jesus said "this woman" (verses 44,45,46). The Pharisee knew what manner of woman she was. He looked on the external. For a woman to kiss a man's feet, and let her hair down in public, displaying loose hair, was a public disgrace. For a "holy man" to be even touched by such a woman of ill-repute of the city, and for her to came in by way of the open courtyard into the house at a meal time – all was such an affront to the religious, respectable Pharisee, undoubtedly seeking to impress Jesus with his hospitality. Then this woman comes and "defiles the whole scene".

The Pharisee looked on the external. Jesus looked on the internal. Jesus saw the thoughts and intents of the heart of the woman, and also of the Pharisee. The Pharisee had not even offered Jesus the common courtesies of the Eastern home. He was cold, hard-hearted, self-righteous – a Pharisee! Man looks on the outward. God looks on the heart (1Samuel 16:7).

The end result was that Jesus pronounced **forgiveness of her sins!** The ones at the table question within themselves asking, Who is this that forgives sins also? Who can forgive sins but God? They did not recognize that Jesus was God incarnate, God in the flesh, and had been given power as the Son of God to forgive sins in behalf of God His Father. He would be the Sin-bearer on Calvary, and through His sacrifice for sin, forgiveness would be available for all on the basis of genuine repentance and faith.

The Jews would forgive sins three or four times at the most (Amos 2:6). Peter felt if he forgave sins seven times, that would be great. Jesus said, forgiveness was to be seventy times seven; that is, until His second advent. The reader is referred back to The Parable of The King and His Servants (Chapter 16), on the matter of forgiveness.

Christ's final word to the woman was a word of comfort, on the basis of faith. "Your **faith** has saved you, go in **peace**." Beyond the external actions of the woman; her weeping, her tears, her wiping His feet with her hair (a woman's glory), her anointing, He saw the **saving faith** in the woman's heart and that she had received Him as her Lord, Saviour and Forgiver of sin! She was cleansed! (Ephesians 2:4-10; 4:32; Matthew 5:7).

The woman was not forgiven because she loved, but she loved Jesus because she was forgiven. John says, "We love Him, because He **first loved** us..."(1John 4:19).

Contrary to what the Pharisee thought, Jesus did know what sort of a woman she was who touched Him. He knew all men and did not need anyone to testify about man to Him. He knew what was in man (John 2:24-25). He knew Simon's proud heart. He knew the woman's humble heart. Simon's heart was legal and Pharisaical. The woman's heart was humble and a heart of faith and love in Jesus.

All of us are bankrupt debtors in the sight of God. We have all sinned and come short of the glory of God (Romans 3:23). We have nothing to pay. The Lord Jesus took our debt and on the basis of repentance and faith, freely forgives us. Our lives should be lives of faith, love and peace because of such wonderful grace.

No one can afford to be the Pharisee, and judge after the sight of the eyes, or by the external. All are guilty sinners, some more, some less, but all need His grace. Jesus is "the friend of sinners", and whether they be "respectable, religious and unregenerate sinners", or, "ungodly, irreligious and unregenerate sinners", all need His grace.

If the Lord should count our iniquities, none could stand. But "there is **forgiveness** with God, that He may be feared" (Psalm 130:1-4). Whether forgiven little, or forgiven much, we should love Him much for His marvellous grace, who first loved us. All will take their stand with the Pharisee or the woman. The moral of the story is: We must have the attitude of Jesus to all who come in deep repentance and faith to Him; that is, an attitude of gratitude for Divine forgiveness!

CHAPTER THIRTY
THE PARABLE OF THE GOOD SAMARITAN

A. The Scripture On The Parable
Luke 10:30-37

And Jesus answering said, A certain man went down from Jerusalem to Jericho, and fell among thieves, which stripped him of his raiment, and wounded him, and departed, leaving him half dead.

And by chance there came down a certain priest that way: and when he saw him, he passed by on the other side.

And likewise a Levite, when he was at the place, came and looked on him, and passed by on the other side.

But a certain Samaritan, as he journeyed, came where he was: and when he saw him, he had compassion on him,

And went to him, and bound up his wounds, pouring in oil and wine, and set him on his own beast, and brought him to an inn, and took care of him.

And on the morrow when he departed, he took out two pence, and gave them to the host, and said unto him, Take care of him; and whatsoever thou spendest more, when I come again, I will repay thee.

Which now of these three, thinkest thou, was neighbour unto him that fell among the thieves?

And he said, He that shewed mercy on him. Then said Jesus unto him, Go, and do thou likewise.

B. The Setting Of The Parable
Luke 10:25-29

And, behold, a certain lawyer stood up, and tempted him, saying, Master, what shall I do to inherit eternal life?

He said unto him, What is written in the law? how readest thou?

And he answering said, Thou shalt love the Lord thy God with all thy heart, and with all thy soul, and with all thy strength, and with all thy mind; and thy neighbour as thyself.

And he said unto him, Thou hast answered right: this do, and thou shalt live.

But he, willing to justify himself, said unto Jesus, And who is my neighbour?

These verses provide the setting for the Parable of the Good Samaritan. A certain lawyer (or scribe) was standing in the crowd and wanted to put Jesus to the test. His motive was not totally right or pure. The lawyers or scribes were the official theologians and interpreters of the law. Their whole business was occupation with the Mosaic Law in the time of Christ. Their work was to relate the law to life. This lawyer was going to test or try and prove Christ on the question of questions. He asks:"Master (Teacher), What shall I DO to inherit eternal life?" Jesus, as the Master Theologian and Hermeneutician answers his question with a question, as often was His custom.

Jesus asks a twofold question:

1. What is written in the Law? This has to do with observation.
2. How do read (understand) this? What has it taught you? This is interpretation.

The lawyer's answer showed that he did have real insight into the law of God and the Scriptures. Beneath all the laws of God is "THE law", and the bottom line was to be found in the two greatest laws, yet both laws are summed up in one word; the one law – the law of love! Note the lawyer's answer.

1. You are to **love the Lord your God** with all your heart (spiritually),

    and with all your soul (emotionally, voluntarily),

    and with all your strength (physically),

    and with all your mind (mentally, intelligently).

2. You are to **love your neighbour** as yourself.

The lawyer was caught into answering his own question. Jesus commented that he had the right answer. "You have answered right".

The lawyer has quoted from the law the two greatest of all commandments. The first commandment to "love God" is from Dueteronomy 6:5. The second commandment to "love your neighbour" is from Leviticus 19:18.

It is a similar scene, but not to be confused with, the lawyer of Matthew 19:16; 22:35-40; Mark 12:28-34; Luke 18:18. In these Scriptures, the lawyer tests Christ by asking Him which is the great commandment of the law. Christ Himself answered by quoting the two commandments of (1) love to God as the first and greatest commandment, and (2) to love your neighbour as yourself is the second great commandment. On these two commandments hang all the law and the prophets.

The problem in the present setting was the lawyer had **the right answer** but **the wrong interpretation** of the commandments, especially the "love your neighbour as yourself" commandment. Jesus said, "You answer is right: do this and you will live". If you want to do something to inherit eternal life, then DO this – love God and love your neighbour as yourself and you will gain eternal life! Jesus knew how impossible this was for fallen man, but the lawyer did not know it.

The lawyer unwittingly exposed what was in his heart. He was out to justify himself, and so he asks another question: "And **who** is my **neighbour?**" It was a 'loaded' question. It was not about the first commandment, as there was no question in his mind about love to God. It was about the second commandment – about love of a neighbour!

Jesus, in the "Sermon on the Mount" had said, "You have heard that it has been said, You shall love your neighbour and hate your enemy, But I say to you, Love your enemies..." (Matthew 5:43-48; Luke 6:27; Romans 12:14).

The Jews counted their fellow Jews as "neighbours", but no Gentile was a neighbour. They were Gentile dogs. So when the lawyer challenged Jesus by asking, "Who is my neighbour?", Jesus gave him the parable of the good Samaritan. For, under the New Covenant laws, there would be a higher law of love; not only to love your neighbour, but also to love your enemies! This was indeed "a new kind of love".

This is the setting in which the parable is given, both to the lawyer and those around who would be listening to Jesus.

C. The Moral Of The Parable

Jesus Himself provides the moral of the parable in Luke 10:37b to this lawyer, and to us all. It is this. Any person in need is our neighbour, regardless of race or culture.

To really love our neighbour as ourself is to show practical mercy and help in their time of need. The good Samaritan has given us the practical example of what we should do.

D. The Exposition Of The Parable

There is absolutely no doubt that Jesus, in the giving of this parable, carefully chose His words, packing the parable with Divine thoughts. It was a very true-to-life parable, and the hearers would have no problem identifying with its contents. Behind the common and every-day elements in this kind of story, there are also timeless spiritual truths being conveyed by the Lord Jesus. It is more of what may be called "a typical parable" than "a symbolic parable". It certainly has a more personal touch than symbolical touch or elements in it. Most expositors, even though they fear falling into allegorization, do glean several lessons from the story, and not merely one moral.

1. A Certain Man

The certain man could be any person, any man or woman. It would seem here that the certain man was undoubtedly a Hebrew, or a Jew travelling.

2. Went Down

Geographically accurate, as one always went "up" to Jerusalem, and travellers always went "down" to Jericho (Acts 18:22). From Jerusalem to Jericho was seventeen miles travelling.

3. From Jerusalem

In spiritual lesson, Jerusalem means "Vision of Peace", and some writers interpret it as "City of Righteousness and Peace" ("Jeru = "Righteousness", and Salem = "Peace"). It was the seat of blessing in history and the city of God, where the tribes would go up to worship in festival times (Psalm 122). One must have to remember all that Jerusalem represented in the Jewish (or Hebrew) mind. Here the name of the Lord dwelt. Here the temple of God stood and all the sacrificial, ceremonial and worship ministry of the priests took place here.

In Scripture, the Lord often used geographical directions to symbolize spiritual directions also. Thus Abraham went "down" into Egypt in time of famine, and after much distress over Sarah, the Lord caused him to go "up" out of Egypt, back to the place of his altar, tent, and to calling on the name of the Lord at Bethel (Read Genesis 12-13 chapters for details). Here Abraham came back to God's will.

Jonah also went "down" to Tarshish as he fled from the will of God and the presence of the Lord (Jonah 1). The geographical points to the spiritual and symbolical truth. This man went "down" from Jerusalem, and all that is represented in spiritual/symbolic truth in the city of God, the city of righteousness and peace. Here God recorded His name; here the temple of the Lord and its Divine services took place.

4. To Jericho

Jericho means "the city of palms"(2Chronicles 28:5-15). Here was the first city conquered by Joshua and Israel as they entered the promised land. Out of this city, Rahab the harlot, and her household came into faith and into the Israel of God (Joshua 2). Here at this city, Joshua had the revelation of the Lord as

Captain of the Lord's Hosts (Joshua 5:13). Here, as the priests with the trumpets, and the people of God, marched around the city for seven days, the walls fell flat by the power of God (Joshua 6).

Joshua placed a curse on the city and anyone who would rebuild it would do it at the cost of the death of their firstborn (Joshua 6:26). In time (about BC.930), Hiel the Bethelite build Jericho, defying Joshua's prophetic word, and his firstborn, Abiram, suffered the judgment of death (1Kings 16:34).

Later on, there was a school of the prophets there. Jericho was beautiful for situation with its palm trees. The city became a priestly city where some priests lived when not in their course at the temple in Jerusalem (2Kings 2:4-5). Thus Jericho had an evil beginning, but in Christ's time, it was a priestly city, and like any city, had the good and the evil in it. The certain man in the parable is going "down" to Jericho.

5. **Fell Among Thieves**

The road from Jerusalem to Jericho was a dangerous road to travel on. There was a rocky and dangerous gorge. The hills were infested with robbers and thieves and travel was very unsafe. Jesus said the thieves and robbers come to rob, to kill and to destroy (Read John 10:1,8,10 with Hosea 6:9). Satan is a thief and a robber. We see what the thieves did to him on the Jericho road.

(a) **Stripped Him of His Raiment**

His covering garment. In spiritual truth, Satan and his demonic 'thieves' come to strip mankind of the garments of salvation, righteousness and praise (Isaiah 61:10). Satan stripped Adam and Eve of their garment of light in Eden and they found they were naked in the presence of a holy God (Genesis 3:1-6).

(b) **Wounded him**

Wounds by beating were inflicted on this certain man by the violence of these thieves. Satan and his demonic 'thieves' inflict great wounds on mankind. Isaiah speaks of man's fallen condition as being covered with "wounds, and bruises and putrifying sores". From the crown of his head to the soles of his feet, man has been wounded by Satan and sin (Isaiah 1:5-6).

(c) **Left him half-dead**

The thieves departed, leaving this certain man half-dead. Though half-dead, he was also half-alive; not totally dead. Where there is life, there is hope. He was helpless to help himself, but he was not hopeless. Mankind, spiritually, is half-dead; dead in trespasses and sins (Ephesians 2:1). But he is alive physically and God can come and rescue him from full death.

6. **A Certain Priest**

By chance, or co-incidence, a certain unnamed priest went that way. The story does not tell us which way he was going. He could have been going home from temple services or he could have been on his way to temple services. The priest is of the Aaronic Priesthood. He saw him and passed by on the other side of the road.

The priest represents the temple ministry, the services of sacrifice, and the law of Moses – the Law Covenant. He is the ecclesiastical ministry of that time.

Generally priests would not be attacked by thieves, for superstitious or other reasons. The priests were supported by the tithes and offerings of the people. They were the spiritual leaders of the Jewish nation.

But here, there was no feeling of mercy in the heart of the priest. He left the man as he saw him. He knew the law, professed to uphold the law, but, for whatever reason, he declined to help the poor man. There was no manifest compassion evidenced in this priest. According to the law, if a priest became defiled by "a dead body", he was unclean for seven days, and could not minister in the temple services (Leviticus 21:1; Ezekiel 44:25; Numbers 19:11-13). Perhaps this was the reason for his by-passing the half-dead man. It speaks of religious failure. The priest thought more of his religious services than a man in desparate need.

7. A Certain Levite

A certain Levite also came by the place. We do not know whether he was going to Jerusalem or Jericho, whether he was coming or going. He looked on the poor, half-dead man and did like the priest, and passed by on the other side. At least he looked at him!

The Levites were the servants of the temple priests for temple services, and instruction in the law of the Lord to the people. They were also spiritual leaders. All priests were Levites but not all Levites were priests, though all were of the priestly tribe. They also were supported by the tithes and offerings of the people. They were supposed to serve the Lord, the priests and the Jewish people.

Again it is possible that the Levite did not want to become ceremonially defiled by touching "a dead body" and therefore, not be able to attend to religious duties in the temple for seven days (Leviticus 21:1; Numbers 19:11-14). Perhaps he was in the temple choir and felt that was more important!

The issue is, both the priest and the Levite, temple ministries, revealed the heartless and religiousness of their profession. There was no compassion, just religion!

8. A Certain Samaritan

Jesus now tells them about "a certain Samaritan" – not a certain Israelite, or a certain Jew! The Samaritans were counted as mongrel nations, half-castes who inter-married with Israelites and corrupted them further. When the House of Israel was taken into Assyrian Captivity (BC 721), various nationalities were placed in the cities of Israel, and became known as "the Samaritans". They had their own worship, their religion, their temple at Mt Gerazim (2Kings 17). The Jews had no dealings with the Samaritans (John 4:9). The religious leaders called Jesus "a Samaritan", and that He had a demon (John 8:48-49). It was no compliment, but a great insult. They were Gentile dogs to the Jews and outside the camp of Judaism. For Jesus to bring in "the certain Samaritan" at this point of the story was a remarkable touch of sattire, to get His point across to the 'loaded' question of the lawyer.

As this certain Samaritan journeyed, he also came where the half-dead man was, and when he saw him, he had compassion of him. In verse 37 it says he had mercy on him. We note some of the important wording that Jesus used about this certain Samaritan.

(a) He came where he was

He came to where the man was. He did not pass by on the other side of the road. He saw his terrible condition; he saw him as he was. So does the Lord Jesus see mankind, just as we are, just where we are. He also came near to us, just where we are. He did not by pass us on the other side of the road!

(b) He had compasion on him

This Gentile Samaritan did not let race, culture or prejudice affect his feelings for a fellow-man in need. What a contrast to the religious priest and Levite. This is why he is called "the good Samaritan", because he had compassion on the poor man. It is possible the poor, half-dead man was a Jew. The Samaritan ignored the fact that he may have been of a different race, or culture. This is the heart of it all – COMPASSION!

Generally the word "compassion" is mainly used of Jesus in the New Testament, and much of the Lord God in the Old Testament. Compassion is a quality in the very being and heart of God towards His creatures, especially fallen mankind.

He is full of compassion (Psalm 86:15; 111:4; 145:8). Jesus was often moved with compassion and healed people out of such compassion (Matthew 9:36; 14:14; 20:24; Hebrews 5:2; 1Peter 3:8). He wants that same compassion to be in our hearts as in His heart.

(c) He went to him

As he came where he was, and saw him as he was, he went to him. There was no by passing on the other side of the road. Here was someone in need of help. That was all that mattered. No questions asked. He went to him.

(d) Bound up his wounds

The man undoubtedly was bleeding, broken and bruised by the thieves. Infection could have set in. He bound up the wounds caused by the evil thieves. Satan and sin has inflicted great wounds on mankind; spiritually, mentally, emotionally, physically and these need to be bound up by Jesus.

(e) Poured in oil and Wine

Oil would soothe the pains, wounds and bruises of the poor, half-dead man. It speaks of healing, and is symbolic of the Holy Spirit's power in a person's life.

Wine, the life blood of the grapes, was used as an anti-septic in ancient times. It would disinfect the wounds in the body. It speaks of the life-blood of the New Covenant.

"Oil and wine" are spoken of in Scripture in both natural and spiritual meanings, as these references show (Numbers 18:12; Micah 6:15; Hosea 2:22). The Lord says in Revelation: "See you hurt not the **oil** and the **wine**" (Revelation 6:6). Oil and wine were used much in the offerings of the Lord (Exodus 29:40; Leviticus 23:13; Numbers 18:12; Deuteronomy 11:14). The Psalmist speaks of "wine that makes glad the heart of man, and oil that makes his face shine" (Psalm 104:15).

(f) Set him on his own beast

The wounded man would be too weak to walk. The wounded man would not have to carry the beast, the beast (perhaps a donkey) would carry him. It spoke of support of another, being upheld by the strength of another when he was weak and strengthless. He would depend on the power of another, not his own.

(g) Bought him to an inn

The inn was the place where they would take care of him. It continued as the place of healing and health. It would be a place of shelter and security and safety. In spiritual sense, it could speak of a home, a haven, or the church, where those who have fallen among thieves of Satan's hosts can be cared for.

(h) Took care of him

The poor man would know that someone cared for him. The Psalmist said,"No one cared for my soul" (Psalm 142:4). But here there would be care. This was the command of the good Samaritan. The shepherd cares for his sheep. The hireling does not care (John 10:13). The priest and the Levite were care-less!

In the church (God's inn), we are to care one for another (1Corinthians 12:25; 2Corinthians 11:28; Philippians 2:20).

(i) Departed on the morrow

The certain Samaritan did not stay at the inn to look after the man personally. He left and continued on his journey on the morrow.

(j) Took out two pence

Two pence, in those times, was two days wages. So for at least, two days, there was enough finance to care for the man and see him restored to full and complete health again. All this was out of compassion. The poor man did not earn it, or merit it. He could not pay for it. He has been robbed of everything, almost to his very life. He was totally dependant on the good Samaritan and his mercy, grace and compassion to cover his costs.

(k) Gave them to the host

The host represented those in the inn who would care for guests who came in their travel times. They would be responsible to protect, feed and care for all who came to their inn. In spiritual sense, God has placed in the church (His inn) various ministries who are to care for those the Lord brings in from the hard world and thieves of mankind. The "host" can represent the oversight, the five-fold ascension gift ministries that the Lord has set in His church to care for the members (Ephesians 4:9-16).

(l) Word to take care of him

The good Samaritan gave the word to the host to "take care of him". The man would need a lot of care to restore him to health and strength, to bring him back to fullness of life again. The host must do what the good Samaritan said as he was covering the cost of it all.

(m) Whatever you spend more

Whatever it would cost, the wounded man must be cared for. Beyond the two pennies, there is more cost in the caring for those who have been wounded and bruised and left half-dead by Satan's thieves. Regardless of the cost, the good Samaritan would pay for it all, out of his own heart of grace and compassion.

(n) When I come again

The good Samaritan promised to come again. He would check to see how the host had looked after the man, how he had been taken care of. His journey would be to and from and back again to the inn. The inn-keeper would be held accountable.

Undoubtedly, Jesus alludes to Himself, who had been called "a Samaritan" from time to time. He was the One who had compassion on the people, and He indeed said He would "come again" (John14:3; Acts 1:10-11; 1Thessalonians 4:16,17).

(o) I will repay you

It would be reward enough for the host to be paid for caring for the wounded man, seeing him restored to health and life again. But the good Samaritan promised to repay any further costs involved in this ministry.

The contrast is seen in the action of the three men:

The Priest	The Levite	The Good Samaritan
Came that way	Came that way	Came where he was
Passed by	Looked on him	He saw him
On the other side	Passed on other side	Had compassion on him
		Bound up wounds
		Poured in oil and wine
		Set him on his own beast
		Brought him to an inn
		Gave two pence to host
		Take care of him
		When I come again
		I will repay you

E. The Practical Application Of The Parable

In Luke 10:36-37, Jesus brings both the moral and practical application home to the tempting lawyer. He faces him with responsibility. Jesus asks, Of these three, who do you think was a true neighbour to the man who fell among thieves? The lawyer answered rightly: The one who showed mercy! He probably did not like to say "the Samaritan!"

Jesus said: You go and do likewise! This is truly loving your neighbour as yourself. If you do this you shall live! (Deuteronomy 5:33; 6:14; Leviticus 18:5).

There are a number of Scriptures in the Old Testament which the lawyer knew, but he applied them only to his "Jewish neighbours", not to Gentile dogs! He "loved his (Jewish) neighbour, and hated his (Gentile) enemy".

The Israelites were to take a lamb for their house and their neighbour (Exodus 12:4).

They were not to bear false witness against their neighbour (Exodus 20:6). They were not to covet their neighbour's house, their neighbour's wife, or their possessions (Exodus 20:17). They were responsible to keep their neighbour's stuff if entrusted with it (Exodus 22:7-14).

They were to love their neighbour as themselves (Leviticus 19:18). They were not to remove their neighbour's landmarks (Deuteronomy 19:14; 27:17).

Jesus enlarged the commandment beyond just "Jewish neighbours" to include "Gentile neighbours" (Matthew 5:43; 19:19; 22:39; Mark 12:33; Romans 13:9-10; Galatians 5:14; James 2:8). This was revolutionary. It was New Covenant kind of love, grace and compassion, which the lawyer did not have, and knew nothing about!

In summary of this, John puts it this way. How can we say that we love God, who we do not see, and not love our brother (neighbour) who we do see? Loving God and loving our neighbour as ourself is the fulfilment of the commandments of the Lord. On these TWO commandments hang all the law and the prophets. LOVE is the fulfilling of the law. Love is expressed in practical care for anyone in need, Jew or Gentile, saved or unsaved (1John 4:12,20; Matthew 22:35-40).

Conclusion:-

A number of expositors seem to recognize that there is a deeper picture behind the parabolic story of the good Samaritan, and that Jesus alludes to Himself in a subtle way, as the religious leaders called him "a Samaritan". In fact, Jesus several times refers to the Samaritans in a positive sense. Of the ten lepers that were healed, nine were Jews and the one who returned and gave thanks was "a Samaritan" (Luke 17:16-18). Here in this parable, it is the "good Samaritan" who showed compassion to the man in need (Luke 10:33).

Behind the parabolic story, all is a picture of mankind, who went down from the city of God and fell among Satanic thieves. Mankind was stripped of his garment of righteousness, left wounded, bruised and half-dead; spiritually dead, but physically alive.

The Law, both moral and ceremonial, represented in the religion of priest and Levite, could do nothing to save man from complete death. Jesus, "the good Samaritan", journeyed from heaven to earth. He came where man was in the incarnation. He saw mankind's sick and dying condition. He had compassion. He poured in the oil of the Holy Spirit and the wine of joy in salvation, made possible by His sacrifice on the cross. He took us by the power of the Holy Spirit to His inn- the church! There He commanded the oversight to take care of the people entrusted to them. Jesus journeyed back to heaven in His ascension. He will cover all expenses needed to care for mankind. When He comes again, as He surely will, He will reward those who have truly cared for their neighbours. He will reward those who have loved God, who they have not seen and loved their neighbours, who they do see!

CHAPTER THIRTY-ONE
THE PARABLE OF THE THREE FRIENDS

A. The Scripture On The Parable
Luke 11:5-8

And he said unto them, Which of you shall have a friend, and shall go unto him at midnight, and say unto him, Friend, lend me three loaves;

For a friend of mine in his journey is come to me, and I have nothing to set before him?

And he from within shall answer and say, Trouble me not: the door is now shut, and my children are with me in bed; I cannot rise and give thee.

I say unto you, Though he will not rise and give him, because he is his friend, yet because of his importunity he will rise and give him as many as he needeth.

B. The Setting Of The Parable
Luke 11:1-4

And it came to pass, that, as he was praying in a certain place, when he ceased, one of his disciples said unto him, Lord, teach us to pray, as John also taught his disciples.

And he said unto them, When ye pray, say, Our Father which art in heaven, Hallowed be thy name. Thy kingdom come. Thy will be done, as in heaven, so in earth.

Give us day by day our daily bread.

And forgive us our sins; for we also forgive every one that is indebted to us. And lead us not into temptation; but deliver us from evil.

The setting of the Parable of the Three Friends is in the context of Christ's example and teaching on prayer.

Jesus had been praying in a certain place. When His time of prayer had finished, one of the disciples said, Lord, teach us to pray as John also taught his disciples to pray. In response to this request, Jesus taught them what is commonly called "The Lord's Prayer". It is more properly "The Disciples Prayer", for Jesus Himself had no need to pray this prayer, as the perfect, sinless Son of God, in unbroken relationship with His Father. The proper "Lord's Prayer" is found in John Chapter 17. However, we note some of the most important things about prayer in the setting for the parable Christ gave about the three friends.

1. **Jesus was a man of prayer – Verse 1**

   Luke records a number of times the prayer life of Jesus, as these few references show (Luke 5:16; 6:12; 9:28,29; 22:32,41,44). The student is referred to the Concordance for other references to Christ's prayer life and His relationship with the Father.

2. **John the Baptist was a man of prayer – Verse 1**

   John the Baptist also was a praying man. He taught his disciples to pray, as a master generally taught the disciples how and what to do as they were either attracted to him or called by him.

3. **The Disciples asked Jesus to teach them to pray – Verse 1**

   They did not ask Him to teach them "how to preach" but "how to pray". Prayer needs to be taught. People need to be taught to pray and how to pray.

4. The Disciples Prayer – Verses 2-4 with Matthew 6:9-15

This prayer is a sample and model prayer, containing in it the basic ingredients of prayer. Luke and Matthew provide the words for us. It is not that the Lord necessarily wanted His disciples to simply "mouth" or "word the prayer", but to follow the basic principles given in the prayer. This is done so many times in various services throughout the church world. Yet, many times, it is prayed with the mouth and not from the heart. True prayer is from the heart, and not merely the mouth!

The Disciples Prayer has been outlined in various ways by preachers and teachers alike. The following is a sample of this.

(a) The Godward Parts

The Paternal	Our Father which is in heaven
The Presence	Hallowed be Your name
The Priority	Your kingdom come
The Principle	Your will be done in earth as it is in heaven

(b) The Manward Part

The Provision	Give us day by day our daily bread
The Pardon	Forgive us our debts as we forgive our debtors
The Protection	Lead us not into temptation, but deliver us from evil
The Power	Yours is the kingdom, the power and glory
The Praise	For ever and ever, Amen.

It is out of this context of prayer that Jesus gave the Parable of the Three Friends. It is actually a "prayer parable".

C. The Moral Of The Parable

The lesson that is to be learnt from the parable is persistency in prayer. In prayer, we are to be insistent, consistent and persistent. It took the friend in need such to keep knocking, asking and seeking until his prayer was answered. If human beings will answer to this kind of importunity in their requests, how much more shall the heavenly Father meet the need of His own children.

D. The Exposition Of The Parable

The story of the parable is a simple and true-to-life story. It is the request of a friend to a friend for a friend. One friend comes in his journey to his friend at the hour of midnight. So he rushes off to his friend and told him the dilemma. His friend is in bed with the children and said he was not going to get out of bed for anyone that hour of the night. The friend persisted asking for three loaves of bread so he could meet the hospitality need of his friend at the midnight hour. The friend arose and gave him the bread – NOT because he was his friend, but because of his "shameless insistence and persistence" (Amplified New Testament).

It is indeed the parable concerning three friends, and its moral is to teach us to be insistent and consistent in prayer. The heavenly Father is much more willing to provide food for His own as they are consistent in prayer.

For the purpose of our exposition, we consider each of these friends and discover what further lessons can be gained from this simple parable. We will liken the three friends to (1) The Saviour, (2) The Saint and (3) The Sinner.

1. The Friend indeed – The Saviour

The first "friend" we consider may be likened to Jesus, the Saviour Friend. One of the charges levelled at Jesus by the Pharisees was "that this Man is a FRIEND of publicans and sinners" (Matthew 11:16-19; Luke 7:31-35; Matthew 9:10-13; Mark 2:15-17; Luke 15:1-10). The Pharisees were exactly the opposite. They were cold, hard, religious, legalistic and most unfriendly.

The word "friend" is **"philos"** (Grk. Strong's SC584), and means, "dear, ie., a friend; act. fond, ie., friendly (still as a noun, an associate, neighbour, etc:- friend. The word is used some fourteen times in the Gospel of Luke. It speaks of someone we love, someone dear, someone who is a real friend and friendly. Jesus was all that. He was a friend of sinners, though He was separate from sinners (Hebrew 7:26).

We may ask: How was Jesus a friend of sinners?

* Jesus called sinners to repentance (Matthew 9:13; Mark 2:16-17; Luke 5:32).

* Jesus was a guest with sinners (Luke 19:7). Zachaeus was such a sinner.

* Jesus came into the world to save sinners (1Timothy 1:15).

* Jesus forgave sinners (Luke 7:36-50).

* Jesus received sinners: This Man receives sinners (Luke 15:1-2).

He loved them, was friendly to them, to win them to the kingdom of God, and bring them into relationship with the Father through Himself. Jesus mingled with them, ate and drank with them. But, though "a friend of sinners", He was "separate from sinners".

Though Jesus mingled with sinners (which the Pharisees shunned to do), there was always that inner separation from sin, because He was "holy, harmless, undefiled and separate from sinners" (Hebrews 7:26).

The Amplified says: "Here is the high priest (perfectly adapted) to our needs, as was fitting, holy, blameless, unstained by sin, separated from sinners and exalted higher than the heavens". The Greek word **"chorizo"**, translated **"separate"** (Strong's SC5563) gives the idea of "empty expance; room, ie., a space of territory; to place room between, ie., part; reflex, to go away, depart, put asunder, separate". So there was that "room between" Jesus, as a friend of sinners, yet separate from sin.

Vine's Expository Dictionary says: "Separated from sinners" by His resurrection, and exalted higher than the heavens, by His ascension and translation!

In the Song of Solomon (Song 5:16), the bride speaks to the daughters of Jerusalem about the bridegroom, and after describing His beauties and glories, she says, "This is my beloved, and this is my friend" (Song 5:1-16a).

The famous Gospel Song, "What a Friend we have in Jesus" was written by Joseph Scriven, born in Dublin, Ireland, in 1820 before he moved to Canada.

His fiancee was drowned on the eve of their intended marriage, and this led to a lonely life. A friend visiting him in a time of illness found the manuscript poem, and inquired as to its origin. Scriven replied that he had written it to comfort his mother in a time of sorrow (1885), and that he had never intended anyone else to see it. The friend made a copy and it soon appeared in religious periodicals. The music was composed in 1870 by Charles C. Converse. It was the Sankey revival meetings that made the Gospel Song so famous, even as it is still in the church world today.

Jesus is indeed the "friend of sinners", a friend in deed and in truth! He is our Saviour Friend!

2. The Friend in need – The Saint

The next "friend" in the parable we liken to a Christian friend. He is the friend in need. The Bible speaks of believers as being friends of God, friends of Jesus, as these references show.

Abraham was called "the friend of God", for even God spoke of Abraham as "My friend" (James 2:23; 2Chronicles 20:7; Isaiah 41:8).

John the Baptist was the friend of Jesus, the friend of the bridegroom, and rejoiced to hear the bridegroom's voice (John 3:29).

Jesus called His disciples His friends, and He laid down His life for His friends (John15:13). He said, "You are My friends if you do what I command you. I have not called you servants, but friends" (John 15:14-15). Christ Jesus is our friend. We are His friends. Believers also should be friends, one of another.

Proverbs 18:24 says, "There is a friend that sticks closer than a brother". And "faithful are the wounds of a friend" (Proverbs 27:6). Yet again, "A friend loves at all times, and a brother is born for adversity" (Proverbs 17:17).

In the parables concerning the lost sheep and the lost coin, both the shepherd and the woman, when they had found the lost, called their friends and neighbours to rejoice together with them over the lost being found. So there is joy over the finding of "lost sinners". As Jesus had the quality of friendliness to sinners, so should Christians be friends of sinners, yet separate from their sinful lifestyle. A Christian becomes a friend of sinners to bring them to Jesus THE Friend of sinners – the Saviour-Friend!

3. The Friend to feed – The Sinner

The third "friend" may be likened to the sinner friend, the friend to feed! The Christian is called, not only to be the friend of Jesus, but also the friend of sinners, as Jesus was.

The friend in the parable was hungry. He wanted and needed food. He needed bread. He needed something to eat. Note the use of "bread" in verses 3,5,11. Every sinner is hungry for something. Man was created to be filled with God. If man is not filled with God, then they will feed on the husks of this world's food.

It is spoken of as "the bread of wickedness" (Proverbs 4:17), and "the bread of deceit" (Proverbs 20:17), and "the bread of idlleness" (Proverbs 31:27). It is eaten to satisfy the emptiness within man's heart and life.

Jesus said He was "the bread of heaven" (John 6 with Psalm 105:40; 132:15). He is the Divine and heavenly manna – God's food for man. As believers, all need to seek to become, as Jesus was, involved in "friendship evangelism", building relationships with sinners to lead them to the Lord, THE Friend of sinners. As has been said, Everybody cannot witness to everybody, but everybody can witness to somebody!

Every believer has different circles of contacts, at work, at business, in the neighbourhood, at school, or college, and other places. All have opportunity to be friendly towards sinners, who are lost souls, going into a Christless eternity, going to hell to be with Satan for eternity.

There are some friendships the Bible says we are to avoid. In Proverbs 22:24 it says, "Make no friendship with an angry man, lest you become like unto him". In James 4:4 it says, "The friendship of the world is enmity with God". James is speaking of the evil, world system. The apostle Paul tells us, "Do not be so deceived and misled! Evil companionships (communion, associations) corrupt good manners and morals and character "(Amplified. 1Corinthians 15:33).

However, it should be remembered that the believer is not asked to go out of the world, but to be kept from the evil that is in the world (1Corinthians 5:9-11 with John 17:15). So believers should be the friend of sinners, yet there is that separation (space between) from sinners in their evils, even as Jesus was. It is not Pharisaical separation, or necessarily physical separation, but that inner and spiritual separation from sin.

4. The Friend to Friend – Three Loaves

The Christian friend finds "he has nothing" to set before the sinner friend. "I have nothing to set before him". It was that sense of inadequacy, emptiness, nothingness in himself. The friend had come at midnight and this friend had nothing to set before him.

The custom was that bread would be baked daily, eaten and gone by midnight. But hospitality was part of the culture, and it was a shame for anyone to come to someones place and no food be available for hospitality, the common courtesy of life.

Christians, of themselves, have nothing to give. But Jesus has all to give to us that we may give to others. The friend in the parable, goes to his friend, and he is shameless and persistent in his asking for "three loaves of bread". It is also the "midnight hour". Both of these phrases provide much food for thought in the Scriptures.

(a) The Midnight Hour

The friend had been asleep for several hours, the doors are locked and barred, and the children are asleep. It was a very awkward hour, a dreadful hour of the night to be wakened up, with someone knocking at the door, asking, insistently for three loaves of bread. The whole house could be wakened by this man.

The midnight hour in Scripture always points to the end of this age, when darkness abounds in the earth. Many significant things took place at the midnight hour in the Bible.

* At midnight the death-angel went throughout Egypt and all who did not have the blood of the Passover lamb on their door experienced the judgment of God (Exodus 11:4; 12:29).

* At the midnight hour, Samson took the gates of the city away (Judges 16:3).

* At the midnight hour, Ruth, the bride-to-be, lay at the feet of Boaz, her kinsman redeemer (Ruth 3:8).

* Midnight can be a time of trouble (Job 34:20), or praise (Psalm 119:62).

* At the midnight hour, the virgins had to arise and trim their lamps to meet the coming bridegroom (Matthew 25:6; Mark 13:35).

And here in this short parable, it is the midnight hour that the friend comes to his friend for bread for his friend. The church is living in the midnight hour, the time of the end, waiting for the coming of the Lord.

(b) The Three Loaves

In Genesis 18:1-8 we have the first occasion of "three loaves". It is here that Abraham asked his wife, Sarah, to prepare three loaves for the heavenly guests, the three angels. Undoubtedly this was a revelation of God to Abraham. Sarah prepared the required three loaves for each person in this angelic visitation.

In the parable here, once again we have the "three loaves". Three is the number of the Godhead; Father, Son and Holy Spirit. In symbolic truth, "three loaves" speak of the fulness of the Godhead, the Divine food for needy man. (The reader is reminded and referred back to the Parable of the Woman and the Leaven and the "three measures of meal").

So the Christian friend is to go to Jesus, his friend, and ask for Divine bread to give to the sinner friend who comes to him hungering after reality! That is the picture that may be seen in this simple parable.

E. The Practical Application Of The Parable

At the conclusion of the parable, Jesus now gives the practical application and spiritual lessons that may be learnt from it. This is seen in the Gospels of Luke and Matthew.

Luke 11:9-13

And I say unto you, Ask, and it shall be given you; seek, and ye shall find; knock, and it shall be opened unto you.

For every one that asketh receiveth; and he that seeketh findeth; and to him that knocketh it shall be opened.

If a son shall ask bread of any of you that is a father, will he give him a stone? or if he ask a fish, will he for a fish give him a serpent?

Or if he shall ask an egg, will he offer him a scorpion?

If ye then, being evil, know how to give good gifts unto your children: how much more shall your heavenly Father give the Holy Spirit to them that ask him?

Matthew 7:7-11

Ask, and it shall be given you; seek, and ye shall find; knock, and it shall be opened unto you:

For every one that asketh receiveth; and he that seeketh findeth; and to him that knocketh it shall be opened.

Or what man is there of you, whom if his son ask bread, will he give him a stone?

Or if he ask a fish, will he give him a serpent?

If ye then, being evil, know how to give good gifts unto your children, how much more shall your Father which is in heaven give good things to them that ask him?

If a son asks bread of his natural father, will he receive a stone? At Satan's temptation of Jesus, he tempted Him to turn stones to bread (Luke 4:1-4). If a son asks his natural father for a fish, will he give him a serpent? If a son asks his natural father for an egg, will he give him a scorpion?

The answer is evident. A natural father wants to give his son good food; bread, or fish or an egg. The application is in verse 13. If evil or natural fathers would only give **good gifts** to their children, **how much more** shall the heavenly Father give the **gift of the Holy Spirit** to them that ask Him, and not give an evil spirit (a stone, a serpent, or scorpion)?

When people come to receive the promise of the Father – the baptism of the Holy Spirit – they need have no room for fear that they will receive a hard stone, a slippery serpent or a deadly scorpion or anything that is evil. The Father is good and gives good gifts to His children. The word is to keep on asking, seeking and knocking and the door shall be opened.

Jesus speaks of the "importunity" of prayer. This is the only place in the Greek New Testament where the word is used. Generally the expositors believe it to mean "shamelessness, insistence, persistence, impudence, and troublesome" kind of prayer! It speaks of stubbornness or unreasonable persistence in prayer – a prayer that does not give up until it is answered! It is not for yourself, but for others in need and this makes it the more persistent kind of praying.

By a play on the English word 'ask', we would see the following, which is implicit in the Greek thought.

    A = Ask and keep on asking!

    S = Seek and keep on seeking!

    K = Knock and keep on knocking until the door is opened to you!

Jesus is our friend. Believers are our friends. Sinners are friends in need, that need the bread of life. Except they partake of Him, they will die. Believers must go to Jesus, and in prayer, ask for the Divine manna to feed those sinner friends who come hungry for reality! These are lessons that may be learnt by the simple parable. The major truth, of course, concerns insistence in prayer, but these are spiritual truths applicable to our lives.

Conclusion:-

A tract printed some years back speaks of an unconverted sinner, standing before the throne of God's judgment. He turns to his friend, who was a Christian, and said to him, "What sort of a friend are you? You never told me about God's throne of judgment, and heaven and hell?" The poem expresses it all.

MY FRIEND

My friend, I stand in the judgment now, And feel that you're to blame somehow,

On earth, I walked with you day by day, And never did you point the way,

You knew the Lord in truth and glory, But never did you tell the story,

My knowledge then was very dim, You could have led me safe to HIM.

Though we lived together on the earth, You never told me of the second birth,

And now I stand this day condemned, Because you failed to mention HIM,

You taught me many things, that's true, I called you friend and trusted you,

But I learnt now that it's too late, You could have kept me from this fate.

We walked by day and talked by night, And yet you showed me not the light.

You let me live and love and die, You knew I'd never live on high,

Yes, I called you "Friend" in life, And trusted you through joy and strife,

And yet on coming to the end, I cannot now call you MY FRIEND!

(Author – Unknown)

The challenge is to consistency in prayer; asking, seeking and knocking, and a trust in the goodness of the heavenly Father. But, beneath the parable are the lessons of the "three friends". What kind of a friend are you? Jesus wants us to be His friends, and, as He was, also a friend of sinners, to lead them to Himself, and give to them the bread of eternal life, through "friendship evangelism", one of the greatest ways to bring people to Christ!

CHAPTER THIRTY-TWO
THE PARABLE OF THE RICH FOOL

A. The Scripture On The Parable
Luke 12:16-21

> And he spake a parable unto them, saying, The ground of a certain rich man brought forth plentifully:

> And he thought within himself, saying, What shall I do, because I have no room where to bestow my fruits?

> And he said, This will I do: I will pull down my barns, and build greater; and there will I bestow all my fruits and my goods.

> And I will say to my soul, Soul, thou hast much goods laid up for many years; take thine ease, eat, drink, and be merry.

> But God said unto him, Thou fool, this night thy soul shall be required of thee: then whose shall those things be, which thou hast provided?

> So is he that layeth up treasure for himself, and is not rich toward God.

B. The Setting Of The Parable
Luke 12:13-15

> And one of the company said unto him, Master, speak to my brother, that he divide the inheritance with me.

> And he said unto him, Man, who made me a judge or a divider over you?

> And he said unto them, Take heed, and beware of covetousness: for a man's life consisteth not in the abundance of the things which he possesseth.

In verses 13-15, Jesus is ministering to the people. Some one in the crowd asked Jesus to speak to his brother to divide the inheritance with him. In response to the hearer's question, Jesus told him that He was not a judge, or in position to divide inheritances. That really belonged to the father of the sons, or else it would have to settled in a court. Custom was that the father's inheritance was divided after his death. On some occasions, the father would give the portion of his inheritance to his sons while yet alive, as in the case of the parable of the prodigal son, at the son's request for his portion.

Perhaps Jesus discerned a motive of covetousness in the man, because it is out of this setting that He gave a warning against covetousness and looking for the abundance of material possessions. True life is not to be found in material things, but in that which is eternal, heavenly and spiritual.

C. The Moral Of The Parable

Jesus Himself gives us the moral of the parable, both preceding the parable and also concluding the parable. This is seen in verses 15 and 21. The warning is against covetousness, materialism and earthly riches. The one who thinks of the present and only for the temporal riches is in danger of neglecting the eternal riches and is indeed a foolish person.

D. The Exposition Of The Parable
1. A Certain Rich Man

It is worthy to notice how often Jesus speaks of "a certain rich man" (Luke 12:16; 16:1,19; Matthew 19:23-24; Luke 18:23).

Paul says, "They that will be rich fall into temptation and a snare, and into many foolish and hurtful lusts, which drown men in destruction and perdition" (1Timothy 6:9-10). The love of money (not money itself) is the root of all evils. Some covet after money and this causes them to depart from the faith, and they pierce themselves through with many sorrows.

2. Ground Of Plentiful Harvest

The blessing of plentiful harvest all came from the Lord. It is the blessing of the Lord on the earth, sending seasonal rains, sunshine, dew and the blessings of heaven. It is the Lord that gives one the power to get wealth, and no one should be lifted up in pride and forget his debt to the God of heaven and earth (Deuteronomy 8:1-20).

3. The Rich Man – Thoughts And Words

"He thought" within himself (verse 17), and "he said" (verse 18) to his soul. It is evident that he had no idea of what "God thought" and "what God said" (verse 20).

* He thought – What shall I do? He had no room to store all his fruits.

* He said – I will do this; I will pull down my barns, and build greater barns; I will bestow all my fruit and my goods; I will say to my soul, Soul you have much goods laid up for many years, take it easy, eat, drink and be merry!

Note the emphasis on "I" - used six times. Note the emphasis on "I will" – used four times. Note the emphasis on "my" – used five times; "my fruits, my barns, my fruits, my goods, my soul". They are all personal pronouns.

It is evident that God is not in any of his thoughts. There is evidence of "self", "self-will" and self-satisfaction, with absolutely no thought of God in his life. He did not seem to recognize or acknowledge that all he had was from God's blessing, that God had given him the power to get wealth and prosperity. He laid up treasure for himself on earth. Where a person's treasure is, that is where the heart is (Matthew 6:19-21).He had no thought of laying up treasures in heaven. As a rich fool, he was high-minded and he trusted in uncertain riches (1Timothy 6:17-19). He did not realize that it was God who gave him richly all things to enjoy.

4. God's Thoughts And Words

God's words reveal God's thoughts. After what the rich fool had thought and said, God has the final thought and word. God spoke His thoughts. "You fool, this night your soul shall be required of you: then whose shall those things be which you have provided?"

God called him "Fool". When God calls someone a fool, it is Divinely serious. The "fool" here is: "one without reason, want of mental sanity, lack of commonsense perception of the reality of things both natural and spiritual" (Herbert Lockyer).

The rich man said "many years"; God said "This night". The rich man said "my soul", but God said "your soul is required of you". The Lord spoke through the prophet Ezekiel saying, "All souls are Mine, and the soul that sins, it shall die" (Ezekiel 18:4).

Paul told Timothy that we brought nothing into this world and it is certain we will carry nothing out. Whatever material wealth one is given between "the gate of birth" and "the gate of death" is all left behind (1Timothy 6:6-8). The rich fool did not understand that it is godliness with contentment is great gain. All that he had gained in life would be left to others, whether wise or foolish, to be used for good or squandered (Ecclesiastes 2:18-19; Psalm 39:6; Jeremiah 17:12).

Perhaps this certain rich man did not believe in life after death, as the Sadducees (Acts 23:8). However, regardless of what he believed, he acted in life as if all were his own possessions, with no thought of after-life and that his very breath was in the hands of the Almighty. He forgot that "it is appointed unto man once to die, and after death, the judgment "(Hebrews 9:27).

E. The Practical Application Of The Parable

In verses 15 and 21, as already noted, Jesus provided the moral of the parable. Jesus gives us (and the questioning hearer!) a warning against covetousness. He shows that the rich fool is an example of those who are not rich towards God. The issue is the difference between laying up treasure for himself, on earth, or laying up treasue, in heaven for God.

Jesus said, "Take heed, and beware of covetousness; for a man's life consists not in the abundance of things which he possesses". Life is more than material possessions.

There are many "take heed" warnings in Scripture and these provide a worthwhile study to the student. We are to "take heed" to ourselves, to the Word of God, to the ministers of God, to the flock of God, to our relationship with the Lord, and take heed that we do not get caught up in the spirit of materialism, which arises out of the sin of covetousness (Read Matthew 6:1; 16:6; 18:10; 24:4; Mark 4:24; 8:15; 13:5,9,23,33; Luke 8:18; 11:35; 17:3; 21:8,34).

The tenth commandment of the Decalogue is a warning against covetousness. "You shall not covet" (Exodus 20:17; Deuteronomy 5:21; Romans 7:7; 13:9). While the previous nine commandments deal with the result of sin, the tenth actually deals with the root of sin. One would not commit adultery, steal, and so forth unless there was the root sin of covetousness there in the heart. To covet is an unlawful desire. Undoubtedly Jesus, who knew the hearts of all men, picked up this covetous desire in the heart of His questioning hearer who wanted Jesus to intervene in the division of the inheritance between these two brothers (Read these Scriptures warning against covetousness also. Mark 7:22; Romans 1:29; Ephesians 5:3; Colossians 3:5; Hebrews 13:5; 2Peter 2:3). Paul tells us that "covetousness is idolatry".

Life does not consist in the abundance of material things a person possesses. True life, that is, eternal life, is found in God through Christ. Material riches are temporal and pass away. Spiritual riches are eternal, enduring for ever.

The rich fool was only interested in this life – not eternal life.

The rich fool was rich toward himself – not rich towards God.

The rich fool laid up treasure for himself on earth – not laying up treasures in heaven.

The rich fool prepared for temporal time – not for eternity.

The rich fool thought only of material things – not of eternal things.

The rich fool thought only of himself – there was no thought for God!

The Book of Proverbs contain numerous warnings against riches. There are more warnings of Jesus and the New Testament writers about "uncertain riches" than any other thing. It is the Lord who makes both rich and poor. All are stewards of what the Lord gives. It is no sin to be rich as long as we are rich towards God, and that we "have riches" but riches do not "have us!" The one who is blessed by God with material and financial riches must be rich towards God, rich in good works, ready to distribute, willing to communicate to those in need, giving to the Lord of his tithes and offerings according to how God has blessed him. He must lay up in store for himself a good foundation against the time to come, so that he may lay hold of eternal life (1 Timothy 6:17-19).

Herbert Lockyer, in "All The Parables Of The Bible" (pages 267-270) outlines his comments of the rich fool, showing that he was:

1. The Godless Fool (Psalm 14:1; Psalm 49:6-13)
2. The Rich Fool (1 Chronicles 29:14; 1 Timothy 6:10)
3. The Self-centered Fool ("I", and "My" and "I will")
4. The Ambitious Fool (Selfish and sensual enjoyments)
5. The Doomed Fool ("Many years", but "This night" – soul is required!).

(The Parable of the Rich Fool can be linked with The Parable of the Rich Man and Lazarus – Luke 12:16-21 with Luke 16:19-31).

CHAPTER THIRTY-THREE
THE PARABLE OF THE WATCHFUL SERVANT

A. The Scripture On The Parable
Luke 12:35-40

> Let your loins be girded about, and your lights burning; And ye yourselves like unto men that wait for their lord, when he will return from the wedding; that when he cometh and knocketh, they may open unto him immediately.

> Blessed are those servants, whom the lord when he cometh shall find watching: verily I say unto you, that he shall gird himself, and make them to sit down to meat, and will come forth and serve them.

> And if he shall come in the second watch, or come in the third watch, and find them so, blessed are those servants.

> And this know, that if the goodman of the house had known what hour the thief would come, he would have watched, and not have suffered his house to be broken through.

> Be ye therefore ready also: for the Son of man cometh at an hour when ye think not.

B. The Setting Of The Parable

The setting of the parable seems to be when the Lord is repeating some things that He had spoken in the Sermon on the Mount, as in Matthew's Gospel.

A comparison of Luke 12:22-34 with Matthew 6:25-34 verifies the truth of these things. He is speaking to His disciples (Luke 12:22). "Then Peter said to Him, Lord, do you speak this parable to us, or even to all?" The Lord then continues with another parable relative to this present parable. Thus, the parable of the watching servant is given in the course of Christ's preaching to His disciples as well as to others who may have been there.

C. The Moral Of The Parable

In verse 40, Jesus Himself gives the moral of the parable. It is a lesson relative to the coming of Christ the second time. He said, "Be you therefore ready also, for the Son of Man comes at an hour when you think not." The key thought is to be watchful. One never knows when the Lord will come. His coming is imminent if not immediate. The truth of watchfulness is applicable to all generations but more especially to that generation which will be alive to the coming of the Lord.

D. The Exposition Of The Parable

The parable is woven throughout with the practical words that Jesus gives. As mentioned, the key word has to do with "watchfulness", the word being used in verses 37,38,38,39; that is, four times.

1. The Servants

The servants are none other than the disciples of the Lord Jesus, whether then or now. Christians are the Lord's servants in every generation.

2. Waiting Servants

These servants were waiting like people who wait for their master returning from a wedding. They were waiting and ready to open the door the moment he arrived and knocked at the door. They were watching and waiting continually because they did not know what hour the master would come.

3. Blessed Servants

When the master came and found his servants ready and watching, he made them sit down at the meal table and he himself served them. They had served him, and now he in turn served them.

4. Watching Servants

The servants did not know which watch of the day or night he would return from the wedding. It could be the second watch, or the third watch. They were not only waiting servants, but also watching servants. It is possible to wait, but not watch!

Hebrew time was divided into several watches. In New Testament times, the Roman division into four watches seems to have been used (Mark 6:48), while in Old Testament times, the Israelites divided time into three watches (Judges 7:19). The servants would take their particular watch and it was their responsibility to be awake, watching and waiting – not sleeping!

5. Thief In The Night

Jesus gave the disciples a simple illustration to enforce the truth of the parable. If the goodman of the house would have known what hour the thief was going to come, he would have both watched and waited, and he would not have had his house broken into. He would have been ready for the thief's coming! This short parable is very similar to The Parable of The Absentee Housemaster (Chapter 26). The reader is referred to the truth therein.

The Scriptures speak of the coming of Jesus as "a thief in the night" (1Thessalonians 5:1-8; 2Peter 3:10; Revelation 3:3; 16:15; Matthew 24:42-44). The Lord will come as a thief in the night to the unwatching and unready world of unbelievers. He will also come as a thief in the night to "Sardis-like" churches, who are unwatchful. But, to those believers who are of the light, and of the day, and are sober and watchful, He will not come as a thief in the night. They will be ready, watchful and waiting for His coming. They will be awake and ready to open the door to Him (cf. Revelation 3:20). Unwatchful believers, who are looking for the Lord to come as a thief in the night are really in darkness, and are linked with the children of the night. Such is the teaching found in the Scriptures listed here.

E. The Practical Application Of The Parable

The lessons learnt from this short parable are several and may be summed up in the following manner.

* Servants must have their loins girded and ready for service.

* Servants must have their lighted lamps shining and burning (Matthew 5:16; Philippians 2:15-16). They will be like the wise virgins, with their lamps trimmed and burning brightly (Matthew 25:1-13).

* Servants must be waiting for their Lord's return.

* Servants must be working for their Lord's return.

* Servants must be watching for their Lord's return.

* Servants do not know what hour the Lord will come.

* Servants know that the Lord comes as a thief in the night, but not to the watchful.

* Servants will be ready when the Son of Man comes.

* Servants will be blessed by the Lord when He comes and finds these qualities in them.

Such are the lessons from the Parable of the Watchful Servant!

CHAPTER THIRTY-FOUR
THE PARABLE OF THE FAITHUL AND WISE STEWARD

A. The Scripture On The Parable
Luke 12:41-48

Then Peter said unto him, Lord, speakest thou this parable unto us, or even to all?

And the Lord said, Who then is that faithful and wise steward, whom his lord shall make ruler over his household, to give them their portion of meat in due season?

Blessed is that servant, whom his lord when he cometh shall find so doing.

Of a truth I say unto you, that he will make him ruler over all that he hath.

But and if that servant say in his heart, My lord delayeth his coming; and shall begin to beat the menservants and maidens, and to eat and drink, and to be drunken;

The lord of that servant will come in a day when he looketh not for him, and at an hour when he is not aware, and will cut him in sunder, and will appoint him his portion with the unbelievers.

And that servant, which knew his lord's will, and prepared not himself, neither did according to his will, shall be beaten with many stripes.

But he that knew not, and did commit things worthy of stripes, shall be beaten with few stripes. For unto whomsoever much is given, of him shall be much required: and to whom men have committed much, of him they will ask the more.

B. The Setting Of The Parable

The setting here is the same as in the previous couple of parables: (1) The Parable of the Rich Fool (Luke 12:13-21), and, (2) The Parable of the Watching Servants (Luke 12:34-40).

It is given as a continuous answer to Peter's question to the Lord about the previous parable, whether it was spoken to them, as His disciples, or to all of Christ's disciples.

C. The Moral Of The Parable

Jesus again, at the conslusion of the parable, provides for us the moral of the parable. "For unto whomsoever much is given, of him shall be much required: and to whom men have committed much, of him will they ask the more".

It is a common life principle. People expect more of those who have the more. Much received means much is required. Much committed is much to ask. Great gifts equal great responsibilities.

D. The Exposition Of The Parable

The parable centers around a steward of the lord who begins doing a good job, but, over time, experiences a change of heart and attitude and becomes an unprofitable servant. The Greek word **"oikonomos"** is used to refer to either:

* A trustworthy slave given authority over his master's household (Luke 12:42), or

* A public official collecting rent (Romans 16:23), or

* A manager (Luke 16:1).

It points to the truth that believers are stewards of the Lord Jesus, and the constant need to watch the heart and attitude during the period of the absent Lord, lest it degenerates from that which the Lord requires – wholeheartedness! The parable shows two possible attitudes and actions of the Lord's stewards. We consider the two possible kinds of stewards in the service of the Lord.

1. A Faithful and Wise Steward

Matthew's Gospel, as has already been seen, speaks of "faithful and wise" servants (Matthew 24:45-51). The parable of the faithful and slothful servants illustrate the first word – "faithfulness". The parable of the wise and foolish virgins illustrate the second word "wise" (Matthew 25:1-13). This parable in Luke follows a similar vein concerning faithful stewards. The qualities of a good servant of the Lord are seen in the following things:

* He is faithful (1Corinthians 4:1-2). Stewards must be found faithful.

* He is wise (Proverbs 1:1-6). Wisdom is the principal thing; get wisdom.

* He is ruler over the household – authority is given to him.

* He gives the people their portions in due season – responsibility is his.

* He is blessed in his doing this until the Lord's coming.

* He is made ruler over all that the Lord has – the reward of a job well done.

2. A Slothful and Unwise Steward

By the law of implication, the opposite to a faithful and wise servant would be a servant that is slothful and foolish. The two parables in Matthew's Gospel have illustrated the slothful servant and the unwise virgins. The qualities of a poor servant are seen in the following things:

* He is slothful. The Book of Proverbs warns against slothfulness (Proverbs. 18:9; 19:24; 24:30 with Ecclesiastes 10:18; Romans 12:11).

* He is unwise. Proverbs warns against folly and foolishness (Proverbs14:8).

* He fails to guard his heart (Proverbs 4:23). The steward thought in his heart that the Lord was not going to come on time.

* He presumes the Lord is delaying his coming and not coming back on the time he had thought he would. Maybe he was a 'date-setter' of His coming!

* He beats the menservants and maidservants of the Lord. This comes out of pride, and anger and abuse of authority. He takes his frustrations out on his fellowservants.

* He eats and drinks and becomes drunken, like the Gentiles given to excess. He is given to excess, indulgence, gluttony and revellings (1Peter 4:1-5).

All these things characterise those stewards of the Lord who become slothful and unwise in their attitudes and actions.

3. Coming, Ready or Not

The lord of the servant came in a day when he was least expected, as a thief in the night, when that slothful servant was not looking for him, when he was not aware. So the Lord Jesus will come when least expected, and catch people unawares. The Lord told His disciples to take heed to themselves, lest at any time their hearts were overcharged with surfeiting, drunkenness, and cares of this life, and that day come upon them unawares. That day will come as a snare on the whole earth. The believer is to watch and pray that he may be worthy to escape the things coming on the earth (Luke 21:35-37). This steward failed miserably in all of this. Jesus is coming, whether we are ready or not!

4. The Penalty
Several things are seen in the penalty given to this unprofitable servant of the Lord.

(a) He is cut asunder
That is, he is "cut off". The expression "cut off" is used many times in Scripture and was a form of disfellowship, judgment, discipline and even, at times, excommunication from the Israel or people of God (Genesis 17:14; Exodus 12:15,19; 30:33,38; 31:14; Leviticus 18:29; Numbers 15:30-31). The wicked also will be "cut off" out of the land of the living (Psalm 37:9,22,34,38; 12:3; 34:16 with Proverbs 2:22).

(b) He is appointed his portion with unbelievers
Instead of taking his place and receiving his portion with the faithful steward and servants of the Lord, the believers, he is placed with the unbelievers and receives his portion of punishment with them. Whatever the full significance of this, it is to be shunned by all means, by the servants of the Lord.

(c) He is beaten with stripes
* Many stripes are laid on those servants who knew the Lord's will and did not prepare themselves to do it. To whom much is given, much is required. So many stripes are given to the servant who knew his Lord's will and did not do it.

* Few stripes are laid on those servants who did not know the Lord's will, and yet did the things worthy of stripes. These will be beaten with fewer stripes.

The issue is doing God's will or one's own will. Self-will characterized the fall of Lucifer when he said "I will" five times, and fell from doing God's will (Isaiah 14:12-14 with 2Peter 2:10). A Christian must not be given to self-will, but present himself a living sacrifice that he may do that good, and perfect and acceptable will of God (Romans 12:1-2). God's will is in His Word. His Word is His will and His will is His Word! There is really no excuse for not knowing the will of the Master.

Again, whatever may be the full significance of the "stripes" here, it is certainly some form of Divine chastening, as a father chastens his sons (Revelation 3:19 with Hebrews 12:5-13).

E. The Practical Application Of The Parable
The Lord Jesus closes off the parable with the practical application – the moral of the parable. This is seen in verse 48. "For unto whomsoever much is given, of him much will be required, and to whom men have committed much, of him will they ask the more".

The more that is entrusted to someone, the more is expected; the more committed to some one (as seen in Matthew's stewardship parable), the more is expected. In other words, the measure of a person's ability, is the measure of their authority, and the measure of their authority is the measure of their responsibility and the measure of their responsibility is the measure of their accountability!

It should be the desire of every believer to be a faithful and wise steward, not slothful and unwise. There is reward for faithfulnes, but penalty for unfaithfulness. Whatever may be the full significance of being "cut off", and "the portion with unbelievers", and being beaten with "stripes" – such Divine chastisement is to be avoided by being faithful and wise stewards of the Lord and His household!

The parable was not just spoken to Peter and the apostles, but is applicable to the Lord's disciples of all ages, and every generation!

CHAPTER THIRY-FIVE
THE PARABLE OF THE BARREN FIG TREE

A. The Scriptures On The Parable

Even though this chapter is entitled "The Parable of the Barren Fig Tree", it will be profitable to bring together in this chapter the several occasions of Christ's word and ministry concerning "the fig tree".

In the course of the Gospels, there is the parable of "Budding Fig Tree" in Matthew 24:32-35; Mark 13:28-31; Luke 2;1:29-33, which is relative to eschatology. Then there is the "Cursing of the Barren Fig Tree", in Matthew 21:18-22 and Mark 11:12-25. Then we have "The Parable of the Barren Fig Tree", as in this present chapter. However, because there is inter-relatedness and a connecting theme throughout these passages, they will be brought together in the exposition of this parable, rather than have separate chapters on each of them. Our study begins with the parable from Luke's Gospel.

Luke 13:6-9

He spake also this parable; A certain man had a fig tree planted in his vineyard; and he came and sought fruit thereon, and found none.

Then said he unto the dresser of his vineyard, Behold, these three years I come seeking fruit on this fig tree, and find none: cut it down; why cumbereth it the ground?

And he answering said unto him, Lord, let it alone this year also, till I shall dig about it, and dung it:

And if it bear fruit, well: and if not, then after that thou shalt cut it down.

B. The Setting Of The Parable

The first few verses of Luke 13 provide the setting for this parable, as the following shows.

Luke 13:1-5

There were present at that season some that told him of the Galilaeans, whose blood Pilate had mingled with their sacrifices.

And Jesus answering said unto them, Suppose ye that these Galilaeans were sinners above all the Galilaeans, because they suffered such things?

I tell you, Nay: but, except ye repent, ye shall all likewise perish.

Or those eighteen, upon whom the tower in Siloam fell, and slew them, think ye that they were sinners above all men that dwelt in Jerusalem?

I tell you, Nay: but, except ye repent, ye shall all likewise perish.

At the time of the telling of the parable, some had talked to Jesus about two incidents that had taken place in Jewry, and was this because these people were worst sinners than others. The incidents concerned:

1. The Slaughtered Galileans

Some of the Galileans, no doubt in insurrection against Rome, had been slaughtered under Pilate and their blood was mingled with the blood of the sacrifices at the altar of the temple in Jerusalem. Jesus asked those present did they think that these Galileans were any worse sinners than all Galileans because they suffered these things! He told them that unless they repent, they would likewise perish.

2. The Tower of Siloam

The next incident was when a tower in Siloam collapsed and eighteen people were killed. The Jews believed that all such calamities came on people because of their wickedness. Jesus asked them again whether they thought these eighteen people were worse sinners than anyone else who dwelt in Jerusalem! Again, he told them, that unless they repented, they would like perish.

It is possible that Jesus, when He spoke of them "likewise perishing", that He had in mind the coming destruction of Jerusalem and the temple, and the desolation of Jewry. In AD 70, untold thousands of Jews were slaughtered, as they offered sacrifices at the temple altar. Many came under worse judgments then than the Galileans and those who perished at the tower of Siloam. Josephus describes the terrible desolations in the city, the temple and the land under Prince Titus and the Roman armies. It is out of this setting that the parable was given.

C. The Moral Of The Parable

In verses 3,5 Jesus gives the moral of the destruction of those of Galilee and those at the tower of Siloam. They all perished by physical death. Jesus said twice in the context, that, unless they repented they would likewise perish. This "likewise perishing" was not necessarily speaking of physical perishing, by physical suffering and death, but spoke ultimately of perishing in the lake of fire and brimstone, where all unrepentant mankind will perish -unless they repent! That is the real issue at hand, and without doubt, this is the thing which Jesus had in mind.

The godless world perished in the flood in the days of Noah (Genesis 6:3). The godless people of Sodom and Gomorrah perished in the fire and brimstone from heaven (Genesis 18:24). God wants all men to come to repentance (2Peter 3:9). He is not willing that any should perish. All will perish unless they repent.

D. The Exposition Of The Parable

1. A Certain Man

Note again "a certain man" as in so many of the parables of Jesus (Luke 16:1,19; Matthew 21:28; Mark 12:1; Luke 10:30; 12:16; 13:6; 14:16; 15:11). No doubt the certain man here represents the Lord Jesus Himself.

2. A Fig Tree

Trees in Scripture are often used to represent or symbolize individuals or rulers or nations. The blessed man is like a tree planted by the rivers of water that brings forth his fruit in his season (Psalm 1:1-3). Jesus likened Himself and His disciples to the vine and the branches (John 15:1-16). King Nebuchadnezzar was likened to a great tree spreading his branches, under which the beasts of the earth sheltered and the birds of the air found rest (Daniel 4).

The fig tree here is used to symbolize the house of Judah, the Jewish nation at this time. Jeremiah speaks of the "good figs" and the "evil figs" when he speaks of the house of Judah (Jeremiah 24). Israel is likened to a degenerate vine in Jeremiah 2:21.

Bethphage means "the house of figs" (Matthew 21:1; Luke 19:29). When Israel dwelt in safety, every one would sit under their fig tree (1Kings 4:25; Micah 4:4). The fig tree represents Jewry in the time of Christ.

3. Planted A Vineyard

The prophet Isaiah interprets for us the vineyard. The house of Israel is God's vineyard and Judah was His pleasant plant (Isaiah 5:1-7). The fig tree, as Judah, was God's planting.

4. He Came

Christ's first coming in the incarnation is pointed to here. He came unto His own people, the house of Judah (John 1:11).

5. He Sought Fruit

When Jesus came the first time, to the house of Judah, He came looking for fruits. He looked for the "fruits of repentance" (Matthew 3:8); the "fruits of righteousness" (Hosea 10:1; Amos 6:12; Hebrews 12:11; James 3:18; Matthew 7:20; 21:41,43), but He found nothing but leaves. Judah was virtually a fruitless nation. He brought forth fruit unto himself.

6. He Found None

It was like the time when He came to the fruitless fig tree, and cursed it at the roots. It had nothing but leaves but should have had some fruit of its present crop (Mark 11:12-21). Jewry had the leaves of professional religion but was devoid of genuine fruit. He found none.

7. The Dresser Of The Vineyard

The dresser here probably points to the Father, who, through Jesus, extends mercy and further ministry to Jewry, hoping yet to obtain some fruit. The certain man and the dresser worked together, even as the Son and the Father worked together (John 5:17).

8. Three Years Seeking Fruit

The three years of seeking fruit undoubtedly points to the three years of Christ's mninistry up to this time, after the six months of John's ministry, where he also called from fruits of repentance (Luke 3:7-9). It points to the first half of the seventieth week of Christ's three and one-half years of ministry (Daniel 9:24-27).

9. Cut It Down – It Cumbers The Ground

The certain man said to the dresser of the vineyard that the fig tree should be cut down. It is injuring the ground, taking good nourishment from the ground and producing no fruit. It was like John the Baptist, when he said that the axe should be laid at the root of the trees when there is no forth coming fruit. It was like the prophet Isaiah also, when he said the vine should be cut down because of no fruitfulness (Isaiah 5:5,6). Every tree that brings not forth good fruit is hewn down and cast into the fire (Matthew 7:19).

10. Leave It One More Year

The dresser of the vineyard intercedes for the fig tree and asks the certain man that it be given one more year's chance and see it brings forth fruit. He said to dig about it, and fertilize it, and if it bears fruit, then well, but if not, after that it should be cut down. There was fixed time, a set year of further grace given to the fig tree.

The three years plus one year would seem to include the six months of John's ministry plus the three and one-half years of Christ's ministry, making four years ministry in total. As noted, Christ's three and one-half years ministry fulfills the first half of Daniel's notable seventy week prophecy (Daniel 9:24-27).

Jewry, as a whole nation, apart from the godly remnant who accepted their Messiah, failed to bring forth the desired and required fruits unto God, the Father, and in AD 70, the "axe was laid to the root", and the nation was "cut down" and cast out of the land of Judah.

This would be the exposition and interpretation of this parable. However, this brings us to the other passages in the Gospels which deal with the fig tree, representing basically the Jewish nation.

E. The Cursing Of The Fig Tree

Mark 11:12-14,20-21 with Matthew 21:18-22 should be read together at this point. Jesus had come from Bethany en route to Jerusalem. Seeing a fig tree having leaves, He came hoping possibly to find some fruit on it. However, He found nothing but leaves. The time of the figs was not yet due. Jesus uttered a curse and said to the fig tree, "No man eat fruit of you hereafter for ever".

The disciples were amazed, as they passed by in the morning, to see the fig tree dried up from the roots. The curse of the Master had caused it to wither and die. What is the significance of this act? Jesus was not in the habit of cursing fig trees, or any other trees, just because they had no fruit, or just to display His power. What is the interpretation of this actual yet symbolic act?

*   The fig tree represents again the Jewish nation. This has already been confirmed in both the prophets of the Old Testament and the New Testament parables of Jesus.

*   Jesus came expecting to find some fruit in Jewry even though it was not the time for the full fruit. It should be explained that the fig tree bears a first crop of figs before the leaves come. Then the leaves come and after that the second crop of figs. Jesus was hoping to find at least some fruit of the first crop, even though the time of the second crop was not yet due. Again, we remind ourelves of the Scriptures which called for "fruits of repentance" and righteousness from the Jewish nation (Luke 3:7-9; Matthew 3:8-10; Acts 6:12; Matthew 21:41-43).

*   Jesus found in Jewry nothing but leaves of ritualism, professionalism, hypocrisy, ceremonialism and legalism. All such were like Adam and Eve "covering themselves with fig leaves" to make themselves presentable and acceptable to God (Genesis 3:7 with Isaiah 64:6). Jewry had nothing but leafy and fruitless formalism.

*   Jesus utters a curse on the fig tree. No fruit ever again will be seen on the fig tree. This Judaism will never again be fruitful in the earth.

*   The end result is the fig tree is "dried up from its roots". It is "cursed" and it "withers away".

If the fig tree represents Jewry, and most expositiors and preachers say it does, then both the parable of Luke 13:6-9 and the cursing of the barren but leafy fig tree in Matthew and Luke show the tragic end and judgment of the Lord on the Jewish nation. The Nation, spiritually, is "dried up from the roots", and "withered away" and under "the curse" of the broken law (Galatians 3:13; Deuteronomy 21:23; Matthew 27:24-25; and Matthew Chapter 23).

Jewish Judasism will never bring forth fruit again. It is "cut down" and the "axe is laid to the root of the trees" (Luke 3:7-9). The only hope for the Jew, as for the Gentile, is "in Christ".

But it will be asked, What about the "budding of the fig tree" that Jesus spoke about? Doesn't this speak of a restoration of the Jewish nation?

In order to discover the answer, the Scriptures in question need to be considered and interpreted properly and in the light of these previous Scriptures already considered. The student should read carefully, once again, Matthew 24:32-35; Mark 13:28-31 and Luke 21:20-33.

Here Jesus is foretelling the events pertaining to the destruction of Jerusalem under the Roman armies, and also on to His second advent. In the midst of these details, He tells another "parable of the fig tree". This parable cannot be used to contradict the previous parable of the fig tree! Luke 21 cannot be made to contradict Luke 13:6-9.

The parable of the fig tree tells us that, when the branch is tender and its leaves begin to come, it is a sign in nature that summer is near. Luke says that it is not only "the fig tree" but "all the trees". When all the trees shoot forth the leaves of their branches, then it is the sign in nature that summer is near.

Each of the Synoptic Gospels give the same interpretation. "SO likewise you, when you see these things (ie., the signs of false Christs, wars, rumours of wars, famines, pestilences and earthquakes, or, in other words, "the leaves"), then know that the kingdom of God is near at hand. Truly I say unto you, THIS GENERATION shall not pass until all these things be fulfilled".

This parable of the fig tree has nothing to do with the restoration of the Jewish nation in a future time. It actually concerned the judgments on the nation under Prince Titus and the Roman armies in AD 70, and the destruction of the city, and temple, and the desolation of the land and the Jewish people – "this generation".

It will be profitable to set down the two parables in contrastive form to show the truth of these things.

Fig Tree Parable – Luke 13:6-9	Fig Tree Parable – Luke 21:29-32
A certain man	The fig tree
A fig tree	All the trees
Vineyard	Shoot forth leaves
Sought fruit	Sign of summer near
Found none	So all "these things" will come
Nothing but leaves	on Jerusalem and Jewry
Three or four years ministry	Kingdom of God is near
If no fruit, then cut it down	This generation not pass until all these judgments are fulfilled

Fig Tree Cursed – Mark 11:12-21
A fig tree afar off
Sought first crop of fruit on it
Found nothing by leaves
Tree cursed – dried up from the roots
Withered away
No fruit hereafter for ever

There is absolutely no way that the latter parable can be used to contradict the previous parable, and the curse of Jesus on the fig tree. There is nothing of a "restoration of the Jewish nation" taught in anything pertaining to the fig tree here.

The only other references to "fig trees" are found in James 3:12; Revelation 6:12; Matthew 7:16 and Luke 6:44.

Undoubtedly it is significant that the New Testament does not specifically liken the Church, or the New Covenant believer to the fig tree. The Church is likened to the olive tree (Romans 11:16-24), and to the vine (John 15:1-16), but it is not likened to the fig tree. The only possible allusion to believers is where Scripture speaks of "the figs" and "the grapes" in Matthew 7:16; and Luke 6:14, and then "the fig tree" and "the olive tree berries" in James 3:12. Jesus does speak of "good trees bringing forth good fruit" and "evil trees bring forth evil fruit". A tree is known by its fruits (Matthew 7:16-19). Jeremiah spoke of the godly Jews in his time as being "good figs", and the evil Jews in his time as being "evil figs" (Jeremiah Chapter 24). They were blessed and judged accordingly.

F.   The Practical Application Of The Parable

Without doubt, there are two major practical lessons to be seen in each of the passages which deal with the fig tree.

The first major lesson has been covered under the moral of the parable. That is, unless all repent, all shall perish. All sinners, great or small, high or low, rich or poor, who remain unrepentant will come under the judgment of God. God so loved the world that He gave His only begotten Son, that whosoever believes on Him should not perish, but have everlasting life (John 3:16). However, unless all come to repentance, all will perish.

The next major practical lesson is seen in the cursing of the fig tree. The New Covenant believer, be they Jew or Gentile, is likened to a tree planted by the rivers of water (Psalm 1:1-3). Believers are called "trees of righteousness, the planting of the Lord, that He might be glorified" (Isaiah 61:3). It is fruit that glorifies the Lord. However, if we, as Jewry, have no fruit and nothing but the leaves of professional religion, then the same judgments will fall on us as on Judaistic Jewry.

"For the earth which drinks in the rain that comes often upon it, and brings forth herbs, meet for them by whom it is dressed, receives blessing from God. But that which bears thorns and briars is rejected, and is nigh unto cursing, whose end is to be burned" (Hebrews 6:7-8). It is this that reveals the goodness and the severity of God on all nations, be they Jewish or Gentiles nations!

These are the great lessons to be learnt from the parable of the fig tree!

CHAPTER THIRTY-SIX
THE PARABLE OF THE TWO GATES AND TWO WAYS

A. The Scriptures On The Parable
Luke 13:22-24

And he went through the cities and villages, teaching, and journeying toward Jerusalem.

Then said one unto him, Lord, are there few that be saved? And he said unto them,

Strive to enter in at the strait gate: for many, I say unto you, will seek to enter in, and shall not be able.

Matthew 7:13-14

Enter ye in at the strait gate: for wide is the gate, and broad is the way, that leadeth to destruction, and many there be which go in thereat:

Because strait is the gate, and narrow is the way, which leadeth unto life, and few there be that find it.

B. The Setting Of The Parable

In verse 22 of Luke 13 we are told that Jesus went through the cities and villages teaching on His journey towards Jerusalem. In Matthew's Gospel, it is a part of the Sermon on the Mount!

C. The Moral Of The Parable

The moral of the parable may be seen in several verses. Many go to destruction. Few go to life. Many go in at the broad gate. Few will enter the strait gate. Many will be lost. Few will be saved.

D. The Exposition Of The Parable

There are two parts that may be considered in this short parable: The two gates and the two ways. Both convey the same truth.

Matthew's Gospel presents the final chapter on Christ's sermon on the mountain. It is especially a chapter of contrasts; a chapter of "twos", one set over against the other, as seen in the following:

Verses 1-5.   The beam and the mote
Verse 6.   The dogs and the swine
Verse 7-11.   The bread and the stones; the fish and the serpents
Verse 12.   The law and the prophets
Verses 13-14. The two gates and the two ways
Verses 15-20. The two trees, the good and the evil fruit
Verses 21-23. The will of God and the workers of iniquity
Verses 24-27. The two builders, the wise man and the foolish man's house.

Two is the number of witness, when it is standing one with one, on the positive side. Two is the number of separation and division, when it is one standing against one, on the negative side. This is what is seen in the short parable of the two gates and the two ways. It is the number of separation and division.

1. The Strait Gate

Someone had asked Jesus a question: Are there only a few that will be saved? The Master's response was the illustration of the strait gate. Jesus told His listeners to strive to enter in at the strait gate. Many would seek to enter in and not be able to. The reason would be that the gate was too strait (John 7:34; 8:21; 13:33).

The gate is the entrance to the way of eternal life. We see the entrance (the strait gate), and the way to walk (the narrow way), and the end of the journey (eternal life).

The word "strait" (not "straight"), means "beset with difficulties". It means "restricted, tight, difficult, compressed", like a "strait-jacket".

Matthew's Gospel brings more of the contrast. He says: Enter in at the strait gate, because strait is the gate, and narrow is the way, which leads to life, and few there be that find it. Wide is the gate, and broad is the way that leads to destruction, and many there be which go in thereat.

What are some of the difficulties that it so hard to enter into the way that leads to eternal life? What is symbolized by the strait gate? The ingredients of repentance and faith are the things that attend the "strait gate".

* Call to repentance of sin, a change of mind about God and sin (Matthew 3:1-2).
* Godly sorrow for sin (2Corinthians 7:9-11).
* Forsaking of sin (Proverbs 28:13).
* Hatred of sin (Ezekiel 36:31-33).
* Restitution where possible (Leviticus 6:1-7; Luke 19:8).
* Faith towards God through Christ (Mark 1:14-15). Repent and believe the gospel.
* Being born again, born from above (John 3:1-5; 1Peter 1:23).

These are the things which attend the "strait gate", and these are the things that people find difficult to come to in order to enter in and walk the narrow way that leads to life eternal. Repentance, faith and the new birth – these are the things that constitute the "strait gate" that one enters the way to life. God has made it difficult to enter life, to be a genuine Christian. He sets before us the entrance to eternal life – the strait gate! That is why FEW there be that find it.

* The rich young ruler was challenged to sell all, take up his cross and follow Jesus. He found this too difficult. It was the strait gate (Mark 10:17-31).
* The disciples that wanted to follow Christ were challenged by Jesus also (Luke 9:57-62). The three would-be disciples had to count the cost. It was the strait gate.
* Those who heard Jesus speak of "eating His flesh and drinking His blood" found this a hard saying, and many of His disciples walked no more with Him. It was the strait gate (John 6:66). It was difficult for them to follow Him. He did not run after them and compromise His truth.
* In the nation of Israel, no matter what tribe a person belonged to, the way of approach to the Tabernacle of the Lord was by way of the court gate (Exodus 27:9-18). It was made of fine linen (righteousness), and embroidered with blue (heavenly authority), and purple (kingship and Lordship of Jesus), and scarlet (the sacrifice of the cross). None could mistake it. This was the one and only way of approach to God in His Tabernacle. It could be likened to the "strait" gate. For any to enter the court by by-passing the gate, and trying to crawl under the court curtains, this

would have been Divine judgment. All must enter by way of the court gate! There was no other way (John 14:6). All must come to God through Christ!

2. The Narrow Way

Once a person enters the strait gate, they find themselves on a way. It is called "the narrow way" – NOT the broad way. The gate is strait. The way is narrow, but it leads to life, eternal life.

The word "narrow" means "restricted, limited". It is the opposite of being wide and broad. People speak of Christians as being "narrow-minded". It is because Christians are on the narrow way which leads to life. Evidences of "the narrow way" are:

* Water baptism, burial of the old self-life, death to self (Romans 6:1-4).
* Self-denial (Matthew 16:24).
* Taking up the cross on a daily basis (Luke 9:23).
* Following Jesus and walking as He walked.

The Bible shows that this way is also:

* The narrow way.
* The way of holiness (Isaiah 35:8).
* The perfect way (Psalm 18:30).
* The way everlasting (Psalm 139:24).
* Jesus is THE Way (John 14:1,6).
* Christians are "people of the Way" (Acts 9:2; 19:9,23).
* The new and living way (Hebrews 9:8; 10:20).

3. Eternal Life

The end of this way is eternal life. The one who enters by the strait gate, and walks the narrow way keeps the end in mind. It is the promise of eternal life. It is the restoration of the tree of eternal life forfeited by Adam in sin. Those that do His commandments will have the right to enter the gates of the city of God and have access to the tree of eternal life (Genesis 3:1-6; Revelation 2:7; 22:14). This promise is to the overcomers.

4. The Few

The FEW only find it. It can be seen why the few only find it because the gate is strait, the way is narrow. The few see the ultimate end of their walk with God. Because they see the end, they can handle the straitness (the difficulties), and the narrowness (the restrictions), for the end is life with God and His Son, eternal life.

As noted already, the young man came to Jesus wanting to know what he could do to inherit eternal life. Jesus told him to sell his all, give it to the poor, take up his cross and follow him. The answer was too strait, the way too narrow. He went away sad. Jesus did not run after him and compromise the cross or the way to eternal life. Jesus never hid His wounds or the cross to gain disciples!

5. The Wide Gate

In contrast to the strait gate, there is the wide gate. It is not beset about with difficulties but is very wide. Here the person can fulfill their own will and wishes. Here they can be a law to themselves. They can enjoy life without having the restraints of the Bible or Christ on them. There is no cross, no repentance, no faith or being born again. They could be religious but unregenerate. It is a wide gate.

6. **The Broad Way**

Opposite the narrow way is the broad way. Here one can be "broad-minded", and not "narrow-minded". Here they can be broad minded on Biblical issues, Divine things, eternal matters. They can be among the atheistic, the agnostic, the humanistic multitudes. They can have loose morals and sinful relationships. They can accept pornography, drugs, alcohol, smoking, drinking, revellings, new age thought and religion, all, without accepting Christ.

7. **Everlasting Destruction**

The people who enter this wide gate, and walk the broad way will have plenty of company. The multitudes walk this way. But "there is A WAY that seems right unto a man but the END thereof are the ways of death" (Proverbs 14:12; 16:25). Being short-sighted, they do not see the end of the way they are travelling.

* It is a way of destruction, destruction of life in this present time.
* It is a way of destruction, destruction and forfeiture of eternal life to come.
* It is a way of destruction, destruction of families, relationships.
* It is a way of destruction at Christ's second coming (2Thessalonians 1:7-10).
* It is final and eternal destruction in the lake of fire (Revelation 20:11-15; Phillipians 3:18; 1Thessalonians 5:3; 1Timothy 6:9; 2Peter 2:1; 3:16).

8. **The Many**

Many there are that enter the wide gate and walk the broad way. There are multitudes on this way, the majority of the people of nations and cultures, and these constitute "the many". It is popular to go with the crowd, with the multitude, where there are no restraints, no restrictions on their life and behaviour. It is much easier for people in this broad way. The millions in the nations who are unsaved are on this broad way which leads to destruction.

E. **The Practical Application Of The Parable**

Each person has to make their choice. The Lord said to Israel, "I set before you life and death, blessing and cursing, good and evil...therefore choose LIFE" (Deuteronomy 30:15-20). There are two gates, two ways, two ends – life or destruction. The Lord says to choose life. All have to choose this day whom they will serve (Joshua 24:15).

All mankind will be divided over what Jesus taught in this short parable. It is their choice.

1. The Two Gates – the strait gate and the wide gate.
2. The Two Ways – the narrow way and the broad way.
3. The Two Groups – the few and the many.
4. The Two Destinies – life and destruction.

Which gate? Which way? There is a way which seems right unto a man but the end thereof are the ways of death (Proverbs 14:12). But the path of the just is as the shining light that shines more and more unto the perfect day (Proverbs 4:18)! Therefore choose LIFE!

CHAPTER THIRTY-SEVEN
THE PARABLE OF THE SHUT DOOR

A. The Scriptures On The Parable
Luke 13:25-30

When once the master of the house is risen up, and hath shut to the door, and ye begin to stand without, and to knock at the door, saying, Lord, Lord, open unto us; and he shall answer and say unto you, I know you not whence ye are:

Then shall ye begin to say, We have eaten and drunk in thy presence, and thou hast taught in our streets.

But he shall say, I tell you, I know you not whence ye are; depart from me, all ye workers of iniquity.

There shall be weeping and gnashing of teeth, when ye shall see Abraham, and Isaac, and Jacob, and all the prophets, in the kingdom of God, and you yourselves thrust out.

And they shall come from the east, and from the west, and from the north, and from the south, and shall sit down in the kingdom of God.

And, behold, there are last which shall be first, and there are first which shall be last.

B. The Setting Of The Parable

The parable is part of the teaching of Jesus as He continues through the different cities and villages on His way to Jerusalem (Luke 13:22-24). It follows after the short parable of the two gates and two ways.

C. The Moral Of The Parable

The moral is clear. Professors of religion, who believe they are first, will be the last. They will be shut out of the kingdom of God while believing Jews and Gentiles will be found in the kingdom of God.

D. The Exposition Of The Parable

This parable, as will be seen, is very much like the words of Jesus in the Sermon on the Mount (Matthew 7:15-23). It is like the parable of the labourers in the vineyard (Matthew 19:30; 20:1-16), and the parable of the wise and foolish virgins (Matthew 25:1-13). However, there are some distinctive thoughts worthy of consideration.

1. The Master Of The House

It is none other than the Lord Jesus Christ. He is the Master of His house, which is the church (Hebrews 3:1-6).

2. The Shut Door

There comes a time when He, as the Master, rises and shuts the door. One may think of the time in the days of Noah, when the door was shut (Genesis 6:16; 7:16), and the door in the days of Lot, which the evil men wearied themselves to find (Genesis 19:6-11). One may also think of the shut door for the foolish virgins (Matthew 25:1-13). Once the door is shut, then no one else can enter it.

3. The Standing Outside

It will like the foolish virgins standing on the outside of the shut door.

4. The Knocking At The Door

Again, it is like the foolish virgins knocking at the door, asking for entrance into the marriage. Undoubtedly those in the days of Noah knocked on the door of the ark of safety once the rains descended, but it was too late!

5. **The Crying Aloud**

Again, the foolish virgins cried to the bridegroom to let them enter in, but there is no record that the door was opened. They were shut out of the marriage.

* Lord, Lord – Luke 6:46; Matthew 7:21; 25:11. Why call Jesus 'Lord' and do not the things He commands us? Many will say in that day, Lord, Lord, have we not prophesied in Your name, and done many wonderful works, and in Your name have cast out devils? But the Lord answers He did not know them.

* Open to us – like the cry of the foolish virgins (Matthew 25:11).

* Eaten and drunken in Your presence – these had been involved in attendance at the house of the Lord, and been in His presence over the years.

* You have taught in our streets – undoubtedly, these had heard the Word of the Lord and heard the teaching of the Scriptures over the years, whether in church life, Sunday School, Bible classes, and so on. But there was something missing in their experience.

6. **The Lord's Response**

The Lord responded to these knocking ones, and their cries to Him.

* I do not know where you are from. He says this twice. It is similar to the word to the foolish virgins (Matthew 25:12).

* Depart from Me. It is similar to the word to the goats in the parable of the sheep and goats (Matthew 25:41).

* You are workers of iniquity. It is like the word to the apostates in Matthew 7:23.

* There will be weeping and gnashing of teeth. Repeated six times in the New Testament Scriptures. It is the symbol of regret, sorrow, lamentation, grief and mourning (Matthew 8:12; 13:42,50; 22:13; 24:51; 25:30; Luke 13:28).

* You will see Abraham, Isaac and Jacob and the prophets in the kingdom of God. These were the men of faith in Old Testament times. "By faith... Abraham, Isaac and Jacob..." (Hebrews 11). It is similar to the word spoken to the Jews in Matthew 8:11-12).

* You yourselves will be thrown out. It is the same as being "cast out" into the outer darkness, into the outer court yard (Matthew 8:12). Refer to those parables which have used the same expression of being "cast out".

* Others will come from the east, the west, the north, the south and sit down in the kingdom of God. This prophetic word pointed to the coming in of the Gentiles from the four corners of the earth. Out of every kindred, tongue, tribe and nation they will come into the kingdom of God (Matthew 8:11-12; Revelation 5:9-10).

7. **The First And The Last**

Those that are last will be the first, and those that are first will be last. Those who are the last to respond to the Lord and His gospel will be the first to enter the kingdom. Those who were the first to be called and did not respond will be the last on the list, and they will be cast out of the kingdom (Refer Matthew 19:30; 20:1-16; Mark 10:31 also).

As can be seen, there is much similarity of language between this and other parables which have been considered.

E. The Practical Application Of The Parable

The message remains the same as in previous parables. Many who are professors of religion but not possessors of Christ in their lives will find themselves shut out of the kingdom of God. They are either found to be religious but unregenerate people, or else religious but apostate people.

The parable corresponds in points to the following parables, and therefore does not need to be over amplified.

1. It corresponds with the parable of the foolish virgins who are shut outside the door (Matthew 25:1-13).

2. It corresponds with the workers of iniquity who the Lord did not know (Matthew 7:21-23).

3. It corresponds with the goats in the parable of the sheep and goats, and the goats who experience the weeping and gnashing of teeth (Matthew 25:31-46).

4. It corresponds to the parable of the man without the wedding garment (Matthew 22:11). He is cast into outer darkness and knows weeping and gnashing of teeth.

5. It corresponds with the parable of the vineyard labourers where the first were paid last, and the last were paid first (Matthew 19:30; 20:1-16).

The issue is, all need to be sure that they have true kingdom faith, as Abraham, Isaac, Jacob and the prophets of old, in order to sit down in the kingdom of God with the saints of all ages, once Jesus comes and the door of salvation is shut – for ever!

CHAPTER THIRTY-EIGHT
THE PARABLE OF THE WEDDING FEAST

A. The Scripture On The Parable
Luke 14:7-11

And he put forth a parable to those which were bidden, when he marked how they chose out the chief rooms; saying unto them,

When thou art bidden of any man to a wedding, sit not down in the highest room; lest a more honourable man than thou be bidden of him;

And he that bade thee and him come and say to thee, Give this man place; and thou begin with shame to take the lowest room.

But when thou art bidden, go and sit down in the lowest room; that when he that bade thee cometh, he may say unto thee, Friend, go up higher: then shalt thou have worship in the presence of them that sit at meat with thee.

For whosoever exalteth himself shall be abased; and he that humbleth himself shall be exalted.

B. The Setting Of The Parable

Luke 14:1-6 provides for us the setting of the parable, as seen in the reading.

And it came to pass, as he went into the house of one of the chief Pharisees to eat bread on the sabbath day, that they watched him.

And, behold, there was a certain man before him which had the dropsy.

And Jesus answering spake unto the lawyers and Pharisees, saying, Is it lawful to heal on the sabbath day?

And they held their peace. And he took him, and healed him, and let him go;

And answered them, saying, Which of you shall have an ass or an ox fallen into a pit, and will not straightway pull him out on the sabbath day?

And they could not answer him again to these things.

Jesus enters into the house of one of the chief Pharisees to eat a meal on the sabbath day. A certain man, who had dropsy, was before Jesus as He is on His way to the Pharisee's house. So Jesus asked the lawyer and the Pharisees: Is it lawful to heal on the Sabbath day? They just held their peace. So Jesus took the man, healed him and let him go. And before they could even speak a word of criticism, Jesus asked whether any one who had a donkey or an ox, if they fell into a pit, even on the sabbath day, would pull the animal out of the pit (Exodus 23:4-5).

The implications were clear. If they would help a poor animal out of the pit, and not feel they had broken the sabbath, surely Jesus could help and heal this poor man of dropsy on the sabbath. This could not be counted unlawful (Compare Matthew 12:10-13 for a similar account). Man is much more than an animal. Therefore, it is lawful to do well on the sabbath days.

None could answer Jesus on these things. All were silenced.

However, as Jesus is sitting at the table, He saw how some of the guests had chosen out the best seats. The parable actually arises out of Christ's observation of this fact.

C. The Moral Of The Parable

Once again Jesus provides for us the moral of the parable. It is a repetition of the lesson of several other parables that Jesus has given. "Whosoever exalts himself shall be abased, and he that humbles himself shall be exalted" (verse 11). Humility leads to exaltation, and self-exaltation leads to abasement. This is the lesson the Lord teaches His own through this parable.

D. The Exposition Of The Parable

1. A Wedding Feast

Any time a wedding takes place, there are always the invited guests who respond to the invitation to attend, celebrating and rejoicing with the married couple.

2. Taking A Seat

Jesus had noticed how some of those who were invited to the Pharisee's house to dine chose out the best seats. It was an outward evidence of inward self-importance. Jesus said, when you are invited by someone to a wedding, do not sit down in the most important place. There may be a more respected, distinguished or honourable person come in that has been invited to the wedding. It would be so embarressing if the host had to come and ask you to give your place to this person. You would then have to take your place in a lower seat, and you would certainly be shamed to have to do this.

"Thus with humiliation and a guilty sense of impropriety you will begin to take the lowest place" (Amp. New Testament).

3. Take The Lowest Place

Jesus told them that the wise thing to do, after you accept the wedding invitation, is to sit in the lowest place. It would be far better for the host to come and say, Friend, take a higher place. Then it will not be so humiliating for you in front of the other guests. The way "up" is "down" in the kingdom of God!

Jesus is really quoting the lesson from Proverbs 25:6-7. "Put not forth yourself in the presence of the king, and stand not in the place of great men. For better it is that it be said unto you, Come up higher; than that you should be put lower in the presence of the prince whom your eyes have seen".

E. The Practical Application Of The Parable

The lesson is seen in the moral of the parable. Take the lowly place and you can always be called up higher, without shame or embarrassment. If you take the high place, you may be asked to step down to a lower place, which could be humiliating.

It is worthy to notice that Jesus speaks this word. "For whosoever exalts himself shall be abased; and he that humbles himself shall be exalted" (Matthew 23:12; Luke 14:11; 18:14). It is the difference between pride and humility; thinking of oneself more highly than they ought to think.

"Before honour is humility" (Proverbs 15:33; 16:19; 18:12).

"Be clothed in humility" (1Peter 5:5,6). Jesus took the lowest place in His incarnation and because of this, God has highly exalted Him (Philippians 2:5-11). "He gives grace to the humble" (James 4:6,10). Peter says, "Humble yourself...that He may exalt you in due time" (1Peter 5:56, with Luke 1:52).

It is simply to have a modest and sober opinion of oneself (Romans 12:1-3). We are not to think more highly of ourselves or even to denigrate ourselves, but to think soberly as God has dealt to every one the measure of grace.

Self-exaltation, or thinking of oneself more highly than he ought to think, always causes one to take the important place. Thinking soberly of oneself and having a contrite and humble spirit is the path of Jesus. A modest opinion of oneself causes one to behave accordingly. As noted previously, in the kingdom of God, "the way up is down".

CHAPTER THIRTY-NINE
THE PARABLE OF THE GREAT SUPPER

A. The Scriptures On The Parable
Luke 14:16-24

Then said he unto him, A certain man made a great supper, and bade many:

And sent his servant at supper time to say to them that were bidden, Come; for all things are now ready.

And they all with one consent began to make excuse. The first said unto him, I have bought a piece of ground, and I must needs go and see it: I pray thee have me excused.

And another said, I have bought five yoke of oxen, and I go to prove them: I pray thee have me excused.

And another said, I have married a wife, and therefore I cannot come.

So that servant came, and shewed his lord these things. Then the master of the house being angry said to his servant, Go out quickly into the streets and lanes of the city, and bring in hither the poor, and the maimed, and the halt, and the blind.

And the servant said, Lord, it is done as thou hast commanded, and yet there is room.

And the lord said unto the servant, Go out into the highways and hedges, and compel them to come in, that my house may be filled.

For I say unto you, That none of those men which were bidden shall taste of my supper.

B. The Setting Of The Parable
Luke 14:12-15

Then said he also to him that bade him, When thou makest a dinner or a supper, call not thy friends, nor thy brethren, neither thy kinsmen, nor thy rich neighbours; lest they also bid thee again, and a recompence be made thee.

But when thou makest a feast, call the poor, the maimed, the lame, the blind:

And thou shalt be blessed; for they cannot recompense thee: for thou shalt be recompensed at the resurrection of the just.

And when one of them that sat at meat with him heard these things, he said unto him, Blessed is he that shall eat bread in the kingdom of God.

This parable is not the same as the parable in Matthew 22:2 where the invitation is given for the wedding feast of the king's son. This parable in Luke's Gospel has its own distinctve features and lessons.

The setting of the parable is the same as in the previous parable, the parable of the wedding feast invitation. Jesus is in the house of one of the chief Pharisees. After He finished this parable, He then turned to the host and spoke to him. Jesus told him that, when he made a dinner, a feast, or supper, he ought to call in the poor, the maimed, the lame and the blind and he would be blessed. The poor could not repay the invitation but he would be rewarded in the resurrection of the just. If he invited his friends, his brethren, his kinsmen and rich neighbours, they could return the invitation. It would be a matter of "You invite and I'll invite you". The poor could not do that.

As Jesus was speaking, one of those who were sitting at the table with Him heard these things and said to Jesus, "Blessed is he that will eat bread in the kingdom of God". The Jews believed that, in the resurrection, there would be a great festival of all those in the kingdom. In other words, this was a nice meal at the house of the Pharisee, but there will be a better one at God's table in the kingdom. It is out of this setting that the parable arose.

C. The Exposition Of The Parable

1. A Certain Man

The certain man here is also called the "master of the house", and "the lord". It seems it could refer either to the Father or the Son.

2. Made A Great Supper

The great banquet or feast, which points to the Gospel Feast which the Father and the Son have provided for all who are interested and respond accordingly.

3. Many Invited

The custom in that time was to send out a preliminary invitation so that those who were invited could mark it on their calendar and be prepared for it when the time came. This first and primary invitation then was the call to Jewry as a nation!

4. The Sent Servant

The servant sent out with the invitations to this great supper could speak of the Son of God or the blessed Holy Spirit.

5. Supper Time

Supper time usually took place in the evening time, the close of the day.

6. All Things Are Ready

The invitation went out: "Come, all things are now ready!" This first or initial invitation, in dispensational setting, would be the invitation which went to the Jew first; to the priests, the scribes, the elders of Jewry, and to the Pharisees. In other words, the Lord always comes to His own first – then to others. The principle of the New Testament was: To the Jew first, and then to the Gentiles (John 1:9-10; Romans 1:16).

7. All Make Excuses

The first group the invitation goes to all make excuses. But each one of the examples given show that they were indeed excuses. An excuse is not a reason! They used these things as reasons to reject the invitation but all were, in reality, simply excuses.

(a) A Piece Of Ground

The first one said he had bought a piece of ground, said, Have me excused. The matter is that, generally one does not buy a piece of ground unless you have seen it first. The ground could not run away. It would still be there the next day. Material possessions, though legitimate, often become an excuse for rejecting the invitation of God's great supper. "Have me excused, accept my apologies" is what he was saying. In reality, he did not want to accept the invitation. He did not want to come.

(b) Five Yoke Of Oxen

This one had bought five yoke of oxen and wanted to test them out. This also was an excuse. One generally does not buy five yoke of oxen without first examining them, and trying them out. He also said, Have me excused. His was an excuse over his occupation. He in reality did not want to come to the supper.

(c) Married A Wife

In Deuteronomy 24:5 a man who had married a new wife was released from war for a year. That was a reason, not an excuse. Here the matter of asking to be excused because he had married a wife was an excuse. He could have brought his wife, at least, to a great supper, no matter how recently he had been married. His apologies simply revealed his unwillingness to accept the invitation. His excuse was a domestic excuse, the claim of human emotion and affection.

The excuses are clear. Each felt that these things, to them, were more important than acceptance of such a great invitation. There was nothing in any of these; buying a piece of ground, or oxen or marrying a wife — but all these were used as excuses to reject the invitation to the supper. "He came unto His own, but His own received Him not..." (John 1:9-11).

8. The Servant's Report

The servant came and reported to his lord all the excuses the invited ones had made; excuses for wilfully refusing the invitation to the great supper. Each were self-centered, uninterested and excuse-makers!

9. The Lord's Anger

The lord was really angry – righteously angry – at the refusal of His generous and gracious invitation. To reject the feast was to reject him. All were excuses, none of their answers were reasons. He said that none of those who had been invited and rejected his invitation would ever get a taste of his supper. They would not get another invitation. It was too late even if they changed their mind. This is Divine anger, and those who reject God's love will know His wrath (Mark 3:5; Judges 2:12,20; Isaiah 1:4). The Bible speaks of both the love of God and the wrath of God!

10. The Second Group

After the first group rejected, the master of the house now sent his servant out into the streets and lanes of the city. He was told to bring in the poor, the maimed, the halt and the blind. Compare verse 21 with verse 13 where the same kind of people are mentioned. These are the ones to invite to the feast. In verse 17 it was "Come to the feast" and here it is "Bring them into the feast".

These are the kind of people who came to Jesus and He ministered the good news of the gospel to them. They responded to His call.

The city represents Jerusalem and the cities of Judea. Those who believed on Jesus became the remnant according to the election of grace (Romans 11:5). As John said, "He came unto His own and His own received Him not (first group invited), but to as many as received Him (the second group), to them gave He power to become the children of God".

11. The Third Group

The servant told the lord of the response of the poor, the maimed, the lame and the blind. These were the ones who were conscious of their need. They had no excuses to offer and were happy to accept the gracious invitation to the supper. But still there was room for others.

The lord of the servant told him to go out into the "highways and hedges" and "compel people to come in so that his house would be filled." The word "compel" has the thought of "constrain, urging people to yield" (Amp.N.T). So Lot was compelled to leave the city of Sodom before it was destroyed by fire and brimstone (Genesis 19:16).

It will be noted that the parable is historical to this point. The invitation of the gospel of the kingdom – God's great supper – went to Jewry first. Then, when the nation as a whole, rejected God's invitation, through Christ, and by the Holy Spirit, the invitation then went out to the Gentiles in the highways and byways of the Roman Empire.

In verse 17, it was "Come". In verse 21 it was "Bring them in", and in verse 23 it is "Compel them to come in" to the feast. So from Jewry to the Gentiles the parable covers in historical and prophetical thought.

D. The Practical Application Of The Parable

The Lord has made a great supper. It is the Gospel Feast. The invitations are sent out by the servant, the blessed Holy Spirit. The Jews were the first to receive the invitations, for the Gospel must go "to the Jew first" (Romans 1:16,17). But many of the higher-up classes; priests, Pharisees, Sadducees, elders and scribes made their excuses. They were too occupied with their own things. In rejecting the invitation, they reject the host Himself. The lower class of people, the common people, the poor, the maimed, the lame and the blind, all responded to Jesus and came to the Gospel Feast.

In due time, the invitation was taken by the Holy Spirit in the church to the highways and byways, the streets and the lanes, of the Gentile world. The Gentiles accepted the invitation and came into His house to enjoy the feast.

There is still room today and all who will receive the Lord's gracious invitation can come. The church is to invite, to bring in, to compel people to come to the Gospel Feast. The Jews who rejected the invitation will not be allowed to enter the feast once they reject the Son of Man, the One who in grace invited them. They will be provoked to jealousy by reason of the Gentiles who accept the free grace of God in Christ.

This is the great lesson which is learnt from this parable of Jesus!

CHAPTER FORTY
THE PARABLE OF THE TOWER BUILDER AND WARRING KING

A. The Scripture On The Parables
Luke 14:25-33

And there went great multitudes with him: and he turned, and said unto them,

If any man come to me, and hate not his father, and mother, and wife, and children, and brethren, and sisters, yea, and his own life also, he cannot be my disciple.

And whosoever doth not bear his cross, and come after me, cannot be my disciple.

For which of you, intending to build a tower, sitteth not down first, and counteth the cost, whether he have sufficient to finish it?

Lest haply, after he hath laid the foundation, and is not able to finish it, all that behold it begin to mock him,

Saying, This man began to build, and was not able to finish.

Or what king, going to make war against another king, sitteth not down first, and consulteth whether he be able with ten thousand to meet him that cometh against him with twenty thousand?

Or else, while the other is yet a great way off, he sendeth an ambassage, and desireth conditions of peace.

So likewise, whosoever he be of you that forsaketh not all that he hath, he cannot be my disciple.

B. The Setting Of The Parable

This dual parable is given in the course of the other parables in Luke Chapters 13-15. Great multitudes are following Jesus, and many of them for mixed reasons. To test their sincerity, Jesus spoke this double parable of the tower builder and the warring king. Each man would need to count the cost lest he be not able to finish what he began and people mock him. We have here two stories, two illustrations, but each belong to the one parable and teach the same moral.

C. The Moral Of The Parable

In verse 33 Jesus once again provides the moral of the parable. Just as the one who was building the tower needed to first sit down and count the cost before he commenced building, and the king going to war, before he started the battle, so any one who would really follow Jesus, needs to count the cost. The cost is all he has. In other words:

> Before building a tower, count the cost,
>
> Before going to war, count the cost, and
>
> Before following Jesus, count the cost!

Do not under-estimate or over-estimate the cost in following Christ Jesus as Lord.

D. The Exposition Of The Parable

The two illustrations Jesus uses are very simple, while the application is rather full.

1. The Tower Builder

If a person decides to build a tower, the sensible thing to do is first, sit down and work out the cost, whether he has enough finance to finish the job. If he lays the foundation and then finds he cannot proceed with the framework and roof of the house or tower and complete it, people will mock him. They will mock the fact that he began and could not finish the tower. It would be evident to all that he did not count the cost (Proverbs 24:27).

So with those who decide to follow Christ. Each person needs to count the cost. If they lay the foundation of repentance (Hebrews 6:1-2), and never continue on with Christ, they will be mocked, ridiculed and even despised. Before following Christ, it is necessary to count the cost. Many times people are invited to follow Christ and are never presented with the cost of following Christ. Then, after accepting Christ, they find the cost is too great, and they fall away.

2. The Warring King
If a king decides to go to war against another king, the first and sensible thing to do is to sit down and see what his standing army totals. If he has only ten thousand men and his opponent has twice that many, twenty thousand soldiers, he had better count the cost of the war. Otherwise, it would be better to send messengers to the king while he is far away and ask for conditions of peace.

So it is with all who decide to follow Christ. All need to count the cost. The Christian life is spiritual warfare. The Christian is enlisted as a soldier in the army of the Lord. He has an enemy. But he needs to know that Jesus is the King of Kings and Lord of Lords and has always won the battle. Otherwise, stay out of the war!

E. The Practical Application Of The Parable
Several of the verses before and after the dual illustration of "counting the cost" are seen to be Christ's own application of the principle. We note several of the things Jesus outlined in counting the cost of following Him.

1. "IF any man comes to Me..." it must be a voluntary or free will coming to Christ. Whosoever will may come. "If" is the conditional word.

2. "HATE father, mother, wife, children, brothers and sisters, and even his own life..." The word "hate" means "to love the less". It seems to be a contradiction. The Scripture says that we are to love our father, our mother, our brothers and sisters. All of this is true. But when it comes to following Jesus, we must not love them MORE than Christ.

   He must come first. Many times, the family members, father or mother or brothers and sisters, may draw one back from following Christ. So they must be "loved the less". This is part of counting the cost in following Christ. Matthew's Gospel puts it this way. "...loves father or mother, son or daughter MORE than Me, is not worthy of Me..."(Matthew 10:34-37). Those who overcame did so by the blood of the Lamb, the word of their testimony and loved not their lives unto the death, John writes in Revelation 12:11.

3. "Deny himself..." Luke's Gospel adds this also (Luke 9:23 with Matthew 16:24; Mark 8:34). This cuts right across the whole "kingdom cult of SELF" and the Self-esteem philosophy of our modern days. While philosophy says to love yourself, esteem yourself, look for your self-image, self-potential, self-actualization, and so forth, Jesus says, "Deny yourself". SELF is to be denied in all its forms of SELF-ishness!

4. "Take up his cross..." Luke's Gospel says, "Take up his cross daily..." (Luke 9:23-26 with Matthew 16:24; 10:38-39; Mark 8:34-39; 2Timothy 3:12). The rich young ruler was not willing to take up his cross, deny self and possessions to follow Christ. He went away sorrowful. Jesus did not compromise to gain His disciples (Mark10:17-22).

5. "Forsake all he has..." Whatever that "all" may be in each individual's life, that is the cost that must be counted to follow Christ.

6. Follow Christ; where He leads, where ever He goes, the disciple will follow Him. In that day, to follow Christ would lead to Calvary and death, and ultimately resurrection.

Jesus said that, unless a person is willing to do these things, "he cannot be My disciple". This is mentioned three times in verses 26,27,33.

This is the message in this twin parable. To follow Christ one must count the cost first. Much Gospel preaching in our day hides the cost of following Jesus. Much is presented of what one can receive or get from Jesus, all of which may be true. But, the cost of self-denial, taking up the cross and loving Christ first and above all others, and following Him, unreservedly, whole-heartedly, and unconditionally – this is indeed "counting the cost" of discipleship. Many believers, after receiving Christ initially, fall away when the going becomes rough, because they never "counted the cost ". Which ever way one may go, the greater "cost" is to reject Christ and enter into a Christless eternity in hell!

Jesus is building His tower, His Church. He has counted the cost. Jesus is fighting a war, spiritual warfare. He has counted the cost. Whether it is building or battling, He has paid the price. When Nehemiah and his people restored the walls of the city of Jerusalem, they had with them (a) The trowel, for building the walls, and (b) The sword, for battle against the enemy. They had counted the cost! (Nehemiah 4:17-18). So should the Christian believer and follower of Christ!

CHAPTER FORTY-ONE
THE PARABLE OF THE SALT

A. The Scriptures On The Parable

Luke 14:34-35

Salt is good: but if the salt have lost his savour, wherewith shall it be seasoned? It is neither fit for the land, nor yet for the dunghill; but men cast it out. He that hath ears to hear, let him hear.

Matthew 5:13

Ye are the salt of the earth: but if the salt have lost his savour, wherewith shall it be salted? it is thenceforth good for nothing, but to be cast out, and to be trodden under foot of men.

Mark 9:50

Salt is good: but if the salt have lost his saltness, wherewith will ye season it? Have salt in yourselves, and have peace one with another.

B. The Setting Of The Parable

Luke's setting is the same as that of several other parables already considered from Luke Chapter 14. Jesus is teaching enroute to Jerusalem. Matthew's setting is seen to be part of the Sermon on the Mount. Mark's setting seems to be in the city of Capernaum as Jesus is enroute to the coasts of Judea (Mark 9:33; 10:1).

C. The Moral Of The Parable

Christians are the salt of the earth. If Christians lose their distinctive flavour – the power and presence of the Holy Spirit in their lives – then they are useless, good for nothing. They have no effect in the corrupting and corrupted world, and may as well be cast out and trodden under foot of men. A "Christian" without Christ is savourless salt!

D. The Exposition Of The Parable

By the law of implication, if the church (the believers) are salt, then the earth must be corrupt. Salt arrests corruption. In the expositon of this short parable, we bring together the similar thoughts from the Synoptic Gospels.

1. The Bible And Salt

The Bible speaks of salt and its various uses, as the following Scriptures show:

The meal offering was to have the salt of the covenant in it, and never to be lacking (Leviticus 2:13; Ezekiel 43:23-24; Numbers 18:19 with Mark 9:49-50).

The barren waters were healed as the cruse of salt was thrown in them (2Kings 2:20-21).

Newborn babies were cleaned in a salt bath (Ezekiel 16:4).

Jesus Himself speaks about salt, using the symbol to speak of believers in the earth (Matthew 5:13; Mark 9:50; Luke 9:34-35).

Paul also spoke of salt, saying, Let your speech be always with grace, seasoned with salt (Colossians 4:6).

2. Salt Is Good

Jesus said, You and you alone are the salt of the earth (Matthew 5:13). There are many, many lessons which can be learned from salt and its use. Salt provides symbolic truth, teaching the believer what he should be in the earth. From the function of salt, and why God created it, and the purpose of its existence, spiritual lessons may be drawn.

(a) Salt Has Many Uses

One Chemist estimates that there are over fourteen hundred uses for salt. It is a fact that, if all the salt was to be removed from the earth, chaos would result and all life would die. So Christians should be useful in the earth – not useless! When the time comes that Christians are removed from the earth, there will indeed be chaos and death. The Christian is useful as savoury salt. He is useless as unsavoury salt.

(b) Salt Has Its Distinct Flavour

Each grain of salt has its distinctive taste, flavour or savour. This is what makes it salt. It is that "mysterious something" (tang) that makes it savoury salt. Salt renders the food pleasant and palatable. Without salt, food can be tasteless, and quite insipid. Job asks, "Can that which is unsavoury be eaten without salt? Or is there any taste in the white of an egg?" (Job 6:6).

So it is "the mystery of Christ is you" that gives the Christian distinctiveness in the earth. Take Christ out of a Christian's life, then he becomes savourless salt, just like a grain of salt without any flavour; he is tasteless, insipid!

(c) Salt Is Distinguished From Earth

Salt may be found in the earth, but it is essentially different from earth, or the sand of the earth. The Christian must be different from the earth. The Christian is in the world, but he is not of the world. The Christian must not let the world squeeze him into its mould or conform to its standards (Romans 12:1-2; John 17). The Christian may be relevant but he is different from the non-Christian.

(d) Salt Can Be A Cleansing Irritant

In the cleansing of sores and wounds, salt can irritate as it cleanses. C.H.Mackintosh in **"Notes on Leviticus"**, when dealing with the salt in the meal offering has these things to say.

"And every oblation of thy meat-offeing shalt thou season with **salt;** neither shalt thou suffer the **salt of the covenant of thy God** to be lacking from thy meat-offering." The expression, "Salt of the covenant" sets forth the enduring character of that covenant.

"Let your conversation be always with grace, seasoned with salt." The whole conversation of the Perfect Man exhibited the power of this principle. His words were not merely words of grace, but words of pungent power – words Divinely adapted to preserve from all taint and corrupting influence. He never uttered a word which was not redolent with "frankincense" and "seasoned wiuth salt." The former was most acceptable to God; the latter, most profitable for man. Witness, for example, the scene in the synagogue of Nazareth (Luke 4:16-29). The people could "bear Him witness, and wonder at the **gracious** words which proceeded out of His mouth, but when He proceeded to season those words with salt, which was so needful in order to preserve them from the corrupting influence of their national pride, they would fain have cast Him over the brow of the hill whereon their city was built." So, also, in Luke 14, when

His words of **"grace"** had drawn "great multitudes" after Him, He instantly throws in the **"salt"**, by setting forth, in words of holy faithfulness, the sure results of following Him." (End quote)

His words certainly had grace in them along with the salt, which irritated those who heard and needed, but rejected, the cleansing His words could bring.

(e) Salt Creates Thirst

It was asked, Why are Christians like salt? The answer "Salt makes people thirsty! True Christians, if they have that Divine flavour in their lives, can make people thirsty for Jesus.

(f) Salt Is A Preservative

Salt is used to preserve meat, as well as many other things. With meat, salt can be rubbed into it and it preserves it from corruption and putrefaction. Meat on its own has the tendency to become corrupt and purtrid. Brine is water impregnated with salt. Think of the ocean, the sea. Think of tears which are impregnated with salt. Salt is used for the preservation of the flesh of animals, fish and even vegetables. So the Christian is rubbed, like salt, into society, trust to preserve, or at least, arrest its corruption. By our lives, by our prayers, Christians preserve the world from entire moral corruption. Although it may not totally stop corruption, it does arrest its working.

(g) Salt Is A Preventative

G.Campbell Morgan, in **"The Parables"** says that "...salt is not antiseptic, but aseptic". That means, not liable to decay, not liable to putrefaction. Antiseptic means, opposing putrefaction, and a substance that resists putrefaction.

"Aseptic is something which is devoid of poison in itself and which tends to cure. Salt never cures corruption. It prevents the spread of corruption. If meat is tainted and corrupt, salt will not make it untainted or pure. But salt in the neighbourhood will prevent the spread of corruption to that which otherwise would become corrupted."

The figure is that of a moral quality operating on the earth level amongst men living in the midst of material things, preventing the spread of corruption. The impurity of an evil man cannot be cured by the good (or Christian) man working at his side in the office, or workplace. But the things the good man (the Christian) will not do, and the things he will not say, will give the person in the same office, a chance, because it will check the evil man. Salt is aseptic." (End quote)

Thus salt restrains putrefaction and total corruption. Salt is really a judgment against sin's corrupting influence and power.

All of this shows, by implication, the state of the world, the state of unregenerate mankind. By reason of the Fall and the entrance of sin, man has a bias towards sin, a pull and tendency to evil and corruption, to rottenness, to pollution, to that which is foul and offensive. It is born in us, because of the fallen, sinful human nature. It speaks of the terrible condition of sinful world. There is no health in the physical body or the human system without salt.

The prophet Isaiah speaks of man's sinful and sick condition. "The whole head is sick (ie., the mind, thoughts, reasons and imaginations), the whole heart is faint (feeble, sick, nauseated, for out of the heart of proceeds all evil – Mark 7:21-23). From the sole of the foot (the walk), unto the head, there is no soundness in it. There are wounds, and bruises and putrifying sores (fresh and bleeding stripes). They have not been closed up (open wound, bruises and sores), neither bound up (not cleansed, or bandaged up), neither mollified (soothed, softened with oil) with ointment" (Isaiah 1:5-6). The language speaks of a leprous condition, a sick and diseased body, sick and diseased in mind, head and heart.

Jesus provides three major periods of time in which corruption abounds in the human race, and the great need of the salt of the Christian life to be manifest.

(1) The Days of Noah

In the days of Noah, man's mind, thoughts and imaginations were evil continually. Wickedness abounded, violence filled the earth, and all flesh had corrupted its way. God used Noah as "salt" in his generation. When the ark of safety was finished, God removed Noah and his family ("salt") and the earth was left to judgment and death by the Flood (Genesis 6-9).

(2) The Days of Lot

In the days of Lot, Sodom and Gommorah were twin and evil cities, corrupted by homosexuality and all forms of evil and pollution ascended to heaven. Lot and his wife and family should have been "salt", but failed. God in His grace and mercy removed Lot and fire and brimstone fell upon these twin cities in judgment (Genesis 18-19). Lot's wife was turned to a pillar of salt – savourless salt, good for nothing, because of disobedience to the warning word of the angels.

(3) The Days of the Son of Man

Jesus said, As it was in the days of Noah...as it was in the days of Lot...so shall it be in the days of the coming of the Son of Man. The same evil conditions prevailing in the days of Noah and in the days of Lot are prevailing in these last days. Violence, murder, crime, vice, immorality, sodomy, perversions, pornography, prostitution, drugs, evil thoughts and imaginations, all reveal the inward state of man's heart and the moral putrefaction that is therein. The filthy are becoming more filthy, and the unrighteous becoming more unrighteous. Flesh is corrupt on the earth (Revelation 22:11).

The world left to itself is like "dead meat", tendering to fester evil and disease. Man's total depravity by sin and the persistent tendancy to putrefaction is seen in the days of Noah, Lot and the last days before the coming of the Son of Man.

It is in this condition that the Church is to be "salt", the restraining influence in the midst of evil. One day, when Jesus comes, the salt will be removed. One can only imagine what it will be like then. There will unrestrained corruption, filth and moral putrefaction. There will darkness, gross darkness which will cover the earth (Isaiah 60:1-2).

3. Savourless Salt

In verse 13 of Matthew 5, Jesus says, "But if the salt has lost its savour, wherewith shall it be salted? It is thenceforth good for nothing but to be cast out and trodden under foot of men".

Jesus did not leave this statement as a nice platitude. You are the salt of the earth, He said to His disciples. But He gave a danger warning. Salt can lose its savour, its taste, and therefore its influence and usefulness. Salt is good...but if savourless...good for nothing (Mark 9:50). "Salt is good, an excellent thing, but if salt has lost its strength and has become saltless (insipid, flat), how shall its salt be restored? It is fit neither for the land nor for the manure heap; men therefore throw it away. He who has ears to hear, let him hear, let him listen and consider and comprehend by hearing!" (Amplified New Testament).

Naturally speaking, salt can lose its savour. Barnes **"Notes on the New Testament"** on this verse says:

"Spiritually speaking, Christians can lose their savour. Christians without Christ in their lives, Christians without the power of the Holy Spirit in them, lose their savour. They lose their tang, their pungency. Christians not in union with the Rock, Christ, lose their influence. By yielding to worldly influences, Christians can lose their quality of Christian influence. They become insipid, tasteless and lose their preventative and restraining qualities as Christians..."

4. Trodden Under Foot

The judgment on savourless salt is: Cast out and trodden under foot of men. In Eastern countries and areas where the salt was impure, where it was mingled with vegetables or earthy substances, it lost the whole of its saltness in time, and such became good for nothing. It was no good for the land, or for the manure heap. It was only used for paths or roads for people to travel on. It was used like gravel, to be walked upon. It was therefore "trodden under foot of men" as people walked on it. This is still the custom in some countries.

One may think of various ministries, believers and "Christian Denominations" in our day who endorse homosexuality and lesbianism in the ministry, or church leadership! Such become salt without savour. They lose their influence in the world. They are trodden under foot of men, cast out, and their influence for God is lost because of endorsement of such immorality, perversions and hypocritical lifestyle. Even the godless world, many times, does not expect "the Church" to endorse, let alone practice these perversions, when it is supposed to uphold the standards of the holiness of God against sin, and uphold the standards of God's Word, the Holy Bible! Those who follow these things, as well as the denial of "the faith once delivered to the saints" are savourless salt – good for nothing, but to be trodden under foot of men! The Church becomes a mockery in the eyes of an evil world. How can the church be good salt when it endorses evil lifestyles? It is impossible!

"Cast out" is the judgment on savourless salt.

"Trodden under foot" is also part of this judgment.

The Scriptures speak of this "casting out" and being "trodden under foot" as seen in these references:

* People without faith are cast out of the kingdom (Matthew 8:12).

* The man without the wedding garment was cast out in outer darkness (Matthew 22:13).

* The slothful servant, failing to use his talents, was cast out into outer darkness also (Matthew 25:30).

* The foolish virgins, lacking enough oil supply, were shut out of the marriage feast (Matthew 25:1-13).

* The outer court, and those therein, was unmeasured, and therefore cast out and trodden under foot for forty-two months, the period of the "great tribulation" (Revelation 11:1-3).

* Apostates from the faith, along with the wicked, are cast down and trodden under foot (Daniel 8:13 with Isaiah 63:18; Nehemiah 4:3).

* Salt which has lost its savour is good for nothing; it is cast out and trodden under foot of men. Salt, along with its usefulness, without its distinctive savour, is also useless. It is also used in Scripture in judgment and destructive sense. Lot lost his influence in the city of Sodom, even though a believer. He offered his two daughters to the evil Sodomites. Then, even when he had escaped the city by the mercy and grace of God, he was made drunk, and in his drunken state, by incest, he fathered two sons, Ammon and Moab, which became enemy nations of the Israel of God in due time. Lot's wife became a pillar of salt because of her disobedience and sinfulness in looking back to Sodom and Gommorah, where her heart was (Genesis 19).

Peter says that Lot vexed his soul with the filthy conversation and **lifestyle** of the wicked people of Sodom. He saw and heard their evil deeds and vexed his soul with their unlawful deeds day by day. He was a man "saved so as by fire" (1Corinthians 3:15).

Salt was also used to destroy the fruitfulness of the land; therefore, such use was destructive and a judgment on the land (Deuteronomy 29:22-23; Judges 9:15; Job 39:6; Psalm 107:34; Jeremiah 17:6; Zephaniah 2:9).

E. The Practical Application Of The Parable

In our day, most houses have a "salt-shaker". In order for the salt to be used and be effective, it has to be shaken out of the salt-shaker! So it is with the believer. The church may be likened to the salt-shaker, but for the Christian to be of use, useful and effective, he has to get out of the salt -shaker and be shaken into the world around him.

The primary task of the church as "salt" is to evangelize the world. The church is not to be in a salt-shaker, in isolation or monasticim. The church is not to compromise and become like the world, though in the world. It is to change people's lives, saving them through the power of the Gospel of Christ, and seeing them come out of corruption, out of sin, into wholeness and righteousness.

To be useful, the Lord has many uses for different ones. Influence, difference, cleansing, preserving, preventing – these are some of the many uses the Lord has for Christians -His salt in the earth!

In **"The Study of the Parables"**, by Ada R. Habershon (p.117), she writes:

"Our lives are intended to be a living testimony against sin and thus to hinder corruption. But if the salt has lost its savour, it will fail in its purpose, it will be just as useless as the life of a Christian who ceases to witness against sin.

If the Holy Spirit fill a believer, He will work through him in convicting the world of sin. In another place, the Lord says, "Have salt in yourselves, and have peace one with another". If there be self-judgment there will be forbearance, and so if there be salt in ourselves, there will be peace for others.

The apostle gives another lesson, "Let your speech be always with grace, seasoned with salt." Graciousness which takes no note of sin is not to be admired or cultivated. It may sometimnes seem more easy, more pleasant, more polite, to take no notice of wrong things said or done in our presence, but there must not be grace without salt. There must be either silent or spoken testimony against sin." (End quote)

If the believer individually, and the church corporately does this, then indeed this parable will be fulfilled, and the Christian will be the salt in the earth. If the believer individually, or the church corporately fails to do this, and loses its savour, then it will cast out and trodden under foot of men! This is the message of this short parabolic illustration. What Jesus said to His disciples then is truth applicable to every generation and to us in our day!

CHAPTER FORTY-TWO
THE PARABLE OF THE LOST AND FOUND SHEEP

Luke Chapter 15 presents, what may be called, a "trinity of parables", all teaching, basically the same truth. It is a unique chapter among the Synoptic Gospels. It contains, according to most expositors, three parables. They could be titled, "The Parables of the Lost and Found", for that is the theme of each parable.

1. The Parable of the Lost and Found Sheep (Luke 15:3-7 with Matthew 18:12-14).
2. The Parable of the Lost and Found Coin (Luke 15:8-10).
3. The Parable of the Lost and Found Son (Luke 15:11-32).

For the purpose of this textbook, Chapters 42, 43 and 44 will take each of this trinity of parables and deal with them accordingly. At the conclusion of Chapter 44, the three parables will be focused more sharply by way of contrast and comparison. This chapter especially considers the lost and found sheep.

A. The Scripture On The Parable

Both Luke and Matthew speak of the lost and found sheep, even though each provides a different setting. For the purpose of the text, both Gospels are brought together here for our exposition.

Luke 15:3-7

And he spake this parable unto them, saying,

What man of you, having an hundred sheep, if he lose one of them, doth not leave the ninety and nine in the wilderness, and go after that which is lost, until he find it?

And when he hath found it, he layeth it on his shoulders, rejoicing.

And when he cometh home, he calleth together his friends and neighbours, saying unto them, Rejoice with me; for I have found my sheep which was lost.

I say unto you, that likewise joy shall be in heaven over one sinner that repenteth, more than over ninety and nine just persons, which need no repentance.

Matthew 18:11-13

For the Son of man is come to save that which was lost.

How think ye? if a man have an hundred sheep, and one of them be gone astray, doth he not leave the ninety and nine, and goeth into the mountains, and seeketh that which is gone astray?

And if so be that he find it, verily I say unto you, he rejoiceth more of that sheep, than of the ninety and nine which went not astray.

B. The Setting Of The Parable
Luke 15:1-2

Then drew near unto him all the publicans and sinners for to hear him.

And the Pharisees and scribes murmured, saying, This man receiveth sinners, and eateth with them.

The setting of this trinity of parables is at a time when the generally irreligious publicans (tax-gatherers) and sinners are gathered around Jesus to listen to His teaching. At the same time, the Pharisees ("the Separatists"), and the scribes (the theologians and official interpreters of the Law) are gathered also.

In Matthew's Gospel, the setting in which the parable was given, pertained to the care and concern of little children of the kingdom. In Luke's setting, it is in connection with lost people.

C. The Moral Of The Parable

The moral of each of the parables is the same. Verses 2,7,and 10 provide this for us. The Pharisees, in critical manner, said, This man receives sinners, and eats with them. Jesus Himself also said, "The Son of Man is come to seek and to save that which was lost" (Luke 19:10; 9:56; Matthew 18:11; 15:24).

The three parables illustrate the truth that is seen when that which is lost is found. There is joy in heaven over one sinner that repents more than over persons who have already repented and are safe in the fold of Christ, the good shepherd.

D. The Exposition Of The Parable

As already seen, this trinity of parables is unique to Luke, although Matthew's Gospel records the parable of the lost sheep in a somewhat different setting. The parables are considered in the order of (a) The Lost Sheep, (b) The Lost Coin, and (c) The Lost Son. Most expositors recognize that, in reality, it is **one parable,** broken up into three **pictures!** All have the same truth, but vary the details of the story and its aspects.

The Parable of the Lost and Found Sheep covers but five verses in Luke. The language and symbolism of the parable is very familiar to Jewry. It did not require much interpretation to a pastoral nation.

1. The Sheep

Many, many Scriptures speak of Israel, or mankind, under the symbol of sheep. "All we like sheep have gone astray, we have turned every one to his own way..."(Isaiah 53:6; Jeremiah 50:6).

"I had gone astray like a lost sheep" (Psalm 119:176). "You were as sheep going astray.." (1Peter 2:25).

Jesus saw the people as sheep without a shepherd (Matthew 9:36; Mark 6:34. Read also Ezekiel 34:5; 1Kings 22:17; Numbers 27:15-23; Psalm 107::41). Jesus came to seek the lost sheep of the house of Israel, as well as, in due time, the lost sheep of the Gentile world (Matthew 10:6; 15:24 with John 10). All would in His time come in to the "one fold" – the New Testament Church.

2. Lost Sheep

Mankind is likened to lost sheep, sheep who have gone astray, turning each to their own way. Sheep have the habit of getting lost, but they never seem to be able to find their way back home. They have to be sought and found. The shepherd seeks for the lost sheep until he finds it.

The lost sheep is the wandering sinner, lost in sin. They are unregenerate sinners (Luke 15:7,10; Isaiah 53:6; 1Peter 2:25).The Son of Man came to seek and to save that which was lost (Luke 19:10; 9:56; Matthew 18:11).

3. The Shepherd

There is no mistaking who the shepherd is. It is none other than the Lord Jesus Christ Himself. Many references attest to this truth. He is:

* The Lord God is our shepherd (Isaiah 40:9-11).

* The Man who is my shepherd (Zechariah 13:7).
* The shepherd of Israel (Genesis 49:24; Psalm 80:1; Psa23:1).
* The shepherd (Isaiah 40:11; Jeremiah 31:10; Ezekiel 34:23).
* The one shepherd (Ecclesiastes 12:11; Ezekiel 34:24).
* The shepherd and bishop of our souls (1Peter 2:25).
* The good shepherd (John 10).
* The great shepherd (Hebrews 13:10).
* The chief shepherd (1Peter 5:4).

In a secondary sense, ministers of the gospel are called to be shepherds. They are under-shepherds of the church, the flock of God (Acts 20:27-35; 1Peter 5:1-4). All need to have the heart of a shepherd. Moses (Exodus 3:1), David (1Samuel 17) were shepherds also, both naturally and spiritually and knew the work of the pastoral life and ministry.

4. The Seeking Shepherd

The shepherd seeks the lost sheep until he finds it. He leaves the ninety and nine that are safe in the fold, whether in the fold in the wilderness or the mountains, and he goes to seek the sheep that is lost, or gone astray.

Ezekiel complains about the shepherds in Israel that do not care about the flock but only care for themselves, what they can get from the flock. Ezekiel speaks of:

* Diseased sheep – needing to be strengthened
* Sick sheep – needing to be healed
* Broken sheep – needing to be bound up
* Driven-away sheep – needing to be brought back
* Lost sheep – needing to be sought and found (Read Ezekiel 34:1-31, and especially verses 4 and 16.

5. The Ninety-Nine Safe Sheep

The ninety-nine safe sheep represents the believers who are already safe in the fold. They cannot represent the Pharisees and scribes who were religious sinners, and needed to come to repentance. They were lost, religious but unregenerate sheep, like the sinnners and publicans around them. The "safe sheep" are those who are just, or justified, and have no need to come to repentance, as they already have come to that and are safe in the fold of Christ. That is the reason the shepherd can leave the fold.

6. The Finding Shepherd

The shepherd seeks the lost until he finds it. The sheep has strayed away, and become lost. The "found sheep" is the sinner that comes to repentance (Luke 15:7,10).

7. The Shepherd's Shoulders

The shepherd lays the sheep upon his shoulders. The shoulders represent the place of strength, responsibility, the place of government. "The government shall be upon His shoulders" (Isaiah 9:6 with Isaiah 22:20-24). The names of the twelve tribes of Israel were upon the two precious onyx stones on the shoulders of the high priest, Aaron (Exodus 28:6-12). The shepherd upholds the lost and found sheep on his shoulders, even as Jesus, the good shepherd does over a lost and found sinner that repents.

8. The Rejoicing Shepherd

Once the shepherd finds the sheep, there is rejoing. He rejoices as he returns home. He calls his friends and neighbours together and asks them to rejoice with him over the finding of the lost sheep.

In John 10, the whole chapter reveals Jesus as the good shepherd, giving His life for the sheep. In the death of Jesus by crucifixion, we see this gracious and loving act of the shepherd of all shepherds. He gave His life that the lost would be found, and be brought into the fold of the church.

E. The Practical Application Of The Parable

There is no mistaking the application of this simple, but beautiful parable here. Jesus Himself gives it to us in verse 7 and later on in verse 10.

Jesus said, "I say unto you, that **likewise** joy shall be in heaven over one sinner that repents, more than over ninety and nine just persons, that need no repentance".

Just as the shepherd and his friends and neighbours rejoice over the finding of the lost sheep, being brought back to the fold, so Christ and His ministers, and His people rejoice over sinners coming into the fold, or back home to God.

Heaven rejoices! Earth rejoices! Christ rejoices! The angels rejoice! The Church rejoices! Religious legalists, like the Pharisees and scribes, murmur, criticize and complain about Jesus receiving sinners and fellowshipping with repentant sinners.

Though there were the priests, the scribes, the Pharisees, Sadducees and the elders of the synagogues, they proved themselves that they had no shepherd's heart for the people. They were religious leaders (Matthew 9:36). All through the ministry of Jesus to lost sheep, the religious leaders murmured and criticized Him, instead of rejoicing over sinners coming to Christ.

They knew their Old Testament Scriptures about Israel being likened to "lost sheep", yet they failed to ever have the heart of a shepherd. They were justly condemned by Jesus for such hypocrisy when He pronounced such woes upon them (Matthew 23).

The lessons are plain for all those in ministry today, who are the shepherds of the people of God. Lost sheep should be sought and found; sick sheep should be healed; bruised sheep should be bound up; broken sheep need to attended to. All ministries, be they called to be apostles, prophets, evangelists, pastors or teachers, should have the heart of a shepherd – for that is the heart of Christ!

CHAPTER FORTY-THREE
THE PARABLE OF THE LOST AND FOUND COIN

A. The Scriptures On The Parable
Luke 15:8-10

Either what woman having ten pieces of silver, if she lose one piece, doth not light a candle, and sweep the house, and seek diligently till she find it?

And when she hath found it, she calleth her friends and her neighbours together, saying, Rejoice with me; for I have found the piece which I had lost.

Likewise, I say unto you, there is joy in the presence of the angels of God over one sinner that repenteth.

B. The Setting Of The Parable

The setting is the same as in Luke 15:1-2. The publicans and sinners are listening to the teaching of Jesus as He receives them. The Pharisees and scribes are murmuring against His receiving such people. The publicans were tax-gatherers for the Romans and therefore much hated by the Jews, as being traitors to their own nation, robbing their own people, and working for the Romans. The publicans were counted as heathen. It is a gathering of the religious and irreligious, but both were unregenerate classes.

C. The Moral Of The Parable

The parable is only to be found in Luke's Gospel. The same moral is consistent through the trinity of parables. Jesus receives sinners. There is more joy in heaven over repentant sinners coming to Christ than over saints who have already repented.

D. The Exposition Of The Parable

The parable is a simple, but true to life story. A woman has ten coins, probably ten pieces of silver, and she loses one. She knows she has lost it in the house. She, therefore, sweeps the house diligently until she finds it. Her joy is great. She calls her friends and her neighbours together to rejoice with her over the lost and found silver coin. The message is the same as that of the shepherd and the lost and found sheep!

1. A Woman

In the shepherd parable, it is a man. In the coin parable, it is a woman. The attitude of the scribes and Pharisees towards a woman is constantly seen throughout the Gospels, especially in Luke's Gospel, which is the "Gospel of Womanhood". Jesus always had kind and courteous thoughts towards the women who were so suppressed in His time by religious leaders, as well as others in Jewry, and other nations and cultures.

2. Ten Silver Coins

It was often the custom to give to a bride-to-be silver pieces as well as other kinds of jewellery. The jewellery was used, at times, for ornamental decorations on the woman's head-dress.

Some expositors say that the silver coins were a gift to a woman, or a part of the dowry given to her, being betrothed or in a marriage relationship. If this was so, then it would make the ten pieces of silver coin more valuable.

Other expositors say that the silver coin was part of the necklace that the woman wore. The full beauty of the necklace is ruined if one of the coins is lost. The loss is more than the value of one single coin, as it is what it represents; it represents the whole.

Other expositors say it represents hard earned money by a peasant woman, and this gave it the value when lost. The woman had either earned it or had been given the same as a gift. The equivalent in our day would be a woman, engaged or married, losing a diamond out of her engagement or wedding ring.

Ten is the number of responsibility in Scripture. One may think of the Ten Commands, the ten virgins, the ten pounds, and so forth, as seen in previous parables. Silver also is symbolic of atonement money (Exodus 30:11-16).

3. One Lost Coin

The one lost coin was of great value because it was part of the whole ten. The woman did not remain satisfied that she still had nine silver coins and did not need to worry about the one lost piece. The whole ten was of value, and so she set about to find the lost coin.

4. Lighting The Candle

Many of the homes in the Middle East were not well lit, either by window light or light from the doorway. They would be dark even in day time. This necessitated the lighting of the lamp to have more illumination to help find the lost coin. Zephaniah speaks of the Lord "searching Jerusalem with candles" (lamps – Zephaniah 1:12) God's Word is a lamp unto our feet and a light unto our path, says the Psalmist (Psalm 119:130). She would search for that which was lost in the light of the Word, so to speak (Matthew 5:14; Philippians 2:15). Light is needed to discover that which is lost!

5. Sweeping The House

The sheep had been lost in the wilderness or on a mountain. The coin was lost in the house; not outside, but inside. The woman had "spring-cleaning" of the house. It was a time for cleansing the house to find the lost coin.

6. Seeking Diligently

Her attitude was that of diligent searching. She was not half-hearted. Hebrews says that God is a rewarder of them that diligently seek Him (Hebrews 11:5-6). God does not respond to half-hearted people. The woman gave herself to diligent seeking of the lost coin. It was lost in the house. She must find it. It would require persistence in cleaning the house, and working in the light of the lamp to find the lost coin. It may not be of much or any value to others, but it was valuable to her.

7. Lost And Found

With the lighted lamp, she kept sweeping and searching until she found that which was lost. The qualities of concern, care and diligence are manifested here.

8. The Rejoicing Woman

After finding the silver coin, like the shepherd, so the woman calls her friends and neighbours together. She told them the story and asked them to rejoice with her that the lost coin had been found.

E. The Practical Application Of The Parable

The message remains the same, with an added thought. Likewise, just like the woman in the story, there is joy in the presence of the angels, there is joy in heaven, over one sinner that repents. One lost coin equals one lost sinner. Searching diligently speaks of genuine concern over the lost sinner. Rejoicing speaks of the great joy in heaven, with the Father God and the angels, over repentant sinners.

The angels are sent forth as guardians of little children. The angels are sent forth to the heirs of salvation. There is much angelic ministry in the Bible, both to the saved and the unsaved. Only eternity will reveal what the angels have done in obedience to the Father's commands in behalf of lost sinners, as well as the saints (Read Matthew 18:10; 24:31; Psalm 104:4; Luke 12:8-9; Hebrews 1:13; 12:22; Revelation 5:11).

The final ministry of angels is to carry the spirit of the redeemed, at death, into the very presence of the Father (Luke 16:22).

If a woman could rejoice over one lost and found coin, and if the Father and the angels in heaven could rejoice over one lost and found sinner, why could the Pharisees and the scribes not rejoice over sinners coming to Jesus? So all leaders and saints should seek to save that which is lost, and when they find lost sinners, should rejoice together with the Father, and the angels and one another over "the lost and found". A "lost and found" sinner is of much more value than a silver coin!

CHAPTER FORTY-FOUR
THE PARABLE OF THE LOST AND FOUND SON

A. The Scripture On The Parable
Luke 15:11-32

And he said, A certain man had two sons:

And the younger of them said to his father, Father, give me the portion of goods that falleth to me. And he divided unto them his living.

And not many days after the younger son gathered all together, and took his journey into a far country, and there wasted his substance with riotous living.

And when he had spent all, there arose a mighty famine in that land; and he began to be in want.

And he went and joined himself to a citizen of that country; and he sent him into his fields to feed swine.

And he would fain have filled his belly with the husks that the swine did eat: and no man gave unto him.

And when he came to himself, he said, How many hired servants of my father's have bread enough and to spare, and I perish with hunger!

I will arise and go to my father, and will say unto him, Father, I have sinned against heaven, and before thee,

And am no more worthy to be called thy son: make me as one of thy hired servants.

And he arose, and came to his father. But when he was yet a great way off, his father saw him, and had compassion, and ran, and fell on his neck, and kissed him.

And the son said unto him, Father, I have sinned against heaven, and in thy sight, and am no more worthy to be called thy son.

But the father said to his servants, Bring forth the best robe, and put it on him; and put a ring on his hand, and shoes on his feet:

And bring hither the fatted calf, and kill it; and let us eat, and be merry:

For this my son was dead, and is alive again; he was lost, and is found. And they began to be merry.

Now his elder son was in the field: and as he came and drew nigh to the house, he heard musick and dancing.

And he called one of the servants, and asked what these things meant.

And he said unto him, Thy brother is come; and thy father hath killed the fatted calf, because he hath received him safe and sound.

And he was angry, and would not go in: therefore came his father out, and intreated him.

And he answering said to his father, Lo, these many years do I serve thee, neither transgressed I at any time thy commandment: and yet thou never gavest me a kid, that I might make merry with my friends:

But as soon as this thy son was come, which hath devoured thy living with harlots, thou hast killed for him the fatted calf.

And he said unto him, Son, thou art ever with me, and all that I have is thine.

It was meet that we should make merry, and be glad: for this thy brother was dead, and is alive again; and was lost, and is found.

B. The Setting Of The Parable

The setting of the parable remains the same as seen in Luke 15:1-2. In contrast to the Parable of the Lost Sheep (five verses), and the Parable of the Lost Coin (three verses), the Parable of the Lost Son has nineteen verses given to it. It is the fullest and most complete of the trinity of parables in Luke 15, It is undoubtedly the richest of the three of God's parables of the "lost and found" department!

C. The Moral Of The Parable

The truth of the parable remains the same. However, there are more supportive truths and lessons to be learnt from this extended parable. God the Father rejoices over sons returning back home, after coming to genuine repentance for leaving the Father's house. Pharisees and scribes, who have the "elder brother attitude" also need to come to repentance and enjoy God's party of reconciliation over lost and found sons! That is the moral of the parable.

D. The Exposition Of The Parable

Besides the major moral of the parable, most all expositors recognize that there are many truths to be gained from the many insights of this extended parable. It is a parable common to daily life. The parable has probably been preached and taught on more than the other two parables over the centuries. Untold numbers of sinners and backsliders have been won to the Lord through an exposition of this pearl of parables. The details are rich and can only be used to provide seed thoughts to the Bible student. This parable also is unique to Luke's Gospel. It cannot be limited to one major moral, for there are a number of other supportive truths to this major moral!

1. A Certain Man

It is one of Christ's favourite introductions to a story (Read Matthew 17:14; 21:28; Mark 12:1; Luke 8:27; 10:30; 12:16; 13:6; 14:16; 15:11; 16:1,19; 18:35; 20:9). The certain man here is a father and points to the heavenly Father, God.

2. Two Sons

Although the emphasis is put on the "prodigal son", the man had two sons. Both sons should be considered, for each reveal underlying attitudes of heart towards their father. The reader is reminded of "The Parable of Two Sons" in Matthew 21:28 over the work in the vineyard. One was an obedient son, the other a disobedient son. The parable here is "The Parable of Two Sons" – the prodigal son and the legal son (Luke 15:11).

3. The Prodigal's Steps Downward

The younger son – not the firstborn son – asks his father for his portion of the goods that would come to him in due time. Sometimes a father would divide his inheritance to his children while he was alive. Other times, it would be divided upon his death (Genesis 25:1-6).

"A good man leaves an inheritance to his children's children" (Proverbs 13:22).

"An inheritance may be gotten hastily at the beginning, but the end thereof shall not be blessed" (Proverbs 20:21).

"Wisdom is good with an inheritance, and by it there is profit to them that see the sun" (Ecclesiastes 7:11).

The father, for whatever reason, divides to his son his inheritance. The younger son does not wait too long before he gathers all together and leaves the father's house. He apparently did not understand Proverbs 20:21, as quoted here. The

Law gave the rules and guidelines for dividing an inheritance between the firstborn and the younger son. The elder son was to receive a double portion, the younger a portion (Deuteronomy 21:15-17).

Thompson's Chain Reference Bible lists seven downward steps in the younger son's story (T.C.R. 4310), which we adapt and amplify here.

(a) Self-will – Verse 12

No longer does the son desire to be subject to his father's will, or his father's authority. Perhaps he is tired of the routine of home life, and the restraints of his parents or being dependant on his father. He is tired of his father's house. He wants to be free, independant, and make his own way in life. Self-will is simply a form of rebellion against the father's will.

(b) Selfishness – Verse 13

It is worthy to note that his request, at the beginning of his journey was, "Give me..." It was what he could get leaving home. At the end of his journey, returning home, his request is, "Make me..." Now it was what he could be (Compare verse 13 and 19).

(c) Separation – Verse 13

Once he obtained his portion of the father's goods, not many days after, he gathered all together and took his journey into a far country; far enough away from all parental control. He is separated from his father, his father's house and authority, and his elder brother, and all that home represented in love and security.

(d) Sensuality – Verse 13,30

In the far country, he wasted his substance in riotous living, in sensual living with harlots. Moral restraints are removed. External restraints of father and home are gone. He becomes reckless, free from restraints, and therefore, loose of living and given to fleshly lusts. The prodigal casts off all internal restraints and lives a riotous life. He forgot Proverbs 23:20-22. He has received his inheritance hastily in the beginning, but he had forgotten that the end would not be blessed!

"Be not among winebibbers, among riotous eaters of flesh; for the drunkard and the glutton shall come to poverty, and drowsiness shall clothe a man with rags. Hearken unto your father that begat you, and despise not your mother when she is old". (Read also Proverbs 28:7; Romans 13:13; 1Timothy 1:6; 1Peter 4:4; 2Peter 2:13, where it warns against those who are "riotous").

(e) Spiritual Destitution – Verse 14

He spent all he had. While he had money, he had friends. He wasted his father's inheritance given to him. A mighty famine came in the land and he is now in dire need. God often allowed famines to come in order to drive His people back to Himself (Psalm 105:16; Ruth 1:1; Jeremiah 2:13; Ezekiel 14:21; Genesis 12:10).

(f) Self-Abasement – Verse 15

He joined (lit. "glued") himself to a citizen of the country who sent him to feed pigs. To feed pigs was the lowest abasement to a Jew. Feeding pigs was feeding unclean animals, abominations to the Lord (Isaiah 65:4; 66:3,17; Matthew 7:6; 8:30-32; 2Peter 2:24; Proverbs 26:11).

(g) Starvation – Verse 16

In this sad state of affairs, he was so hungry that he would have eaten the pigs food. No man really cared for him. The husks were bean-like pods of the carob tree. His physical need is evident.

4. The Prodigal's Steps Upward

Thompson's Chain Reference (4310) lists seven steps of the prodigal as he comes to himself and returns to his father, which are adapted and amplified here.

(a) Realization – Verse 17

"He came to himself". He never would have come to his father if he had not first come to himself! He came to a realization of his spiritual and desolate condition, how far he had gone down since leaving his father's house and his home. He realized that even his father's hired servants were far better off than him, and how they had enough and to spare, and here he was dying of hunger.

(b) Resolution – Verse 18-19

"I will arise and go to my father and say to him, Father, I have sinned against heaven and before you. And I am no more worthy to be called your son. Make me like one of the hired servants". This was an act of the will after realizing his low and evil state.

(c) Repentance – Verse 18-19

Repentance is a change of mind. It also involves confession of sin. "I have sinned" was his word. It involves a sense of unworthiness. "I am not worthy to be called your son". It also involves an attitude of humility. "Make me as one of the hired servants". A different attitude was needed in order to come back to the father's house.

The fruits of repentance are:

* Godly sorrow for sin – 2Corinthians 7:10; Psalm 38:18
* Confession of sin – Psalm 32:5; Proverbs 28:13; 1John 1:9
* Forsaking of sin – Proverbs 28:13
* A complete change of mind and attitude – Matthew 3:1-3; Luke 3:1-19 with Acts 26:20.

(d) Return – Verse 19-20

"I will arise and go to my father... And he arose and came to his father..." It was not enough to complain about the pigs and the pigsty. Repentance is a change of mind. Return is a change of direction. It is "turn" and "re(again)turn". He had turned away from his father. Now he is re-turning back to his father.

How often God spoke through His servants, the prophets, calling to people of Israel to "turn" and "return" to Himself (2Chronicles 30:6,9; Jeremiah 8:4; Isaiah 55:7; Jeremiah 3:22; 4:1; 24:7; Hosea 6:1).

(e) Reconciliation – Verse 20

While he was yet far off, the father saw him, and filled with compassion, ran to him, met him and gave him the kiss of reconciliation. This was unusual in the Middle East for a father to run at all, let alone run to a prodigal son.

Undoubtedly the father had watched day after day for his son's return. He knew in time the inheritance would be squandered. The son confessed his sin before his father. He confessed his unworthiness. He never finished the rest of his confession. It was in his heart, but it never fully got to his lips.

So the Father God sees sinners "afar off". He is filled with "compassion" and longs for their return. He waits and watches daily.

(e) Restoration – Verse 22,25

The father commanded his servants to bring forth:

* The best robe – reclothed, rags taken away, righteousness is restored (Isaiah 61:10).

* The ring on his hand – assurance and authority restored, the ring of the father's acceptance (Genesis 41:42).

* The shoes on his feet – slaves were generally bare-footed, only household members wore shoes; his sonship is restored (Ephesians 6:11-17).

* The feast of rejoicing – a festival occasion, the father's supper of joy.

* The music and dancing – literally, "a ring-around-dance", praise and worship from the tabernacle of David. Instruments of music and group dancing in the father's house (Psalm 150; Jeremiah 33:11; Psalm 149). It was a time to rejoice and be merry. Note the word "rejoice" in verses 6,9,23,24,29.

(f) Rejoicing – Verse 23,27

The father is delighted to have his son back home. It was one thing to lose a sheep, and another thing to lose a coin, but here was a lost son. A sheep is indeed valuable, a silver coin and money more valuable, but a son is the most valuable of all (Herbert Lockyer, p.281, **"All The Parables Of The Bible"**).

The fatted calf was killed, the feast was spread, and great merriment took place at the father's party for his "lost and found" son. See what the father said about his prodigal son.

* My son was dead, but is alive again. So people are "dead in trespasses and sins" but can be made alive again (Ephesians 2:1-4). He was a dead son.

* My son was lost, but is found. He was a lost son.

* My son was unsafe, but now he is safe and sound at home. Full sonship is restored by the father.

An old writer put it this way. For the prodigal there were three stages with relation to his father's house:

1. The rejection of love – while at home
2. The return to home after being – away from home
3. The reception at home – back home.

5. **The Elder Brother – Verses 25-32**

While many times the prodigal son and brother is preached about, the elder brother is often over-looked. The parable actually involves **two sons, two brothers,** even though the major part is given over to the prodigal son and brother.

The prodigal needed to come to repentance. So did the elder brother, as these verses clearly indicate. We note some of the things about this son and the list of sins seen in the elder brother's attitude, both to his father and his brother.

(a) **Complete Inheritance**

As the firstborn son, he had a double portion of his father's inheritance (Deuteronomy 21:15-17). All that the father had was his. While his brother had squandered his portion of the inheritance, he still had his.

(b) **Sinful attitudes**

If the prodigal son was guilty of "filthiness of the flesh", with harlots and riotous living, the elder son was guilty of "filthiness of the spirit", evidenced by his sinful attitudes (2Corinthians 7:1).

(1) **An Angry Attitude – Verses 25-28**

When he came in from working in the field, and heard the music and the dancing, he called one of the servants and asked him what it all meant. The servant told him the good news of his brother's return. Instead of being glad, rushing in to see his brother and rejoicing with him and his father, he was angry. This was a sinful anger, not a righteous anger.

"Anger" here means he was provoked, enraged, becoming exasperated. It arises out of excitement of mind. He was "angry without a cause" (Matthew 5:22; Ephesians 4:26).

(2) **A Legalistic Attitude – Verse 29**

He had served his father as a slave for years. He served his father because he felt he had to, not because he loved to. Literally, he says, "I am your slave!" He had a wrong concept of a proper father/son relationship. You never gave me a party so I could celebrate with my friends, was in effect his reply. He had served his father, as a slave, with a legal attitude, not as a son.

(3) **A Self-Righteous Attitude – Verse 29**

He tells his father that he had not transgressed any of his father's commands at any time. This evidenced a self-righteous attitude. His attitude was like that of the self-righteous Pharisees.

(4) **A Resentful Attitude – Verse 28**

He would not go into the celebration even though his father entreated him. He was proud and jealous and resentful. These things robbed him of the rejoicing and joy at his brother's return home.

(5) A Disrespectful Attitude – Verse 29,20,32

The father entreated the elder son and brother, yet the attitude of disrespect is seen in some of the words of reaction to the father's appeal. The elder brother says, "This **your son...**" while the father says, "This **your brother...**" The whole attitude is one of disrespect towards his father, and contempt for his brother.

(6) An Unforgiving Attitude

The father received the prodigal back as a son, forgiven and restored. The elder brother should receive him back as a brother. But the elder brother throws into his father's face the prodigal brother's sins, his wasted and sensual living. All this speaks of an unforgiving attitude in the elder brother.

(7) A Pharisaical Attitude

The prodigal son represented the "publicans and sinners company" in the crowd, who had come to repentance. The elder brother represented the "Pharisees and scribes company" in the crowd, who needed to come to true repentance for their self-righteous attitude. They, like the elder brother, would not receive the repentant prodigals. They reacted against Jesus receiving sinners. Later on, in the Book of Acts, that same Pharisaical and Judaistic spirit and attitude would react against God receiving the Gentiles into His kingdom.

But the whole matter is: Christ came not to call the righteous but sinners to repentance. The self-righteous also needed to hear the call and also come to repentance.

E. The Practical Application Of The Parable

An overview of this magnificient parable shows us several major things.

1. The Father In The Story Represents The Father God

He is full of compassion, forgiveness and love, and He waits to reconcile mankind to Himself.

2. The Prodigal In the Story Represents Repentant Sinners

All who have wasted the Father's goods in the far country of sin, and have come to true repentance, and back to the Father are the prodigals. They represent both Jews and Gentiles. They are represented by the "publicans and sinners" who were gathered around Jesus at this time of the parable.

3. The Elder Brother In The Story Represents The Religious Sinners

All who look with disdain on prodigals coming to the Father in genuine repentance are the elder brothers. The religious, the self-righteous yet unregenerate sinners are the scribes and the Pharisees of Jesus day. They also include the priests, the Levites, the Jewish elders, along with the Sadducees who constantly criticized Jesus because He was the Friend of sinners, and received and forgave sinners. This company is great through out the whole world in every generation.

4. The Father's House

Jesus spoke of the temple as "His Father's house" (John 2:16-21; John 14:1-6). Since the cross, the church now is Father's house. The church is God's New Covenant temple (Ephesians 2:19-22; Hebrews 3:3-6; 1Timothy 3:15; 1Peter 2:5). All, both repentant Jews and Gentiles, are welcome to the Father's house, where these is feasting, and rejoicing, and music and dancing together as the Father reconciles prodigals and elder brothers are reconciled to their prodigal brothers!

The attitudes of anger, legalism, self-righteousness, resentfulness, disrespect and the spirit of Pharisaism have to be repented of in order to enjoy Father's house together!

In Summary:

A number of commentaries bring out rich truths by way of contrasts and comparison in this trinity of parables. The major thoughts are summarized here in a three-column approach for better focusing of the truths in each of the parables.

The Triune Parables

The Lost and Found Sheep	The Lost and Found Coin	The Lost and Found Son
Luke 15:3-7	Luke 15:8-10	Luke 15:11-32
Lost in the wilderness	Lost in the house	Lost in the far country
Sheep lost by wandering	Coin lost through no fault	Son lost deliberately, wilfullly
Vaguely sensed it	Did not consciously know	consciously lost
Sheep could not find itself	Coin could not find itself	Son could come to himself
Represents 1% loss	Represents 10% loss	Represents 50% loss
Shepherd sought the sheep	Woman sought the coin	Father not seek the son
Lost and found	Lost and found	Lost and found, Dead and alive
Rejoicing	Rejoicing	Feast of merriment with Father
Friends and neighbours	Friends and neighbours	Music, dancing with servants
Lost publicans and sinners	Lost publicans and sinners	Lost prodigal sons
Joy in heaven	Joy among the angels	Joy in Father's house
Over repentant sinners	Over repentant sinners	Over repentant prodigals
Pharisees, scribes murmur	Pharisees, scribes murmur	Elder brother angry at Father's
at Jesus receiving sinners	at Jesus forgiving sinners	receiving and forgiving prodigal
Parable of the Son of God	Parable of the Holy Spirit	Parable of the Father God
as the Good Shepherd	working with the bride-church	as the compassionate God

CHAPTER FORTY-FIVE
THE PARABLE OF THE UNRIGHTEOUS STEWARD

A. The Scripture On The Parable
Luke 16:1-13

And he said also unto his disciples, There was a certain rich man, which had a steward; and the same was accused unto him that he had wasted his goods.

And he called him, and said unto him, How is it that I hear this of thee? give an account of thy stewardship; for thou mayest be no longer steward.

Then the steward said within himself, What shall I do? for my lord taketh away from me the stewardship: I cannot dig; to beg I am ashamed.

I am resolved what to do, that, when I am put out of the stewardship, they may receive me into their houses.

So he called every one of his lord's debtors unto him, and said unto the first, How much owest thou unto my lord?

And he said, An hundred measures of oil. And he said unto him, Take thy bill, and sit down quickly, and write fifty.

Then said he to another, And how much owest thou? And he said, An hundred measures of wheat. And he said unto him, Take thy bill, and write fourscore.

And the lord commended the unjust steward, because he had done wisely: for the children of this world are in their generation wiser than the children of light.

And I say unto you, Make to yourselves friends of the mammon of unrighteousness; that, when ye fail, they may receive you into everlasting habitations.

He that is faithful in that which is least is faithful also in much: and he that is unjust in the least is unjust also in much.

If therefore ye have not been faithful in the unrighteous mammon, who will commit to your trust the true riches?

And if ye have not been faithful in that which is another man's, who shall give you that which is your own?

No servant can serve two masters: for either he will hate the one, and love the other; or else he will hold to the one, and despise the other. Ye cannot serve God and mammon.

B. The Setting Of The Parable

Verses 1 and 14 seem to be the setting of the parable. The parable here is particularly spoken to Christ's disciples. But, among the disciples there were a number of Pharisees who derided Jesus when they heard His teaching. Jesus reproved them for their evil hearts and their self-justification before men and God (verse 15).

The parable here is quite similar to the "Parable of the Talents" in Matthew 25:14-30, and teaches similar truths, but there is some variation in its details.

C. The Moral Of The Parable

It would appear that Jesus, once again, provides the moral of the parable in verses 9-13. The disciples of Jesus must learn how to wisely use money in the kingdom of God. He must invest in time for eternity. He must be faithful in the little things before being trusted with greater things. He must be faithful in earthly riches before receiving eternal riches. Money is a means to an end, not the end in itself. One must not be deceived by the means and miss the end!

D. The Exposition Of The Parable

The parable is a true to life story of a rich man and his steward. Behind the earthly story is a heavenly meaning.

1. A Certain Rich Man

Christ's usual parable formula is seen once again. Luke 16 centers on a certain rich man in the two parables given by Jesus.

"A certain rich man" – verse 1.

"A certain rich man" – verse 19.

"A certain beggar" – verse 20.

The certain rich man in this present parable may point to the Lord, who is the owner of all things in heaven and earth, and to whom all are accountable. The earth is the Lord's and the fulness therein. The silver and gold is His and the cattle on a thousand hills (Genesis 14:19,22; Psalm 24:1; 50:11-12; 68:19; 89:11; Haggai 2:8). He is the possessor of heaven and earth.

2. A Steward

This rich man had a steward, a manager or overseer of the affairs of his house. A steward was responsible to provide food for the household and manage the business of his master. The master of the house entrusted him with his goods and expected faithfulness in the handling of his goods. The steward was not the owner, but a steward and therefore, responsible and accountable to the master (1Chronicles 28:1; Luke 16:1; 1Peter 4:10; Luke 12:42).

In spiritual sense, all ministers of the Gospel, as well as all believers, are called to be stewards of the things of God, and the Word of God. Paul says we are "stewards of the mysteries of God", and a steward is required to be found faithful (1Corinthians 4:1-2). The things God gives are His goods. The Pharisees and scribes were called to be stewards of the Old Testament Scriptures, along with the priests and elders of the Jewish nation.

3. Wasting The Master's Goods

The steward, instead of properly managing the master's goods, was accused of being wasteful, and squandering, and mismangament of these affairs. He wasted money on things. Instead of use, there was abuse of the master's goods.

Unbelievers and believers can waste the things God has entrusted to them. They can squander away the goods God has given them. They can mismanage their time, their talents, gifts and finance and life. All are a trust from God. All can be wasted: wasted time, wasted talents and gifts; wasted money and a wasted life.

4. Give Account Of Stewardship

The rich man of the house called for the steward and told him that he had heard rumors about his mismanagement. He called him to give an account of the property, and because of his mismanagment, he could no longer be steward. He forfeited his position; he lost his job. He was dismissed!

The truth here is clear. All men, believers or unbelievers, are accountable to God. All will be called to account one day. All have to give an account to the Lord for all He has entrusted to them.

5. A Steward's Unrighteous Shrewdness

In verses 3-7 we see a shrewd steward acting in an unrighteous way to look after himself.

After being told of his dismissal, he asked himself what he could do for a living. He said he was not strong enough to go digging ditches for a living, and he was certainly too proud to go begging. He decided on what he felt was a good idea. By doing this, when he had no job and no house to live in, there would be those friends who would receive him into their houses, once he lost his stewardship. He called his master's debtors and asked each one what they owed his master. He promptly told them to cut the debt down.

* The one who owed a hundred measures of olive oil wrote down quickly that he owed but fifty (That is, about 1000 gallons to 500 gallons of oil).

* The one who owed one hundred measures of wheat wrote down quickly eighty measures of wheat (That is, from 1000 bushels to 800 bushels of wheat).

Undoubtedly, each of the debtors were pleased to cut down their accounts so much. Each thought the steward was kind and generous to do that for them. It was his decision, not theirs, after all. They would certainly be his friends. His action was dishonest. His action was shrewd. His action was wrong, it was unrighteous!

6. Received Into Their Houses

The parable does not round off the end of the story for us. But we may safely assume that the steward's hope, "that they may receive me into their houses" (verse 4) was fulfilled. He had used money, his master's accounts, to make friends in order to have someone receive him into their house once he was dismissed from his job!

7. The Rich Man's Commendation

The master found out about it and praised the dishonest steward – NOT for being dishonest – but for his being so shrewd! It was dishonest shrewdness. The manager did a wrong thing, but it was a wise thing. Wise things are not always right things!

The last part of verse 8 says: "For the children of this world are, in their generation, wiser than the children of light."

The Amplified New Testament says: "And his master praised the dishonest (unjust) manager for acting shrewdly and prudently; for the sons of this age are shrewder and more prudent and wiser in relation to their own generation – that is, to their own age and kind – than are the sons of light".

The steward's lord did not commend the steward for his wrong and unjust actions he took with his creditors. He commended him for his **wisdom** (shrewdness) relative to the unrighteous mammon.

E. The Practical Application Of The Parable

The Lord's comments on the parable are particularly found in the latter part of verses 8 on through verses 9-12. They center around **wisdom** and **faithfulness.** The steward was **wise** but **unfaithful** in that which was entrusted to him. Disciples of Jesus should be both **wise and faithful** with what the Lord has entrusted to them. That is the message.

1. **Wisdom – Verse 8b**

   The children of this age are often shrewder, wiser, and more prudent than the children of light. The Lord wants His children to be wiser, shrewder and more prudent because He can give them wisdom that is from above, not from beneath (James 3:13-18). If any one needs wisdom, the God of wisdom is more than willing to give it (James 1:5-8). The Book of Proverbs is a book of Divine wisdom for every area of human life, including the handling of money. If the children of this world – this age – are wiser in handling worldly matter, the children of light should be wise, because they also handle heavenly matters (Luke 20:34; John12:36; 1Thessalonians 5:5; Ephesians 5:8). Christians are "children of the light", not "children of the darkness".

2. **Faithfulness – Verses 8,10-12**

   The second word is "faithfulness", and it is required of stewards that a man be found faithful (1Corinthians 4:1-2).

   "Confidence in an unfaithful man in time of trouble is like a broken tooth and a foot out of joint" (Proverbs 25:19). One cannot depend on or rely on these in trouble.

   There are measures of faithfulness the Lord speaks of in:

   * Faithful in that which is least, faithful in much. Honesty in little things and matters prepares one for greater things.

   * Unjust in that which is least leads to being unjust also in much. Dishonesty leads to further dishonesty. If not faithful in the unrighteous riches (mammon), then one cannot be trusted with true riches. The material riches of earth are temporal. Spiritual riches of heaven are true and eternal. If we cannot be trusted with worldly wealth, can we handle heavenly wealth?

   * If one is faithful in that which is another man's, then he can be prepared to be faithful in that which is his. The steward was not faithful with his master's goods. He was not trustworthy. How could he handle his own things?

   The Lord's word at His coming is: "Well done, you **good AND faithful** servant. You have been faithful over a **few things**. I will make you ruler over **many things.** Enter into the joy of your Lord" (Matthew 25:21-23).

3. **Friends Of The Unrighteous Mammon – Verse 9**

   Without doubt, verse 9 has been the most difficult part of the Lord's teaching in this parable to be understood.

   "Make to yourselves friends of the mammon (riches) of unrighteousness, that, when you fail, they may receive you into everlasting habitations" (KJV). Several other translations help to clarify the point of the Lord here.

   "Now My advice to you is to use 'money', tainted as it is, to make yourselves friends, so that when it comes to an end, they may welcome you into the houses of eternity" (Phillips Translation).

"So I say to you, use your worldly wealth to win friends for yourselves, so that when money is a thing of the past, you may be received into an eternal home" (New English Bible).

"I tell you, use worldly wealth to gain friends for yourselves, so that when it is gone, you will be welcomed into eternal dwellings" (New International).

"And I tell you, make friends for yourselves by means of unrighteous mamon (that is, deceitful riches, money, possessions), so that when it fails, they (those you have favoured) may receive and welcome you into the everlasting habitations (dwellings)" (Amplified N.T.).

Translations use either, "When you fail", or "When it fails". So, when a person fails in health and dies, or when money fails or come to its end, the truth is applicable. When "it" fails is the mammon a man has made use of. Money shall fail. Health shall fail. Both are true of real life.

The **"they"** who receive the wise steward into **"everlasting houses"** are those who have been won to Christ through the wise investment of filfthy lucre (unrighteous mammon) in the kingdom of God. These are **"the friends"** won by use of money for the kingdom. The **"everlasting habitations"** speak of heaven itself and the dwelling places for the redeemed of this age.

Eternity alone will reveal and bless those who have supported financially the church, and the extension of God's kingdom in both home lands and foreign lands and missionary work! Eternity alone will reveal the souls which have been converted to Christ because of financial support from wise and faithful stewards of money.

By way of contrast and comparison:-

The Steward	The Believer
(a) Wasted his master's good	Does not waste his Master's goods
(b) Called to account	Day of account is coming
(c) Dismissed from his work	Rewarded for good works
(d) Dishonest with unrighteous mammon	Honest with unrighteous mammon
(e) Wise, shrewd, prudent man of this age	Should be wiser as child of light
(f) Made friends for himself by dishonesty	Makes friends by honesty dealings
(g) When he failed in his job over money matters	When a believer fails in health or money fails
(h) He was received into their temporal and earthly homes	Believers will be received into eternal and heavenly home
(i) Unfaithful in his trust	Faithful in little will be trusted with much

Truly, eternity alone will reveal "the friends" – the souls – who have been won to Christ and helped by a Christian steward's honest and wise and faithful use of money, wealth and possessions with which he was trusted. It is not making friends of money or riches, but making friends by means of it, using it for the kingdom of God.

Even though verses 13-14 do not seem to be part of the parable, the truth therein is applicable to the parable. No one can serve two masters. He either hates the one or loves the other. He either holds to one and despises the other. The two masters are either God or Mammon.

"Mammon" simply means "money" or "riches". The Pharisees were covetous (more lit. "lovers of money"), and after hearing the teaching of Jesus derided Him. They scoffed and sneered at Him.

Money is not evil in itself. It is the **love of money** which is the root of all evil. It has drowned men in destruction and perdition (1Timothy 6:6-10). It is a means to use for the glory of God, the necessities of life, the building of His church, the salvation of souls and the extension of the kingdom of God. This is being a **wise AND faithful** steward of the unrighteous mammon.

Once again, the measure of a man's ability is the measure of his responsibility and the measure of a man's responsibility is the measure of his accountability!

CHAPTER FORTY-SIX
THE PARABLE OF THE RICH MAN AND LAZARUS

A. The Scripture On The Parable
Luke 16:19-31

There was a certain rich man, which was clothed in purple and fine linen, and fared sumptuously every day:

And there was a certain beggar named Lazarus, which was laid at his gate, full of sores,

And desiring to be fed with the crumbs which fell from the rich man's table: moreover the dogs came and licked his sores.

And it came to pass, that the beggar died, and was carried by the angels into Abraham's bosom: the rich man also died, and was buried;

And in hell he lift up his eyes, being in torments, and seeth Abraham afar off, and Lazarus in his bosom.

And he cried and said, Father Abraham, have mercy on me, and send Lazarus, that he may dip the tip of his finger in water, and cool my tongue; for I am tormented in this flame.

But Abraham said, Son, remember that thou in thy lifetime receivedst thy good things, and likewise Lazarus evil things: but now he is comforted, and thou art tormented.

And beside all this, between us and you there is a great gulf fixed: so that they which would pass from hence to you cannot; neither can they pass to us, that would come from thence.

Then he said, I pray thee therefore, father, that thou wouldest send him to my father's house:

For I have five brethren; that he may testify unto them, lest they also come into this place of torment.

Abraham saith unto him, They have Moses and the prophets; let them hear them.

And he said, Nay, father Abraham: but if one went unto them from the dead, they will repent.

And he said unto him, If they hear not Moses and the prophets, neither will they be persuaded, though one rose from the dead.

B. The Setting Of The Parable

This parable is peculiar to Luke's Gospel. It would appear that the setting is the same as the previous parable of the Unjust Steward. It is another undesignated parable concerning the rich and their attitude to the poor before God. It arose out of Luke 16:14 where the Pharisees sneered at Jesus teaching on using money for selfish ends. This parable in Luke 16:19-31 is really a rebuke to them who were covetous. The Pharisees were "respectable sinners", and they were filled with unbelief.

C. The Moral Of The Parable

As mentioned, though not specified as a parable, the moral is clear. It is summed up in verse 31. If people will not believe the Word of God, and Moses and the prophets, they will not believe even if one rose from the dead to speak to them. Salvation must be received in Time. There is no second chance after death. Eternal states are settled here in Time. The parable can certainly be applied to any true to life account of a rich and poor man.

D. The Exposition Of The Parable

This parable is only to be found in Luke's Gospel. The interpretation and exposition thereof must arise out the Bible as a whole. Biblical theology about the after-life undergirds the parable. The parable takes away the veil for a short while and gives us a glimpse into the next world. It shows the condition of the saved and the unsaved. There are basically two scenes in the parable.

1. Scene One – Deals with life and death on earth, and three verses are given to it.
2. Scene Two – Deals with heaven and hell in eternity, and nine verses are given to it.

1. A Certain Rich Man

See again verses 1,19,20, on "a certain rich man" and "a certain beggar". The scene we have is the rich man in life. It could be any real life situation. The certain rich man is unnamed but most expositors speak of him as "Dives", which simply means "a rich man".

He is clothed in purple – the colour of royalty, and the clothing often of idols (Esther 8:15; Daniel 5:17; Jeremiah 10:9). It is the colour of luxury and pride.

He is cothed in fine linen – the colour of purity, and very costly linen.

He fared sumptuously every day – luxurious living, rich food.

The rich man is well fed, and well clothed. Food and clothing are the basic necessities of this temporal life. He had these things (Matthew 6:25-34; 1Timothy 6:6-10). He did not have to be concerned with what he would eat or drink, or what he would be clothed in. He was healthy and wealthy but self-centered. It is not sinful to be rich but if one is not rich towards God, then riches can lead to destruction and perdition.

2. A Certain Beggar

The certain beggar is named, his name being Lazarus, "Whom God Helps". It is a picture of Lazarus in this life. Lazarus was laid at the rich man's gate day by day by some good friends. His condition is pitiful in contrast to the certain rich man.

He is poverty stricken. He is a poor man.

His body is full of sores, putrifying sores; unhealthy, sick condition.

His sores are licked by the street dogs, unclean animals.

He is hungry and longs to be fed just with the crumbs from the rich man's table. The crumbs were probably thrown to the dogs.

What a contrast to the certain rich man. Both were sons of Abraham, after the flesh, but one was a son of Abraham, after the spirit.

3. Lazarus Died

Death passes on all men, rich or poor. "In Adam all die" (Romans 5:12-21; Genesis 2:16-17). He became a disembodied spirit. His body, no doubt, was thrown outside the city, into the place of burning, called "Gehenna", where all the refuse and bodies of criminals and lepers were burnt.

4. Rich Man Died

"It is appointed unto man once to die, and after this the judgment" (Hebrews 9:27). Death is the great leveller of all mankind, rich and poor, free and bond. He also became a disembodied spirit.

5. Lazarus In Abraham's Bosom

When Lazarus died, he was carried by the angels into Abraham's bosom. This speaks of intimate friendship and relationship, a place of love and care. The angels are sent forth as ministers to the heirs of salvation (Hebrews 1:14). The final ministry of any person's guardian angel is to take the spirit of the redeemed through the trackless universe into the very presence of God (Matthew 18:10; Luke 16:22).

"Abraham's bosom" was symbolic of a place of love and peace. Abraham is the father of all who believe, whether Jews or Gentiles. The spirit of Lazarus was taken into Abraham's affections (Romans 4:11). As the woman, who had a physical infirmity was a daughter of Abraham, so Lazarus was a true son of Abraham (Luke 13:16; 19:9).

"Abraham's bosom" is generally accepted by expositors as referring to Sheol or Hades, the place of the spirits of the righteous dead until the time of Christ's ascension to heaven. It becomes symbolic of heaven because the **angels** carried him there. It is seen by Dives "afar off", and there is a "great gulf" between hades and Abraham's bosom. No one can pass across from one place to the other.

"Abraham's bosom" then is:

* A place where the angels dwell – Verse 22
* A place of fatherhood – Verses 22,23,24,25,27,29,30. Abraham is here.
* A place of loving affection – Verse 22,23.
* A place of comfort – Verse 25.
* A place of good things – Verse 25 with Revelation 21:1-7. There are no more tears, sorrow, crying, pain, rags, sores, dogs, begging, hunger, or death.

6. Rich Man In Hades

The rich man, after he died, and his body was given a decent burial, found himself in hell (Grk. "Hades" in the NT, and "Sheol" in the OT), the place for departed human spirit beings. It is the spirit world. Hades is like a jail, a waiting room, where the spirits of the departed human beings wait for the coming day of the great white throne judgment. Death is not annihilation, or unconsciousness or soul-sleep. It is a place of conscious existence.

The Bible reveals that there are "three hells". Hades or Sheol is the "hell" for human spirit beings. Tartarus is the place for fallen angelic spirit beings. Gehenna is the final and eternal hell for all fallen and unregenerate created beings, whether human or angelic (2Peter 2:4; Jude 6; Revelation 20:11-15). After the great white throne judgment, death and hades are cast into the lake of fire, the final hell.

7. Voices From Hades

In verses 23-31 we have a vivid account of conditions in Hades of a man waiting for the final judgment. There is no conversation between Dives and Lazarus in Abraham's bosom. It is a conversation between Dives and Abraham only and this in the spirit realm.

(a) Hades was a place of torment for Dives.

(b) Hades was a place where he could see Abraham afar off.

(c) Hades was a place where he could see Lazarus in Abraham's bosom.

(d) Hades was a place where no mercy could be shown, though Dives cried to Abraham for mercy. Three times he called "Father, Abraham..." But, though he was a son of Abraham after natural birth, he was not a son of Abraham in faith (Matthew 3:8-9; John 8:33-39). He was like the Pharisees; Abraham's seed after the flesh, but not Abraham's seed after the spirit.

(e) Hades was a place where there was no water to quench his thirsting tongue.

(f) Hades was a place of torment and flame – verses 23,24,25,28. Note also Matthew 8:29; Mark 5:7; Luke 8:28; Matthew 18:34; Revelation 8:5; 18:7,10,15; 9:5; 20:10. The torment is in the presence of the holy angels, and the Lamb of God – for ever!

(g) Hades was an actual place. It was a place of unfulfilled desires, a place of lost spirits, of self-reproach. All the things he said were his torments.

(h) Hades was a place of sharpened faculties. He could hear (vs 25). He could feel (vs24). He could taste (vs24). He could smell (vs24). He could remember (vs25). It was the torment of memories. He could speak (vs24,27). He had a conscience. This is the worm that never dies (Mark 9:49-40).

If the flame of fire is but a symbol, then the reality of a thing is always greater and more real than the symbol used to symbolize it!

Thus Dives had all his faculties, in spirit, of feeling, knowing, seeing, reasoning, hearing, and remembering. He was in a state of consciousness, conscious suffering!

8. **Father Abraham's Words**

Abraham had some words to say to him in this invisible spirit realm.

(a) The rich man was told to remember the good things he had in his earthly life.

(b) The rich man also was told to remember the evil things Lazarus had in his life.

(c) The rich man was told that Lazarus now is comforted in heavenly life.

(d) The rich man is told now that he has to suffer torment. All is reversed hereafter.

(e) The rich man was told of a great gulf that was fixed between the two realms.

(f) The rich man was told that no one from Abraham's side could go to Hades, and no one from Hades could cross over to Abraham's side. There was no bridge between heaven and hades. There was a great gulf between Abraham's bosom and Hades. It was fixed. It was uncrossable. None could visit each other from either side. There was a way from earth to heaven, but none from heaven to hades!

"A great chasm has been established. so that those wanting to cross hence to you may not be able, nor yet those there ferrying to us" (Concordant Lit. Translation).

"But that is not all; between us and you a great gulf has been fixed, to stop anyone, if he wanted to, crossing from our side to yours, and to stop anyone crossing from your side to ours" (Jerusalem Bible). There is no chance beyond the grave.

9. The Rich Man's Plea

The rich man suddenly feels concern for his father's house and his five brothers. He almost wanted to become "an evangelist". He asked Abraham to send Lazarus back to earth, from the dead, by resurrection, to testify to his brothers. He would like Lazarus to warn his brothers not to come to this place of torment. He did not help the beggar in TIME, but wanted the beggar to help him in ETERNITY!

10. Abraham's Final Words To Dives

Abraham clearly said, "They have Moses and the prophets, let them hear (listen to) them". Dives pleaded with Abraham, arguing that if one (maybe Lazarus) went to them, raised from the dead, they would repent!

Abraham's final word is clear. "If they will not hear Moses and the prophets, neither will they be persuaded though one rose from the dead". If Dives did not take the Scriptures seriously, when he was on earth, neither will his brothers, even if one rose from the dead. With all the resurrections that took place in the Bible, how many people did come to faith?

Think of the various resurrections which did take place in Bible times:

* Moses – Jude 9 with Deuteronomy 34:5-6; Matthew 17:1-9
* The widow's daughter – 1Kings 17: 17-24
* The widow's son – 2Kings 4:18-37; 8:5
* The soldier who touched Elisha's bones – 2Kings 13:29-31
* Jarius daughter – Matthew 9:18-26
* The widow's son – Luke 7:11-23
* Lazarus – John 11:43-44; 12:1,9,17
* The company of saints – Matthew 27:51
* Dorcas – Acts 9:36-42
* A young man – Acts 20:7-12

(**Note:**- It is significant that Jesus did raise another Lazarus from the dead, from the spirit realm. Did the religious leaders believe? No! They actually sought to put Lazarus to death again because many Jews believed on Jesus! (John 11—12:1-11).

The greatest resurrection of all times was the resurrection of Jesus Himself (1Corinthians 15:1-8; Acts 1:3). But every one will not believe or repent, or be persuaded even though Christ has risen from the dead.

E. The Practical Application Of The Parable

The issue here is not to do with riches or poverty. The issue is that the certain rich man had been blessed with material wealth but lived for himself. He was self-centered, lived luxiously and his "god" was the unrighteous mammon. He was an unbeliever. He was not a true son of faith or son of Abraham. He saw Lazarus laid at his gate daily, as a beggar, and did not minister to him in any way. Lazarus was a poor and needy believer, a true son of Abraham.

Neither riches nor poverty are evidence of spirituality or acceptance before God. It is, however, important to note some Scriptures pertaining to the "rich" and "poor". Under Hebrew laws, there were laws concerning the rich and the poor, and they have a bearing on the parable here.

It is God who gave Israel power to get wealth (Deuteronomy 8:18).

The rich and the poor meet together, and the Lord is the maker of all (Proverbs 22:2).

The Lord makes rich and the Lord makes poor (1Samuel 2:7).

He who has mercy on the poor, happy is he (Proverbs 14:21).

If a man oppresses the poor, he reproaches his maker. The poor need mercy (Proverbs 14:31).

If a poor man is in the land, then the rich should minister to their needs. The poor will never cease out of the land (Deuteronomy 15:7-11). The rich are to open their heart and hand and give to the poor.

In festival seasons, the poor were to be ministered unto (Leviticus 19:10; 23:22; 25:25,35,39,47).

He who has pity on the poor, lends to the Lord, and that which he has given will he pay him again (Proverbs 19:17).

Whoever stops his ears at the cry of the poor, he also shall cry but shall not be heard (Proverbs 21:13, 18:23).

The New Testament also confirms ministry to the poor, and more especially a poor, fellow believer (1John 3:17-18; Galatians 2:10).

The Lord tested this certain rich man by Lazarus. He was unmoved by Lazarus poor and beggarly condition. Mammon was his god! He forgot all the Scriptures pertaining to the ministry to the poor. He spent his wealth on himself and his own house. He never received the charge to the rich, that the love of money is the root of all evil, which, some covet after and drown themselves in destruction and perdition (1Timothy 6:9-10,17-19). He trusted in uncertain riches. He was irreligiously rich.

The Bible shows that God makes some rich in order for them to bless the poor. The rich have to learn to give. The poor have to learn to receive.

Because the Lord Jesus spoke this word, it may not be limited to being a parable but to a true life situation of which Jesus Himself perfectly knows. He died to save all from this place of torment.

If the rich man became burdened and concerned for his brethren, after death, when it was too late, what should the Christian be for those who have contact with the living? Everybody cannot witness to everybody, but everybody can witness to somebody. All believers have contacts with unbelievers. Every one can witness to some one and point them to the Word of God and the resurrected Son of God who will come to judge the world in righteousness. Time is the place to prepare for eternity!

Such are the many important lessons to be learnt from the parable of the rich man and Lazarus.

(Note:- Trench, in **"Notes on The Parables of our Lord"**, pp169-170, uses this in an allegorical manner. He writes that the certain rich man is like the Jewish nation. The purple and fine linen pertains to the priests. Jewry was rich with the blessings of God (Romans 9:4, 3:1-2). Jewry was selfish, and cared not for the Gentile dogs. They boasted that they were Abraham's seed, and Abraham was their father. The Gentile dogs, like Lazarus, became Abraham's seed, by faith, and those who were not a people became the people of God (1Peter 2:10; Ephesians 2:10-13). The Jews fell into great torments because of rejecting the Law and the Prophets, and finally the resurrected Son of God (Leviticus 26:14-39; Deuteronomy 28:15-68; Luke 13:28-30.

While not endorsing any allegorization of the parables, undoubtedly there is truth that is applicable from Trench's comments).

CHAPTER FORTY-SEVEN
THE PARABLE OF THE UNPROFITABLE SERVANTS

A. The Scripture On The Parable
Luke 17:7-10

But which of you, having a servant plowing or feeding cattle, will say unto him by and by, when he is come from the field, Go and sit down to meat?

And will not rather say unto him, Make ready wherewith I may sup, and gird thyself, and serve me, till I have eaten and drunken; and afterward thou shalt eat and drink?

Doth he thank that servant because he did the things that were commanded him? I trow not.

So likewise ye, when ye shall have done all those things which are commanded you, say, We are unprofitable servants: we have done that which was our duty to do.

B. The Setting Of The Parable

Jesus is still enroute to Jerusalem, passing through the borders of Samaria and Galilee. He is particularly speaking to His own disciples as Luke 16:1-6 and 17:1,11 show. It is possible that some Pharisees were still around (Luke 16:14-15).

C. The Moral Of The Parable

Once again, Jesus Himself provides the moral of the parable. In verse 10 He said to His disciples: "So likewise you, when you shall have done all those things which are commanded you, say, We are unprofitable servants: we have done that which is our duty to do".

Even though, in other parables, the Lord commends His servants, yet, when all is said and done, whatever we do for the Lord is our duty to do. He is not obligated to thank us, although He does.

D. The Exposition Of The Parable

1. A Servant

The word for "servant" or "servants" as used in the parable speaks of bond-slaves. In a number of the parables of the Lord Jesus, He refers to His disciples as His servants. The bond-slave was really a love-slave, who had chosen not to be free after six years of servitude to his master. Because he loved his master, he did not want to go out free but was content to be his master's slave – for ever (Exodus 21:1-6).

The apostles were pleased to refer to themselves as bond-slaves of the Lord Jesus Christ (Romans 1:1; Philippians 1:1; James 1:1; 1Peter 1:1; Revelation 1:1). All true believers are bond-slaves, the love-slaves of Christ. As servants, we are not our own but we are bought with a price. All that we are, all that we have, all that we will ever be is our Master's – the Lord Jesus Christ.

2. Ploughing Or Feeding

The servant's work consisted of ploughing his master's field or feeding his master's cattle, whether sheep or oxen. The bond-slave simply is there to do what he is told. His is not to question why. His is unquestioning obedience to His master's voice.

Herbert Lockyer (**"All The Parables of the Bible"**, pp297-298) says, "Ploughing or feeding cattle" are symbolic images of spiritual labour, to which Christ has called His own (John 21:16; Acts 20:28; 1Peter 5:2).

3. **Serving The Master**

   When the servant has finished his work in the field, or looking after his master's cattle, he is still not finished. A slave's work is never done. The servant cannot come in and expect the master to tell him to sit down and for the master to give him supper. The servant's work is to gird himself, get supper ready and then serve the master his food and drink. Then, afterwards, he himself can have his supper. The master comes first in everything as far as the slave is concerned.

   His whole life is to be His master's servant. This is his obligation, to do all that is commanded and expected of him. He is totally at his master's disposal. So the believer, Christ's disciples, are totally at His disposal. The disciple is to seek first the kingdom of God. The Master comes first (Matthew 6:33).

4. **A Thankless Master**

   The parable points out that the master of a slave is generally thankless. It was not the custom to thank or commend slaves for any work they did. The servant does not do his work just to receive praise and thanks from his master. His work is a thankless task. His master may seem thankless for his servant's work, but the servant is there to fulfill his obligations. That is why he is a bond-slave. He is not here to do his own will, but his master's will. If he is doing work just to receive praise, or rewards, then he will be very disappointed.

   So for the believer, who is a love-slave of Jesus Christ. Motives must be pure in serving Him. We do not serve Him for what we get out of Him. We serve Him because of who He is, and who we are. God is no man's debtor. We are debtor to Him, and we fulfill our service in a spirit of humility and with a servant spirit and attitude.

E. **The Practical Application Of The Parable**

   As in many of Luke's parables, Jesus Himself provides the practical application, which is seen in the moral of the parable. In verse 10, Jesus said to His disciples: "Even so on your part, when you have done everything that was assigned and commanded you, say, We are unworthy servants – possessing no merit, for we have not gone beyond our obligation; we have merely done what was our duty to do" (Amplified New Testament).

   A study of the Gospels shows that the disciples had wrong views of themselves. Often seeking position, and who would be the greatest among them in the kingdom – these things reveal an undue projection of themselves. They believed their obedience to the Master merited some place and position, recognition, thanks and commendation (Mark 9:33-37; 10:35-40; Luke 22:24-30). They were simply unworthy, undeserving servants, who simply did what was expected of them as bond-slaves.

   The parable must be considered in the light of the whole of the Gospel story. The disciples, the Master's love-slaves, even when they had fulfilled His will, were simply doing what He commanded them. They simply did what was their duty to do. If they did His work and will simply to receive praise, their motive was not pure.

   For believers today, all that we do is for the Lord Jesus, our Master. As His redeemed bond-slaves, it is our obligation, our duty to do His will. Our motive must not be to do it in order to receive thanks and praise, but because we are His love-slaves. None of our services for the Master are totally perfect. All that we do has the blemish of our human fallenness and imperfections of a sinful nature. Nothing is perfectly done from imperfect beings, but all is done out of our love for Him, as His love-slaves – for ever!

This parable, however, is not the complete story. While on earth, there may not be any commendation or praise from the Master. In heaven, all is changed. Our Lord and Master gives commendation: "Well done, you good and faithful servant... enter into the joy of your Lord" (Matthew 25:14-30). In that time, the Master will gird Himself, and make His servants to sit down at the table, and He Himself will serve them, as they have served Him. The following comparisons from Luke's Gospel shows the truth of these things.

Parable – Luke 17:7-10	Parable – Luke 12:35-37
1. A servant	Servants
2. Ploughing and feeding	Watching and waiting
3. Serving the Master	For the Master to come
4. Gird himself, serve the Master	Gird Himself and serve servants
5. At the table	At the table
6. Master to eat and drink	Servants to eat and drink
7. No thanks or praise	Well done, good and faithful
8. Done our duty	servants... enter into joy of the Lord (Matthew 25:21-23).

By comparing and contrasting these Scriptures in Luke, it would seem that the parable in Luke 17:7-10 has more of an **earthly setting,** while the parable of Luke 12:35-37 is a second coming parable, and therefore, more of a **heavenly setting!**

The issue is, as servants of the Lord, we ourselves do not do the Lord's service for praise, but because it is our duty. But He, out of His graciousness, does give us praise, commendation and even rewards for our service, regardless of our imperfections. After all, the Master is also Servant, and the Servant became our Master!

CHAPTER FORTY-EIGHT
THE PARABLE OF THE UNJUST JUDGE AND WIDOW

A. The Scripture On The Parable
Luke 18:1-8

And he spake a parable unto them to this end, that men ought always to pray, and not to faint;

Saying, There was in a city a judge, which feared not God, neither regarded man:

And there was a widow in that city; and she came unto him, saying, Avenge me of mine adversary.

And he would not for a while: but afterward he said within himself, Though I fear not God, nor regard man;

Yet because this widow troubleth me, I will avenge her, lest by her continual coming she weary me.

And the Lord said, Hear what the unjust judge saith.

And shall not God avenge his own elect, which cry day and night unto him, though he bear long with them?

I tell you that he will avenge them speedily. Nevertheless when the Son of man cometh, shall he find faith on the earth?

B. The Setting Of The Parable

By a reading of Luke 17:11-12 and 18:31, it would appear that Jesus and His disciples are enroute, through Samaria and Galilee, to Jerusalem, as in the previous parable. During the course of the journey, Jesus healed ten lepers, answered questions of the Pharisees about the kingdom of God, and also spoke of His second coming. It is out of this setting the parable arises.

C. The Moral Of The Parable

Jesus Himself provides the moral of the parable for us, as He does in most of the parables in Luke's Gospel. The moral is found in verses 7-8. By means of the parable, He shows that God is far more willing to avenge His elect and answer prayer, though He is longsuffering in dealing with mankind. However, prayer should be consistent and persistent and the one who prays must not become faint-hearted because God does not instantly answer their prayers. One must pray constantly (1Thessalonians 3:10. Ephesians 5:18). It is given to His disciples. It is a prayer parable. Both this parable (verses 1-8) and the next parable (verses 9-14) are about prayer.

D. The Exposition Of The Parable

1. A Certain City

The city could be a city anywhere, in any nation of the earth. The Authorized Version in the marginal reference says, "A certain city..."

2. A Judge

Judges were set in Israel as a nation and called to be righteous and impartial in their judgments, as they dealt with the causes of the people. Justice and mercy were to be the scales of their judgments (Exodus 18:13-22; Leviticus 19:15; Deuteronomy 16:18; 1Kings 3:9; Psalm 9:8; Genesis 18:19; Psalm 89:14). They were to be just in their dealings with people, even as God is just in all His judgments.

3. Unjust Judge

This judge, in this parable, did not fear God and did not respect or consider man. He was a godless judge and contemptuous to the people he had to judge. His attitude to God and his attitude to man is revealed in these words. He did not care for God or for widows. "He cared not for God "- which has to do with the first four commandments of the Decalogue; there was no relationship with God. "He cared not for man" – which has to do with the last six commandments of the Decalogue; there was no relationship with people. Business was business.

4. A Widow

A widow in that same city came to the judge appealling for justice on her adversary. She asked the judge to protect and defend her, and give her justice against an adversary she had. She came often to him asking him to vindicate her. It was a legal case needing justice, vindication and avenging of the widow's adversary, her enemy.

The Old Testament abounds with laws God had given for the protection and care and cause of the widows in Israel. This widow had an adversary which needed judgment (Read these references concerning God's laws for the protection, care and concern for widows. Exodus 22:22-24; Deuteronomy 10:18; 24:17; Psalm 68:5; Isaiah 1:23; James 1:27; Malachi 3:5). There was Divine judgment on any who oppressed the widow and the fatherless.

The very fact that she was a widow should have moved the judge to action. As these Scripture references reveal, the laws of God were to protect the widow. This judge cared not for God nor for widows. He had no real heart for anyone, let alone widows.

5. An Adversary

The widow has an enemy, an adversary, someone who was against her in a very serious manner. This adversary of the widow should be brought to justice.

6. A Persistent Widow

The widow persistently and consistently kept coming to the judge appealling for justice, for him to take up her cause. This was a quality in the widow to be commended.

7. The Avenging Judge

Even though the judge would not listen to her for a while, he finally was worn down with her persistency. Different translations use words like, "intolerable annoyance", "wear me out", "bothers me", "nuisance", "pestering", "trouble me", all showing the persistency, consistency and insistence of the widow in her request.

The judge says, "Though I fear not God, nor regard man; yet because this widow troubles me, I will avenge her, lest by her continual coming she weary me".

Different translations say, "weary", "wear me out", "wear me out with her persistence", "she will persist in coming and wearing me to death", or, the Amplified New Testament says, "at the last she come and rail on me, or assault me, or strangle me".

The point is, the widow just kept coming and coming until the judge's resistence gave in, in spite of his lack of the fear of God and respect for mankind. He dealt justice (or vengeance) to her adversary and thus settled her from continual troubling of his peace. The Lord told His hearers just to listen to what the unjust judge said.

E. The Practical Application Of The Parable

In verses 7-8, the moral and practical application of the parable is seen. If the unjust judge eventually responded to the widow's persistent appeals, how much more will God, the Judge of all mankind, respond to His people.

God's people are His very own elect, elect according to the foreknowledge of God (1Peter 1:2). The church is God's elect since the cross (Matthew 24:22,24,31; Romans 8:33; Colossians 3:22). God is the Divine and righteous Judge, though the judges of earth may be human and unjust.

The elect cry to Him day and night, continually praying for Him to answer their prayers. The souls under the altar cry that their blood will be avenged. They are given white robes and told to rest until the number of martyrs is complete (Revelation 6:9-11).

This present age is a time of mercy and forbearance. But the time will come when it will become "the day of vengeance of our God". Then "the avenger of blood" (our Kinsman Redeemer, Jesus Christ) will execute vengeance on all them that know know God, and obey not the gospel of our Lord Jesus Christ (Read these Scriptures: Isaiah 61:2; 63:1-6; 34:8; 2Thessalonians 1:7-10; Isaiah 59:;17; Luke 21:22; Revelation 6:9-10).

Jesus told His disciples they should always pray and not faint. Come continually to the Father God, as the widow to the judge. Do not give up. Keep perservering in prayer.

By way of contrast and comparison, we consider, in summary, the unjust judge and widow and God, the just Judge and the Church elect.

Unjust Judge and Widow	God the Just Judge and Church
1. The widow in need	The Church in her need
2. The unjust judge	God, the just Judge
3. The widow's adversary	Satan is the Church's adversary
4. Persistency of request	Pray always, do not faint
5. Need for vengeance	God will avenge His Church
6. The judge brings about justice	God will bring eternal justice
7. Delayed a long time	Will not delay for ever.

It is worthy to note the Lord's question as He closes off the parable. The Amplified New Testament says, "However, when the Son of Man comes, will He find persistence in the faith on the earth?" Some expositors will answer in the negative, some in the positive. The answer is, He will find faith in His elect, the true church, while unbelief abounds in the earth.

The widow was persistent. She believed if she kept continually coming to the judge, he would eventually respond, no matter how reluctantly. She had persistency, but it was also persistent faith. So should the church have this persistency of faith before the Lord, the true and righteous Judge of all the earth (Genesis 18:25). He will answer the prayers of the church, according to His will, His way and time, and vengeance shall be executed on Satan, the adversary and all the hosts of evil arrayed against the church, His elect.

CHAPTER FORTY-NINE
THE PARABLE OF THE PHARISEE AND PUBLICAN

A. The Scriptures On The Parable
Luke 18:9-14

And he spake this parable unto certain which trusted in themselves that they were righteous, and despised others:

Two men went up into the temple to pray; the one a Pharisee, and the other a publican.

The Pharisee stood and prayed thus with himself, God, I thank thee, that I am not as other men are, extortioners, unjust, adulterers, or even as this publican.

I fast twice in the week, I give tithes of all that I possess.

And the publican, standing afar off, would not lift up so much as his eyes unto heaven, but smote upon his breast, saying, God be merciful to me a sinner.

I tell you, this man went down to his house justified rather than the other: for every one that exalteth himself shall be abased; and he that humbleth himself shall be exalted.

B. The Setting Of The Parable

As seen in the previous several parables, the setting is Jesus enroute to Jerusalem via Samaria and Galilee (Luke 17:11-12, 18:31). The parable is especially spoken to the Pharisees and others like them who trusted in themselves, were self-righteous and despised others. It is rebuke to all pride.

C. The Moral Of The Parable

Jesus Himself provides the moral of the parable for us in verse 14. Anyone who exalts himself, like the Pharisee, shall be abased and brought down before God. Anyone who humbles himself, like the Publican, shall be exalted and brought up before God.

D. The Exposition Of The Parable
1. Two Men

Two men went up into the temple to pray. The contrast is vividly seen in the parable.

(a) A Pharisee

The Pharisees were the Separatists of Christ's time. They had actually begun in a reformation movement, to uphold the holiness of God, and separation from the evils of the time. Over the years, the Pharisees had degenerated into externalism, formalism, and legalism. Jesus saw them as whited sepulchres. They were "white-washed" but not "washed white!" Christ's greatest denunciations were given upon the scribes and the Pharisees for their hypocritical self-righteousness (Matthew 23).

(b) A Publican

The Publicans were the tax-gatherers in Christ's time. They, as Jews, were then employed by the Romans to collect taxes from their brethren for the Roman Empire. They were hated by their fellow Jews, and looked upon as traitors for working for the Romans. They, more than often, over-taxed their fellow Jews and pocketed the extra taxes for their own benefit. When

Zacchaeus, who was a tax-collecter, came to Jesus, he promised to make four-fold restitution of all the excess taxes he had robbed off his own people. Salvation came to his house (Luke 19:1-9). Zacchaeus was a chief among the publicans.

2. The Temple

The temple was the centre of priestly ministrations, the place of sacrifices and oblations, the offering of the incense, worship, and the annual festivals occasions. The temple was the focal and binding power of the Jewish nation. They would live and die for the protection of the temple and its priestly services.

3. Time Of Prayer

Probably the two men, the Pharisee and the Publican, went up at the hour of prayer (cf. Acts 3:1). Solomon's prayer, at the dedication of the original temple was, that it would be a house of prayer for all nations (1Kings 8; Isaiah 56:7; Matthew 21:13). In the parable we have two kinds of prayers that were offered before God. Undoubtedly the Pharisee prayed in the Court of the Temple, not the Court of the Priests, or the Court of the Gentiles.

4. The Pharisee's Prayer

The Pharisee's prayer is worthy of much attention, for it is not the kind of prayer that the Lord in heaven would hear. "If I regard iniquity in my heart, the Lord will not hear me", the Psalmist said (Psalm 66:18). Note the words and motives of his prayer.

* He stood and prayed with himself. That is, in a class by himself. He stood alone and aloof. He prayed about himself. It was the custom to stand and pray (Psalm 135:2). Sometimes Jews would prostrate themselves in prayer (1Kings 8:22; 2Chronicles 6:12-13; Matthew 6:5; Daniel 6:10; Acts 21:5).

* He began his prayer with "God..." but that was the only place "God" had in it.

* He prayed a very self-centred prayer, filled with his own self-righteousness. Five times he mentioned the self pronoun, "I". "I" thank You, "I" am not as other men are; extortioners, unjust adulterers, or even as this publican..." "I" fast twice a week, "I" give tithes of all "I" possess!

His prayer is like the action of Lucifer in Isaiah 14:12-14. Five times Lucifer expressed his own SELF-WILL! He said:

1. I will ascend into heaven (Self-ascension)

2. I will exalt my throne above the stars of God (Self-exaltation)

3. I will sit on the mount of the congregation in the north (Self-enthronement)

4. I will ascend above the heights of the clouds (Self-glorification)

5. I will be like the Most High (Self-deification).

The Pharisee moves from the negative (what he does not do and is not like), to the positive (what he does and is like)! The Pharisee sees two classes of people.

One Class	His Class
Extortioners	Fast twice a week
Unjust	Tithes of all he has
Adulterers	Not like other men
The Publican	Not like this Publican

The Law only recognized one national day of fasting, that being the Day of Atonement (Leviticus 16:27). The Law confirmed tithes of all one earned (Numbers 18:21; Deuteronomy 14:22; Leviticus 27:30; Matthew 23:23, Luke 11:42). The Pharisees tithed more than was required of the Law.

The whole prayer was a self-righteous, arrogant kind of prayer. Pharisaical righteousness saturated his whole prayer. Paul speaks of his own kind of Pharisaical and self-righteousness, by works of the Law (Philippians 3). But the Pharisees went about to establish their own righteousness and would not submit to the righteousness which was by faith (Romans 9:30-10:4). There was no confession of sin on his part, only his own righteousness, all of which were "good things" in God's sight, but all done out of wrong motives and from a position of works before God.

The Pharisees generally prayed "a daily prayer", which said: "I thank You, O God, that I am not a woman, or a Gentile dog, or a Roman citizen!"

5. The Publican's Prayer

What a contrast is the publican's prayer to that of the prayer of the Pharisee, as the wording of the parable shows. As a publican, he was counted a renegade Jew, a traitor to his people, working as a tax-collector for Rome.

* He stands afar off. Israel was a people near to God, the Gentiles a people afar off (Psalm 148:14). In Christ, Paul shows that those that were "near" (Israel), and those that were "afar off" (Gentiles) would become one through the cross (Ephesians 2:12-22). Probably the publican was standing in the Court of the Gentiles. It would be death for any one to go into the Court of the Priests. The walls of separation kept all in their respective places. The publican does not feel he can draw near to God.

* He would not lift his eyes to heaven. There is no arrogance here, but self-effacement and humility of prayer. Ezra was ashamed to even lift his eyes to the Lord because of Judah's sins (Ezra 9:6 with Isaiah 57:15; Psalm 138:6).

* He smote or beat upon his breast, the place of the human heart. Here is remorse, contrition and self-abasement (1 Kings 8:38-40).

* He prayed a simple but powerful prayer. "God be merciful to me a sinner".

It is worthy of deep consideration to weigh the few short words of the publican's prayer, for it is full of meaning.

The publican's prayer begins with GOD and ends with his acknowledgement of being a SINNER! In between, there is the word **"merciful"**. The Greek word for "merciful" is **"hilaskomi"** (SC2433), and means "to conciliate, to atone for sin, be propitious". It is translated by the English words, "be merciful, make reconciliation for". The inter-related words are **"propitiation"** (1John 2:2; 4:10; SC 2434) and **"mercy-seat"** (SC2435).

The publican's prayer was actually saying: "**God** be **mercy-seated** to me a **sinner**". It is like David's cry (Psalm 51:1), and Paul's testimony (1Timothy 1:15). Both recognize their need of the mercy of God as sinners needing His grace and forgiveness.

The whole thought brings one to the Ark of the Covenant and the blood-stained mercy seat (Exodus 25:12-22). On this mercy-seat was sprinkled the blood of atonement. God communicated to His people, by the High Priest, off that blood-stained mercy seat. God has nothing to say apart from the blood.

The publican realized his need of the **mercy** of God; the need for God to be gracious to him. He realized his need to be reconciled to God through the atonement, by means of the blood-stained mercy-seat!

The New Testament clearly shows that Jesus Christ is our **"propitiation"** (lit. our "mercyseat", Romans 3:25; 1John 2:2; 4:10). We come to God by Him and through His atoning and reconciling blood.

6. **The End Result**

The end result of the prayers of the Pharisee and the publican were:

(a) The publican went down to his house justified before God (Romans 5:1,9; 4:5-6).

(b) The publican humbled himself and was exalted (Luke 14:11).

(c) The Pharisee went home self-justifed, and therefore condemned (Job 9:20; Luke 10:29; 16:15).

(d) The Pharisee exalted himself and was abased (Matthew 23:12; James 4:6; 1Peter 5:5).

E. The Practical Application Of The Parable

The message is simple. A person must be willing to humble himself before God. He must come in a spirit of contrition. There must always be that recognition of the need of the blood-stained mercyseat of God. Justification before God is by the mercy of God, a humble and contrite spirit, confession of sin and faith towards God. There is no self-trust. There is no self-righteous attitude. There is no despising of others. There is no comparison of self with others. These things are the characteristics of the religious yet unregenerate sinner and find no acceptance before God.

The contrast between the prayers of the Pharisee and the Publican are most evident:

The Pharisee	The Publican
Prayed with himself	Prayed to God
He stood	Prayed afar off
In pride	In humility
Commended himself	Condemned himself
Thirty-four word prayer	Seven word prayer
Five times "I" in his prayer	God and me, a sinner

Eyes lifted up	Not lift his eyes to heaven
Compared himself with others	Acknowledged he was a sinner
Did not ask God for mercy	Ask for the mercy-seat of God
Went home self-justified	Went home justified before God
Exalted himself	Abased himself
Abased before God	Exalted before God

The reason for this parable is given in verse 9. Jesus spoke this parable to those who:

1. Trusted in themselves – Self-trust
2. That they were righteous – Self-righteous
3. Despised others – Self-conceit.

The Pharisee's prayer revealed each of these things. He trusted in himself, not God. He was self-righteous, and did not have a faith-righteousness, and he depised others, including the publican praying afar off (Luke 10:29; 16:15). The publican's prayer revealed that he put God first, himself last – as a sinner – and between himself and God he asked for the mercyseat and blood atonement to cover his sin!

What a lesson in prayer is this for all!

CHAPTER FIFTY
THE PARABLE OF THE POUNDS

A. The Scripture On The Parable
Luke 19:11-27

And as they heard these things, he added and spake a parable, because he was nigh to Jerusalem, and because they thought that the kingdom of God should immediately appear.

He said therefore, A certain nobleman went into a far country to receive for himself a kingdom, and to return.

And he called his ten servants, and delivered them ten pounds, and said unto them, Occupy till I come.

But his citizens hated him, and sent a message after him, saying, We will not have this man to reign over us.

And it came to pass, that when he was returned, having received the kingdom, then he commanded these servants to be called unto him, to whom he had given the money, that he might know how much every man had gained by trading.

Then came the first, saying, Lord, thy pound hath gained ten pounds.

And he said unto him, Well, thou good servant: because thou hast been faithful in a very little, have thou authority over ten cities.

And the second came, saying, Lord, thy pound hath gained five pounds.

And he said likewise to him, Be thou also over five cities.

And another came, saying, Lord, behold, here is thy pound, which I have kept laid up in a napkin:

For I feared thee, because thou art an austere man: thou takest up that thou layedst not down, and reapest that thou didst not sow.

And he saith unto him, Out of thine own mouth will I judge thee, thou wicked servant. Thou knewest that I was an austere man, taking up that I laid not down, and reaping that I did not sow:

Wherefore then gavest not thou my money into the bank, that at my coming I might have required mine own with usury?

And he said unto them that stood by, Take from him the pound, and give it to him that hath ten pounds.

(And they said unto him, Lord, he hath ten pounds.)

For I say unto you, That unto every one which hath shall be given; and from him that hath not, even that he hath shall be taken away from him.

But those mine enemies, which would not that I should reign over them, bring hither, and slay them before me.

B. The Setting Of The Parable

The time is not long before the cross. Jesus is enroute to Jerusalem. He is passing through Jericho. Here in Jericho, Zacchaeus was blessed with salvation. Jesus said He had come to seek and to save that which was lost (Luke 18:31-34; 19:1-10,11,28,41).

He is about to enter Jerusalem in triumph on the donkey amidst the loud praises of the people, and the criticisms of the Pharisees. It is about the close of His ministry and shortly before the crucifixion.

As the people heard Jesus speaking, some had misunderstood Him and they thought that the kingdom of God was about to appear, because of His close approach to

Jersualem. They had a national and political concept of the kingdom. Because of this, Jesus **added** and spoke this parable of the pounds. It is one of those parables that spread out over this dispensation, from the first coming to the second coming of Christ. It covers the interim period bertween the first and second advents. It shows that the kingdom "is here" but "not yet". This is the setting of the parable.

C. The Moral Of The Parable

The moral is basically the same as the Parable of the Talents in Matthew (Matthew 25:14-30, with 25:29; 13:12; Mark 4:28; Luke 8:19). The moral is found in Luke 19:26. To everyone who uses what he has been given, more shall be given. But the one who does not use what he was given, he will lose what he has got. Use it or lose it, is the message. You lose what you do not use. It is a parable of responsibility and accountability. It is a kingdom parable, it is a prophetic parable. Although it has the same truth as the Parable of the Talents in Matthew, it is not the same parable.

D. The Exposition Of The Parable

Jesus added and spoke this parable (1) Becasue He was near Jersualem, and (2) Because they thought the kingdom of God should immediately appear. As noted, this parable is quite similar to the Parable of the Talents, but there are some slight differences, even though the major moral of both parables is basically the same.

1. A Certain Nobleman

It is the Lord's general opening formula of a parable, as seen in previous parables about "a certain man". The nobleman here is none other than the Lord Jesus Himself as subsequent thoughts confirm.

2. Went To A Far Country

The far country is none other than "the heavenly country" that Abraham, Isaac and Jacob looked for (Hebrews 11:10-16 with Matthew 25:14; Mark 13:34). This going into the far country points to the Lord's ascension after the work of the cross (Hebrews 1:3; Philippians 2:8-11; Ephesians 1:17-22). It includes the Lord's ascension and exaltation to the Father's right hand.

3. To Receive For Himself A Kingdom

The Book of Daniel clearly shows the Son of Man receiving a kingdom from the Father, the Ancient of Days, and it is a time when "the saints possess the kingdom" (Daniel 2; Daniel 7:18-27; Hebrews 12:28). It is an unshakeable and eternal kingdom.

4. And To Return

Jesus promised His disciples, "And If I go away, I will come again and receive you unto Myself, that where I am, there you may be also "(John 14:1-6). This points to the second coming or the return of Jesus again.

5. He Called His Servants

The servants are His disciples, His apostles, and represent all believers. All have been called out of the kingdom of darkness into the kingdom of light. It is a high and holy and heavenly calling (Romans 11:29; Ephesians 1:18; 4:4; Philippians 3:14; 2Timothy 1:9; Hebrews 3:1).

5. Ten Servants

Ten servants were called to the Lord. The number must be taken beyond the actual number of the significance of the ten servants. The parable presents ten servants, but in reality, the Lord has untold thousands of servants in His kingdom. Ten is the number of law and order, the number of responsibility and accountability, as we have seen in previous parables. We think of the ten virgins, the ten talents, the ten toes, the ten horns, as well as many other "tens" in the Scriptures. Ten is a multiple of two fives. The fingers and toes are in two lots of five and responsible to look after the human body. In the temple of Solomon, there were ten tables of shewbread, and ten golden lampstands in the holy place, and ten washing lavers in the outer court, all being set in two groups of five. It was the responsibility of the priests to attend these articles of furniture in the house of the Lord.

7. Ten Pounds Distributed

A pound at this time was a **mina**, the value of a few English pounds and shillings in currency, or a few dollars in our currency. One pound was given to each servant, making responsible and therefore accountable to the nobleman. They were His pounds. Each had equal opportunity for all received a pound each. This is not like the Parable of the Talents, where one received ten talents, another five talents, and another one talent. Here, all received exactly the same, all had equal opportunity to use their pound.

In symbolic sense, we may say "the pound" could point to "the gift of salvation", which every believer receives. It is the same salvation "common to all" believers (Jude 3). In another sense, because each receive **exactly the same pound,** the analogy is not quite the same. "The pounds" have been likened to a talent, a gift, a skill, a ministry or ability which the Lord gives to every member of the Body of Christ. These are to be used for His glory and to spiritually trade with others and gain for the kingdom by using what the Lord gave us. But, without doubt, "the pound" speaks of that which the Lord gives in common to all believers! Believers are to use what the Lord gives them, they are to reproduce in others what the Lord has given them.

8. Occupy Until I Come

The word "occupy" means "to do business with", "to gain by trading". The servants were to do this until He came back from the far country the second time with the kingdom. Amplified New Testament says, "Buy and sell with these while I go and return". It meant each of them were to trade, do business, and traffic with what the nobleman had given them. Equal responsibility meant equal opportunity and accountability!

9. His Citizens Hated Him

The citizens here were the nobleman's fellow-citizens, those really relating to the nobleman. It is clear here that Jesus is referring to His own fellowmen, the Jews. His own people, His own nation hated Him. "He came unto His own, and His own received Him not..." (John1:11; 4:22; Romans 9:3). His kinsmen after the flesh said they had no king but Caezar (John 19:21; Acts 17:7). They rejected king Jesus.

10. The Message

The citizens sent a clear message to the nobleman. "We will not have this man to reign over us..." Compare verse 14 and verse 27. It is the cry of the crowd at Christ's trial and crucifixion. "Away with Him, crucify Him...We have no king but Caezar" (John19:15).

11. When He Returned

The language leaps over this whole period of time, from Christ's ascension to His second coming. Jesus is going to return again as He promised. This will be His second advent in glory at the end of this age. He left physically, actually, bodily and gloriously and will return the same way (Acts 1:9-11). It is a dispensational parable covering from Christ's crucifixion, ascension, intercessory ministry, right to His advent; from first to second coming.

12. Having Received The Kingdom

The prophet Daniel sees the Son of Man in vision receiving a kingdom from the Father, as the Ancient of Days. The beastly kingdoms of this world were destroyed by the power of the Son of Man (Daniel 7:1-28). The saints of the Most High shall rule and reign in that kingdom with Him also. It is this which balances out the truth of the kingdom "now" and the kingdom "not yet" (Luke 17:20-21 with 19:11-15). Believers are born into the kingdom "now" (John 3:1-5), but the full manifestation of the kingdom is "not yet" but shall be at Christ's – the nobleman's – second coming.

In an earlier chapter, it was shown how the aspect of the "kingdom present" and the "kingdom future" must be kept in view. In this parable it points to the future aspect of the kingdom. The kingdom is here and now, but the kingdom is not yet. But when Jesus returns again, the kingdom will appear in full glory and manifestation.

13. Servants Called To Accountability

In the rest of the parable, we see the nobleman calling his servants, who he had entrusted his money with, to accountability. Responsibility brings accountability. There is no responsibility given where there is no accounability required. He wanted to know how much each man had gained by trading. It points to the accountability of all believers to the Lord at His reurn.

(a) The First Servant

The first man was pleased to say he had gained ten pounds with the one pound entrusted to him. The Lord's reward was, "Well done, you **good** servant; you have been **faithful** in a very little, have authority over ten cities".

(b) The Second Servant

The second was pleased to say that his pound had gained five pounds. The Lord's reward to him was the same commendation. He was a **good** and **faithful** servant and he would rule over five cities.

(c) The Other Servant

This servant, undoubtedly with hesitancy said, "Lord, here is your pound. I kept it in a handkerchief. I was constantly afraid of you. I knew You were a stern (hard, severe (AmpN.T) man. You pick up what you did not lay down. You reap what You did not sow".

All this was but lame excuse. He had shrugged his responsibility. He had not been good or faithful with what the Lord gave him.

There is no reward. There is no commendation, only words of reprimand and judgment. In contrast to the others, who were **"good and faithful"** servants, this one was a **"wicked and slothful"** servant. Compare this with Matthew 25:24.

Out of his own mouth he was judged and stood condemned (Matthew 12:37; Job 15:6)..

The nobleman told the wicked servant that, at least he could have put his money into the bank where he could have received some interest on the deposit when he returned. This would have been little, but certainly better than nothing!

14. Use Or Lose

The nobleman told those that stood by to take from this wicked servant the one pound and give it to the good and faithful servant with ten pounds. They remarked that he already had ten pounds. But then the nobleman gave the moral of the parable.

In this writer's paraphrase form, it reads like this: "For I say to you, That unto every one who has used what he has been given shall more be given; and from every one who has not used what he has been given, shall be taken away what he was given".

It is the same message of the unused talents in Mathew 25:14-30 (verse 29), with Matthew 13:12; Mark 4:25; 8:18. The wicked servant learnt that you lose what you do not use. The measure of responsibility is the measure of accountability.

15. The Final Judgment

The enemies of the nobleman, who had now returned with the kingdom, were brought before him and suffered the death penalty. They did not want him to reign over them and they were slaughtered in his presence by the executioners. Just as Joshua had the wicked kings of the Canaanites slaughtered in his presence as Israel took the land, so it is here (Joshua 10:24).

This points to the Jewish nation, who became the enemies of Christ and rejected His kingdom, and because of this came under Divine judgment. Other Scriptures also show that all the Gentile nations who reject the rule and reign of Christ shall be judged. The ultimate and eternal judgment of all mankind takes place at the great white throne judgment (Revelation 20:11-15). The final judgment of all unrepentant mankind, Jew or Gentile, shall be in the lake of fire and brimstone – eternally!

E. The Practical Application Of The Parable

Enough lessons have been woven throughout the exposition of the parable, besides its major moral.

The Lord Jesus gives to His people "so great a salvation". He gives them various talents, giftings, ministries, skills and abilities and all are to be used for His glory during His absence from earth, while He is away in heaven.

Believers are to reproduce in others what they have been given. It is "spiritually trading" with the Lord's "pounds". The measure of responsibility is the measure of accountability. There is a day of account, a day of reckoning coming. Each of the stewardship parables teach the same truth.

The message is clear. We lose what we do not use. We gain what we do use. The reward of the Lord involves (1) His commendation, "Well done, you good and faithful servant", and (2) His authority, "Rule over cities". Whatever may be the full meaning and significance of those words, His coming will tell. It takes place at His return.

There is also (1) Condemnation for the "wicked servant" and (2) Loss of what he had. The pound is taken from him because he did not use it. He had false concepts of the Lord and acted accordingly by not using his pound.

The choice is ours. Use or lose, gain and retain; rule or be ruled over; commendation or condemnation. The difference between the Parable of the Talents is, they had unequal privileges, and received the "Well done" according to use, and here in the Parable of the Pounds, they had equal privileges, and received the "Well done" according to use. In both the Talents and the Pounds Parable, those who did not use what was given forfeited it.

Regardless how expositors may interpret "the pound", the message is clear: Use or lose what the Lord Jesus has given. Choose the "Well done, good and faithful servant" commendation, or "You wicked servant" condemnation! The choice is ours.

PART FIVE

Supplemental Section

SUPPLEMENTAL SECTION

1. **Mixture and Separation in the Kingdom Parables**
2. **Parabolic Groupings**
   a. Kingdom Parables
   b. People Parables
   c. Seed Parables
   d. Vineyard Parables
   e. Feast/Supper Parables
   f. Discipleship Parables
   g. Marriage Parables
   h. Prayer Parables
   i. Judgment Parables
   j. Israel's History Parables
   k. Stewardship Parables
   l. Second Coming Parables
3. **The Godhead in the Parables**
4. **The Christology of the Parables**
   a. His Incarnation
   b. His Ministry
   c. His Crucifixion
   d. His Ascension
   e. His Absence
   f. His Advent
   g. His Judgments
   h. His Kingdom
5. **Table of Scriptures on the Parables**
6. **The Golden Lampstand and Matthew 13**
7. **Overview of the Kingdom of God - Diagram**
8. **Overview of World Kingdoms - Diagram**
9. **Matthew 13 in Dispensational Setting**
   BIBLIOGRAPHY

SUPPLEMENTAL ONE
MIXTURE AND SEPARATION

Most of the parables of Jesus teach the truth that the kingdom, in its present, mystery form and manifestation, has mixture in it. This state of mixture will continue unto the second coming of Christ when all mixture will be taken out. The coming of Christ is the time of the separation. This is seen in the list of the parables here. The student is referred to the Supplemental "Table of Scriptures" for the references.

1. The Sower and the Seed and the Evil Birds.
2. The Wheat and the Tares.
3. The Mustard Seed Tree and Birds.
4. The Woman and the Leaven in the Meal.
5. The Dragnet of Good and Bad Fish.
6. The King and His Servants, Forgiven and Unforgiving.
7. The Vineyard Labourers – The Happy Hired, and Murmuring Hired.
8. The Two Sons in the Vineyard – Obedient and Disobedient.
9. The Vineyard and the Husbandmen – The Wicked and the Good Husbandmen.
10. The Marriage of the King's Son – Those with or without a Garment.
11. The Wise and Foolish Virgins – Oil or no Oil.
12. The Used and Unused Talents.
13. The Sheep and the Goats and the Great Separation.
14. The Pounds – Used and Unused.
15. The Old and New Wine and Wineskins.
16. The Old and New Garments and Patches.
17. The Fig Trees – Barren and Fruitful.
18. The Strait and Wide Gates, and the Narrow and Broad Ways.
19. The Salt – Savoured and Unsavoured.
20. The Wise and Foolish Builders – with or without the Foundation.
21. The Good Samaritan or Religious Priest and Levite.
22. The Watchful or Unwatchful Servants.
23. The Faithful and Wise Servant or Unfaithful and Unwise Servant.
24. The Lost and Found Sheep and Coin.
25. The Lost and Found Prodigal Son and Elder Brother.
26. The Rich Man and Lazarus – Hades or Abraham's Bosom.
27. The Unjust Judge and Widow.
28. The Pharisee and the Publican – Hypocritical or Genuine Prayer.

There are basically two groupings in every parable. The mixture can be of saints and sinners, the backsliders and apostates from the faith. The Divine reward or punishment is according to their spiritual status before the Lord. All will stand in their lot at the end of the age, at the second coming of Christ. Mixture will cease and the great separation for all eternity will take place.

SUPPLEMENTAL TWO
PARABOLIC GROUPINGS

A number of expositors have endeavoured to classify the parables of Jesus into specific groupings. No full or complete grouping can be perfect. Following are groupings worthy of the student's consideration without being locked into the same.

A. Kingdom Parables

As a general rule, the Gospel of Matthew provides the fuller listing of the "Kingdom of Heaven" Parables. Mark and Luke supply others which may be added to the list. Generally speaking, the formula is: "The kingdom of heaven is like...". Several parables do not have this specific formula, nevertheless they are recogized as kingdom parables. The dominant ones are listed here.

1. The Parable of the Sower and Seed (Matthew 13:1-23).

2. The Parable of the Wheat and Tares (Matthew 13:24-30).

3. The Parable of the Mustard Seed Tree (Matthew 13:31-32; Luke 13:18).

4. The Parable of the Woman, Leaven and Meal (Matthew 13:33).

5. The Parable of the Treasure in the Field (Matthew 13:44).

6. The Parable of the Pearl of Great Price (Matthew 13:45-46).

7. The Parable of the Good and Bad Fish (Matthew 13:47-51).

8. The Parable of the Scribe and Householder (Matthew 13:52-53).

9. The Parable of the King and His Servants (Matthew 18:23-35).

10. The Parable of the Labourers in the Vineyard (Matthew 20:1-16).

11. The Parable of the Marriage of the King's Son (Matthew 22:1-14).

12. The Parable of the Ten Virgins (Matthew 25:1-13).

13. The Parable of the Talents (Matthew 25:14-30). "The kingdom of heaven is as..."

14. The Parable of the Kingdom Seed (Mark 4:26-29). Only to be found in Mark.

Matthew's Gospel was written to the Jewish world, with the emphasis on Messianic predictions and fulfilment. There is much more symbolism in the parables of Matthew which need to be interpreted to understand the parable. A number of the symbols from the Old Testament Feasts of Israel are also used, such as; leaven, oil, meal, etc. Therefore other portions of the Scriptures must be used to help interpret the New Testament parables. Parables include the total Bible.

B. People Parables

Luke's Gospel is especially a "People Parable" Gospel. While Matthew's parables are far more frequent in the use of symbolic elements, Luke's parables deal much more with real people and human relationships, as the following shows.

1. The Wise and Foolish Builders (Luke 6:46-49; Matthew 7:24-27).

2. The Creditor and Debtors (Luke 7:41-50).

3. The Good Samaritan (Luke 10:30-37).

4. The Three Friends (Luke 11: 5-13).

5. The Rich Fool (Luke 12:16-21).

6. The Watchful Servant (Luke 12:35-40; Matthew 24:42-44).

7. The Faithful and Wise Steward (Luke 12:42-48; Matthew 24:45-51).

8. The Lost and Found Sheep, Coin, and Son (Luke 15:1-32).

9. The Unrighteous Steward (Luke 16:1-13).

10. The Rich Man and Lazarus (Luke 16:19-31).

11. The Unprofitable Servants (Luke 17:7-10).

12. The Unjust Judge and Widow (Luke 18:1-8).

13. The Pharisee and the Publican (Luke 18:9-14).

14. The Pounds – Used and Unused (Luke 19:11-27).

C. Seed Parables

Jesus made use of nature and the things God, His Father, had created. The language of creation became the language of the symbol, and the language of the symbol became the language of redemption, and the language of various parables.

1. The Sower and the Seed (Matthew 13:3-23; Mark 4:2-20; Luke 8:4-15).

2. The Wheat and the Tares (Matthew 13:24-43).

3. The Mustard Seed Tree (Matthew 13:31-32; Mark 4:30-32; Luke 13:18-19).

4. The Kingdom Seed (Mark 4:26-29).

D. Vineyard Parables

The vineyard of various trees was a very familiar one to the Hebrew mind. Jesus used the known, the natural, to impart the spiritual truth. Creation pointed to redemption.

1. The Vineyard Labourers (Matthew 20:1-16).

2. The Two Sons and the Vineyard (Matthew 21:28-32).

3. The Vineyard and the Husbandmen (Matthew 21:33-45; Mark 12:1-12; Luke 20:9-19).

4. The Barren and Budding Fig Tree (Matthew 24:32-44; Mark 13:28-32; Luke 13:6-8).

E. Feast-Supper Parables

The Hebrew mind and culture was saturated with the Feasts of the Lord, and Supper times in their lifestyle.

1. The Guest at the Wedding Supper (Luke 14:7-11).

2. The Supper for the Rich or the Poor (Luke 14:12-14).

3. The Great Supper of the Kingdom of God (Luke 14:15-24).

F. Discipleship Parables

The parables of discipleship especially emphasize "counting the cost" before following the Lord Jesus Christ.

1. The Tower Builder (Luke 14:25-30).

2. The Warring King (Luke 14:31-33).

G. Marriage Parables

The Hebrew mind was totally familiar with weddings and the various marriage customs and celebration of such a great event. Jesus used the known to point to the heavenly.

1. The Marriage of the King's Son (Matthew 22:1-14).
2. The Wise and Foolish Virgins and the Marriage (Matthew 25:1-13).

H. Prayer Parables

The Hebrew mind was also filled with the concept of prayer. The temple was God's house of prayer for all nations. Jews would gather there at the hour of prayer.

1. The Unjust Judge and the Widow (Luke 18:1-8).
2. The Pharisee and the Publican (Luke 18:9-14).

I. Judgment Parables

The Judgment Parables have to do with "Outer Darkness, Weeping, Wailing, Gnashing of Teeth, and Furnace of Fire".

1 The Jews without faith into Outer Darkness (Matthew 8:11-12).
2. The Man without a Wedding Garment into Outer Darkness (Matthew 22:13).
3. The Unprofitable Servant cast into Outer Darkness (Matthew 25:30).

   Read also Matthew 13:42,50; 24:51; Luke 13:28.

J. Israelic Parables

These parables deal with Old Testament Israel and are prophetic and Messianic parables. They involved the overview of the whole Bible, especially an overview of Israel's history in Old Testament times, through to the coming and rejection of their Messiah, and then on through New Testament Church history to the second coming of the Lord Jesus Christ.

1. The Vineyard and the Husbandmen (Matthew 21:33-45; Mark12:1-12; Luke 20:9-19).
2. The Barren Fig Tree (Matthew 24:32-44; Mark 13:28-32; Luke 13:6-8).
3. The Great Supper (Luke 14:16-24).

K. Stewardship Parables

Stewardship parables emphasize ability, responsibility and accountability.

1. The Scribe and the Householder (Matthew 13:51-52).
2. The Wise and Foolish Virgins (Matthew 25:1-13).
3. The Used and the Unused Talents (Matthew 25:14-30).
4. The Rich Fool (Luke 12:16-21).
5. The Faithful and Wise Steward (Matthew 25:45-51; Luke 12:42-48).
6. The Rich Man and Lazarus (Luke 16:19-31).
7. The Pounds – Used and Unused (Luke 19:11-27).

L. Second Coming Parables

Most of the parables point to the second advent of Christ. Several only are listed here as the fuller list is noted under the Supplemental, "Christology".

1. The Separation of the Wheat and Tares (Matthew 13:24-43).
2. The Separation of the Good and Bad Fish (Matthew 13:47-50).
3. The Separation of the Wise and Foolish Virgins (Matthew 25:1-13).
4. The Separation of the Sheep and Goats (Matthew 25:31-46).

SUPPLEMENTAL THREE
THE GODHEAD IN THE PARABLES

In a number of the parables, there is a distinct representation of the Godhead, especially of the Father and the Son. Only the most prominant representations are given here. For the Scriptures, the reader is refer to Supplemental "Table of Scriptures".

A. The Father In The Parables
1. The Parable of the Prodigal Son, the Elder Brother and the Father.
2. The Two Sons and the Vineyard.
3. The Marriage of the King's Son (ie., The Father's Son).

B. The Son In The Parables
As will be seen more fully in "Christology", the Son of God is seen in most of the parables in His various roles and representations. He is seen in the parables as:

1. The Sower of the Word
2. The Seed of the Word
3. The Man (by incarnation)
4. The Fisherman
5. The King
6. The Certain Man
7. The Husbandman
8. The Son
9. The Heir
10. The King's Son
11. The Shepherd
12. The Bridegroom
13. The Nobleman
14. The Absentee Householder
15. The Wise Builder
16. The Good Samaritan
17. The Friend
18. The Scribe or Teacher

C. The Holy Spirit In The Parables
The Holy Spirit is primarily "the unseen One", working in conjunction and unity with the Father and the Son. He is the symbolized One more especially in the operations of the Godhead in the plan of redemption.

1. The Oil in the Believer's Lamp
2. The Lighted Lamp
3. The Savour in the Salt
4. The New Wine in the Wineskin

The student is referred to the exposition of the various parables for appropriate references.

SUPPLEMENTAL FOUR
THE CHRISTOLOGY OF THE PARABLES

Without doubt, Christ Jesus is pre-eminent in most of the parables. The parables cover His incarnation, life, ministry, rejection and crucifixion, ascension, intercessory ministry and His second coming. The doctrine of Christ is seen in many of the parables.

While it is recognized that one does not build doctrine on the parables, yet parables are the doctrine (teaching) of Christ, and such can be used to **illustrate** doctrine. This is seen in the following outline of Christology in the parables.

A. His Incarnation

In many of the parables, Jesus alludes to Himself as "a certain man", or "a man". Jesus became a man in the incarnation, by the miracle of His virgin birth. There He took upon Himself the form of man after being in the form of God (Phillipians 2:1-12).

B. His Ministry

In His ministry over three and one-half years, Christ is seen as the sower of the good seed of the word of the kingdom (Matthew 4:17; 9:36).

C. His Crucifixion

The specific parable that speaks of the death of the Son is the parable of the vineyard and the husbandmen. They recognized Jesus as the Son and Heir, and caught Him, took Him out of the vineyard and killed Him. This points to His rejection and crucifixion of Jewry and especially of the Jewish leaders.

D. His Ascension

The man who "goes into a far country" to receive for Himself a kingdom is none other than the Lord Jesus in His ascension (Luke 19:11-27). He came from the Father. He returns to the Father. This completes the cycle of the Father's will (John 16:26-27).

E. His Absence

The absence of the householder, and the certain man who gave talents and pounds to His own, along with other parables, point to the time that the Lord is in heaven, during His mediatorial ministry and work. It is during His absence that much of the language of the parables have to be fulfilled by His disciples, by the church. During His absence the servants are to:

* Sow the seed of the gospel of the kingdom
* Be good scribes of the kingdom word
* Labour in the Master's vineyard
* Keep the lamps burning brightly and watch for His return
* Use the talents the Lord has given
* Build a wise man's house that will stand the storm
* Be a good Samaritan to the poor and needy
* Invite people to the Gospel Supper
* Be salt and light in the midst of a corrupted and darkened society

* Seek and save that which is lost
* Be faithful and wise stewards of the Lord's goods
* Be sincere and humble in prayer
* Use the pounds the Lord has given, and all the other things the parables teach us to be doing for the Master in His absence.

F. His Advent

Christ's second coming brings about the end of the age. The "time element" in the parables confirms this.

"The harvest is the end of the age..." (Matthew 13:39).

"At the end of the age..." (Matthew 13:40).

"When the king came in to see the guests..." (Matthew 22:11).

"When He comes...the bridegroom came..." (Matthew 24:19; 25:6).

"After a long time, the Lord of that servant came...." (Matthew 25:18).

"When the Son of Man comes in His glory..." (Matthew 25::31).

"To receive for Himself a kingdom and to return..." (Luke 19:12).

"That when He was returned, having received the kingdom..." (Luke 19:15).

"Come as a thief in the night..." (Matthew 24:43; Luke 12:39; 1Thessalonians 5:1-4; 2Peter 3:10; Revelation3:3; 16:13).

"When He returns from the wedding..." (Luke 12:30).

"My Lord delays His coming..." (Luke 12:35-48).

The Old Testament said He is coming. The New Testament said He has come. The Revelation and the Parables say He will come again (Matthew 24:48)!

G. His Judgments

Most of the parables point to Christ's second coming again. The parables use varying expressions, but all point to His advent from heaven, His return to earth and the time of judgment for sinners, hypocrites as well as rewarding of His own. It will be a time of accountability for all before Him. The parables teach this truth.

1. The separation of the wheat and tares.

2. The separation of the good and bad fish.

3. The taking of the treasure and the field.

4. The reception of the pearl of great price.

5. The reward of the righteous labourers.

6. The marriage of the king's Son.

7. The bridegroom and the wise and foolish virgins.

8. The separation of the sheep and goats.

9. The reward and punishments of those who used their talents or did not use talents.

10. The reward of those who used or did not use their pounds.

11. The return of the absentee householder.

12. The reward of the faithful and wise steward.

13. The shut door at His coming.

14. The great supper, or the marriage supper of the Lamb.

H. His Kingdom

At His second coming, the great separation takes place and all mixture that is in the kingdom in its present form comes to an end. Only the righteous enter the kingdom, that is, the millennial kingdom of 1000 years, and then on into eternity. Each of these kingdom of heaven parables reveal this to be so.

1. After the separation of the wheat and tares, only the righteous enter the kingdom and shine forth as the sun in the kingdom of the Father (Matthew 13:36-43).

2. When the nobleman returns, after receiving the kingdom in the far country, He rewards His own servants (Luke 19:11-27).

3. After the separation of the sheep and goats, the righteous only enter into the kingdom prepared for them of the Father from the foundation of the world (Matthew 25:31-46).

Thus the whole life of the Lord Jesus is seen in outline form in the Christology of the parables!

THE PARABLE TITLE	MATTHEW	MARK	LUKE
1. The Sower and The Seed	13:3-23	4:2-20	8:4-15
2. The Wheat and The Tares	13:24-30,36-43		
3. The Mustard Seed	13:31-32	4:30-32	13:18-19
4. The Woman, Leaven and Meal	13:33		
5. The Hid Treasure in the Field	13:44		
6. The Merchant Man and Pearls	13:45-46		
7. The Dragnet and the Fish	13:47-50		
8. The Scribe and Householder	13:51-52		
9. The King and His Servants	18:23-35		
10. The Vineyard Labourers	20:1-16		
11. The Two Sons of the Vineyard	21:28-32		
12. The Vineyard and Husbandmen	21:33-45	12:1-12	20:9-19
13. The Marriage of the King's Son	22:2-14		
14. The Wise and Foolish Virgins	25:1-13		
15. The Used and Unused Talents	25:14-30		
16. The Sheep and the Goats	25:31-46		
17. The Lighted Lamp and City	5:14-16	4:21-22	8:16-17
18. The Kingdom Seed		4:26-29	
19. The Absentee Householder		13:33-37	
20. The Old and New Wineskins	9:16-17	2:21-22	5:36-38
The Old and New Garments	9:16-17	2:21-22	5:36-38
21. The Wise and Foolish Builders	7:24-27		6:46-49
22. The Creditor and Two Debtors			7:41-50
23. The Good Samaritan			10:30-37
24. The Three Friends			11:5-13
25. The Rich Fool			12:16-21
26. The Watchful Servant	24:42-44		12:35-40
27. The Faithful and Wise Steward	24:45-51		12:42-48
28. The Barren or Budding Fig Tree	24:32-44	13:28-32	13:6-8
			21:29-33
29. The Two Gates and Two Ways	7:13-14		13:22-24
30. The Shut Door			13:25-30
31. The Wedding Feast Invitation			14:7-11
32. The Great Supper			14:16-24

SUPPLEMENTAL SIX
THE GOLDEN LAMPSTAND AND MATTHEW 13

As seen in the course of the textbook, Matthew 13 has seven specific parables of the kingdom, and an eighth parable of the scribe and householder. There are many illustrations in the Scripture of the numbers seven and eight. One of the illustrations, upon which the parables can be super-imposed, is the illustration of the golden lampstand in the Tabernacle of Moses, or, the Tabernacle of the Lord.

In brief, the golden lampstand had a central shaft, out of which came six branches. The six branches were in pairs, therefore making three pairs of two branches. Upon the top of the seven branches were the seven golden lamps, filled with holy oil, that caused the lamps to shine, sending forth the Divine light. The six branches came out of the shaft, the central branch, yet all were part of the whole. There was but one golden lampstand. The seven lamps threw light upon each other and also the lampstand itself.

Though there were seven lamps of light, yet there was but one light manifested. The high priest attended to these seven lamps in the daily ministrations, trimming the lamps and supplying the golden oil.

This is a beautiful illustration of the mystery parables of the kingdom in Matthew 13. In all there are seven distinct kingdom of heaven parables. The first parable (The Sower and The Seed) is like the shaft of the lampstand, for Jesus told His disciples that, if they did not understand this parable, then how would they know and understand the other parables. This first parable was "the seed parable", out of which other "seed parables" came (Mark 4:13).

The six other parables are in three pairs, like the three pairs of branches out of the side of the golden lampstand. The first pair of parables, like the first pair of branches, consist of the Mustard Seed Parable, and the Woman and Leaven Parable. The second pair of parables, like the second pair of branches, consist of the Treasure in the Field, and the Pearl of Great Price. The third pair of parables, like the third pair of branches, consist of the Parables of the Wheat and Tares and Net of Good Fish and Bad Fish. Each of the pairs, or twin parables, teach the same truth, even as the branches had the same ornamentation in them. Yet altogether, the seven branches consisted of one golden lampstand, even as the seven parables consist of one truth – the mystery of the kingdom.

Parable One = The Word of the Beginning of the Kingdom (The Shaft of the Lampstand).

Parables Two and Seven = The Mixture in the Kingdom and Final Separation (Two Branches).

Parables Three and Four = The External Growth and Internal Corruption of the Kingdom (Two Branches).

Parables Five and Six = The Priceless Value and Cost of the Kingdom (Two Branches).

The eighth parable is the scribe and householder and may represent the priest who had to attend to the seven lamps of the golden lampstand. As each of the lamps threw light on the lampstand, so the seven parables of the kingdom throw light on each other in the light of the whole of the Scriptures, both Old and New Testament. The Holy Spirit, as the Divine oil, causes light to shine forth in the study of the Mystery Parables of the Kingdom. The diagram of the golden lampstand here places the parables in the numerical order of their respective truths, including the shaft parable and the three twin parables.

THE KINGDOM OF HEAVEN PARABLES
(MATTHEW CHAPTER 13)

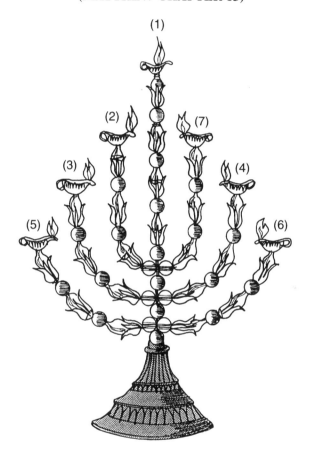

Parable # 1	The Word of the Beginning of the Kingdom
Parable # 2 & 7	The Mixture in The Kingdom and Final Separation
Parable # 3 & 4	The External Growth & Internal Corruption of The Kingdom
Parables # 5 & 6	The Priceless Value and cost of The Kingdom

SUPPLEMENTAL SEVEN
OVERVIEW OF THE KINGDOM GOD

In simple over-view, the kingdom of God, in its manifestation on earth has three phases: The Kingdom Past (Patriarchs & Israel), The Kingdom Present (The New Testament Church), and The Kingdom Future (The Millennial Kingdom). The kingdom itself is "from everlasting to everlasting", but in relation to earth it has its successive stages. The diagram illustrates this overview.

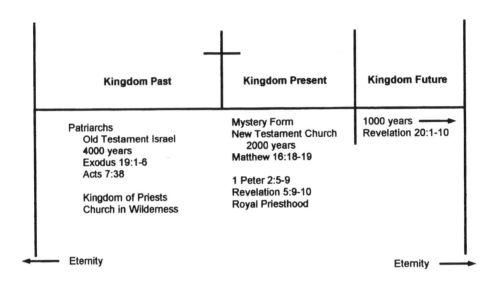

SUPPLEMENTAL EIGHT
OVERVIEW OF WORLD KINGDOMS
DANIEL TWO
WORLD KINGDOMS — GOD'S KINGDOM

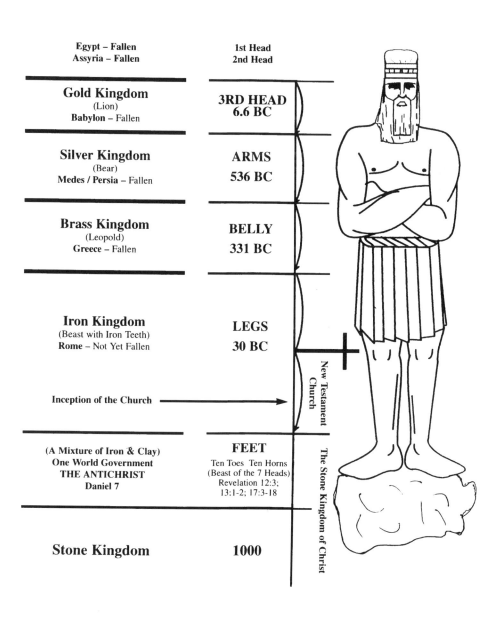

Egypt – Fallen
Assyria – Fallen

1st Head
2nd Head

Gold Kingdom
(Lion)
Babylon – Fallen

**3RD HEAD
6.6 BC**

Silver Kingdom
(Bear)
Medes / Persia – Fallen

**ARMS
536 BC**

Brass Kingdom
(Leopold)
Greece – Fallen

**BELLY
331 BC**

Iron Kingdom
(Beast with Iron Teeth)
Rome – Not Yet Fallen

**LEGS
30 BC**

New Testament Church

Inception of the Church →

**(A Mixture of Iron & Clay)
One World Government
THE ANTICHRIST
Daniel 7**

FEET
Ten Toes Ten Horns
(Beast of the 7 Heads)
Revelation 12:3;
13:1-2; 17:3-18

The Stone Kingdom of Christ

Stone Kingdom

1000

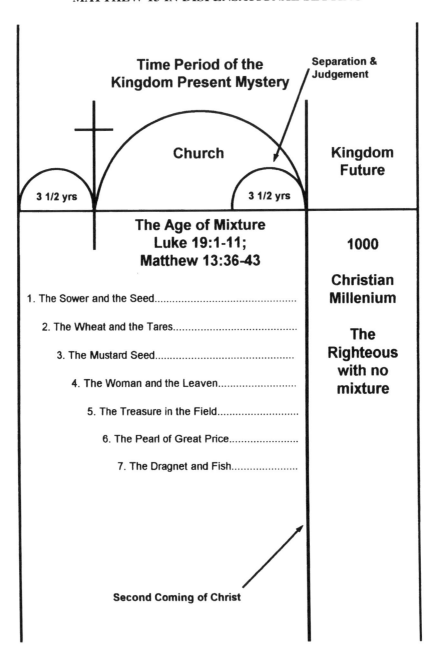

**Time Period of the
Kingdom Present Mystery**

Separation &
Judgement

Church

**Kingdom
Future**

3 1/2 yrs

3 1/2 yrs

**The Age of Mixture
Luke 19:1-11;
Matthew 13:36-43**

1000

**Christian
Millenium**

1. The Sower and the Seed...

2. The Wheat and the Tares...

3. The Mustard Seed...

4. The Woman and the Leaven...........................

5. The Treasure in the Field...........................

6. The Pearl of Great Price.......................

7. The Dragnet and Fish.....................

**The
Righteous
with no
mixture**

Second Coming of Christ

BIBLIOGRAPHY

1. Bailey, Kenneth E., *Poet & Peasant AND Through Peasant Eyes,* Grand Rapids, Michigan, W.B. Eerdmans, 1976.

2. Bible Dictionary, New Bible Dictionary, "Parables" (pages 877-879).

3. Chitwood, Arlen L., *Mysteries of the Kingdom,* Norman, Oklahoma, The Lamp Broadcast, Inc., 1980.

4. Chitwood, Arlen L., *Parables of the Kingdom,* Norman, Oklahoma, The Lamp Broadcast, Inc., 1979.

5. Conner, Kevin J., *The Gospel of Matthew,* Melbourne, Australia, (Unpublished Exposition), 1977.

6. Conner, Kevin J and Kenneth P. Malmin., *Interpreting the Scriptures,* Portland, Oregon, USA., Bible Temple Publishing, 1976.

7. Fausett, A.R., Dictionary, "Parables" (page 538).

8. Fee, Gordon D and Douglas Stuart., *How To Read The Bible For All Its Worth,* London, Scripture Union, 1983.

9. Habershon, Ada R., *The Study of the Parables,* Grand Rapids, Michigan, Kregel Publications, 1957.

10. Kistemaker, Simon., *The Parables of Jesus,* Grand Rapids, Michigan, Baker Books, 1980.

11. Lockyer Herbert., *All The Parables of The Bible,* Grand Rapids, Michigan, Zondervan Publishing House, 1963.

12. Morgan, G. Campbell., *The Parables & Metaphors of our Lord,* Fleming H.Revell Company, Old Tappan, New Jersey, 1900.

13. Seagren, Dan., *The Parables,* Wheaton, Illinois, Tyndale House Publishers, Inc. 1978.

14. Spurgeon, C.H., *Miracles & Parables of our Lord,* Vol I-II-III, Grand Rapids, Michigan, Baker Book House, 1992.

15. Trench, R.C., *Notes on the Parables of our Lord,* Grand Rapids, Michigan, Baker Book House , 1948.

16. Strong, James., *Strong's Exhaustive Concordance,* Madison, New Jersey, 1890.

17. The Holy Bible, *Authorised Version* (1611. Public Domain).

Other Books by Kevin Conner

Are Women Elders Biblical? (NEW)
Biblical Principles of Leadership
The Book of Acts
The Book of Daniel (An Exposition)
The Book of Deuteronomy (NEW in the OT Commentary Series)
The Book of Hebrews (An Exposition)
The Book of Jude (An Exposition)
The Book of Revelation (An Exposition)
Christian Millennium
The Church in the New Testament (best-selling book)
The Church of the Firstborn and the Birthright
The Daily Ministrations (NEW)
The Day After the Sabbath (NEW)
The Death-Resurrection Route
The Feasts of Israel
Foundations of Christian Doctrine (best-selling book)
Foundation Principles of Church Membership
Foundation Principles of the Doctrine of Christ
Headship, Covering and Hats
The House of God
Interpreting the Book of Revelation
Interpreting the Symbols and Types
Interpreting the Scriptures
The Kingdom Cult of Self
Kings of the Kingdom
Law and Grace
The Lord Jesus Christ our Melchizedek Priest
The Manifest Presence (NEW)
Marriage, Divorce and Remarriage
Methods and Principles of Bible Research

Ministries in the Cluster
The Ministry of Women
Mystery Parables of the Kingdom
The Name of God
New Covenant Realities
Only for Catholics
Passion Week Chart
Psalms - A Commentary
The Relevance of the Old Testament to a New Testament Church
Restoration Theology
Romans (An Exposition)
The Seventy Weeks Prophecy
The Sword and Consequences
The Tabernacle of David
The Tabernacle of Moses
The Temple of Solomon
Table Talks
Tale of Three Trees
This is My Story (Kevin Conner's best-selling autobiography)
This We Believe
Three Days and Three Nights (with Chart)
Tithes and Offerings
Today's Prophets
To Drink or Not to Drink
Understanding the New Birth and the Baptism of the Holy Spirit
Vision of an Antioch Church
Water Baptism Thesis
What About Israel? (NEW)

Visit www.kevinconner.org for more information.
Visit www.amazon.com/author/kevinjconner for a list of other books by Kevin Conner.

Made in the USA
Coppell, TX
18 December 2020